Bradt

Slow
Norfolk &
Suffolk

Local, characterful guides to Britain's special places

Laurence Mitchell

Edition 1

Bradt Travel Guides Ltd, UK
Alastair Sawday Publishing Co Ltd, UK
The Globe Pequot Press Inc, USA

CHAPTER LOCATION MAP

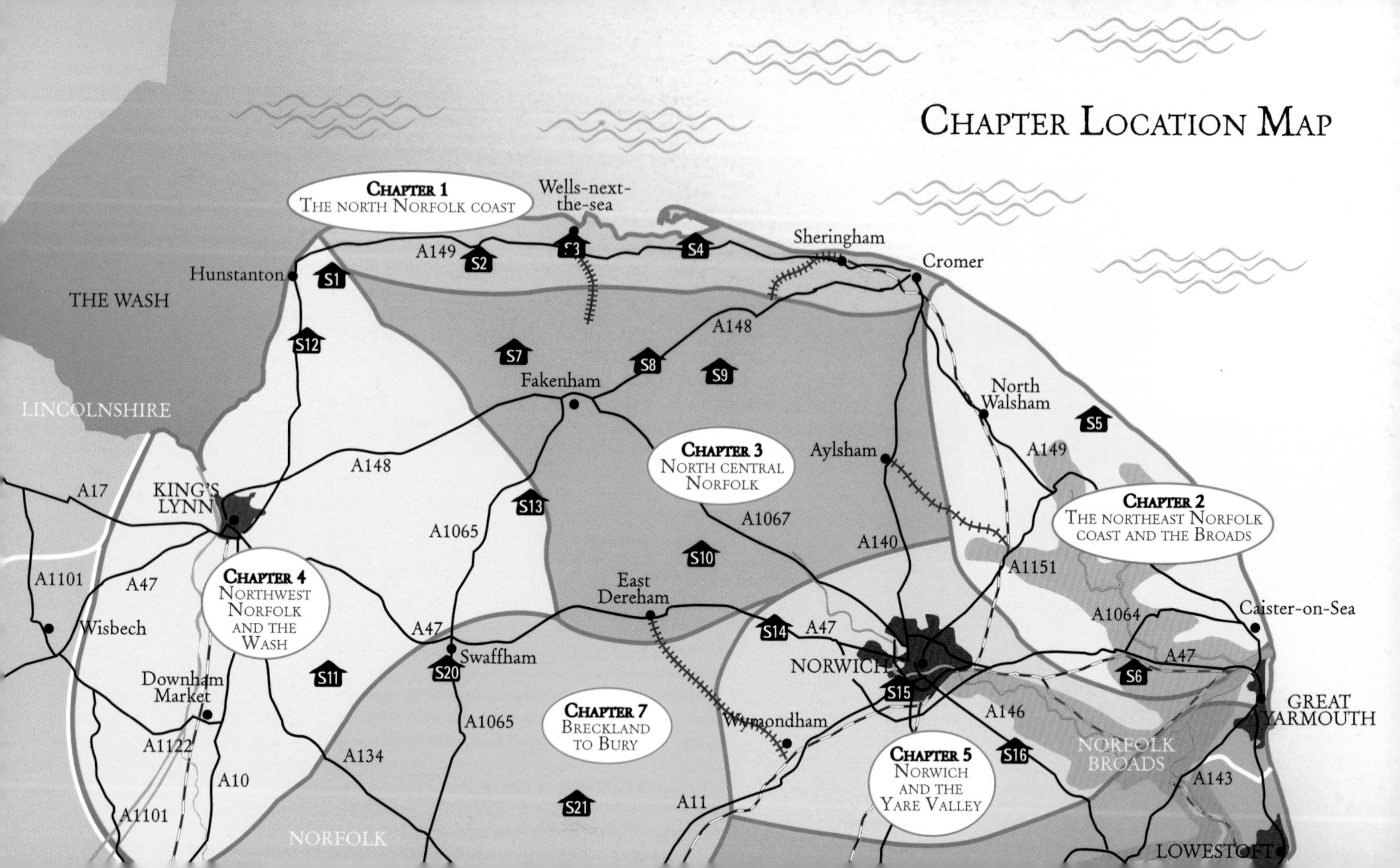

THE WASH

LINCOLNSHIRE

Hunstanton

CHAPTER 1
THE NORTH NORFOLK COAST

S1

S2

A149

Wells-next-the-sea

C3

S4

Sheringham

Cromer

North Walsham

CHAPTER 2
THE NORTHEAST NORFOLK COAST AND THE BROADS

S5

Caister-on-Sea

GREAT YARMOUTH

LOWESTOFT

A143

A47

S6

NORFOLK BROADS

A1064

A1151

A149

A148

S9

S8

S7

Fakenham

Aylsham

CHAPTER 3
NORTH CENTRAL NORFOLK

A1067

A140

S10

S13

East Dereham

A146

S16

A47

CHAPTER 5
NORWICH AND THE YARE VALLEY

S15

NORWICH

S14

Wymondham

A11

A47

S20

Swaffham

A1065

CHAPTER 7
BRECKLAND TO BURY

S21

A1065

A148

CHAPTER 4
NORTHWEST NORFOLK AND THE WASH

S11

A134

KING'S LYNN

S12

A47

A17

A1101

Wisbech

Downham Market

A10

A1122

A1101

NORFOLK

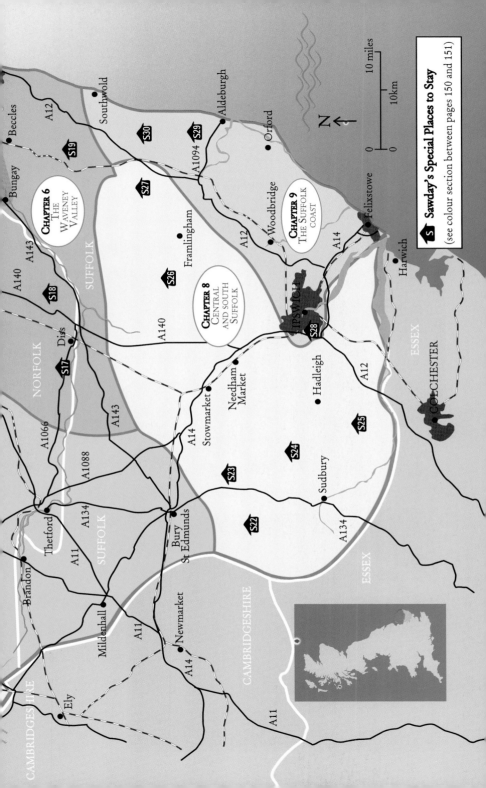

A Norfolk & Suffolk Gallery

Buildings along the Norfolk coastline make good use of the plentiful supply of beach pebbles. This one in Cley-next-the-Sea has a red pantile roof and Dutch gables typical of the region. (LM)

Go about your Busines

This sundial at the church of St Peter and St Paul in Clare at the western end of Suffolk's Stour Valley has a curt message to discourage stragglers. (LM)

The National Trust-owned Dunwich Heath in Suffolk is a rare example of unimproved sandlings habitat with heather and gorse bushes. (RG/PL)

The sign might seem to say it all but it's not so boring really, just a quiet – and very pretty – north Norfolk village. With typical Norfolk contrariness, the neighbouring village of Little Snoring is actually slightly bigger. (LM)

Taking time to explore

This is the ultimate Slow region with its forest and coastal walks, sleepy villages, steam railways and magnificent skyscapes.

The Mid-Norfolk Railway between Wymondham and East Dereham is staffed entirely by volunteers. The route passes through quiet outposts of central Norfolk like Thuxton and Yaxham, whose stations were closed at the time of the 1960s Beeching cuts. (LM)

Walking in a bluebell wood, one of many in the region. (LP/PL)

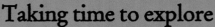

Barton Broad is the second largest body of water in the Broads system. Once badly polluted, it has improved enormously in water quality over the past few decades. (LM)

Norfolk and Suffolk landscapes

Norfolk and Suffolk deserve to be explored at leisure. Take time to meander through the Broads, cycle between flint and pebble villages or delve into vast areas of woodland.

Warham, just inland from the north Norfolk coast, is a flint-and-pebble village with a good pub and the site of an Iron Age settlement nearby – excellent terrain for exploring by bike. (DB/FL)

The region where the Brecks and Fens meet in west Norfolk is sometimes fancifully described as a coastline. Not so many years ago, the Fens to the west really were underwater. (LM)

Thetford Forest covers a vast area of southwest Norfolk and northwest Suffolk. Planted partly to combat soil erosion, it consists mostly of conifers, but there are areas of deciduous trees and sandy heaths too. (TLL/SS)

Windmills like this one near Horsey in the Norfolk Broads are still a common feature of Broadland. Built to drain the marshes in the 18th and 19th centuries, they are now mostly in a picturesque state of disrepair. (LM)

Constructed in 1790, Happisburgh's red-and-white banded lighthouse is the oldest working lighthouse in East Anglia and an iconic sight along the northeast Norfolk coastline. (AF/SS)

Gurneys in Burnham Market is just one of a number of specialist food shops in this smart Georgian village. The produce on sale here is lobsters, crabs and fresh fish from the nearby north Norfolk coast. (TC/FL)

Cromer crabs are highly popular for their sweet flesh. It is thought that their distinctive taste may be a result of their slow-growing habit or the lack of mud on the local seabed. (LM)

Picnic Fayre in Cley-next-the-Sea on the north Norfolk coast is a long-established delicatessen selling locally sourced organic vegetables, specialist breads and takeaway pastries. (AF/SS)

South Quay in King's Lynn was once the embarkation point for thousands of maritime adventures, with a roll-call of Norfolk mariners – Captain Vancouver, Captain John Smith and Admiral Nelson – all setting off from here. (LM)

Village shops and pubs

This region's long coastline means that all manner of seasonal seafood is on offer, while village stores and pubs provide ideal fuel for walkers and cyclists.

Southwold's lighthouse is sandwiched between terraced streets away from the shore close to the Adnams brewery. The Sole Bay Inn is one of many Adnams pubs in this Suffolk town. (LM)

Bury St Edmunds has the largest brewery in East Anglia... and the smallest pub. The Nutshell consists of just a single tiny bar. Nevertheless, it is big enough to be said to be haunted. (LM)

Before being silted up in the 17th century, Cley-next-the-Sea was an important port. These days, the reed-beds and marshes of its neighbouring nature reserve provide enough specialist habitats to make it a birdwatching Mecca. (LM)

Blakeney's former seafaring tradition is reflected on its village sign. The fiddler and dog represent a legend in which a local man and dog entered a secret passage below the village guildhall, never to be seen again. (DP/PL)

Towns and villages

From picturesque hamlets of thatched cottages to Norwich's Tudor lanes and elegant cathedral, the region's towns and villages reveal a surprisingly rich history.

Framlingham Castle, Suffolk's largest castle, was where Mary Tudor proclaimed herself queen in 1553. Her successor, Elizabeth I, used it as a prison. (LM)

The village of Thornham in north Norfolk was once well known for its fancy wrought ironwork, hence the forge on the village sign. (DP/PL)

Norwich Cathedral, whose construction began just after the Norman invasion, has the second highest spire in the country. (SV/SS)

Elm Hill in Norwich has some of the city's finest Tudor buildings, although its eponymous tree was a victim of Dutch elm disease back in the 1970s. (HT/PL)

Cavendish in the Stour Valley is a picture-perfect Suffolk village with thatched pink cottages arranged around a large green. Sir John Cavendish, killer of the rebel leader Wat Tyler, unsuccessfully attempted to find sanctuary at the village's church of St Mary in 1381. (LM)

Wells-next-the-Sea is a popular place for north Norfolk sailors. Numerous muddy creeks meander out from the harbour through salt marshes to the sea. (TLL/SS)

Blakeney Harbour in north Norfolk was an active port until the early 1900s but, like other ports along this coast, it lost its trade with the silting up of its estuary. (DP/PL)

Cromer pier was badly damaged by storms on several occasions in the late 20th century. You can still catch an end-of-the pier show at the Pavilion Theatre here. (LM)

Southwold's colourful beach huts are an iconic feature of the Suffolk coast. For some, they represent a desirable and expensive piece of seaside real estate. (RE/PL)

The coast

The glorious Norfolk and Suffolk coasts encompass landscapes of sand ridges, cliffs, sweeping beaches, salt marshes and charming harbours.

The distinctive red-and-white cliffs at Old Hunstanton in west Norfolk are composed of layers of red limestone and chalk. This is the only part of the East Anglia coastline that faces west, into the sunset. (LM)

Orford on the Suffolk coast has a 12th-century castle overlooking Orford Ness, a huge spit across the estuary that was once home to a secret military testing zone. (JM/PL)

The Slipper Chapel at Houghton St Giles just outside Little Walsingham is the important last staging point on the Catholic pilgrimage to 'England's Nazareth'. Pilgrims are supposed to walk the last stretch barefoot – even Henry VIII did this. (LM)

Wymondham Abbey, now a twin-towered parish church, started life as a Benedictine priory but its monastic buildings were destroyed during the Dissolution. (LM)

Churches

This region is replete with remarkable churches; enigmatic woodcarvings and exquisite stained-glass windows are to be found in the unlikeliest places.

Salle's church of St Peter and St Paul in north central Norfolk has some wonderfully expressive bench carvings. This one shows monks deep in conversation. (LM)

Round towers are common in Norfolk and Suffolk. This one at the church of St Andrew at Little Snoring in north Norfolk is unusual in having a conical windmill cap and being detached from the church. (LM)

The winter rook roost at Buckenham Carrs in the Yare Valley is a timeless, spectacular event that was even recorded in the Domesday Book. (LM)

Birds

With its astonishing range of habitats, this is one of the best regions in Britain for birdwatching.

The bearded tit (or bearded reedling), is a beautiful rare bird found only in reed beds. Numbers have increased since the advent of milder winters in recent years. (AF/SS)

Barn owls are often seen flying at dusk in rural Norfolk and Suffolk. As their name suggests, they were once encouraged to nest in barns in order to keep down vermin. (AF/SS)

This house at Snape Maltings in Suffolk is so covered with Virginia creeper that you might think it to be some sort of art installation. (LM)

The House in the Clouds at Thorpeness in Suffolk is a much-photographed local landmark. The house is built on top of a five-storey plinth that was originally a water tower. (RE/PL)

'The Pyramid', tucked away in the Great Wood on the Blickling Hall estate in north central Norfolk, is actually an eccentric mausoleum built in the late 18th century. (LM)

Quirky buildings

Norfolk and Suffolk have more than their share of eccentric buildings, from a crow's-top style dwelling to ivy-smothered houses.

This holiday home at Potter Heigham in the Norfolk Broads makes use of the top of a helter-skelter salvaged from Great Yarmouth's Britannia Pier. (TLL/PCL)

Author

Laurence Mitchell holds a degree in environmental science and at various times has worked as an English teacher in Sudan, surveyed farm buildings in Norfolk, pushed a pen in a local government office and taught geography in a rural secondary school. Having finally settled for the uncertain life of a freelance travel writer and photographer, he specialises in places firmly off the beaten track like the Balkans, Central Asia and the Middle East when not wandering around his home patch of East Anglia. As well as writing several guides for Bradt, his work has appeared in publications including *Geographical, Discovery Channel Magazine* and *hidden europe*. He is a member of the British Guild of Travel Writers and has a website at www.laurencemitchell.com.

Author's story

I am not a native of East Anglia but, in my defence, I have lived here a long time – since the 1970s in fact. I stayed on in Norwich after graduation from the University of East Anglia, like many other 'UEA refugees', unable – or perhaps unwilling – to go anywhere else. Months led to years, years led to decades and eventually I just merged into the scenery. This is not to say that I have been twiddling my thumbs at home for the past thirty years. I have travelled widely in the interim period but Norwich has become the place to which I return. For someone with a foot in both urban and rural camps, I have found the city to be something akin to the best of both worlds.

Although I have lived in Norwich for most of my East Anglian life, I have always made frequent expeditions into the surrounding hinterland, especially to north Norfolk, the Broads and the Suffolk coast. Slowly, I have learned to unravel the region's calm beauty and arrive at the realisation that perhaps mountains aren't everything.

I was delighted to be given the opportunity to write this guide. As someone who has written about some pretty odd, far-flung places, it seemed strange at first to be focusing so close to home. But this just made me take a closer look at my own back yard and helped restore an appreciation that I may have been starting to take for granted.

Researching this book, I ended up revisiting many old stomping grounds and also discovered quite a few villages that I did not know existed – wonderful little places like Boulge, Middleton, Northwold and Mendham, to name just a few. I even came to appreciate places that I had hitherto dismissed. I had forgotten just how attractive the old part of King's Lynn is and how vividly maritime history permeates the very bricks of Great Yarmouth's rows. It has been the small things though, the things that you could not plan for, that have really brought home to me why I live in this eastern curve of the country: fresh details that reveal themselves on oft-trodden walks, serendipitous sightings of wildlife and magnificent fleeting skyscapes. In a way it feels like a homecoming.

First published May 2010
Bradt Travel Guides Ltd
23 High Street, Chalfont St Peter, Bucks SL9 9QE, England
www.bradtguides.com
Alastair Sawday Publishing Co Ltd
The Old Farmyard, Yanley Lane, Long Ashton, Bristol BS41 9LR
www.sawdays.co.uk
Published in the USA by The Globe Pequot Press Inc, 246 Goose Lane,
PO Box 480, Guilford, Connecticut 06437-0480

ISBN-13: 978 1 84162 321 4

Photographs, illustrations and maps
Photographs Flickr: David J W Bailey (DB/FL), Tim Caynes (TC/FL); Laurence Mitchell
(LM); Photolibrary: Rod Edwards (RE/PL), Roz Gordon (RG/PL); John Miller (JM/PL),
Lewis Phillips (LP/PL), Dave Porter (DP/PL), Howard Taylor (HT/PL); SuperStock: age
fotostock (AF/SS), Steve Vidler (SV/SS), Travel Library Limited (TLL/SS)
Maps and illustrations Chris Lane and Chris Nairne-Clark (Artinfusion Ltd)
Cover artwork Neil Gower (www.neilgower.com)

Typeset from the author's disc by Artinfusion Ltd
Production managed by Jellyfish Print Solutions and manufactured in the UK

CONTENTS

Acknowledgements

My thanks go to the team at Bradt for their support throughout the production of this book – in particular Adrian Phillips, Helen Anjomshoaa, Donald Greig, Anna Moores, Debbie Hunter and Deborah Gerrard. I am particularly indebted to Tim Locke for his patient editing and enthusiastic overseeing of the project, and to Janice Booth for her painstaking proofreading and suggested improvements. I am also grateful to my Slow colleagues, Hilary Bradt and Mike Bagshaw, for their encouragement and comradeship in what is a new venture for all of us.

Several individuals provided fascinating boxes to accompany the main text and I would like to mention all of them: Hilary Bradt, Penny Edwards, Donald Greig, Poppy Mathews, Janice Booth, Anne Locke and Tim Locke. Thanks also go to Andy Paxton, John Hiskett, Penny Edwards, David Vince and Caroline Davison for suggestions on what to include, and to Wendy Ellis of Boydell & Brewer for permission to quote from John Seymour's *Companion Guide to East Anglia*. I would also like to thank Henry Head at Norfolk Lavender, Neil Featherstone of The Brecks Partnership and Helen Sibley for her information on Thornham Walks. A big 'thank you' also goes to Sheila Rattray for the informal 'interview'. Keep on pedalling, Sheila! Last, but by no means least, I owe gratitude to my wife Jackie, a Norfolk native, for her valued insider's perspective and unstinting support throughout.

Reference books

Blythe, Ronald *Borderland* Canterbury Press, 2007.

Deakin, Roger *Wildwood: A Journey Through Trees* Penguin, 2008.

Deakin, Roger *Notes From Walnut Tree Farm* Penguin, 2009.

Dutt, William *A Highways & Byways in East Anglia* Macmillan & Co, 1901 (out of print).

Cocker, Mark *Crow Country Vintage*, 2008.

Jenkins, Simon *England's Thousand Best Churches* Penguin, 2009.

Mabey, Richard *Flora Britannica* Sinclair-Stevenson, 1996.

Mabey, Richard *Nature Cure* Vintage, 2008.

Parker, Rowland *Men of Dunwich* Collins, 1978 (out of print).

Pevsner, Nikolaus *The Buildings of England – Norfolk 1: Norwich and Northeast* Yale University Press, 1997.

Pevsner, Nikolaus *The Buildings of England – Norfolk 2: Northwest and South* Yale University Press, 1999.

Pevsner, Nikolaus *The Buildings of England – Suffolk* Yale University Press, 1974.

Sebald, W G *The Rings of Saturn* Vintage, 2002.

Seymour, John *The Companion Guide to East Anglia* Companion Guides, 1996 (out of print).

The Slow mindset

From Alastair Sawday, founder of Alastair Sawday Publishing
One of my early literary 'heroes' was John Stewart Collis, a poet who wrote about his work as a farm labourer during World War II. "Now, as far as I can see in any direction, a plantation free (of entanglements) meets my eye, accomplished by the labour of my hands alone. Nothing that I have ever done has given me more satisfaction than this, nor shall I hope to find again so great a happiness." If you are a gardener, have an allotment, make things or simply revel in the slow creative labours of others, you will know what Collis meant.

Going Slow is a way of thinking, living, eating and being. It is also a sophisticated response to unsophisticated, vacuous commercialism – the Slow movement offering something that is life-affirming, rooted in a deep understanding of human needs.

Slow is serious, yet it is fun too. The ideas go deep, but so do the pleasures – for Slow can be seen as a 'bridge from panic to pleasure'. These Slow books are awash with stimulating examples of people who have turned their backs on hectic and empty lives to find deep pleasure in living in a different gear.

Sawday's *Go Slow England* book has enabled thousands of people to enjoy themselves innocently, slowly and greatly. This collaboration with Bradt Guides, a delightful company with whom we have much in common, will lure readers more deeply into the crannies and nooks of England in pursuit of deeper and even slower pleasures.

From Hilary Bradt, founder of Bradt Travel Guides
At a Bradt editorial meeting some years ago we started to explore ideas for guides to our favourite country – Great Britain. We pretty much knew what we wanted: to recruit our best authors to write about their home areas. They had shown that they could write wittily and perceptively about distant lands, so why not ask them to explore closer to home? We wanted a series of books that went beyond the usual tourist attractions and found something different, something extraordinary in familiar villages and landscapes. To quote T S Eliot: 'We shall not cease from exploration, and the end of all our exploring will be to arrive where we started and know the place for the first time'. Exactly.

We have long been impressed with Alastair Sawday's approach to life and travel, and he prepared the way for this series. The Slow philosophy matched our concept perfectly: the ideal partnership. So take time to explore. Don't rush it, get to know an area – and the people who live there – and you'll be as delighted as the authors by what you find.

GOING SLOW IN NORFOLK AND SUFFOLK

So why Slow Norfolk and Suffolk? Surely the region is 'slow' enough already? What is so special about this part of the country? Well, for a start, both counties were largely bypassed by the Industrial Revolution. This is not to say they had no part to play in shaping England's history – far from it – it is just that they tended to be greater movers and shakers back in medieval times rather than over the last few hundred years. Norfolk and Suffolk are both highly distinguished in terms of geography too. Where else in the country could you find such a diversity of landscapes – the flooded peat-diggings of the Broads, the saltmarshes of the north Norfolk coast, the saltings and silted harbours of the Suffolk coast, the sandy wastes of Breckland or the wool-rich, timber-framed villages of the Stour Valley – all within a two-hour drive?

Cynics might argue that both counties are forever a step behind the rest of the country. 'Normal for Norfolk' is a common jibe, as is 'Silly Suffolk', but it's good to see these expressions being turned upside down. 'Normal for Norfolk' has

Norfolk and Suffolk churches: some personal favourites

Hilary Bradt

When I was young – late teens, early twenties – I became obsessed with brass rubbing. I had a guide to the memorial brasses of England, and spent my holidays making rubbings (which, to the uninitiated, are made by spreading paper over the brass memorials found on church floors, and rubbing them with black wax to create a picture). Only those in Buckinghamshire were accessible by bicycle, and I looked with envy at the large section of the book describing the exceptional churches of East Anglia.

Many years later I wrote a walking guide to eastern England and once again took notice of country churches, featuring some in the book. Then came the publication of *England's Thousand Best Churches* by Simon Jenkins, and the die was cast. I set out to see all of the churches described in the book. No, of course I haven't achieved this yet, and probably never will, but it brings an extra dimension to any car journey in England. Meanwhile, here are some of my favourites in Norfolk and Suffolk.

Glandford (Norfolk) This little church is at the centre of a 'model village' built by the Victorian benefactor, Sir Alfred Jodrell. Sir Alfred rebuilt St Martin's church as a memorial to his mother and crammed the tiny interior with all that is typical of East Anglian churches: elaborate woodcarving, gorgeous stained-glass windows, and a marble angel in memory of his mother. My favourite whimsy was the carved bench end in memory of his dog.

Ludham (Norfolk) The church of St Catherine has her emblem of martyrdom incorporated into the roof. The painted rood screen Is special, beautifully carved and recently been deconstructed and adopted as a slogan by Norfolk County Council in the sense of meaning 'world class'; and you should know that 'Silly Suffolk' originates from the expression '*Selig*' Suffolk, selig meaning 'holy' or 'blessed' in Old English, on account of the vast number of fine churches in that county.

I first came to Norfolk three decades or so ago to attend university. I went away for a year or two but I have pretty well based myself here since then, mostly in Norwich but also for a few years in south Norfolk. It has been a slow burn of appreciation. To be honest, it took a while for the subtle charms of the region to grow on me. Birdwatching in north Norfolk, the Broads and the Suffolk coast got me out and about in the region, as did a bit of cycling around my own patch in Norwich and south Norfolk. Then, in the mid 1980s, I got a job as team leader on a project that was carrying out an extensive survey of farm buildings and agricultural practices in Norfolk. This got me interested in vernacular architecture and the way that the rural landscape had been shaped by farming and feudalism. I interviewed many north Norfolk farmers as part of this work and some of these were just old enough to remember working with horses.

Even just 25 years ago, things were different. Large-scale agribusiness had not taken such a firm hold and the majority of the farms were family-run, 200-acre affairs that, besides mechanisation, were not managed all that differently from

with paintings of some obscure saints including a gloomy-looking St Appolonia, patron saint of dentists, holding one of her own extracted teeth. The font is unusual here – and rather gratifying – since among its wildmen in skins and wielding clubs, is a woman. Nice!

Blythburgh (Suffolk) Popularly known as the Cathedral of the Marshes, this is one of the county's most celebrated churches. Building began in 1412, and completed some 80 years later. In those days it had a steeple but during a violent thunderstorm in 1577 the steeple crashed through the roof and was never rebuilt. This was the devil's work: they found scorch marks near north door made by his fingers as he made his escape. The church's glory is its life-sized roof angels, spreading their wings across the central beam. Cromwell's men did a thorough job on this church, smashing the stained glass windows and the crucifixes and statues, but they couldn't reach the angels. Below, are some earthly sins carved into the bench ends, including Sloth who is just considering getting out of bed.

Mildenhall (Suffolk) Another 'angel church', where every available beam or wooden structure is carved into a guardian angel. They hover with outstretched wings or peer down at the congregation below, complementing other carvings of biblical or secular scenes.

Thornham Parva (Suffolk) This is a still-to-be-looked-at-properly church. I only caught a glimpse of it as I passed by bus, but the image of this little thatched church is still vivid in my mind. Jenkins describes the wall paintings inside, and 14th-century painted saints. I will just have to come back.

the way they had been in the inter-war period. Memories of many of the farms I visited have blurred with the passing of time but I vividly recall visiting one small and rather old-fashioned place near North Walsham, more of a large smallholding than anything else, which was lovingly farmed by a wonderful old couple. After I had looked around and made my notes, the farmer gave me a mug of tea and took me to one side, 'Some people might cart right across the world looking for beautiful scenery but we are blessed, we've got it right here.' He gazed across a dung-covered farmyard alive with feeding swallows, past a rickety old barn to the fields beyond. 'Have a look at that view, will you? Have you ever seen anything better than that? Me and the missus never go on holiday and we've never been abroad either. What's the point when you've got all this on your doorstep?' I didn't have the slightest doubt about his sincerity – and he was absolutely right, it *was* a lovely view in a bucolic, John Constable sort of way. He was a wise and happy man, this old farmer; perhaps the perfect ambassador of what the Slow outlook is all about.

Hamish Fulton, whose art results from the experience of walking, once staged an exhibition entitled *An Object Cannot Compete with an Experience*. It's a mantra that stands me in good stead. The Slow movement is all about savouring the moment. A good meal taken slowly is an experience, so is a long walk with never-to-be forgotten views. So is a conversation that gives you an insight into someone else's life and celebrates a shared humanity. It's about a sense of being where you are, what makes it special, what makes it unique.

While I was writing this book, I was fortunate to attend a talk by the writer Richard Mabey who was discussing the paintings of Mary Newcomb, a recently deceased local artist whose works were on display in a special exhibition at Norwich Castle Museum. Mary Newcomb's gloriously naive, almost Zen-like, paintings, along with Richard Mabey's insightful appraisal, helped me realise that an appreciation of the subtle beauty of rural East Anglia depends on having an eye for detail and a fondness for the drama of small events.

Perhaps that is what the essence of Slow is: finding the extraordinary in the commonplace – that which makes a place distinctive. Everywhere has these qualities to some extent; it is just that, in terms of distinctiveness, Norfolk and Suffolk probably have more than their fair share. Let's not get carried away, there are places here as humdrum as anywhere else but the thing to do is to scrape away the veneer a little and see what is beneath.

People who have close contact with the land generally know this. The Northamptonshire shepherd poet John Clare, who modestly and perhaps disingenuously claimed, 'I found the poems in the fields, and only wrote them down, extolled the spirit of Slow when he wrote:'

O who can pass such lovely spots
Without a wish to stray
And leave life's cares a while forgot
To muse an hour away?

I hope this book will help to inspire some happy musing.

Request for feedback

Norfolk and Suffolk are stuffed with people who have specialist knowledge on their part of the region, and although we've done our best to check our facts there are bound to be errors as well as the inevitable omissions of really special places. You can post your comments and recommendations, and read the latest feedback from other readers online at http://updates.bradtguides.com/norfolk&suffolk.

How to use this book

The **colour map** at the front of this book shows which area falls within which chapter. Each chapter begins with a more detailed **chapter map** highlighting places mentioned in the text.

(1) (2) (3) To guide you round, each featured place is given a **circled number** corresponding to the same circled number on the map. Points are numbered consecutively as they occur in the text, making it easy to locate them on the map.

S) This symbol denotes a **pub** recommended in Alastair Sawday's *Pubs & Inns of England & Wales*.

S1 **S2** These symbols appear on the chapter maps at the start of each chapter, as well as on the colour map at the start of the book. These refer to the 30 **Sawday's Special Places to Stay**, which are described fully in the second colour section.

To give clarity to some descriptions of localities – particularly walks – simple **sketch maps** are included. They are intended merely to set the scene rather than to provide detailed information.

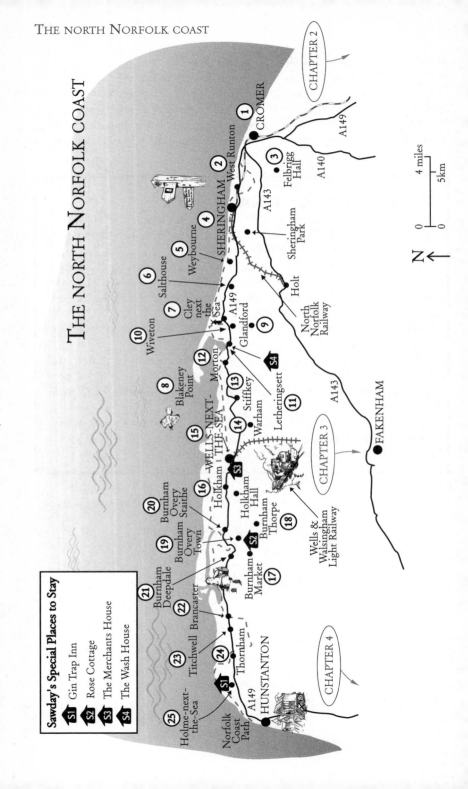

THE NORTH NORFOLK COAST

Sawday's Special Places to Stay

S1 Gin Trap Inn
S2 Rose Cottage
S3 The Merchants House
S4 The Wash House

CHAPTER 2

CHAPTER 3

CHAPTER 4

N

0   4 miles
0   5km

CROMER

West Runton

Felbrigg Hall

A149

A140

A143

Sheringham Park

SHERINGHAM

Weybourne

Holt

North Norfolk Railway

Salthouse

Cley next the Sea

A149

Wiveton

Glandford

Morton

Blakeney Point

WELLS-NEXT-THE-SEA

Stiffkey

Warham

Letheringsett

A143

FAKENHAM

Holkham

Holkham Hall

Burnham Thorpe

Wells & Walsingham Light Railway

Burnham Overy Staithe

Burnham Overy Town

Burnham Market

Burnham Deepdale

Titchwell

Brancaster

Thornham

Holme-next-the-Sea

Norfolk Coast Path

A149

HUNSTANTON

1. THE NORTH NORFOLK COAST

From the slightly faded Victorian resort of **Cromer** to the village of **Holme-next-the-Sea**, the north Norfolk coast stretches resplendently east to west (which is how this chapter is ordered): a classic landscape of wide beaches, salt marshes, offshore sandbanks, muddy tidal inlets and all-too-rare harbours. This is the Norfolk that most city-dwellers hanker after: big skies, golden beaches and neat pebble-built cottages; mewing gulls and fishing boats beached in the mud. This stretch of coastline is quite unlike any other place in the British Isles,

and has been designated an AONB (Area of Outstanding Natural Beauty). The icing on the cake is that there are even some modest hills here, with **Beacon Hill** near Cromer – a tad over a hundred metres high – marking the highest point of the ridge where the southbound glaciations of the last ice age finally gave up the ghost as they deposited chunks of Scandinavia and North Sea seabed on Norfolk soil.

In spring, the road verges are emerald green with alexanders, a plant related to celery (of which it tastes strongly) that is particularly abundant at the coast and was recently considered for selection as the county flower of Norfolk. Predictably, the powers that be chose the poppy instead – a safe, if less representative, choice. In summer, the saltings glow purple with large swathes of sea lavender, and, with bright blue skies, the coastal marshes become an impressionist painting of sea, sand and sky. Autumn brings waves of migrating birds, and the bushes twitch with freshly landed migrants at this time of year, as do the salt marshes where exotic waders feed cheek by jowl much to the delight of birdwatchers. In winter, the sky is often alive with noisy flocks of geese in their thousands. In fact, if you can put up with onshore wind that seems to hail directly from the Arctic, a bright, crisp winter's day is hard to beat for a bracing walk along the seashore followed by lunch in a cosy pub.

With a range of distinct habitats for wildlife that include salt marshes, sand dunes, pebble banks, reed beds and woodland, it is hardly surprising that birds – even some rarities – are found everywhere, and that conservation bodies like the RSPB and NWT (Norfolk Wildlife Trust) have several reserves along this coast, as does the National Trust. In fact, **Cley-next-the-Sea**, a village with the vast **NWT Cley Marshes Nature Reserve** of salt marshes and reed beds, has long been considered one of the best sites for birding in the entire British Isles. Seals are easy to see too, and a boat trip out among them is invariably a hit with visitors of all ages.

This coast is largely a place of small fishing villages that have turned, in part

1

at least, to tourism. Flint and pebble rules supreme, with whole villages – houses, pubs, churches, even bus shelters constructed out of these plentiful beach materials. It's almost a surprise that public phone boxes aren't made out of them – since public conveniences generally are.

Getting around

Public transport

This is surprisingly good – far better than the dire situation a decade or two ago when travelling the coast required either a car or a willingness to hitchhike. Thankfully, the excellent and convenient **Bittern Line** (www.bitternline.com) links Norwich with Cromer and Sheringham on the coast. This, in turn, connects with the superbly useful **Coasthopper** bus service that runs regularly – every half hour or so in summer – between Sheringham and Hunstanton, calling at each village along the way as well as stopping on request – very useful indeed for walks along the coast. Easy connections can be made from Hunstanton down to King's Lynn, which is connected to Cambridge (but not Norwich) by rail. Coasthopper drivers are generally excellent ambassadors for the north Norfolk coast and are courteous and helpful in the extreme, so if you are unsure as to where to get off, just ask. A **Bittern Line Rover ticket** at £7 per adult, £3.50 per child, entitles unlimited travel at weekends and any time after 8.45am Mondays to Fridays, as well as free travel on the Coasthopper 36 bus service – a veritable bargain. Trains

run more or less hourly during the daytime and evenings Monday to Saturday, with a two-hourly service on Sundays. As well as the Bittern Line, there are a couple of short-distance, privately owned heritage railway lines that, while tourist-oriented, can sometimes come in useful for getting about. The **North Norfolk Railway** (01263 820800; www.nnrailway.co.uk), also known as the **'Poppy Line'**, runs between Sheringham and Holt (see Sheringham) and the **Wells and Walsingham Light Railway** (01328 711630; www.wellswalsinghamrailway.co.uk) plies the eight miles between Wells-next-the-Sea and Little Walsingham.

Walking

Exploring on foot can be sublime along this stretch of coast. It's flat certainly, but here you'll find some of the best marsh and coast walking anywhere in the country. The **Norfolk Coast Path**, which links to the **Peddars Way** at Holme-next-the-Sea before meandering 44 miles eastwards to Cromer, takes in nearly all of the best bits: the whole thing, known rather clumsily as the Peddars Way & Norfolk Coast Path, is a National Trail, with the route shown with acorn markers. Quite a lot of the coastal portion leads along grassy sea walls that zigzag between drained grazing land (much of it drained by Coke of Holkham, the agricultural pioneer) and vast expanses of seemingly impenetrable saltmarsh cut by countless creeks and gulleys. Sections of the Peddars Way and Norfolk Coast Path make for excellent day walks, although circular walks will sometimes entail a stretch along the busy A149 coast road, which is tolerable but not really that much fun. In all honesty, with the exception of the paths through the Holkham estate and the sandy heaths behind Cromer and Sheringham, the walking is not nearly so good away from the coast anyway, even if you do manage to avoid the awful coast road. This is where the Coasthopper bus service really comes into its own: walk in one direction along a stretch of coast; take the bus back – the ideal solution. Those expecting stereotypical Norfolk flatness may be surprised when they venture a little way inland from the coast, but ropes and climbing gear are not required.

Away from the coast, three magnificent estates have free year-round access for walkers, with lots to look at: **Felbrigg**, **Holkham** and **Sheringham Park**.

North Norfolk coast walking highlights

Cromer to Sheringham, following the Norfolk Coast Path, which ventures inland to take in some modest hills and Norfolk's highest point. Returning from Sheringham, you can either take the train back or walk along the beach beneath the cliff.

Blakeney to Cley-next-the-Sea, following the North Coast Path, taking the dyke out through the marshes to Cley Channel before heading inland towards Cley village along the bank of the River Glaven.

Cley-next-the-Sea to Salthouse, alternating between the beach and sea wall.

Burnham Overy Staithe to Holkham Gap, walking along the dyke and beach, then returning by bus. You can extend the walk through the Holkham estate, across fields to Burnham Overy Town, and back.

Burnham Deepdale to Burnham Overy Staithe, along the dyke, returning by bus.

Holme-next-the-Sea to Thornham, following the North Coast Path along the beach and dykes, perhaps having a drink at the Lifeboat on the way back.

Cycling

Along the coast itself the prospects are not as good for two wheels as they are for two legs. The Norfolk Coast Path is a footpath, not a bridleway, and so it's out of bounds for cyclists (and horses). In summer, the A149 has far too much motor traffic along it to be enjoyable for most cyclists, and inattentive holiday drivers rubber-necking the scenery are an additional hazard.

A better bet is to make use of the **Norfolk Coast Cycleway**, a route just inland from the coast that links King's Lynn with Cromer (and Great Yarmouth), using National Cycle Network Route 1 between King's Lynn and

Wighton (southeast of Wells-next-the-Sea) and Regional Route 30 on to Cromer and Great Yarmouth. Felbrigg and Sheringham Park estates also have some very family-friendly traffic-free cycle routes.

The **Norfolk Coast Partnership** North Norfolk District Council (Holt Rd, Cromer, Norfolk NR27 9EL ☎ 01263 513811) has produced a map of the entire Norfolk Coast Cycleway that is available for £2 from tourist information centres or direct by post from them (postage is extra). Ten Explorer tours of between six and forty miles are also offered as circular day routes.

> **Huff and Puff Cycles** Kelling Heath Holiday Park in Weybourne ☎ 07788 132909 ✆ www.cyclenorfolk.co.uk. They have cycles for hire and useful suggestions for routes, some easy, some more demanding, that may actually require a degree of huffing and puffing.
>
> **On Yer Bike Cycle Hire** Nutwood Farm, Wighton ☎ 01328 820719 or 07799 647330 ✆ www.norfolkcyclehire.co.uk. Situated on Norfolk Coast Cycleway Route 30, they have bikes for hire that may also be collected from, or delivered to, Burnham Deepdale Information Centre further west along the coast.

Tourist information

Cromer Prince of Wales Rd ☎ 0871 200 3071.
Sheringham Station Approach, Station Rd ☎ 01263 824329.
Wells–next-the-Sea Staithe St ☎ 01328 710885.
North Norfolk Coast Area of Outstanding Natural Beauty see ✆ www.norfolkcoastaonb.org.uk.

The end of the line: Cromer and Sheringham

Cromer and Sheringham, the last places on the Bittern Line, are a long way from any notion of wild, remote Norfolk. With origins as modest fishing ports they were both developed as resorts during the late Victorian period. They were fashionable once but nowadays are often dismissed as old-fashioned or faded. I still have a soft spot for them both, though – especially Cromer, and especially out of season when winter wind whips up the sea and rattles the pier.

If you find yourself at a loss as to what to do in Cromer, East of England Tourism have produced a practical guide to sustainable tourism in the town, which is available both online (www.eet.org.uk) and as a printed booklet.

① Cromer

'I am not enjoying myself very much,' a young, homesick Winston Churchill once wrote home to his mother regarding his stay in Cromer. For some reason – hurt pride, perhaps – Cromer's town council have seen fit to commit these words to posterity and Churchill's youthful words are now engraved in the town's seafront promenade. As they say, there is no such thing as bad publicity.

Cromer became popular as a family resort in the late 19th century when the **railway** link to Norwich and London was established and those who could afford it would escape the capital's infernal smog and come here to grab a healthy lungful of north Norfolk air. Cromer's first railway station came into service in 1877, somewhat inconveniently located at the town's outskirts, but ten years later 'Cromer Beach' station was opened right in the centre of town.

Even before the steam age, city dwellers had come to Cromer to breathe its bracing salt air. Daniel Defoe came here in the 1720s and Jane Austen visited in the early 19th century and later wrote of it in *Emma*: 'Perry was a week at Cromer once, and he holds it to be the best of all the sea-bathing places.' Although popular in the Victorian period with the families of Norfolk's banking aristocracy like the Gurneys, it took a prince – and a railway – to really put it on the map. The future King Edward VII did just that when he started coming here to play golf at the end of the 19th century (probably one of the more innocent activities that the prince got up to whilst gallivanting in Norfolk away from the watchful gaze of his mother and wife). Around the same time, the journalist, Clement Scott, started to write about the resort in the London papers and inevitably, with its easy access by train, and prior royal approval, it soon became a popular holiday resort with the late-Victorian chattering classes. The German Kaiser, Oscar Wilde and the aforementioned Winston Churchill all subsequently came to see for themselves.

These days, Cromer is probably best known for two things: crabs and its pier. **Crabs** are still caught here and are as sweet and delicious as ever. The **pier**, however, has had a rather troubled life over the past half-century or so. It was badly damaged by storms in 1953 and 1989, and in 1993 suffered the ignominy of being sliced in half by a  storm-tossed drilling rig that had broken adrift. Currently it is in rude health and the only place in the country where you can still take in a genuine end-of-the-pier show of the likes of the Grumbleweeds or a Patsy Cline tribute show, or the annual **Folk on the Pier** weekend held in May (www.folkonthepier.co.uk); these take place at the **Pavilion Theatre** (01263 512495; www.cromer-pier.com). Otherwise just do what everybody else does and take a stroll along it. Looking back towards land from its end you can admire Cromer's grand neo-gothic hotels along the cliff-top beach road with their towers, turrets and elegant picture windows. Sadly, with British seaside holidays spiralling out of favour over recent decades, many of Cromer's hotels have gone the way of those in other resorts and struggle for business. Directly facing the pier, the **Hotel de Paris** manages to maintain an air of slightly faded elegance. It bids 'non-residents welcome' above its door, but I could not find any staff on duty when I last ventured inside in search of afternoon tea. There again, this was on an exceptionally blustery day in mid-winter. TV polymath Stephen Fry claims to have worked here as a waiter in his youth – so perhaps they are still looking for his replacement?

The true heart of Cromer is not in the narrow streets of the railway-age resort that stretch behind the main promenade, pleasant though they are, but in the far older **fishing community** that lies immediately east of the pier. This is Cromer's 'crab central', where small, clinker-built boats are launched from the beach, and where Cromer's redoubtable *Number One Lifeboat* is housed. The indisputable hero of the Cromer Lifeboat tradition is Henry Blogg (1876–1954), who remains the most decorated of any lifeboatman in the United Kingdom. Cromer's central **Church of St Peter & St Paul** has a stained-glass window commemorating the man (and another lovely window by Burne-Jones) as well as the tallest church tower in the county. The **RNLI Henry Blogg Lifeboat Museum** (01263 511294; www.rnli.org.uk/henryblogg) is dedicated to the history of the Cromer Lifeboat and, naturally enough, Henry Blogg also figures prominently. There is a life-size figure of the former coxwain with his dog here, as well as the *H F Bailey*, a rescue vessel that came into service in 1935 and saved over 500 lives during its tenure as the town's lifeboat. The **Cromer Museum** (01263 513543; www.museums.norfolk.gov.uk) also has some absorbing exhibits, mostly concerned with the Victorian 'bygone days' theme. Its geology gallery features a few bones from the famous 'West Runton Elephant', whose skeleton was found propping up the cliffs just to the west of here (see page 8).

Cromer is not a place for fancy dining, rather it's somewhere for fish and chips on the promenade or afternoon scones in a teashop.

Buttercups Tearooms 5 High St ☎01263 510990. Tucked away behind the Esplanade, this is a good place for afternoon tea. Scones come with a choice of jam.

Davies' Fish Shop 7 Garden St ☎01263 512727. Considered by many to be the best place to buy freshly boiled or dressed crabs. The Davies family have been catching and cooking them for generations. Lobsters and wet fish are also available.

Flint Cottage Restaurant & Coffee Shop 1a Church St ☎01263 513178. A cosy place for a cooked breakfast or afternoon tea.

Mary Janes Fish Bar & Restaurant 27–29 Garden St ☎01263 511208. Of the fish and chip shops, this is considered by many to be the best.

Rocket Café The Gangway, Promenade ☎01263 514334. A bright modern café and restaurant conveniently situated directly above the Lifeboat Museum. Have your coffee outside on the balcony and watch the crab boats go about their business.

Cromer crabs

Cromer crabs may be a little on the small side but they are universally loved for their plump, sweet meat. The best come from the waters just offshore from Cromer and Sheringham. The crabs are *Cancer pagarous*, exactly the same species as other British edible crabs, so it is hard to tell what it is that makes them so special and distinctive in taste. It may be that they are especially slow growing and so fill their shells with meat more plentifully, or that they contain more sweet white meat than their counterparts do. Alternatively, it may be that the seabed here has less mud than other parts of coastal UK and this influences the flavour. Whatever it is, their reputation has ensured a decent living for Cromer and Sheringham's small crabbing community over the years. Not that long ago, around fifty crab boats used regularly to put out to sea from Cromer's beach, but these days just a handful remain.

Crabbing technique involves the setting of long lines of baited pots called 'shanks' in the rocky offshore waters. These are marked with buoys and left overnight, to be hauled in again the next day and re-baited with white fish once the catch has been removed. Men work in pairs to haul in the lines, remove the crabs and re-bait the pots. Sorting takes place at sea and a good four-fifths are returned to the water simply because they are too small.

The crabbing season usually begins in March when crabs can be found relatively close to shore – they tend to retreat further out to sea to deeper waters during the colder months. The season lasts until the autumn, although there is a lull in high summer when the crabs breed and grow new shells. As the saying goes, crabs should be eaten only in those months that do not have an 'R' in them – sound seasonal advice. Because it is on a relatively small scale, crabbing is also reassuringly sustainable, but in recent years, there has been concern about dwindling stocks, probably the consequence of offshore dredging and rising seawater temperatures caused by global warming disrupting breeding patterns. There may also be competition for food and habitat from velvet crabs, which are usually found in the South West but have been moving north thanks to warmer sea temperatures.

The crabber's secret, of course, is to know exactly where to lay his pots, and when to check them: the sort of thing that can only be learned by hard experience. Some Cromer crab dynasties like the Davies family have been catching and selling crabs – and manning the lifeboat – for generations. Cromer has a number of marvellous fish shops and the same families that catch the crabs often run these – Bob Davies' excellent fish shop is a case in point. Whether boiled or dressed, the important thing is freshness, so buying and eating one here is about as close as it gets to crustacean perfection.

② West Runton

The A149 coast road runs west through East Runton and West Runton to Sheringham, along manicured green cliff tops that are home to regimented caravan sites and golf courses. Arriving by train on the Bittern Line gives a slightly different perspective, and you may notice that West Runton station with its pretty garden has won awards for 'Best Unstaffed Station of the Year 2004' and 'Best Small Station 2006 (and 2007)'. Nothing since then though; have they let things slide?

A choicer but slower route to Sheringham is – tide permitting – on foot along the **beach**. Here you'll find chalky rock pools and soft crumbling cliffs that are home to fulmars and the odd fossilised mammoth. The so-called **West Runton Elephant** was discovered in the cliffs here by two locals back in 1990. The 'elephant' was, in fact, a steppe mammoth and turned out to be the largest, near-complete *Mammuthus trogotheni* skeleton ever found. The 600,000 year-old beast, which would have stood four metres tall and weighed around ten tonnes, twice the weight of an African elephant, was not fully excavated until 1995 when the Norfolk Archaeological Unit completed the task. Because of its weight and size, it is not possible to see the animal in its full, reconstructed glory but a few selected bones may be viewed in the Cromer and Norwich Castle museums.

Elephants aside, West Runton's other taste of fame comes from being home to the **West Runton Pavilion**, a venue that was used back in the 1970s and early 1980s by big-name rock bands wishing to begin national tours in a no-pressure, rural location. The Clash, Joy Division, Slade and, most famously, the Sex Pistols all played here in their heyday – not bad for a village of 1,600 with a rather elderly demographic. A blue plaque commemorates the venue on the original building today. West Runton is also the base of the **Norfolk Shire Horse Centre** (01603 736200; www.hillside.org.uk), which now goes under the name of Hillside Animal and Shire Horse Sanctuary as it operates under the auspices of the Hillside Animal Sanctuary at Frettenham near Norwich. The centre, which is open for visitors between April and October, has five breeds of heavy horse – Shire, Punch, Clydesdale, Percheron and Ardenne – as well as a collection of old farming machinery. Ploughing demonstrations are held each day and special blacksmith's days and sheepdog events are organised from time to time.

Shire horses are magnificent creatures and farmers used to form strong bonds with their beasts of burden. Horse ploughing was a common practice right up until the 1950s in some parts of Norfolk. I can remember talking to some older farmers back in the 1980s who spoke fondly of their working horses: the unquestioning companionship that these gentle giants offered ('gentle giant' may well be a dreadful cliché but here it is wholly appropriate), and the magic of the farmyard at dusk when the horses settled down for the night, snorting with satisfaction at the prospect of fresh hay and a warm stable.

West Runton parish is home Norfolk's highest point – **Beacon Hill** – that rises behind the southern reaches of West Runton as part of Cromer Ridge. The views from here, as you might expect, are good, as 345 feet of elevation counts for quite a lot in vertically challenged East Anglia. **Roman Camp**, just to the west, belongs to the National Trust and, despite the name, is not Roman at all but a set of Saxon and medieval iron workings. The Norfolk Coastal Path doesn't follow the coast hereabouts but instead passes just south of the camp en route to Cromer.

③ Felbrigg Hall

This 17th-century Jacobean country house is a magnificent National Trust property, just south of the A149 coast road and the rolling, rather un-Norfolk-like slopes of the hall's 520-acre Great Wood. Felbrigg's construction straddled the period of the English Civil War and the house's elegant Stuart architecture is beautifully complemented by its sumptuous Georgian interior and Gothic-style library. Outside, there is a nicely restored, and still productive, walled garden and a splendid 18th-century dovecote that stands centrepiece to a kitchen garden with potagers. Also of horticultural interest are extensive orchards filled with traditional 19th-century fruit varieties, a fine collection of camellias, an 18th-century orangery and a Victorian pleasure garden. The 1,760 acres of parkland, lakes and mature woodland have a number of waymarked trails that allow free access to walkers and cyclists in daylight hours.

Felbrigg Hall ☏ 01263 837444 ∽🖰 www.nationaltrust.org.uk. Open early Apr–end Oct; closed Thu and Fri. Gardens also open Mar.

④ Sheringham

As with Cromer, Sheringham is a crab- and lobster-fishing centre that became a resort with the arrival of the railway. Like supporters of rival teams at a local football derby, the Cromer and Sheringham crabbing communities were historically antagonistic towards each other until the realities of modern life required them to cooperate.

Although Sheringham has its neon-bright amusement arcades and might seem a bit tacky and 1960s in feel it is a nice enough place for gentle pursuits like walks on the beach and afternoon tea, and does have tangible civic pride. As plaques outside the Poppy Line station will inform you, Sheringham has won numerous Anglia in Bloom awards and, in season, the town has more bedding plants than you can shake a trowel at. For entertainment beyond pubs and strolls, the **Sheringham Little Theatre** (01263 822347; www.sheringhamlittletheatre.com) in Station Road is just that: a 170-seat regional theatre that manages to survive by putting on a mixture of repertory plays and blockbuster Hollywood films.

West of the town, south of the coast road, lies **Sheringham Park** (National

Trust, free access 01263 820550; www.nationaltrust.org.uk), landscaped by Humphry Repton in 1812 and with a dazzling purple display of rhododendrons in early summer. Many consider the park to be Repton's finest work – he described it as his 'favourite and darling child in Norfolk'. There's an exhibition of the landscape architect's life and work at the Wood Farm Barn visitor centre at the southern edge of the park. The park surrounds Sheringham Hall, which is privately owned and may not be visited, but high above the hall there's a hilltop gazebo that is worth climbing to for its panoramic views along the coast and the wooded country behind it. As well as numerous waymarked walks through the extensive woodland at the south of the park, there's also a special Tree Trail taking you past some rare and unusual trees. The park is open dawn to dusk year-round, while the visitor centre is open daily from March 15 to September 30, Wednesday to Sunday in October, and weekends only in winter.

Close to Sheringham's main railway station, the terminus of the Bittern Line from Norwich, is the privately run **Poppy Line** station of the **North Norfolk Railway** (01263 820800; www.nnrailway.co.uk) that runs between Sheringham and Holt, with an intermediate station at Weybourne and a request stop at Kelling Heath. Both diesel and steam trains ply this route regularly in summer and there are special events like steam galas and family days held throughout the year. Weybourne station is convenient for Sheringham Park (a one mile walk to the entrance), while the request stop at Kelling allows for strolls among the heather and gorse bushes of **Kelling Heath**, which has a nature trail and offers a reasonable chance of witnessing nightjars whirring around at dusk in high summer. You can sometimes hear nightingales, quite rare this far north, singing from the blackthorn thickets too.

Station Road has a selection of cafés, fish and chip shops and pubs scattered along its route down to the sea.

The Lobster 13 High St, Sheringham ☏ 01263 822716 ⌂ www.the-lobster.com) has decent pub grub and a good range of beers, with fancier offerings in its Stables restaurant. **Craske's Bakery** at 36 High St is a decent bakery that sells rolls in the shape of crabs and lobsters.

⑤ Weybourne

Weybourne is a pretty, leafy village with a windmill that clings to the twisting coast road just west of Sheringham. Weybourne's North Norfolk Railway station lies a mile or so from the village. The station's greatest claim to fame is its use as a location for an episode of *Dad's Army* ('The Royal Train'). Norfolk featured quite prominently as a backdrop for this classic TV series – more on this elsewhere (see page 183).

The shingle beach at **Weybourne Hope** lies just north of the village past the ruins of an Augustinian priory founded in 1200. The beach is sloped steeply here, with relatively deep water offshore, enough to allow invading Danes to bring their boats right up to the shoreline in the 9th and 10th centuries. Such vulnerability was well-noted and, in keeping with an old saying that claims, 'He who would all England win, should at Weybourne Hope begin', defences were built in the 16th century to prevent possible attack by the Spanish Armada. The Spaniards never came but smugglers did, bringing 'tax-free' gin and tobacco to shore here, taking advantage of the ideal natural facilities of the beach and, indeed, all the coast between Sheringham and Weybourne. This strategic nervousness continued into the 20th century, when World War II anti-invasion measures included pillboxes, barbed wire and landmines. The garrison here, Weybourne Camp, became a top-secret military site during World War II and a training ground for anti-aircraft gunners. The camp continued with fresh intakes of national servicemen until it closed in 1959, a year before conscription was abolished.

Ship Inn The Street ☎ 01263 588721 🖥 www.shipinnweybourne.co.uk. A convivial pub that makes a point of only serving beers that are made within the county such as Woodforde's from Woodbastwick and Yetman's from Holt. The bar menu mostly incorporates local ingredients like Marston mussels and Weybourne crab.

Saltmarshes and samphire: from Salthouse to Stiffkey

West of Kelling, the north Norfolk coast starts to take on the character that brings delight so many: glistening silver channels snaking through saltmarshes, marram-tufted sand dunes and shingle banks. And birds of course – mewing, piping, quacking and warbling – everywhere, birds.

⑥ Salthouse

Salthouse is a typical north Norfolk coastal flint village with an impressive church for such a small place. Its name actually does derive from 'salt' as salt-panning was a viable industry in medieval times all along England's east coast. Being this close to Cley-next-the-Sea, this is superb birding territory and the Norfolk Wildlife Trust owns the saltmarshes that shelter behind the shingle bank. In winter, large flocks of Brent geese cloud the sky here, and a variety of slender waders probe the marshes for food. Even more exotic, Arctic species like snow buntings and shore larks can be found on the beach at this time of year. Other migrants often turn up in the marshes and dunes on passage. As with all of this coastline, the quietest time of year in avian terms just happens to coincide with that which is busiest for human activity – August.

Cookie's Crab Shop The Green ☎ 01263 740352 🖰 www.salthouse.org.uk. On The Green next to the 'Lug Bait' sign, Cookie's is well known locally as a place to buy shellfish and order seafood platters, sandwiches and salads. A large selection of fishy combinations are available, including delicacies like kipper-and-tomato soup, and smoked-mackerel-and-horseradish-sauce sandwiches. Although the premises are not licensed, customers are welcome to bring their own drinks.

Dun Cow Coast Rd ☎ 01263 740467 🖰 www.theduncow-salthouse.co.uk. A conveniently placed pub in a 17th-century building that served as a blacksmith's in a former life. It has local cask ales and a good range of pub grub on the menu. Birders will be pleased to know that there is a telescope in the pub garden.

⑦ Cley-next-the-Sea

As anyone with even a passing interest in birds will tell you, Cley is *the* birding Mecca – it really is. All of the north Norfolk coast is good, of course, but Cley-next-the-Sea has that bit extra, those few essential ingredients: a wide range of natural habitats for breeding and feeding, a prime position on bird migration routes, sensible and long-established farming practices and, above all, plenty of goodwill towards feathered creatures. At peak times of spring and autumn migration, Cley can get very busy, with cars nose-to-tail on the A149 and the NWT car park filled to bursting. Usually, it is perfectly manageable though; the reserve is a big place and, with wonderful walks across the marshes and along the pebble bank and out to Blakeney Point, there is something for everyone here, even those who don't quite know their dunnocks from their dunlins.

The **NWT visitor centre** and car park are on the A149 just east of the village, with the entrance to the reserve and access to some of the hides just across the road. You'll find a very decent range of bird books and birding paraphernalia at the visitor centre, while the café has a choice view over the reserve's marshes. You can peruse the bird log at reception.

With birders and twitchers in abundance, most of the colour on show in the Cley area is green – ex-military camouflage clothing, green binoculars (preferably Zeiss) and probably a 'scope and tripod. It must be said that the total value of the 'optics' (for that is what birders call their 'bins' and telescopes) on display here at any given time probably exceeds the GNP of a small African country.

This is very much birding nirvana. There cannot be many places where you can savour a Danish pastry and cappuccino while enjoying the spectacle of dense flocks of Brent geese rising above the marshes, avocets tirelessly scything the mud or even the rare public appearance of a bittern. If this is not enough you can always peruse the bookshelves and fantasise about the exotic birdlife of southeast Asia, where kingfisher species run to dozens.

A beginner's guide to Norfolk birders

So what differentiates a birder from a twitcher? If you are visiting Cley for the first time then it is better that you know. Simply put, a common or garden **birder** is someone who is knowledgeable about birds, likes them, wants to protect them and goes out of his (and increasingly *her*) way to seek them out in their natural habitat. A **twitcher** is all of the above, but with the extra dimension of being preoccupied with listing new and rare species. Of course, the really rare species are in anything but their natural habitat – they are supposed to be in a North American forest or the Siberian taiga rather than stranded in a lonely north Norfolk marsh with no ticket home. The defining characteristic of a twitcher is his (and rarely *her*) 'list', or rather, lists: UK list, Norfolk list, year list, life list etc. Some twitchers will also extend their lists to other life forms such as butterflies or dragonflies (or more personally, to girlfriends or real ales sampled). It is a man thing: try not to judge them too harshly.

Occasionally, the live theatre of a 'twitch' can be seen being played out at Cley or its environs. It is an easy phenomenon to identify: a murmuring green-camouflage army, brandishing telescopes like bazookas, will remain motionless and silent for some considerable time before a sudden flurry of activity occurs and there is a mass movement to a fresh viewpoint. The simple explanation: the elusive and rare bird that had fled from view some time ago has just been 'relocated'.

Cley-next-the-Sea has far more than just birds, of course. It is a charming flint-and-pebble village with wonderful walking potential right at its doorstep. You could easily enjoy a stay here without having the remotest interest in birdlife.

Cley Mill, the windmill here, is a north Norfolk icon, featuring in innumerable guidebooks and articles about the county. It is, indeed, rather beautiful, and, serving as a B&B, a wonderful place to stay.

Otherwise, just stand back, admire, and take your own souvenir photograph. The mill dates from the 18th century and first went up for sale in 1819. It changed hands frequently over the next hundred years, eventually falling into disrepair after World War I. In 1921, the mill was converted into a holiday home by Sarah Maria Wilson, who later passed it on to her grandson Hubert Blount in 1934. Although the 1953 floods damaged the building, it managed to survive and, in 1979, Charles and Jane Blount, parents of the army officer turned singer-songwriter James Blount, took over the running of the place. It passed into its present ownership in 2005.

Cley's High Street has some lovely buildings and a handful of quaint shops that include an excellent **smokehouse** and **delicatessen** (see below). There is quite a diversity of building styles: a mixture of flint and brick, with some pebble dash and the odd Dutch gable. The terrace next to the George pub even has an interesting art deco front to the street. But it is Cley's unsung nooks and crannies that make it such a pleasure to wander around. There is a heavily weathered stone arch on the High Street – the entrance to two cottages – that has a framed poem on the wall inside: *The Hardest Heart* by Anne Clark. Elsewhere, charming little alleyways lead down to the mill and marshes from the high street. If you head down the one that lies opposite Crabpot Books, turn around after passing under the archway to see the panel of St George and the Dragon set in the wall above. Cley also has an excellent pub, **The George**, which in those halcyon days before mobile phones, the internet and Twitter served as an operational centre for birders on trips to the coast. So did the café, now closed, next door. I recall many an occasion scouring the visitors' bird book there while I scoffed large chunks of bread pudding and toyed with the idea of braving the winter wind out on the marshes. The old café in the beach car park also had a similar book that recorded bird sighting and was filled with enigmatic entries like 'V. Scoter ?, out to sea, flying W'. Sadly, this convivial place has recently disappeared along with the car-park toilet block, the result of savage storm tides, but there are still a couple of excellent teashops in the village.

Strictly speaking, Cley (pronounced 'Cly' by the way, not 'Clay') is no longer 'next-the-Sea', but it once stood at the mouth of the River Glaven. Although it is hard to believe looking at it today, in the Middle Ages the river was navigable for even quite large boats as far as Glandford. Cley subsequently became a prosperous port exporting wool, grain and fish to the Low Countries until it began to silt up in the 17th century, mainly the result of unsuccessful land reclamation work carried out by Sir Henry Calthorpe.

St Margaret's Church

A little way along the Holt road stands St Margaret's Church, the largest in the Glaven Valley, overlooking the village green with the Three Swallows pub (01263 740526) – the perfect name for bird-mad Cley. Appropriate too, as swallows – usually far in excess of three – tend to gather on the telegraph wires above the green, taking turns to swoop down for flies.

Back in the days when Cley served as a port the church would have looked straight down on the harbour. Silting up has left this magnificent building high and dry, and it is sobering to think that it would have been even larger and more impressive had work not ceased when the Black Death devastated the village in 1349. The church has a bright, unusually cheerful interior, with graves among the flagstones and secondhand paperbacks for sale. Its porch, stained glass and carved bench ends are all of interest but some might find themselves more drawn to the display that documents the arrival of an American white-crowned sparrow to a nearby garden in January 2008. Naturally, the arrival of this extremely rare bird, which looks rather like an ordinary sparrow wearing a cycle helmet, heralded a vast influx of birders eager to tick it off. The sparrow was amenable enough to hang around until March of that year, although there was much nervousness as to whether a local cat, 'Hooligan', might end up making a meal of it.

I came across a local man in the church who had taken on the responsibility of managing the church's resident **bat population**. 'The bats are a real nuisance', he told me, 'There are two sorts – one that flies straight out after waking up, and another that needs to have a good old fly around before it leaves the church. We've got both sorts here and it's my job to clear up their mess.' The guano-removal man was eager to show me around, pointing out a wooden boss in the porch that depicts a country woman seeing off a fox attacking her goose – a charming vignette of no religious significance whatsoever. He took me back inside to show me the roof. 'It looks as if the walls are twisting outwards doesn't it? They're not of course – it's just an optical illusion. When they rebuilt the roof, some of the resin soaked into the masonry so they skimmed it and that created the effect of the walls falling outwards.' He went on to demonstrate the church's remarkable acoustics, which had not been lost on me anyway, as an acoustic guitarist had been using the church as a practice space since I had first arrived. As I made my move to leave, the bat-man chimed, 'It's a wonderful church, don't you think? So full of light.' He was quite right: the high clerestory windows seem to gather light of such quality that you can sense you are close to the coast without even stepping outside. Besides, a church that has resident bats and acoustic guitarists can do no wrong in my book.

Cley Smokehouse High St ☎ 01263 740282 ✆ www.cleysmokehouse.com. This excellent Cley institution has a wide range of quality smoked goods, all hand crafted on the premises.

Cley Windmill ☎ 01263 740209 ✆ www.cleywindmill.co.uk. Although primarily a place to stay, this serves three-course, set-menu evening meals by candlelight to non-residents. Advance booking is essential.

Cookes of Cley Tearoom High St ☎ 01263 740776 ✆ www.cookes-of-cley.co.uk. With lobster pots lined up outside, this traditional tearoom is a good bet for coffee, a light lunch or an afternoon cream tea.

⑤ George Hotel High St ☎ 01263 740652. A rambling Edwardian Inn with a small outdoor beer garden overlooking the saltmarshes. It comes as no surprise that the Norfolk Naturalists' Trust first formed here. The extensive menus champion local produce as much as possible; there is a comprehensive wine list and a choice of real ales.

Picnic Fayre The Old Forge ☎ 01263 740567 ✆ www.picnic-fayre.co.uk. Where else could you expect to buy lavender bread, or have an antipasta bar to choose from? This delicatessen, established in 1984, is the place where north Norfolk's foodies come for their cheese, wine and speciality breads. It also has a good selection of organic vegetables and sumptuous takeaway pastries.

West Cottage Café New Rd. A cosy, convenient place for home-cooked light meals and cream teas. Located at the end of the village opposite the delicatessen, this has a sheltered walled garden for sunny tea-sipping and scone-nibbling.

To the sea and back from Cley

A recommended **walk** from Cley is to follow the footpath across the nature reserve from the pond (Snipes Marsh) on the main road, about half a mile east of the NWT visitor centre. To reach Snipes Marsh, turn right from the visitor centre and follow the coast

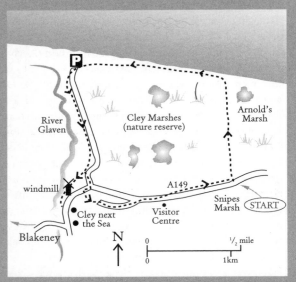

road east you reach it. Fortunately, there is a grass verge so you don't need to dodge the traffic too much. Just before the shingle bank is a large shallow pond called Arnold's Marsh, which is often full of wading birds. Climb up the shingle bank and admire the view back over the marshes to the low hills behind the village then follow the bank west to the beach car park.

The nature reserve is spread out beneath you as you walk scrunching gravel to the low background roar of the seas. In summer, there will be yellow horned poppies emerging improbably out of the shingle, seemingly existing on nothing other than stones and salt; in winter, you are likely to see small flocks of snow buntings flittering about like sparrows dipped in icing sugar. The onshore wind can be pretty keen in winter, vicious even, but it is my favourite time to be here when the elements seem to be at their most primordial. Even then, it is never completely deserted – this is Cley and birders are a tough breed.

At the beach car park, a road follows the course of a dyke back into Cley, where, just before the village, a footpath (part of the Norfolk Coast Path) veers off to the right to skirt the windmill before returning to the High Street. You'll then need to follow the coast road east back to the Visitor Centre. You might well prefer to avoid the A149 as much as possible – it is, after all, rather a busy road. One alternative might be to skip the little detour to the windmill and instead return directly to the A149 by way of the beach car-park road, cross over the coast road and take the little road left that runs parallel to it. This will bring you back to the A149 just before the Visitor Centre at the junction with Old Woman's Lane.

⑧ Blakeney Point

Blakeney Point is one of several spits along this coastline, the result of drifting sand and pebbles being deposited by offshore currents. The 'point' is a curious place that starts out as a narrow strip close to Cley beach car park before widening out to where marram-grass-covered dunes rise on its landward side opposite Blakeney harbour. As Norfolk's most northerly point (although, admittedly, inaccessible Scolt Head Island does just have the edge, but we're talking yards here) this is the Ultima Thule of East Anglia – a genuinely wild place, with nothing but open sea between here and the Arctic.

The point's western extremity is curved like a bird's claw – quite fitting really – and home to a visitor centre and colonies of nesting terns, also both common and grey seals. From Cley, it is a marvellous walk out to the end of the point: about four miles each way, but quite a tough four miles, as for most of the way it is a matter of trudging along pebbles – noisy work and tiring for the feet. Halfway along the spit is a hut called, rather unimaginatively, 'Halfway House'. Many years ago, I camped near here for a night (which I am not recommending, by the way: this is a nature reserve and, quite rightly, it is not now allowed). What struck me most was the eerie sensation of hearing the sea slap against the pebbles on both sides of me, inducing an odd sense of claustrophobia.

⑨ Glandford

Cley lies at the mouth of the **Glaven River** and the village of Glandford immediately to the south stands on the same river. There is a ford here by the watermill, too deep and tricky for most cars, and a footbridge. It's a charming spot full of birdsong and buzzing bees and the perfect objective for a gentle circular walk that might also take in Wiveton village and Wiveton Downs.

It may be just a tiny estate village, with Dutch-gabled cottages dating from the early 20th century, but Glandford does have its very own **Shell Museum** (01263 740081; www.shellmuseum.org.uk; closed in winter) next to the church – an eccentric place that has thousands of seashells in addition to quite a collection of fossils, birds' eggs and oddities such as a sugar bowl used by Queen Elizabeth I and a dried puffer fish. There is also the **Wildflower Centre** (01263 711091) nearby, just south along the road to Letheringsett, within the walled confines of the Bayfield estate, which, unlike Glandford, has a tearoom.

⑩ Wiveton

A little inland from the coast on the Blakeney to Letheringsett road is the small village of Wiveton, with a church, an excellent pub and a neat row of cottages overlooking a village green – a sleepy place in the best sense of the word. You may notice a road sign here that says 'Slow You Down', which is Norfolk-speak

17

for 'Slow'. Depending on your outlook, you might find this witty, slightly annoying or downright patronising. I tend to opt for both of the first two, while my wife, a Norfolk native, favours the third.

Wiveton Downs

Southwest of Wiveton stands the gorse-covered viewpoint of Wiveton Downs where there is an **esker**. An 'esker', as the information board will tell you, marks the past course of an underground river beneath a glacier. Some geologists scoff at this idea, however, arguing that if this were a true esker then it would be at right angles to the coast not parallel to it. Whatever, most locals come to walk their dogs rather than ponder Quaternary geomorphology. The gorse is particularly impressive here in spring, with a custard-almond pungency that almost knocks you off your feet. The views are lovely too: Cley Mill and Blakeney's St Nicholas' church are clearly visible, as is Blakeney's Old Rectory snuggled away in the lee of the hill behind the church. Looking inland, you should see a well-appointed metropolis of pigs just to the south; that is, unless the bottom has dropped out of the bacon market by the time that you read this.

S **The Wiveton Bell**, Blakeney Rd **☎** 01263 74101 ⌂ www.wivetonbell.co.uk. The whitewashed 18th-century Wiveton Bell, next to the village green and church, offers rustic charm and a sophisticated gastro-pub menu that utilises local ingredients. Adnams, Yetman's and Woodforde's ales are all on draught and there is a carefully selected wine list.
Wiveton Hall Fruit Farm Wiveton Hall, Holt NR25 7TE **☎** 01263 740525
⌂ www.wivetonhall.co.uk. Located on the A149 between Cley and Blakeney this has soft fruit and asparagus in season, and a café that is open between May and October.

⑪ Blakeney

The village of Blakeney slopes down narrow streets towards the harbour from the coast road where its magnificent 13th-century church of St Nicholas is located. Blakeney is picture-perfect north Norfolk in every sense, with all the classic coastal village ingredients: a tiny harbour, flint-pebble cottages, fishing boats and quaint little shops.

This was an active port far more recently than Cley, functioning as such until the early 1900s. Blakeney's eventual fate would be the same, however: the silting up of its estuary. It is this silting that characterises the coastal landscape here, with twisting muddy channels and creeks meandering out across the tidal flats of Blakeney Channel. Thankfully, the channels out to the sea are still navigable for smaller private craft at high tide and this is where Blakeney really comes into its own, as the village has become a favourite of north Norfolk's yachting set both for its moorings and for the unspoiled feel of the village itself. It is undoubtedly lovely but just a little unreal: a well-behaved ghost of the thriving port that it used to be. Even John Seymour writing about Blakeney back in the late 1960s in his *Companion Guide to East Anglia* reflected that: 'Certainly no fisherman could afford to buy a "fisherman's cottage" today,' adding, 'Blakeney is now what is called "select", meaning that many of its inhabitants have a lot of money. There is no "pin-table and Bingo culture" there'. Well, it is undoubtedly still select, and there is still no 'pin-table and Bingo culture' or 21st-century equivalent.

St Nicholas' Church, on the hill above the village, is well worth a look. You may notice something distinctly odd about this 13th-century church, sometimes referred to as 'the cathedral of the coast', when you first glimpse it. Above the chancel is a second tower that is much smaller than the main one to the west. This smaller tower was a 15th-century addition but its function is still a matter of debate. It used to burn a light as a beacon for Blakeney boats, but there is no reason why a second tower needed to be constructed especially for this purpose. Some think this incongruous addition may have been intended as a bell tower but, again, this makes little sense when the older, larger tower is far more suitable. The current church committee does not seem to have a firm opinion on this matter and invites visitors to write down their own suggestions on the pieces of paper provided. Simon Jenkins offers the thought that it may have been a private venture by a local patron wishing to rival the sponsor of the main tower. Undoubtedly, it does have something of the sense of a proud, if misguided, folly about it. Whatever the answer to this mystery, it is worth having a scout round and helping yourself to the generous free literature made available inside the church and, for a reminder of the long fishing tradition of this now somewhat sanitised village, take a look around the churchyard where you'll see plenty of fishermen's gravestones decorated with ropes and anchors.

You can buy excellent **fresh crabs, lobsters and oysters** from the house on the main road that lies just west of the church and displays the sign: **Blakeney Crab Shed**.

The Moorings High St ☎ 01263 740054 🖥 www.blakeney-moorings.co.uk. This modern, stylish bistro serves snacks and cappuccinos during the day and a full dinner menu in the evening. Booking is recommended for dinner or Sunday lunch. Local seasonal produce is used wherever possible.

Weston's Fish Shop 5a Westgate St ☎ 01263 741112 🖥 www.westonsofblakeney.co.uk. This small fish shop, which also does business from a trailer parked at Morston quay, specialises in Cromer crabs, Norfolk lobster and other local seafood products. It also sells home-cooked seafood platters to take away.

S⃝ White Horse Hotel 4 High St ☎ 01263 740574 🖥 www.blakeneywhitehorse.co.uk. The seafood here includes smoked salmon from Cley Smokehouse and mussels from Morston. As well as the cosy polished bar, which serves lunchtime food, there is an airy conservatory and the 'Long Room' for more formal dining. Adnams, Yetman's and Woodforde's ales are all served on draught, while Adnams of Southwold are responsible for the wine list.

Kayaking from Blakeney to Cley

Penny Edwards

I recently joined some friends on a Sunday morning in July when the tide was unusually high. We unchained the kayaks from the grassy area next to Blakeney Harbour and set off about 90 minutes before high tide, at about 9am. I had cycled out to Blakeney from Norwich and it felt good to be continuing to power myself, yet in a different medium. We made our way slowly past sailing boats and into New Cut – a channel joining Blakeney to Cley, created about three years ago to prevent flooding by the River Glaven.

It took us less than an hour to reach Cley Windmill. We didn't disembark because we were aware that the tide would not remain high for very long. On our return journey we stopped in New Cut to have a quick swim. We did this when the tide was near enough at its highest, and consequently the water was flowing so fast away from Blakeney that we found ourselves swimming on the spot making no forward progress whatsoever.

After a large breakfast, I set off back to Norwich feeling as revived as if I had been away on a week's holiday instead of just out for the day.

⑫ Morston: a seal-spotting boat trip

There is not that much to Morston, another medieval port that has since silted up and now lies two miles from the open sea. Nevertheless, this is the place to come to take a **boat trip** out to Blakeney Point to see the seals. Beans Boat Trips (01263 740505 or 740038; www.beansboattrips.co.uk) run from Morston Quay, with one-hour trips to view the seals and longer ones that land on Blakeney Point and spend up to an hour there. Times are dependent on tides. Temples Seal Trips, which have a ticket office in The Anchor pub (01263 740791; www.sealtrips.co.uk), and Bishop's Boats (01263 740753, freephone: 0800 0740754; www.norfolksealtrips.co.uk), operating from Blakeney Quay, all offer similar services. £8 for adults, £4 for children seems to be the going rate.

Viewing the **seals** is a slightly hit-and-miss business, despite their being 'guaranteed' by the boat companies. On an early May boat trip, Jason, one of the Beans Boats skippers, told me, 'We do get a few common seals but they come mostly later in the year. This time of year it's mostly grey seals – you can tell them from the common by their long, grey heads.' Out in Morston harbour, the seals were certainly a bit thin on the ground. 'You might want to call me a liar but, believe it or not, there are maybe

around a thousand seals out around here altogether. They do well here – there's plenty of fish to eat and no predators for them.' Although the seals were not out in number, the birds certainly were. 'There's four sorts of tern out here. There's common tern, with their red beaks, and Arctic, who look pretty similar. Little terns are quite a bit smaller, of course, and then there's Sandwich terns, which are the biggest of all of them and have a sort of crest on their heads.' Terns were, indeed, everywhere, gracefully dive-bombing the water for sand eels, but I had also spotted some poetic skeins of sleek, dark geese flying about in the distance. 'They're Brent geese,' said Jason, 'They come all the way from Russia and they should have gone back home by now. I don't know what they are doing here this late. Maybe they know something we don't.'

Chugging back to Morston harbour, past the bright blue warden's building out on Blakeney Point, Jason tells me about Morston's maritime history. 'That building was at the very end of Blakeney Point when it was first built but the spit has grown a lot longer over the last hundred years. Originally, it was a lifeboat station and the crew had to row three and a half miles out there from Morston just to reach it. They kept horses in stables out on the point and when the crew got there, they had to hitch the horses up to the lifeboat and drag it down to the shore. Then the crew had to row the lifeboat out to wherever the incident was. There was supposed to be a crew of 16 to man the boat but sometimes they had to make do with 12 or less. It took three or four hours just to get the lifeboat launched and when they had the job done they had to spend the same amount of time getting home again.' Clearly, the old days were not a time to be in any hurry to be saved. Still, the Morston lifeboat did manage to rescue over a hundred lives during its lifetime so it must have been doing something right. It finally went out of service in 1936 when Morston's rescue crew combined forces with the lifeboat at Wells.

SǪ The Anchor The Street ☎ 01263 741392. This cosy, whitewashed flint building has a number of intimate rooms to choose from for drinking and dining, as well as a beer garden for fine weather. The Anchor serves honest pub food that includes local seafood and has some good Norfolk beers on offer.
Morston Hall ☎ 01263 741041 🖰 www.morstonhall.com. A luxurious hotel, which opens its Michelin-starred restaurant to non-residents for breakfast, afternoon tea, dinner and Sunday lunch. Booking is essential.

⑬ Stiffkey

Heading west from Morston towards Wells-next-the-Sea along a road bright green with shiny fresh Alexanders in spring, you'll pass through Stiffkey, a village with both an odd name and an eccentric reputation. Stiffkey has earned local renown for being the home of 'Stewkey blues', blue cockles that are gathered on the Stiffkey Salt Marshes north of the village. It is said to be the mud that gives them their distinctive blue coloration.

The village is an attractive place of flint and pebble houses, and even the motor traffic on the busy A149 that passes right through can do little to assuage its obvious charm. The jury is still out on whether the village – and the river that passes through it – should be pronounced 'Stiff-key', as it is spelled, or 'Stew-key' in keeping with its famous shellfish. Opinions seem to differ, even between locals, so it's probably best to stick with the phonetic version lest you appear to be trying a bit too hard.

The east end of the village has the church of **St John the Baptist** alongside the ruins of an earlier church, St Mary's, in the same churchyard. South of this, **Stiffkey Old Hall**, the once spectacular property of the Bacon family, now lies in ruins and all that remains today is a gatehouse and part of one wing of the house. One of Stiffkey's former rectors, the **Reverend Harold Davidson**, who preached at the church and occupied the village's grand Georgian rectory during the interwar period, was a controversial figure who gained notoriety for attending the spiritual needs of fallen women from London. The Rector went on to become known as the 'Prostitutes' Padre' as a result – hardly the best moniker for a man of the cloth, especially in an isolated north Norfolk village. Such a crusade was an invitation to scandal whatever his true motives and, following accusations of licentious behaviour and falling out with the ecclesiastical powers that be, he was eventually defrocked at Norwich Cathedral and a more suitable replacement found. Bizarrely, Harold Davidson (no longer 'the Reverend' but still wearing full clerical regalia) met with a sticky end when he was mauled by a lion in a show at Skegness Amusement Park. His act had consisted of entering a lion's cage and talking about the injustices that had been meted out to him by the establishment. Unfortunately, one of the lions, Freddie, was unsympathetic to his plight and attacked him when he tripped over the tail of the other lion. These days, it is generally accepted that the charges against him were ill-founded and that he had inadvertently become one of the very first anti-celebrities created by the press.

Another controversial one-time resident of the village was Henry Williamson, the writer and naturalist alternately famous and notorious respectively for his admiration of both otters and Nazism. Williamson bought a farm in the village in 1936 and lived here during World War II before eventually moving to Devon. The next time that you order an Indian meal it might be helpful to remember Williamson's most famous book if you wish to know the difference between plain dhal and *tarka* dhal: *tarka* is, of course, a little 'otter.

For walkers and self-caterers, the **Stiffkey Stores** stocks cakes, savouries and organic produce.

🆂 **Red Lion**, 44 Wells Rd ☎ 01328 830552 🖥 www.stiffkey.com. This unpretentious pub is a warren of small rooms with bare floorboards and quarry tiles. Serving fresh local seafood like crab and mussels, and beers from a number of Norfolk breweries, this is a busy place for birdwatchers, coastal path hikers and thirsty locals alike.

Marsh samphire

'Half-way down,
Hangs one that gathers samphire; dreadful trade!'
William Shakespeare, *King Lear*

The Shakespeare quotation above comes from a scene set near Dover and probably refers to the practice of gathering rock samphire, but it is marsh samphire (*Salicornia europaea*), sometimes known as glasswort or sea asparagus, that is the speciality of the Norfolk coast. The old name 'glasswort' comes from the medieval use of the plant's ashes to manufacture soap and glass.

Although it can be found at other locations around the British coastline, the best comes from the saltings of north Norfolk. Enjoyed as part of the local diet for centuries, samphire has started to appear on fancy upmarket menus in recent years, usually as an accompaniment to fish and seafood. It is harvested anytime between June and August before the plant flowers, but the sweetest is usually gathered early on in the season. Samphire can be bought from a limited number of outlets in north Norfolk in season but it is altogether more rewarding to forage for your own at low tide, providing you know what you are looking for and do not mind getting muddy.

Like most seasonal foods, samphire's short-lived availability is actually part of its appeal. It can be eaten raw in salads although the saltiness is quite pronounced; a light boiling or steaming helps to remove much of this. With its taste like asparagus dipped in seawater, eating samphire is a pleasure akin to stripping edible beads from a necklace with your teeth.

⑭ Warham

Halfway between Stiffkey and Wells-next-the-Sea, and a little further inland, is the flint and cobble village of Warham, which has a good pub and the site of an Iron Age settlement nearby. There were two parishes here before the reformation, hence the village's two churches. Half a mile or so south of the church of **All Saints**, along a quiet lane, lie the round grass-covered earthworks of the Iron Age camp. Covering three acres, this was built by the Iceni in the second century BC and is usually referred to as **Warham Fort**, although for many years it was known as 'Danish Camp' because it was thought to be the work of Viking invaders.

S☞ Carpenter's Arms High St, Wighton ✆ 01328 820752. The interior is brightly painted and decorated with kilims and bold paintings, and both bar and dining room are warmed by a single, double-sided wood-burner. An imaginative menu makes good use of local ingredients.

Mrs Temple's Cheese Copys Green Farm, Wighton ✆ 01328 820224. Produces a range of farmhouse cheese from the milk of their own cows. Varieties include Binham Blue (soft and blue-veined), Walsingham (crumbly), Wighton (creamy) and Warhans (Gouda-like).

S **Three Horseshoes**, Bridge St ✆ 01328 710547. This 300-year-old village pub, a convenient place to eat before or after a walk, has plenty of interest other than its excellent beer and pies. It has gas lighting and stone floors and is full of agricultural and village memorabilia. There is a pleasing absence of fruit machines but you can try your hand at one of the two one-armed bandit machines that date from 1936 and the 1960s respectively. The best things on offer here, other than the Woodforde's beer, are the filling homemade pies and puddings. Neither credit card nor telephone booking are accepted, so it is first-come, first-served for a table.

Wells-next-the-Sea and Holkham

⑮ Wells-next-the-Sea

The largest settlement between Cromer and Hunstanton, Wells-next-the-Sea is also the only real working harbour along this stretch of coast, even though it stands well over a mile inland. Really the suffix '-next-the-Sea' might be better described as '-quite-near-the-Sea'. Wells has seen service as a port for at least seven centuries although, as with the rest of this coastline, silting-up has been a major problem over the years. Lord Leicester of nearby Holkham Hall constructed a high embankment ('The Bank') in 1859 to reclaim 800 hectares of saltmarsh and as an attempt to protect the harbour. Unfortunately, this proved ineffective against the floods that devastated the coast in 1953 and 1978. These days, **The Bank** is a favourite walk out to the beach, woods and caravan and camping site that lie north of the town, and you can continue along the pine forest and on to the vast **beach** that extends past Holkham Gap. The Bank also marks the stretch of the Norfolk Coast Path that leads into Wells. A miniature railway runs alongside The Bank. This might be a little too quaint for some tastes, but don't let this put you off – Wells has plenty more to offer.

Considerably less precious than Blakeney, Wells is an appealing little town with narrow streets of flint houses and an atmospheric waterfront that still has vestiges of its former life as a busy port. Most prominent is the granary with its overhanging gantry, which has been converted into holiday flats. The granary building itself on Staithe Street, the town's main shopping street, now serves as a small theatre. This is the main venue for the annual **Poetry-next-the-Sea Festival** (01328 711813; www.poetry-next-the-sea.com) that features poets and writers from East Anglia and beyond.

You may observe that there are notably more bungalows here than in Blakeney, as well as a few amusement arcades and tacky gift shops along the harbour, but I think these humanise rather than devalue the place. One of the harbour fish and chip shops used to have a resident cormorant outside that would pester customers for a bit of cod as they sat on the quayside benches to eat. The bird has long gone but the chips remain as good as ever, as does the pleasure of tasting salt air along with your alfresco meal. The harbour wall is also a great place for children who seem to love hoisting up small crabs on a line from the water below just as much as I did when I was a boy.

Crabs and shellfish continue to be caught be local fishermen in Wells but **whelks** were the main industry here half a century ago when the port had its own fleet of special clinker-built boats. Once landed, the whelks were boiled in the town's boiling sheds close to the East Quay before delivery around the country by train. Whelks are still brought in for processing today but the industry is a shadow of what it once was.

The *Albatross*, a 100-year-old Dutch clipper that resides in Wells harbour on a more or less permanent basis, has an interesting history. The boat may have been used to assist Jewish refuges escaping from Nazi Germany and to supply the Dutch resistance with weapons. The boat was used to ship soya beans from Belgium to Norfolk from 1990 to 1996 and since then she has been used by Greenpeace as an environmental study centre for schoolchildren. These days she spends most of her days in Wells harbour, apart from occasional charter trips across the North Sea to her native Dutch waters. When last seen, the *Albatross* was moored at the quay near the fish and chip shops, selling beer and pancakes from its deck – something of a fall from grace for a sea-going vessel. What I cannot understand is the choice of the boat's name. Have I, a confirmed landlubber, fallen into the trap of believing the old chestnut that the albatross is an unlucky bird for seafarers, or is it that Dutch sailors are exempt?

As well as the mile-long miniature railway that runs along The Bank, Wells is also the home station of the **Wells & Walsingham Light Railway** (01328 711630; www.wellswalsinghamrailway.co.uk). This claims to be the longest 10½-inch gauge steam railway in the world, running all the way to Walsingham, a distance of some nine miles, along the track bed of the old Great Eastern Railway. The service operates between April and October and takes 30 minutes with halts made at Warham St Mary and Wighton en route.

The coffee shop at the **Mermaid's Purse** (42 Staithe St ☎ 01328 711744 🖰 www.mermaidspurse.com), which doubles as a clothing and gift shop, has a tasty selection of homemade cakes and scones for afternoon tea as well as seafood platters in season. The sunny garden has picnic benches made from recycled plastic bottles – eco-friendly if not necessarily attractive. **Café 38** (38–40 Freeman St ☎ 01328 710456) is another option that is conveniently close to the harbour.

SD The Crown The Buttlands ☏ 01328 710209 ⊕ www.thecrownhotelwells.co.uk. Set in a 16th-century coaching inn overlooking the town green known as the Buttlands, The Crown serves modern British cuisine and Pacific-Rim-influenced dishes like steamed cod with ginger, lemongrass and lime, and Thai marinated duck breast with seared scallops and chilli jam. Simpler pub food like Brancaster mussels or crab claws can be ordered in the bar and eaten in the lounges or the modern conservatory.

SD Globe Inn The Buttlands ☏ 01328 710206 ⊕ www.globeatwells.co.uk. This 19th-century coaching inn, also on Buttlands Green and owned by the Coke family, has a restaurant that serves excellent seasonal food, much of which originates from the Holkham estate. There is a courtyard for sunny weather and Adnams and Woodforde's ales on draught.

The Real Ale Shop Branthill Farm, NR23 1SB ☏ 01328 710810 ⊕ www.therealaleshop.co.uk. Just off the B1105 Wells to Fakenham road, and selling over 50 ales by 15 different Norfolk brewers, this must have the widest choice of locally produced brews in Norfolk.

Wells Deli 15 The Quay ☏ 01328 711171 ⊕ www.wellsdeli.co.uk. Stocks a wide range of regional produce, including Mrs Temple's cheeses, bread from Grooms of Burnham Market and venison from the Holkham estate.

Whin Hill Cider Stearman's Yard ☏ 01328 711033 ⊕ www.whinhillcider.co.uk. This Wells shop sells cider, perry and nine varieties of apple juice made from fruit from their 13-acre orchard at nearby Stanhoe. All products are unfiltered and pasteurised at low temperatures to retain flavour and contain no added water or artificial sweeteners.

⑯ Holkham

The estate village of Holkham serves as a mere appendage to the extensive grounds of **Holkham Park** and **Holkham Hall**. It also allows access to the grandest of Norfolk's beaches. The hall and park have walled gardens, a lake and a deer park, garden centre, gift shop and cafe, in addition to a Bygones Museum filled with artefacts of every description. The hall's grounds are used to stage regular summer musical events that range from Jools Holland to José Carreras, while the marble hall is occasionally used for chamber music concerts.

Holkham Hall

Holkham Hall, the property of the Coke family, is a sumptuous Palladian mansion that dates from the mid 18th century, its construction inspired by the Italian travels of Thomas Coke, the 1st Earl of Leicester, whilst undertaking a grand tour. Building began in 1734 under the guidance of Lord Burlington and the architect William Kent, who were both keen admirers of Andrea Palladio's Renaissance style. The hall contains a highly impressive collection of classical statuary and art that includes paintings by Van Dyck and Rubens. What is most impressive is that the hall remains completely unchanged from its original form. It is undoubtedly striking but perhaps not to everyone's taste: purists might consider an Italian-Renaissance-style house to be somewhat incongruous up here in north Norfolk.

You can walk or cycle through the estate's extensive grounds at will (for no charge) but since this is a working farm dogs have to be kept on a lead.

Holkham Hall ☎ 01328 710227 🖰 www.holkham.co.uk. Closed Wed, Fri, Sat, plus Tues in Oct and all Nov–May.

Coke of Norfolk: the great agricultural improver

With the hall finally built – it took 28 years in all – and the Coke family's vast art collection installed, later generations, most notably **Thomas William Coke** (1754-1842), Thomas Coke's nephew, concentrated on improving the estate itself. Thomas was far more interested in earth than architecture and would subsequently become known as 'Coke of Norfolk'. He went on to become the standard-bearer for the Agricultural Revolution with his application of four-crop rotation, an innovation for which modern farmers and even humble allotmenteers owe a debt for today. Although often credited with inventing this practice, it was more likely that 'Turnip' Townshend of Rainham Hall was the actual innovator here. North of the hall, a tall column with sheep and cows carved around its plinth serves as a fitting memorial for this agricultural aristocrat and, if stately homes do not float your boat, then you might enjoy this more. This being Norfolk, even aristocratic pronunciations are not all that they might appear to be: Coke should be pronounced *cook*.

Holkham Beach

No question, Holkham Beach is one of the finest in all England: a wide swathe of glistening sand backed by dunes and a thick stand of Corsican pines; the sea, a softly lapping presence or a thin line on the horizon, depending on the tide. This is the very beach that Gwynneth Paltrow walked along in *Shakespeare in Love* and it features too in Stephen Fry's ITV drama, *Kingdom*.

Whatever the state of the tide, it's a wonderful beach for bathing and about as safe as it gets for children. Access is via Lady Ann's Drive opposite the Victoria Hotel and Holkham village. The provision for parking here is considerable but so are the crowds that come here on warm summer days. Once parked up, however, there is plenty of sand for everyone – the beach is a vast expanse that stretches as far west as the dunes at Gun Hill next to Burnham Harbour creek, and east to The Run at Wells-next-the-Sea. Given the volume of traffic, arriving here on the Coasthopper bus makes an awful lot of sense, as long as you don't mind the half-mile walk along Lady Ann's Drive from the main road.

A Holkham Beach walk

It can be breezy here – it usually is – and the idea of lazing on the beach may not be to everyone's taste. Birdwatchers should find plenty of interest in the pinewoods behind the beach – rarities have turned up here over the years – but otherwise the best thing to do after a swim or a picnic is to go for a stroll. An enjoyable five-mile walk that takes an unhurried couple of hours is to bear right at Holkham Gap and head along the beach as far as the lifeboat station by the embankment at Wells-next-the-Sea. Then, reversing direction, follow the way-marked Norfolk Coast Path back west, keeping the pine plantation to your right all the way to the car park at Lady Ann's Drive. A shorter alternative is to turn left at Holkham Gap and follow the track that leads along the southern flank of the pinewoods until you pass a large pond and reach a bird hide where there is access to the beach along a boardwalk. The path continues past the hide and past Meals House until reaching a crossroads in the woods. Turning right here will bring you to the beach at Burrow Gap, from where you can turn right and walk back to Holkham Gap and Lady Ann's Drive. An even shorter option, barely more than a mile, is to turn right at the boardwalk by the hide and return to the start point by walking through the woods or by turning right along the beach.

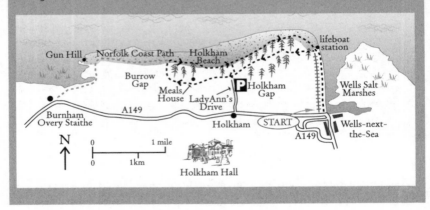

Stables Café Holkham Estate ☎ 01328 713114 🖰 www.holkham.co.uk. Next door to the Pottery on the estate, this has a decent range of snacks and is a good choice for afternoon tea. Best of all is the homemade ice cream made from locally sourced milk and cream and flavoured with lavender and plums grown on the estate.
Victoria Park Rd ☎ 01328 711008 🖰 www.victoriaatholkham.co.uk. This fully renovated and spruced-up brick and flint pub at the entrance to the Holkham Estate enjoys considerable repute as both a restaurant and a convivial place to stay. Like the Globe Inn at Wells-next-the-Sea, this is owned by the present incumbents of the estate, Tom and Polly Coke. Fresh local produce features strongly – Cromer crabs, Brancaster mussels and beef, game and eel from the estate. There is also a simpler pub menu served at lunchtimes.

The Burnhams

A whole family of Burnhams lie just west of Holkham in the valley of the unassuming River Burn: Burnham Overy Staithe and Burnham Norton on the coast road; Burnham Market, with its appendages of Burnham Westgate and Burnham Ulph, just to the south; and Burnham Overy Town and Nelson's birthplace, Burnham Thorpe, a little further inland. Burnham Deepdale lies a mile or two to the west of this group, and both Burnham Overy Staithe and Burnham Deepdale straddle the route of the Norfolk Coast Path. Such a tight cluster of villages means that six medieval churches lie within just three miles of each other. Ironically, Burnham Overy Town is the smallest of the group, hardly a village, although it was once the port in the medieval period. Similarly, Burnham Norton also has little to it other than a round tower church with a restored rood screen (at the very edge of the parish, almost in Burnham Market). In contrast, Burnham Overy Staithe, with its delightful boat-strewn creek, is perhaps the very epicentre of northwest Norfolk's yachting set, although Brancaster Staithe, which adjoins Burnham Deepdale to the west, might also claim this prize.

It is the largest Burnham, Burnham Market, that seems to charm the most, judging by the traffic weaving through it and the impressive array of smart cars parked in its narrow streets on any given summer's day. It is here where people gravitate to 'escape London' and discuss skiing holidays in the village's posh eateries. You might even spot a famous face 'getting away from it all'.

⑰ Burnham Market

A picture-perfect village of attractive Georgian houses surrounding a green – is it any wonder that Burnham Market is so popular? How many villages of this size have such a selection of galleries and boutiques and even a posh hat shop? How many have such potential for fine dining? And how many get labelled 'Little Chelsea' because of their unashamed metropolitan atmosphere? More than anywhere else in the county, this reminds me of the Cotswolds or even parts of Wiltshire.

While it is certainly true that the village has attracted a disproportionate number of affluent second-home owners it is easy to see what all the fuss is about. If you are looking for a smart, yet unmodernised, rural idyll then look no further; if you seek the rural Norfolk of old then you might do better to try elsewhere. Either way, come and have a look around at least. The predominant dialect spoken around here may be that of Kensington these days but that is not to say that genuine locals have disappeared from the scene altogether. There is a **farmers' market** here on the first Saturday and third Friday of each month.

A Burnham Market stroll

A pleasant short walk around Burnham Market starting from the Hoste Arms with the pub on your left is to turn left down Herrings Lane, then right on to Cross Lane after about half a mile towards Burnham Norton's St Margaret's church with its Anglo-Saxon tower and Norman font. Turn right

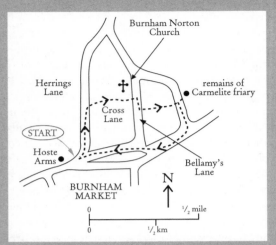

here along Bellamy's Lane (or you can extend the walk by taking the first path on the left, to see the remains of a Carmelite friary, with its gatehouse and one wall of its church standing) and then right again at All Saints' church into Burnham Market passing the Fairfax Gallery on your way back to the green.

As well as the celebrated Hoste Arms, Burnham Market has **Lucy's Tea Shop** on the Market Place (✆ 01328 738908) for a light lunch or home-baked scones, **Gurney's Fish Shop** (✆ 01328 738967 ✆ www.gurneysfishshop.co.uk) for locally caught wet fish, and **Groom's Bakery** (✆ 01328 736289 ✆ www.groomsbakery.co.uk) for cakes, pastries and 20 varieties of bread. **Humble Pie** (✆ 01328 738581) is a sumptuously stocked delicatessen and cook shop, a Mecca for foodies.

S **Hoste Arms** The Green ✆ 01328 738777 ✆ www.hostearms.co.uk. This luxurious inn at the heart of things in the village is open for breakfast, morning coffee, lunch, afternoon tea and dinner. Afternoon tea, in particular, is an occasion to savour. More a pleasure dome than an inn these days, the Hoste Arms buzzes with efficient bonhomie throughout the year. The food is fancy and luxurious, featuring local produce like crabs and oysters cooked with an oriental twist.

⑱ Burnham Thorpe

Horatio Nelson's birthplace no less and, although the original rectory in which he was born has been torn down and replaced long ago, there is a plaque on the wall that commemorates the man whom many regard as one of the very greatest of Englishmen. The village pub, which unsurprisingly goes by the name of The Lord Nelson, does in fact date from Nelson's time and serves as something of a shrine to his memory with all manner of memorabilia and paintings of marine battle scenes on its walls. The church next to the Manor House has more: a crucifix and lectern fashioned from wood taken from *HMS Victory*.

⑤ Lord Nelson Walsingham Rd, Burnham Thorpe ☎ 01328 738241
🕁 www.nelsonslocal.co.uk. This, the only pub in Burnham Thorpe, is both atmospheric and unspoiled, and despite its claims to be 'Nelson's local' remains remarkably unpretentious. There is no bar as such, just a serving hatch. With a stone flagged floor and original wooden settles, it is easy enough to imagine the famous mariner lingering over a rum here. What Nelson would have made of the occasional quiz nights and local R&B bands that sometimes perform here is less certain. The Lord Nelson serves pub grub with a Mediterranean flavour, and Greene King and Woodeforde's ales as well as the strong (5.1%) Nelson's Blood Bitter from Heacham's Fox brewery. The pub's speciality is a herb and spice-infused brandy it calls Nelson's Blood – an allusion to the story of Nelson's body being preserved in a barrel of brandy whilst shipping home for a state funeral.

Plumbe & Maufe Farming Nelsons Barn, Burnham Thorpe PE31 8HW
☎ 01328 738311. This farm close to Burnham Market has a **plum orchard** with over 30 varieties of this much-overlooked native fruit. Offering both ready picked or pick-your-own, the orchard is open for business between mid-July and September.

⑲ Burnham Overy Town

In a car at least, by the time you have said the name you have driven through it. Burnham Overy Town does have the rather odd church of **St Clement's**, with its squat central tower. Historically, this village on the River Burn served as the harbour but this function switched to Overy Staithe at the end of the medieval period. One of the small cottages at the road junction has some curious recycled classical statues flanking its front door and there are the remains of an ancient cross, now reduced to little more than a hitching post, in the middle of the junction's central reservation.

⑳ Burnham Overy Staithe

Along with Brancaster Staithe further west, this small coastal village is a favourite of the sailing set. The fact that it has a chandlery but no shop or café says it all. The creekside harbour may be modest in the extreme but the village's seafaring credentials are impressive: Nelson learned to row and sail on the creek here and Richard Woodget, captain of the *Cutty Sark*, retired here to farm. As elsewhere, the harbour has long since silted up and these days Burnham Overy Staithe sees a very different type of craft sailing up its creek.

The Hero Wells Rd, Burnham Overy Staithe ☎ 01328 738334
🕁 www.theheroburnhamovery.co.uk. Burnham Overy Staithe's village pub is an unpretentious and cosy place for a drink or a tasty homemade meal after a walk.

A sea wall stroll

For a wonderful short **walk** out to the beach from Burnham Overy Staithe, take a stroll along the sea wall that starts at the end of the road by the little harbour and zigzags its way above the saltings to reach the dunes; to the left you can carry on round past a point known as Gun Hill . Over the water is Aster Marsh, the eastern end of **Scolt Head Island**, mauve with sea asters in late summer. Keep going past Gun Hill (or take a short cut through the dunes) and you're on the same beach that extends round to Holkham Gap (see page 28).

㉑ Burnham Norton and Burnham Deepdale

Coming from the bright, fashionable lights of Burnham Market, **Burnham Norton** has the round-tower church of St Margaret but no shop, café or pub. **Burnham Deepdale**, a little further on, has all of these facilities, along with the added appeal of easy walks out to the saltings and marshes. Other than that, the village centres on a strip of shops on the main road just before the eastern limits of Brancaster Staithe.

Burnham Deepdale's church of **St Mary** is also well worth a look inside, having a Saxon round tower and a square Norman font that is carved to depict the Labours of the Months. Depending on the month when you visit, you can check what you ought to be doing in the agricultural calendar. In July, the 'labour' is mowing; in August, harvesting; winter is far more relaxed, with feasting in December and drinking in January.

Besides a handy garage and supermarket, there is a clothing store and a café here as well as the reception of the **Deepdale Backpackers Hostel** and the excellent **Deepdale Camping** (see box) situated just behind it that offers the opportunity to stay in a heated tipi or Mongolian yurt. The reception doubles as the **Deepdale Information Centre** (☎ 01485 210256 ⌂ www.deepdalebackpackers.co.uk), which is helpful with suggestions for local walks and has a good range of books and maps, including a stock of the wonderful hand-drawn Wilfrid George footpath maps. Deepdale Leisure Ltd, which runs all of these enterprises under the same green umbrella, promotes green tourism in the locality and organises an annual **Earth Day** event in April and a Conservation weekend in February. Courses, guided walks and other activities are on offer throughout the year. Deepdale Camping was awarded the East of England Sustainable Tourism award in 2009.

Deepdale Café ☎ 01485 211 055 ⌂ www.deepdalecafe.co.uk. Serves everything from practical to posh, snack to slap-up. They open early (7.30) in good time to provide a full English breakfast for hungry cyclists and walkers but do not serve food after 4pm.

Camping at Burnham Deepdale

Donald (Managing Director of Bradt Guides) and Darren (from the RSPB) spent a weekend polishing up their rusty camping skills in north Norfolk – and survived to tell the tale.

'Whether you're a seasoned camper or a first-timer just wanting to see what it's all about, the campsite (Deepdale Camping) at Burnham Deepdale is an ideal spot for a slow experience. Days are filled with lots of low-impact outdoor activities, evenings are all about simple cooking on a stove or BBQ, or eating in one of the local pubs, and come bedtime you can retire weary but satisfied to the cosy interior of your canvas "bedroom".

We hadn't camped for more than 15 years when we visited for the bank holiday weekend at the end of May, but soon got into the swing of things. Over the three days we were there we walked, cycled, went birdwatching and took umpteen photographs of the timeless coastal and inland landscapes, with their ever-changing skies, historic flint-built houses and churches, and captivating light that has inspired generations of artists. One evening, we cooked easy but nutritious meals on our stove; another day we spent a wonderfully memorable evening in the conservatory restaurant of the local pub watching a brilliant sunset over the marshlands, and sat in the outdoors wrapped up in fleeces with a bottle of wine as dusk turned to night. By the time we left we felt as if we had had a complete escape filled with three days of really healthy living, and what's more, we didn't use the car once.'

Brancaster to Hunstanton

㉒ Brancaster

Further west along the A149 coast road, Burnham Deepdale morphs almost seamlessly into **Brancaster Staithe**, which in turn leads into **Brancaster** proper. These villages have developed more than most as smart holiday centres and have more than their fair share of holiday lets and weekend sailors. If you doubt this, try **The Jolly Sailors** for a drink or a meal on a Saturday night and see if you can detect many Norfolk accents. Despite this, Brancaster Staithe has not given itself over to leisure craft entirely and there is still a viable whelk and mussel industry here. Leisure craft and fishing boats have separate staithes linked by a path. To reach the fishermen's sheds walk down the lane opposite The Jolly Sailors pub. The neighbouring leisure-craft staithe (see page 34) has a highly attractive row of 17th-century cottages at its entrance; the National Trust owns the 'Dial House', the one with a sundial above its porch.

The Romans built a fortress, **Branodunum**, in what is now Brancaster and used it as a base to tame Boudica's wild tribes but nothing remains to be seen. Other than sailing, the biggest draw in Brancaster these days is the Royal West Norfolk Golf Club with a course that stretches with the sea on three sides nestled between the beach and the saltings, its clubhouse and car park by the dunes. Private boats can sometimes be hired for the trip across to **Scolt Head Island**, another spit rather like Blakeney Point that is a nature reserve and even more isolated and difficult to reach. There are nesting colonies of Sandwich terns here in summer, the largest in the country.

Up to Barrow Common

For a good overview of the coast at Brancaster, take a walk or cycle inland up Common Lane. In less than a mile, this narrow, Alexander-lined road leads gently uphill to **Barrow Common**, where there is parking, gorse bushes a-plenty and fantastic views over Brancaster Harbour, Scolt Head, Brancaster golf course and even west across the Wash. On a clear day, you can easily see the wind turbines over on the Lincolnshire shore.

In Brancaster Staithe harbour, Letzers Seafood at **The Crab Hut** (www.letzersseafood.com) has crabs, lobsters and all manner of seafood caught from their own boat for sale.

The **Brancaster Millennium Activity Centre** (☎ 01485 210719) based in the Dial House building at the entrance to the staithe, organises a wide range of courses throughout the year that are mostly connected with art or wildlife. There are also activity days for children and family fun weeks that involve sailing, kayaking and mountain biking.

Brancaster Midsummer Music is a modest, local music festival that makes use of local churches and houses for its concerts (☎ 01485 210527; www.brancaster.net)

🅢 **The Jolly Sailors** Brancaster Staithe ☎ 01485 210314 ⌐ www.jollysailors brancaster.co.uk. This traditional 18th-century pub is known to everyone in these parts and has the advantage of a Coasthopper bus stop right outside its door. The pub has its own Brancaster Brewery ale and serves decent pub grub and pizzas.

🅢 **White Horse** Brancaster Staithe ☎ 01485 210262 ⌐ www.whitehorsebrancaster.co.uk. With wonderful views over the marshes and estuary and the coastal path right outside, this is a great place to watch the sunset from the Room at the Top, a split-level room with French windows and a telescope. The interior is tastefully modern and the food good, featuring local seafood like oysters and mussels. The selection of beers includes Adnams and Woodforde's, and there is a lengthy list of wines from around the world.

㉓ Titchwell and ㉔ Thornham

The coast road passes through **Titchwell** on its way here from Brancaster, a village with marshes that are home to a 420-acre **RSPB bird reserve**. The reserve has a swishly modern visitor centre and offers a good chance of seeing bearded tits and bitterns among its many breeding species, and geese, plovers

and harriers in winter. If you still have not seen an avocet, the graceful bird that symbolises the RSPB, a sighting here is virtually guaranteed.

Thornham was once a busy port but trade peaked here back in the 17th century when the River Hun was diverted in order to drain the marshes. Predictably, silting, and the inevitable arrival of the railway put an end to its harbour commerce. The floods of 1953 sounded the final death knell.

The village marks the western end of the transition zone of north Norfolk's vernacular architecture. East of here, to well beyond Cromer, the building material of choice is mostly flint (although the transition starts somewhere around Brancaster); here at Thornham, chalk is the main material, a clue to the local geology. The village is a spread out, attractive place of neat gardens and well-maintained houses. Quietly affluent, it seems geared more to retirement than to second-home ownership.

A Thornham coastal walk

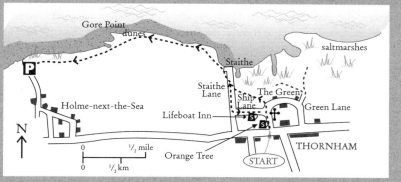

A pleasant, varied but easy, **circular walk** can be made starting at the Orange Tree at Thornham. The Coasthopper service has a bus shelter here. Walk north past the church, bearing immediately right at the junction to continue as far as the wood, bearing left at the edge of the wood along the signed footpath. The Norfolk Coast Path soon turns left over a stile. Follow this path alongside a vast reed-bed where you may well see marsh harriers quartering for prey in summer – blissfully unaware that they are supposed to stay within sight of birders at the nearby RSPB Titchwell reserve. The path emerges close to the staithe, with its chalk-built coal barn, where you can have a look at the boats. If you want to extend the walk, you can carry on westwards along the coast path from here, past Gore Point to Holme-next-the-Sea, and return the same way back to the staithe. Then from the staithe head along Staithe Lane, turn left along Ship Lane past the Lifeboat Inn and the wooded grounds of Thornham Manor before turning right at the end past the terrace of white cottages and back to the main road.

S♥ Lifeboat Inn Ship Lane ☎ 01485 512236. This traditional 16th-century pub used to be the haunt of smugglers but these days it sees a more cosmopolitan clientele. The old bar has an open fire and gas lamps but there is also a new extension for swankier dining.

S♥ Orange Tree High St ☎ 01485 512213 ✆ www.theorangetreethornham.co.uk. The Orange Tree is a modern food pub with an imaginative menu that incorporates local produce as much as possible. A sound choice for a memorable meal in cool, stylish surroundings.

㉕ Holme-next-the-Sea

Once again, the village here can hardly be described 'next-the-sea'. Holme is the point where the Norfolk coastline starts to twist south to face The Wash. It is also the 'elbow' of the combined Peddars Way & Norfolk Coast Path: the place where one ends and the other begins. It's a sudden change of coast and scenery, whichever direction you walk.

The village has a nice sandy **beach**, very popular on hot summer days, which can be reached by walking down Beach Road and turning right, or by turning just before the car park along a sandy path that leads through a NWT nature reserve. The boardwalk leads into a shady conifer plantation where the path continues, to reach a sea defence bank near the tip of a pool called Broadwater. This path, the beginning of the Norfolk Coast Path, continues inland along sea defence walls to Thornham.

If you keep your eyes peeled on the beach, you may come across groups of what appear to be black peaty discs. These are the fossilised remains of a large, **prehistoric forest** that once extended across the North Sea. More of the same can be seen on the beach at Titchwell, just west of the sea wall and Brancaster golf clubhouse. The beach at Holme-next-the-Sea was put firmly on the map just over a decade ago with the discovery of a far more enigmatic arrangement of ancient wood, the so-called '**Seahenge**' (see box). A second timber circle has recently been discovered nearby, this time dating back to 2400BC, which predates Seahenge by several hundred years. Holme may well have several more like this buried away in its vicinity.

With a leisure beach and wildlife reserve located next door to one another, there has always been the potential for a conflict of interests at Holme. The discovery of Seahenge added further tensions to the people-versus-wildlife debate. The word on everyone's lips these days, though, is global warming and what can – or should – be done to protect coastal wildlife against the effects of **rising sea levels**.

John Hiskett, Senior Conservation Officer at the Norfolk Wildlife Trust, gave me his view. 'As sea levels rise, higher tides will squeeze coastal habitats against the shoreline and this will mean less habitat for wildlife. The main losers will be those species that depend on these habitats and the bittern, for example, may be lost as a breeding species in north Norfolk if coastal reed-beds disappear completely.' So how can conservation bodies respond to this threat? 'We should help wildlife adapt to these changes by moving towards a more natural coastline.

Freshwater habitats that are currently protected by seawalls will gradually be replaced by saltmarsh – it is inevitable. At Holme, increased erosion means that we need to start considering some form of planned retreat now rather than live with possibility of a catastrophic breach of the dunes sometime in the future.'

White Horse 40 Kirkgate St ✆ 01485 525512. A 17th-century, oak-beamed inn serving good pub food, this is conveniently situated for Peddars Way & Norfolk Coastal Path walkers.

The Seahenge saga

Back in 1998, a particularly low tide at Holme beach revealed a circle of 55 oak timbers surrounding a massive upturned tree stump. The peat that had protected and hidden the circle for so many years had been washed away by the tide and there were fears that further tides would sweep away the newly discovered site. As this was clearly some sort of ritualistic site, there was a strong argument for removing the timbers for preservation along with an equally vehement call to leave it well alone.

Debate raged as to what the original function was of what had become known as 'Seahenge' in the newspapers. Archaeologists suggested that the circle may have been a mortuary enclosure, while those of a less rigidly academic persuasion mooted more fanciful interpretations, such as a ley-line centre. Spirits ran high and tempers frayed as those who would have the timbers removed clashed with those who wished to leave them be. Although this was mostly good-natured debate, the once-quiet beach at Holme became the setting for noisy argument between sensibly clothed archaeologists and neo-druids in dreadlocks and home-knit jumpers, the latter performing improvised rituals accompanied by distinctly non-druidic instruments like didgeridoos and African drums.

The saga took an even more bizarre turn when, at a public meeting at the Le Strange Arms Hotel in Hunstanton, archaeologists, council officers and druids chanted together and used a 'talking stick' to symbolise the individual's right to speak uninterrupted. The meeting lasted five hours and reached some degree of accord but the circle's fate was already sealed.

The oak timbers were excavated and taken to Flag Fen near Peterborough. Analysis revealed that the circle was 4,500 years old and that the posts had not been positioned individually but placed in a circular trench. It was estimated that between 16 and 26 trees were used to build the monument, with at least 51 bronze axes employed, suggesting a community endeavour.

For many local objectors, the greatest fear was that the timbers might end up in the British Museum or somewhere similar, far away from Norfolk. These fears were unfounded, however: since 2008, the recreated Seahenge has taken pride of place in the Lynn Museum (01553 775001; www.museums.norfolk.gov.uk) just down the road from its original site.

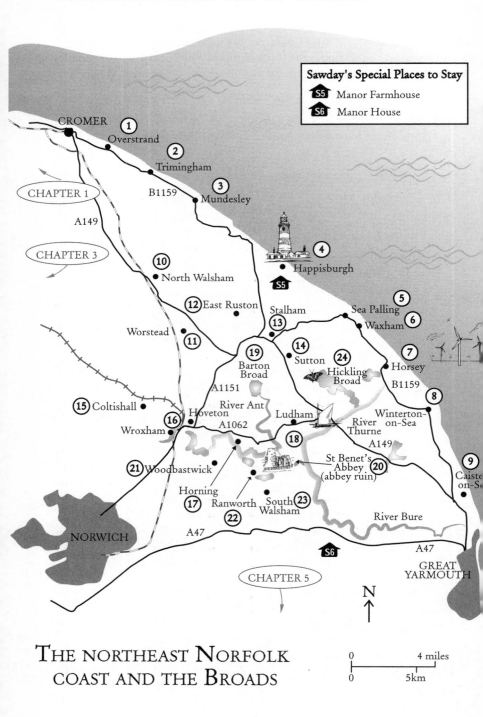

2. THE NORTHEAST NORFOLK COAST AND THE BROADS

E ast of **Cromer**, the north Norfolk coast curves gently southeast towards **Great Yarmouth** and the border with Suffolk. The coast here is less spectacular than that further west but provides locals with pleasant spots for dog-walking and fishing, as well as sunbathing and swimming in the summer months when the wind drops. It is an uncomplicated, calming landscape of sand, slate-grey sea, pebble banks and dunes, set against a backdrop of fields of grazing cattle and great swathes of sugar beet and barley. Thousands of hedgerows were enthusiastically grubbed out in this part of the county back in the 1960s but, that said, even some of the larger expanses of grain seen inland from the coast are a far cry in scale from the geometric prairies in the Fens further west. With quiet, old-fashioned villages like Overstrand and Mundesley, along with the slightly more bucket-and-spade atmosphere of places like Sea Palling and Winterton, Norfolk's northeast coast is likeable but it's hardly super-distinctive. Nevertheless, its safe sandy beaches and marram-grass-covered dunes make for great places for young families to potter about in.

The villages that punctuate this stretch of the coast have little of the cosmopolitan gloss of places like Blakeney or Burnham Market in northwest Norfolk, but there are enjoyable corners: this is workaday Norfolk, and there are far fewer incomers and second-home-owners than elsewhere in the county.

The timber groynes that push out to sea along the length of this shoreline – sometimes mysteriously erased from view by the frequent sea mists – give a clue to the nature of the coastline in these parts. West of Cromer, it is a landscape in the making, with transported sand creating spits and extensive offshore sands. Here, it is one of occasionally brutal erosion. Dotted sporadically along this stretch of coast are houses perched precariously on the edges of crumbling cliffs, with livelihoods hanging in the balance as the North Sea threatens to breach dunes and seawalls to flood valuable farmland. Measures to slow down the rate of coastal nibbling by the sea are hugely costly and ultimately often don't solve the problem. This can be hard to explain to those whose lives have always been centred here and whose King-Canute-like faith in the possibility of stemming the waves remains undaunted.

Global warming is an altogether more sinister Sword of Damocles hanging over the region. With virtually all of northeast Norfolk sitting less than twenty feet above sea level, things do not bode well for the future. Worst-case scenarios suggest that much of this coastline may disappear underwater by the middle of the century: a radical redrafting of the map of lowland Britain. For many, it is more palatable to limit concern to receding cliffs and menacing high tides.

The northern Broads

Just inland from the coast is an area that really could not belong anywhere else in the country. **The Broads** dominate the landscape south of the small market town of Stalham: a sprawl of inland lakes linked by the River Bure and the shallow but navigable tributaries of the Thurne and Ant. Another collection of broads lies further south, east of Norwich along the River Yare, while a few more can be found across the border in Suffolk, although they are all generally referred to as 'The Norfolk Broads'. For the purposes of this chapter, we will include just those northern broads clustered around the Rivers Bure, Ant and Thurne – the very heart of Norfolk Broadland.

These sparkling bodies of water, previously assumed to be natural phenomena, were only proved to be manmade in the early 1960s, when research by Dr Joyce Lambert, a botanist, revealed that they had originally been medieval peat diggings that had become flooded over the centuries. With unique wildlife and landscape, and 28 Sites of Special Scientific Interest and nine National Nature Reserves within their boundary, the Broads have been awarded national park status, with the **Broads Authority** responsible for the area's management since its establishment in 1989.

The Broads are the one place that everyone associates with Norfolk (even though part of the area overlaps into Suffolk). Even David Bowie has made mention of them in one of his songs, although he was singing about 'Life on Mars' at the time. He also mentioned Ibiza in the same line, which hints at the frenzy that some parts of the Broads experience in high summer. At this time of year, the 'tourist honeypot' principle is amply demonstrated in the streets of **Hoveton**, where wannabe ship captains from the Midlands crowd the pavements, and Potter Heigham's medieval bridge has a lengthy tailback of floating gin palaces queuing to pass underneath. But this is just one face of the Broads; the other is a serene, watery wonderland of windmills, dykes and reed-beds so rich with butterflies, dragonflies and exotic looking birds that it can feel almost tropical. It very much depends where you go... and when.

Not surprisingly, the busiest part of the Broads is around the boat hire centres – **Wroxham**, **Hoveton** and **Ranworth Broads**, and the River Thurne around **Potter Heigham**. Far quieter and more rewarding for landscape and wildlife are **Barton**, **Cockshoot** and **Hickling Broads**, the latter two having boarded walkways and water trails. **How Hill** near Ludham has special activities for children and a delightful walking trail through grazing marshes and woodland, and standing at a towering 40 feet above sea level, the highest point for miles, also offers one of the best panoramas in the area. It is also one of the most reliable places to see swallowtail butterflies around midsummer. Another excellent place for an overview of the Broads is the tower of **Ranworth Church**.

Few of the settlements in and around the Broads are particularly attractive. Red-brick rules supreme and bungalow estates are the norm – perhaps the reality of living at sea level inhibits the urge to build a second storey. **North Walsham**, just outside the Broads network, is an unremarkable but nice-enough market town, while **Stalham** is mostly bungalow-land centred upon a workaday high street. **Wroxham/Hoveton** is very much a holiday centre between Easter and September when the Broads cruiser hire trade is at its peak. Outside this season, it is pretty humdrum. What comes as a surprise is the lack of really good **pubs** in the region. The fringes of the Broads are more fruitful territory, and recommendable places for a drink can be found in Winterton, Horsey and Woodbastwick.

Getting around

Travelling around the Broads can be problematic, given so much water. It's far from ideal car-touring terrain as it is so divided by rivers and great expanses of wetland that long, circuitous detours are necessary to travel from A to B. More frustratingly, you see virtually nothing from a car, other than the number plate of the vehicle in front. This is low-lying terrain and it is rarely possible to get views over the reed-beds to the water beyond even when a road does pass nearby. The good news is that you don't really need to travel the length of the Broads to get the idea: you can very much slow down and get the Broads flavour just by exploring a very small area in detail.

Railways

Luckily, a surprisingly decent **rail service** passes through the western part of the Broads, which, with a bit of ingenious bus timetabling and a willingness to walk, makes much of the region reasonably accessible. The more-or-less hourly **Bittern Line** train service (www.bitternline.com) links the Broads with both Norwich and Sheringham on the north coast. Salhouse station lies some distance away from the quiet broad of the same name, but Hoveton station, at least, is convenient for Wroxham Broad, the epicentre of boating activity in summer, and also handy for occasional bus links deeper into the Broads.

Particularly useful stations for starting country walks from include Worstead and Gunton. The steam-powered Poppy Line from Sheringham to Holt, and the Bure Valley Steam Railway (01263 733858; www.bvrw.co.uk) between Aylsham and Wroxham, also link with the Bittern Line.

Buses

Bus services are rather sketchy but the 12A **First Eastern Counties** service runs from Norwich Castle Meadow, Monday to Saturday, to Stalham via Hoveton, Horning, Ludham and Catfield. **Sanders Coaches** run between Norwich, Wroxham, North Walsham, Mundesley and Cromer, and **Neaves** have their 36 service between Norwich and Sea Palling via Wroxham and Stalham, although none of these operate on Sundays. **Anglian Coaches** fill the gap here, with their 54B service between Norwich and Wroxham on Sundays and bank holidays.

The website www.travelineeastanglia.org.uk is useful for timetables and routes.

River craft

Obviously, the very best way to see the Broads is on **water**. Self-drive boat hire options are numerous, and several companies like Broad Tours (01603 782207; www.broads.co.uk) at Wroxham, Fineway Launch Hire (01603 782309; www.finewayleisure.co.uk) at Hoveton and Ludham Bridge Boatyard (01692 631011; www.ludhambridgeboats.co.uk) offer quieter and less polluting electric boats for hire. Even more eco-friendly boat excursions worth considering are leisure trips on Barton Broad using the solar-powered *Ra* (booked from the Hoveton Broads Information Centre – see below) or following a wildlife water trail around How Hill National Nature Reserve near Ludham using the *Electric Eel* (booked from Toad Hole Cottage – see below).

Canoeing

Paddling your way around by canoe is probably the ideal way to get the authentic Broads experience and is one of the best means of sneaking up on wildlife too. Canadian canoes are very stable and easy to paddle even for beginners. They can hold up to three people and are great fun for children. Hire centres can advise on routes and suitability according to experience but, generally speaking, headwaters are the most rewarding for novices while lower reaches tend to require more experience – more strength too, given the need to cope with tidal waters.

Starting from hire centres, you might for instance try heading upstream along the River Bure from Wroxham Bridge past Belaugh towards Coltishall, or exploring the Dilham canal as far as the disused lock from Wayford Bridge, or south along the River Ant to reach Barton Broad. Staff at canoe hire centres are generally happy to advise on times and distances for planned itineraries. Both **Bank Dayboats** at Wayford Bridge near Smallburgh (01692 582457; www.urwins.co.uk) and **Barnes Brinkcraft** at Riverside Rd, Wroxham (01603 782625 or 782333; www.barnesbrinkcraft.co.uk) have canoes for hire.

Canoeing for novices

For the uninitiated, canoeing is fairly intuitive really. I have a hopeless sense of balance but even I can manage it without too much trouble. The secret is to not stand up once you're in the canoe. It's best to make sure that anything that doesn't go well with water – cameras or electrical devices for example – is well-protected. In fact, it's easier just to leave these sorts of things behind.

Paddling is not especially hard work, although your shoulders and back may ache a bit if you are not used to it. Three hours is probably enough for novices – a six-hour canoeing session would leave most beginners pretty tired. Tidal currents probably should not present much of a problem unless you are a long way downstream but wind can slow you down and make it harder work just like on a bike.

As a humble canoeist, expect power boats to regard you in the same way that car drivers do cyclists – their attitude can range from courteous consideration to total contempt. The further you can get away from them the better. Many anglers aren't very keen on canoeists either, because they think you scare the fish away; give them a wide berth out of courtesy.

The positives are considerable. You'll be getting good exercise and seeing river life close-up. You are bound to see plenty of kingfishers, herons and dragonflies and, with luck, you might even glimpse an otter.

A recent innovation is to take a **guided canoe trail** through the Broads, ideal for beginners who might otherwise lack the confidence to strike out alone. Mark Wilkinson, otherwise known as **'The Canoe Man'** (07810 838052; www.thecanoeman.com) offers a variety of guided canoe trails. Guided short, half-day and full-day trails are available every Saturday between Easter and September, and more frequently during the school holidays. One- or two-night guided canoe and bushcraft trails take place about twice a month in the summer with camping or bivouacking on sites arranged with local farm owners ('wild camping' as such is not permitted in the Broads).

More comfortable are the canoe trails (from one to four nights) that make use of local B&Bs – these also offer an unguided option.

Cycling

Exploring the back lanes by bike is a delight, but not the busy main roads like the A149 and A1151. The terrain is almost perfectly flat, and you won't be needing those low gears. Using bridleways and minor roads, it is possible to travel around the region far more efficiently than in a car, avoiding long detours. There's still a lot of water to get round though, and it takes very careful routing to avoid the main roads. The summer-only foot ferry across the River Bure from Woodbastwick Fen to Horning will take bicycles and this makes for an excellent short cut.

East of England Tourism have produced a practical guide to sustainable tourism in Wroxham that is themed around cycling (and boating) in the area. This is available both on line (www.eet.org.uk) and as a printed booklet.

For those without their own bikes, cycle hire is available at Clippesby Hall (01493 367800; www.clippesby.com), which incidentally has an excellent touring and camping park with pitches set out in natural woodland, Broadland Cycle Hire in Hoveton (01603 783096), BeWILDerwood near Hoveton (07887 480331; www.norfolkbroadscycling.co.uk) who provide free cycling maps, Bike Riders in North Walsham (01692 406632), Ludham Bridge Stores (01692 630322) and the tearooms at Stokesby (01493 750470).

The **Bittern Line** is a highly convenient means of taking your own bike in or out of the area. Those turning up on the day can transport their bike on a first come, first served basis – each train is able to take up to four bikes. In summer it is probably best to book in advance (0845 600 7245).

The Broads Authority produce a useful leaflet entitled *The Broads by Bike* that can be picked up from any visitor centre. This shows an orbital cycling route around the Broads and suggests a variety of day and half-day itineraries. One really good ride of around 15 miles that takes in Potter Heigham, How Hill and Ludham, begins and ends in Clippesby and gives a good overview of the region. A similar-length route starts at Hoveton's BeWILDerwood and follows quiet country lanes to Neatishead and Barton Turf where there is access to the boardwalk and viewing platform at Barton Broad. Another possibility is to follow the nine-mile Bure Valley Path that follows the Bure Valley Railway between Wroxham and Aylsham. Bicycles can also be carried on the trains, space permitting, for £3.

Walking

The **Weavers' Way** takes a meandering 58-mile route through the Broads from Great Yarmouth to Cromer following footpaths, bridleways, riverside tracks and the occasional minor road. The whole route takes at least three days, although sections of it are ideal for half-day or day excursions. A particularly enjoyable section is between Potter Heigham and Hickling Green, taking in a stretch of the River Thurne and snaking around the south side of Hickling Broad. The seven-mile section from Stalham and North Walsham is also appealing as it has decent bus links between the two.

Another walking route through the northern part of the region is the **Paston Way**, which meanders between North Walsham and Cromer, taking in 15 historic churches as it goes. The spidery, wandering route, waymarked in the North Walsham to Cromer direction, is anything but a straight line but does offer rewarding walking and some intriguing detours.

In contrast to the rather linear walking available along Norfolk's northwest coast, the area has many other walking possibilities, and circular routes are easy to organise if you don't mind the odd short section of minor road. With few contours on the map, it goes without saying there are no uphill struggles. The downside of this is that, away from water, the terrain can sometimes be a bit dull, but alongside river or broad, it can be a delight. Several of the rivers have footpaths that follow them for miles but seeing the broads themselves on foot is not so easy as most lack waterside paths.

Tourist information

Hoveton Station Rd ✆ 01603 782281.
Ludham Toad Hole Cottage Museum, How Hill ✆ 01692 678763.
Potter Heigham The Staithe, Bridge Rd ✆ 01692 677016.
Ranworth The Staithe ✆ 01603 270453.
Broads website ✆ www.broads-authority.gov.uk.

The coast: Overstrand to Caister-on-Sea

① Overstrand

Overstrand lies just two miles east of Cromer as the gull flies. Originally a place of crab fishing like its big-sister neighbour, it has slowly developed into a quiet resort with a safe, sandy beach. Much lauded in the writings of Clement 'Poppyland' Scott, the village was favoured by the Victorian upper classes and soon became known as 'the village of millionaires'. Some of its grandest buildings date from this period. Overstrand Hall was designed by a young Edward Lutyens for Lord Hillingdon, while Gertrude Jekyll was is said to have been responsible for the gardens at The Pleasaunce. The rather grand Overstrand Hotel, built at the turn of the 20th century, became a very popular hangout for the aristocracy and upper classes, and one of the most prestigious hotels along the east coast. Unfortunately, the architects built it rather too close to the cliff edge and its foundations started to crumble within a matter of years. It finally collapsed in 1947, ironically as the result of a fire.

Erosion is a serious concern all along this coast. In the neighbouring village of Sidestrand, the village church was moved back, stone by stone, from the cliff edge in the 19th century, although the tower was left standing where it was. Overstrand's original church had been swallowed up by the sea centuries before, in the late 1300s. A new church, of the same name – St Martin's – was built in 1399 but this too fell into disrepair by the middle of the 18th century and was a ruin by the mid-1800s (see page 47). A replacement church was built and consecrated in 1867 but this proved to be too small for local congregations and so in 1911 it was decided to restore and re-consecrate St Martin's.

A cliff walk to Cromer

A favourite outing from Overstrand is the **walk along the cliffs to Cromer**: a short, often windy, hike of just a couple of miles that gets a marvellous view over the resort and its pier as you approach from the east. This route, which also coincides with the last couple of miles of the Paston Way, is very popular all the year round. In autumn and winter, bushes that bear the brilliant orange berries of sea buckthorn flank the clifftop path. The berries look good enough to eat and they were, apparently, part of the diet of prehistoric man. Appearances can be deceiving though, as they taste unbelievably bitter – not the sort of things you'd want to put in a pie.

② Trimingham

Further southeast along the coast road from Overstrand towards Mundesley, the village of **Trimingham** has the rather unusually named church of **St John the Baptist's Head**. There is only one other church in Britain with the same macabre dedication, and that is in Kent. Needless to say, neither of these is the true repository of the apostle's cranium (which, to my knowledge, rests in the Ummayad mosque in Damascus): the name dates from a medieval scam in which hapless pilgrims were lured by the promise of holy relics. Certainly, as holy relics go, the head of St John would have been a very impressive attraction – if only it had been true. It does raise the question too: exactly what did they put on display here so as not to send away disappointed pilgrims? The church itself is a little on the squat side but it makes up for this by standing, like Napoleon on a soap box, at one of the highest points along the northeast coast – around 200 feet above sea level.

South of here, beyond tiny Gimingham, is **Trunch**, a place that sounds like a dull blow to the head but is, in fact, rather more pleasant. The gazebo-like, Gothic font canopy of Trunch's **St Botolph's Church**, carved with animals that include squirrels, monkeys, dogs and even a pig wearing a bishop's mitre, is by far the most striking feature of this 14th–15th-century building, although its hammerbeam roof is quite splendid too. **Knapton**, the village immediately east of Trunch, also has the interesting church of **St Peter and St Paul**, with its early 16th-century hammerbeam roof timbers lavishly decorated with angels with outspread wings, 138 in total (according to Nikolaus Pevsner), although the church itself claims 160 – or count them yourself and arrive at your own figure. The cockerel weathervane on the tower here is reportedly the design of the eminent Norwich School artist, J S Cotman, who gave drawing classes at nearby Knapton Hall.

The Legend of Black Shuck

'And a dreadful thing from the cliff did spring, and its wild bark thrilled around, his eyes had the glow of the fires below, 'twas the form of the Spectre Hound.'
Old Norfolk saying

Tales of Black Shuck, a dark ghostly hound with terrifying fiery eyes, are commonplace throughout East Anglia, especially along the coast. The legend may have arrived with Danish raiders, with 'Shukr' being the name of the faithful, yet ultimately abandoned, canine companion of the Norse god Thor. Alternative derivations may come from *scucca*, an Anglo-Saxon word that means demon, or even 'shucky', a local dialect word meaning 'hairy'.

One of Shuck's most notable appearances was at Blythburgh in Suffolk in 1577 (see page 237) when he appeared at the church and terrified the congregation, killing a man and boy, causing the tower to collapse and leaving scorch marks in his wake. Not content with this, Shuck was reported to appear at Bungay the very same day and put on much the same sort of performance at the parish church (see page 159).

The Overstrand version of the Shuck legend has it that two friends, a Dane and a Saxon, were drowned whilst out fishing together with their dog. The Dane washed up at Beeston and the Saxon at Overstrand, while the dog's ghostly presence roamed the coast in search of both his masters. Anyone unfortunate enough to encounter Shuck on his nightly patrol would generally find himself dead within the year. Along with any number of supposed sightings elsewhere, Shuck was reported to have made his home in the ruins of Overstrand's St Martin's Church until the restoration work of 1911 drove him away. He is rumoured to haunt the coast road between Overstrand and Sheringham.

Legend or not, Shuck has been quite an influential figure in literature. Sir Arthur Conan Doyle probably heard of the legend whilst on a golfing visit to Cromer in 1901 and a terrifying spectral dog character subsequently appeared in his *Hound of the Baskervilles*, published the following year. The setting was transposed from north Norfolk to Dartmoor but the descriptions of fictitious home of the Baskerville family are strongly reminiscent of Cromer Hall.

③ Mundesley and around

Mundesley is more of a large village than a town. The railway station that brought the Victorian elite here in the 19th century has long since closed and the nearest station these days is the Bittern Line station in North Walsham. John Seymour describes Mundesley as 'a good solid respectable seaside town, and that is all there is to say about that.' He has a point, but it also has a fine Blue Flag beach for bracing walks and safe swimming – a great place for children to splash about. The beach has a neat terrace of brightly painted beach huts next to the beach café, which add a splash of colour to an otherwise grey scene on an

overcast winter's day. It may not quite be Southwold in the charm stakes but at least it makes an effort. The tiny **Maritime Museum** (01263 720879) on Beach Road, one of the smallest in Britain, which is housed in an old coastguard lookout point, is worth 50p of anyone's money.

Stow Mill (01263 720298; www.stowmill.co.uk) lies just outside the village on the road south to Paston. Built in 1827 as a flour mill, it saw service for over a hundred years until 1930 when it was stripped of its machinery and converted into a dwelling. Since 1960, the four-storey structure has been slowly restored by a number of private owners. It is open for visitors most days and has a small shop attached. You enter through the side door by millstones and, after feeding your £1.50 into the honesty box at the entrance, are free to climb up a steep narrow ladder to explore each of the four storeys as far as the top dust floor. There's plenty to read on the walls telling you among other things that Stow Mill is a tarred, brick-walled, wooden-capped, tower mill, the third and final type in England, and that the gear on top of the main upright shaft is called the 'wallower'.

A little further along the B1159 coast road you reach the small village of **Paston**, where there is a magnificent flint and thatch **barn** built by Sir William Paston in 1581. At 160 feet long and 60 feet high it is one of Norfolk's largest, which is noteworthy even in this county of cavernous barns. The Paston family's dominant role in the village's history is brought to life through the legacy of the famous **Paston Letters**, a hugely historically important collection of 15th-century correspondence now kept in the British Museum and Oxford's Bodleian Library. The village's 14th-century St Margaret's Church has several memorials to the family; the most striking is that of Katherine Paston, sculpted in fine alabaster in 1628.

Bacton, a little further east still, is another small seaside centre but the name is more frequently associated with the enormous North Sea Gas Terminal that lies north of the village. The terminal is actually closer to Paston than Bacton. You can't miss it, as you drive right past on the coast road, although perhaps you might like at least try to do so. Both Paston and Bacton are quite attractive villages in their own right, although it is hard to see the attraction of the caravan site that is right next to the gas terminal itself: it offers an industrial outlook that only those homesick for Teeside could love.

Just south of Bacton, the ruined **Bromholm Priory** was an outpost of the Cluniac priory at Castle Acre in the Middle Ages, and an important pilgrimage centre as it claimed to have a piece of the True Cross.

Bacton Farm Shop On the coast road ☎01692 650271. Has a wide range of local products that include cheese, milk and ice-cream in addition to pork and ham from the farm's own rare-breed Gloucester Old Spot pigs.

Café B 2 Cromer Rd, Mundesley. A multi-tasking sort of place that serves teas, coffee, pastries and panini, as well as selling second-hand books and Kaffe Fassett knitting yarns.

Ship Inn Beach Rd, Mundesley ☏ 01263 722671. A decent enough local pub serving Woodforde's Wherry, Black Friar's Bitter from Yarmouth and other locally brewed guest beers and ciders.

④ Happisburgh

Continuing southeast along the coast past Walcott, which, frankly, is a bit of a grim sprawl of houses next to a bleak-looking beach, you arrive at Happisburgh, an instantly recognisable place thanks to its distinctive red and white banded **lighthouse**, the oldest working lighthouse in East Anglia. Happisburgh, pronounced 'Hazeboro', was put on the map back in 1990 when the repainting of the lighthouse became the object of a *Challenge Anneka* television programme, in which the presenter landed her helicopter and ran about badgering locals into revamping their village icon. The 'challenge' was to smarten up the dowdy-looking structure with a repaint in 48 hours. The task took almost two weeks apparently – although they didn't mention this in the television programme as this went rather against the spirit of things. They used the wrong type of paint too, which soon start to peel, so the lighthouse required an expensive repaint later on. They still talk about this event in the village – the next best thing to *Antiques Roadshow* coming to town. 'Put on the map' is perhaps an unfortunate choice of words as the twin threats of coastal erosion and rising sea levels currently threaten to erase parts of the village from the map altogether. Take a look at the cliffs from the end of Beach Road if you are in any doubt about this.

The lighthouse (www.happisburgh.org), which is occasionally open to the public in summer, was built in 1790 following a severe winter storm off the northeast Norfolk coast in 1789 in which 70 ships were wrecked and 600 men lost. Before that, apart from distant light from Cromer and Winterton, the only navigation aid had been the tall tower of Happisburgh's **St Mary's Church**.

Hill House Happisburgh ☏ 01692 650004. This converted 16th-century coaching inn is a good local pub that serves tasty, home-cooked food, including local fish, and a wide range of real ales. The Solstice Beer Festival takes place here each June, when up to 40 ales and ciders may be sampled. Sir Arthur Conan Doyle is said to have frequented the place and actually wrote a Sherlock Holmes story while staying at the inn.

Lessingham Manor Farms Heath Rd, Hempstead ☏ 01692 583053. A local producer of organic lamb and Red Poll beef that sell at Stalham Farmer's Market and also at the farm by prior arrangement.

Smallsticks Barn Café Cart Gap Beach, Happisburgh. Close to the new lifeboat station at Cart Gap, halfway to Lessingham along the coast, this is a small converted barn with good views from its courtyard and the usual range of coffee, tea, cakes and snacks.

⑤ Sea Palling and ⑥ Waxham

Sea Palling, south of Happisburgh and four miles east of the market town of Stalham, is another fairly nondescript coastal village with a nice beach that has boasted a Blue Flag award for several years now. The drone of jet skiers speeding along the foreshore might help spoil your peace, however. Right next door is **Waxham**, a smaller village that has a derelict church (St John's) next to a 15th-century gatehouse that once belonged to Waxham Hall. Originally there were two villages, Waxham Magna and Waxham Parva, but the latter has gone the way of much of this coastline and been washed away to sea.

Waxham Great Barn is one of the longest historic barns in the country. The building, which has featured in the BBC's *Restoration* series, was built in the early 1580s by the Woodhouses, a wealthy local family. Architectural salvage was common in those days if any material other than flint was to be used, and the barn's construction recycled parts of three monasteries closed by Henry VIII. The barn is actually a little larger than the slightly earlier one at nearby Paston and the roof may well have been built by the same carpenters.

Caroline Davison from Norfolk County Council's conservation department told me, 'The roof structure at Waxham barn is the same and was built only two or three years later. I like to think that the Woodhouses were making the point that they were the dominant family in the area, so they deliberately built their barn a bit bigger.' The Norfolk Historic Buildings Trust now manages the barn as a visitor centre on behalf of Norfolk County Council. It is open to the public in July and August and on Sundays throughout the year and has a café run by volunteers.

⑦ Horsey

The coast road from Sea Palling turns inland slightly to pass through the village of Horsey, which has the best of both worlds in being close to the coast but also at the very edge of the Broads. Standing only a couple of feet or so above sea level, the village has always had a fractious relationship with the North Sea just over the dunes and was cut off completely for four moths in 1938 when all of the villagers had to be evacuated. The village is tiny but manages to boast a good pub, a nice old barn and thatched church, and easy access to a beach. Roman coins have been found in the area on several occasions and so despite its obvious vulnerability, Horsey has been settled for a very long time.

A Horsey Mere circuit

One of my favourite **walks** in Broadland begins and ends at **Horsey Mere**, a broad just west of the village. The handy car park next to the staithe is alongside a four-storey windmill, lovingly restored by the National Trust. Horsey Mere, which also belongs to the

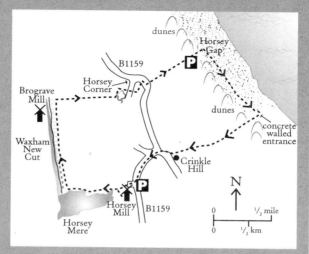

National Trust, is a small, picture-perfect broad with thatched boathouses and sedge warblers calling from the reed-beds. If you are lucky, marsh harriers may be flying overhead – I have seen them here on several occasions – and, in the winter months, hen harriers and day-flying barn owls too. There is also a permanent colony of cranes in the fields around here, although for some reason I have never come across them. The lovely thing about this walk, which is probably at its best on a clear, crisp winter's day, is that it gives you a taste of everything the area has to offer in the space of an easy five miles: reed-beds, lake, river, farmland, marsh, beach, dunes and the North Sea itself.

A marked footpath leads through reed-beds around the north side of the mere, along Waxham New Cut and over grazing marshes to a picturesque drainage pump before turning right to cross fields to the coast road. From here, a track leads over dunes at **Horsey Gap** to the beach, a favourite haunt of grey seals and their pups in winter. A mile or so southeast along the dunes, there's a muddy, pot-holed track that leads inland to reach the road at Crinkle Hill. The 'hill' part of the name should be taken with a pinch of salt – round these parts 'hill' can mean almost anything above the horizontal; this one is about six feet above sea level, perhaps a little less. The road leads back to the village past the Nelson Head pub – a tempting enough stopping point – opposite a picturesquely weathered flint barn. At Christmastime, you also cannot fail to notice the playful village garden filled with Santa's little helpers and other yuletide characters like red-nosed reindeer and cheery snowmen.

For coffee, cake and light meals there is a **teashop** at Horsey Corner on the coast road just before Horsey Gap. 'Well-behaved' dogs are welcome upstairs in the gallery where old postcards, bric-a-brac and second-hand guitars make for interesting browsing while you are waiting for your tea to arrive.

Nelson Head The Street ☎ 01493 393378 🖥 www.nelsonheadhorsey.co.uk. With a red telephone box immediately in front of the entrance and a log fire and cheery, warm interior within. Steak and ale pie is a mainstay; good Woodforde's beer.

⑧ Winterton-on-Sea

Winterton's Holy Trinity and All Saints' church is distinguished by its noticeably tall tower, the third highest in Norfolk, but steeples on steroids make good sense along this occasionally treacherous coastline: they stand out as beacons in this pancake-flat terrain. Local tradition sometimes claims that Winterton's church tower is 'a herring-and-a-half higher than Cromer'. Unfortunately, this is not true: it is, in fact, 35 feet shorter.

Daniel Defoe, who visited the village in 1722, remarked that all its houses seemed to be constructed out of the timbers of wrecked ships – a reflection on the hazardous nature of the coastline here. Most of the ones he commented on would have come from the fleet that was wrecked in the fatal storm of 1692. The danger of shipwreck can seem real enough if you come here on a winter's day when thick sea mist blankets the shoreline and stretches for a mile or so inland obscuring everything from view.

The **Winterton Dunes Nature Reserve**, north of the village, is a large hummocky stretch of sand dunes stabilised by marram grass that are home to a large colony of rare natterjack toads. Plenty of birds nest here too – little terns, ringed plovers and stonechats – and dragonflies flit above the ponds. You can often see seals offshore here too: there is usually a colony of them on the beach to the north. Other colonists found among the dunes to the north here are the odd naturist (and, perhaps, even odder naturalist) along with concrete pillboxes

constructed during World War II as anti-invasion defences. In 2005, a landslide resulted in some of these toppling on to the beach near the car park.

Clearly visible from Winterton is the **Blood Hill wind farm** at nearby Somerton, one of the first erected in the UK, as well as the more extensive offshore wind farm at **Scroby Sands**, built in 2003 and 2004. Of course, wind farms are not popular with everyone, least of all those who fear living in their shadow. 'Nimby' might sound rather like a Danish place name but around here it means something completely different.

A Winterton walk: dunes, fields and woodland

Starting and ending at Winterton, a rewarding **circular walk** can be made that takes in pretty well all that the area has to offer: sand dunes, wildlife, wind turbines and woodland. It is about five miles – two hours – in total, but easy going and varied. You might prefer to do the whole walk in the other direction if you want to keep the coastal stretch for the finale.

Starting at the beach car park, head towards Winterton Dunes Nature Reserve to the north until you reach a marked footpath beyond the nature reserve sign. Continue north along the sand dunes keeping the perimeter fence to your left. After a mile or so, the reserve ends at Winterton Ness; turn left here along the public footpath to Winterton Holmes in the Burnley Hall Farm. Turn left again towards the wind farm along a concrete farm road, which turns sharply right after another few hundred yards. When the track finally divides, turn left along the estate wall, heading south towards the wind turbines alongside woods. At the end of a small plantation to your right, turn left and then follow the path past the entrance and left towards Manor Farm. To the right, hidden in the woods, is the ruin of St Mary's Church. From Manor Farm, head east down Low Road past the duck pond to return to Winterton.

While Winterton retains the slightly isolated feel of the northeast coast, **Hemsby**, the neighbouring village, just a mile away, seems to belong firmly to Great Yarmouth's gravitational field. In Hemsby, you are starting to venture into a hinterland of caravan parks, amusement arcades and crazy golf that stretches all along the coast from here through Yarmouth and Lowestoft as far as Kessingland in Suffolk.

⑨ Caister-on-Sea

Virtually a suburb of Great Yarmouth, Caister offers much the same as Hemsby, except for the nearby remains of **Caister Castle**, a 15th-century moated castle built between 1432 and 1446 by Sir John Falstaff, the inspiration for the Shakespeare character. The Pastons inherited the castle from Sir John but before long the Duke of Norfolk, an enthusiastic and serial castle-grabber, took control of it having laid siege for a year. When he died, it passed back into Paston hands until the 17th century when the new London owner decided to tear most of it down. The castle (www.caistercastle.co.uk) now serves as home to the largest private collection of motor vehicles in Britain, and includes a minor star of *Chitty-Chitty-Bang-Bang*. Caister is also well known for its lifeboat and never-say-die fishermen, whose slogan, 'Caister men never turn back', says it all.

The word Caister comes from *castrum*, the Latin for camp: hidden rather unglamorously behind back gardens of semis and bungalows are the labelled knee-height walls of the late **Roman fort** (free access), built as a defence against Saxon raiders around AD200 and in use until the end of the following century, that gives the village its name. This is not to be confused with another Roman 'Caister' in the county – Caister St Edmund (Venta Icenorum) close to Norwich, a Romano-British settlement which has altogether more impressive town walls.

The Fisherman's Return The Lane ☎ 01493 393305 or 393631 ⌨ www.fishermans-return.com. This 300-year-old traditional brick and flint pub has a good range of local ales, including Woodforde's and Blackfriars, and bar food.

Into the Broads proper: North Walsham to the River Bure

⑩ North Walsham

This market town, just beyond the Broads, is the most important urban centre in northeast Norfolk. Having said that, it is still pretty low-key. The Bittern Line between Norwich and Sheringham passes through the town, as does the Weavers' Way long-distance footpath. There is no river but the now-disused North Walsham and Dilham Canal, which connects with the River Ant and Broads system, skirts the town to the northeast.

In keeping with Norfolk's radical tradition, the town became a focus for a rural uprising in support of Wat Tyler's Peasants' Revolt back in 1381, when a local dyer Geoffrey Litester headed a group of rebels calling for the abolition of serfdom. Workers' rights were not high on the agenda in the 14th century and, unsurprisingly, their pleas fell on deaf, and highly unsympathetic, ears. The rebels were attacked by none other than the Bishop of Norwich himself, Henry Despencer, who, if historic accounts are correct, rather enjoyed the bloodshed. The bishop, being a man of the cloth, was at least good enough to grant Litester absolution before having him drawn and quartered. Litester's quarters were subsequently dispatched to Norwich, King's Lynn, Great Yarmouth and his home village 'so that rebels, and those that rise above their place, may learn how they will end' – they did not do things by halves in those days. Bishop Henry erected three crosses to mark the crushing of the uprising, one of which can still be seen on the Norwich road just south of North Walsham.

Like Holt, most of Tudor North Walsham went up in flames, on this occasion in 1600, and most of the town's larger buildings date from the Georgian period. The town centre is a pleasant enough place to wander but the only real sight as such is the **Market Cross**, sometimes referred to locally as 'the gazebo', which has stood on the spot since 1550.

The North Walsham and Dilham Canal

Few expect to find canals here in Norfolk, far away from England's industrial heartland, and this modest stretch in northeast Norfolk is the county's sole example. It was created by the canalisation of the upper reaches of the River Ant and the locks installed were made a little wider than average in order to accommodate Norfolk wherries. The canal is a little less than nine miles long and begins at Swafield Bridge, just north of North Walsham, ending where it reaches the River Ant at Smallburgh near Stalham. Opened in 1826, it was mainly used to transport animal bones and phosphates to the bone mills at Antingham, although grain, coal and building materials were also carried by the wherries. The canal was sold off in 1885, but the money from the sale – some £600 – mysteriously went missing in the care of the company solicitor. He was never seen again.

Today, very little of the original canal, last used for a cargo journey in 1934, is navigable – just a couple of miles at the Smallburgh end – although there are plans to restore some parts of it for pleasure craft. It is best explored by following footpaths along its banks south of the villages of East Ruston and Honing. A canoe is an even better option: hire one at Wayford Bridge and paddle along Tyler's Cut to reach the staithe at the Honing Road bridge at the end of the channel, from where you can easily walk into Dilham village with its Cross Keys pub.

The Bluebell Bacton Rd ☎01692 404800. Just outside the town, this has the usual choice of bar food and Norfolk and Suffolk real ales on tap.

Tavern Tasty Meats The Street, Swafield, NR28 0RQ ☎01692 405444
🖰 www.taverntasty.co.uk. Norfolk's only accredited rare-breed butcher, selling gourmet sausages and excellent pork at their Swafield outlet and also at Holt's The Sausage Shop and the farmers' markets at Fakenham, Norwich and Aylsham.

Antingham bone mills

North of North Walsham, you find yourself in classic north Norfolk 'light-land' farming country of redbrick farmsteads and old, straight hedgerows. Much of this land formerly belonged to the **Gunton Estate**, centred upon Gunton Hall just north of the village of Suffield. **Antingham**, northwest of North Walsham, is a village of bone-crushers, or rather their descendants. The two Antingham bone mills took bones from butchers, slaughterhouses and knacker's yards and crushed them together with phosphates transported by rail and canal from North Walsham in order to make fertiliser (see box).

⑪ Worstead

This solid, distinguished-looking village with its seemingly oversized church has a long historic association with the medieval Norfolk wool trade. The clue, of course, is in the name, as the village became well-known for producing a particular type of cloth. 'Walsham' cloth was light and for summer wear, while 'Worstead' was heavier. The first cloth description soon went out of common use, but the village still gives its name to worsted, even though it has not been produced in the village for centuries. Worsted cloth was introduced to East Anglia by Flemish immigrant weavers and the soft-textured but hardwearing material became highly sought-after from the 13th century onwards. Back in the medieval heyday of Norfolk's weaving industry, Worstead was a thriving place with two churches – more of a town than a village – but as the wool trade shifted to the mill towns of the north of England, its economy started to dwindle. There are still a few weavers' cottages there, characterised by their high ceilings, lofty enough to accommodate a loom. Perhaps more remarkable is that Worstead still has an active, if rather symbolic, Guild of Weavers who sometimes put on demonstrations of their ancient craft.

St Mary's church, built with wool money in 1379, stands tall in the centre of the village and has a number of noteworthy features other than its sheer size: an impressive hammerbeam roof, box pews and a finely painted dado.

The **Worstead Festival** (www.worsteadfestival.org), the largest village festival in Norfolk, held each year on the last weekend in July, gives villagers the chance to show off a bit and makes for a fine day out. This is the perfect excuse for displaying rare breeds and prize farm animals and demonstrating country crafts from ploughing with heavy horses to sheep shearing, beekeeping and falconry. Classic farm vehicles and vintage cars are dusted off to take part in a parade and there is usually live music in the village square.

The **Bittern Line** has a station a couple of miles west of the village. Be aware that not all of the trains between Norwich and Sheringham stop here between Monday and Saturday. On Sundays, all trains stop at Worstead.

Crown Inn Smallburgh; ✆01692 536314. This thatched 15th-century coaching inn in the neighbouring village is probably the best bet in the area, with home-cooked food, a choice of real ales and a beer garden.
New Inn Church Plain ✆01692 536296. Worstead's village local has Adnams ales and home-cooked pub grub.

⑫ East Ruston

Halfway between North Walsham and Stalham, close to the route of the Weavers' Way, this sprawling village is home to the rather splendid **East Ruston Old Vicarage Garden** (01692 650432; www.e-ruston-oldvicaragegardens.co.uk), a rather special 32-acre garden open to the public from Wednesday to Sunday between April and October. It's less than two miles from the coast and vulnerable to onshore winds but the shelter of a belt of pines helps to maintain a relatively warm microclimate. Themed garden areas include the Californian Border and Desert Wash, a Tree Fern Garden, Sunken Garden and so on, as well as a wildlife flower meadow and cornfields sown with native species that have become rare in this age of herbicides. A pot of tea on the lawn here on a hot summer's afternoon with bees buzzing in the borders is an unbridled pleasure. The garden is not in the village itself but further east towards the coast along the Bacton Road, just beyond East Ruston church: guided tours on the second and fourth Tuesday of the month.

Butcher's Arms Oak Lane ✆01692 650237. A cosy, friendly village local with real ales and decent pub grub.

⑬ Stalham and ⑭ Sutton

These are two separate villages on the bend of the A149 at the northern limit of the Broads, both linked to the River Ant and Barton Broad by staithes. **Stalham** High Street is a hotchpotch of small shops and architectural styles but the town is probably best known locally for its supermarket that shall be nameless (but which rhymes with 'al fresco'), which, after years and years of planning permission being turned down, eventually took over the traditional saleground next to the bypass. It was inevitable, I suppose, that something as unfashionable as a weekly market and auction would finally give way to yet another 'out of town' shopping centre.

So what does Stalham have to recommend it now? Well, there is the rather interesting **Museum of the Broads** (01692 581681) down at the staithe, where you can see a mock-up of a wherry's cuddy (see box *Black sails in the sunset – the Norfolk Wherry* on page 66) and plenty more relating to the working life of the Broads. The museum, which is open seven days a week between Easter and October, puts on occasional events in the summer. The tiny **Firehouse Museum** (01692 580553) on the High Street is a fittingly eccentric place, the second-oldest fire station in the UK, with a 1902 fire engine and an array of fire-fighting paraphernalia on display.

Sutton has **Sutton Mill** just east of the village: at nine storeys high, the tallest remaining windmill in the UK (awaiting restoration and currently not open for visitors). The mill was built around 1789 on the site of a former tower mill. The Weavers' Way goes right past the mill before venturing west into Stalham.

Swan Inn Sea Palling Rd, Ingham ☎01692 581099. A 14th-century thatched inn in Ingham village, between Stalham and the coast, that was originally part of Ingham Priory and is one of two tied houses belonging to Woodforde's (the other is at Woodbastwick). The menu here is similar to that of Woodbastwick's Fur and Feather Inn, as is the selection of Woodforde's beers.

⑮ Coltishall

Coltishall gives its name to the RAF base that existed to the north of here until recently. It's actually quite a pretty village that sits in a bend of the River Bure. Formerly important for its malthouses and as a loading point for wherries travelling the Bure as far as Aylsham, the village's river trade fell into decline with the arrival of the railway line in 1879. Navigation beyond Coltishall became altogether impossible when the lock gates at Horstead were destroyed in a flood in 1912, and even today this remains the end of the line for boats venturing up from Wroxham.

Coming from Wroxham, the river bends sharply at **Belaugh** before it reaches Coltishall, and having passed the village meanders sluggishly through lovely woodland west of **Great Hautbois** – superb, safe canoeing territory that is often frequented by school groups. Great Hautbois – pronounced 'Hobbis' – gets its odd name not from 'high woods' or oboes but from the Alto Bosco or Haut Bois family, who acquired land in the area just after the Norman conquest. The village of Great Hautbois was the head of navigation of the River Bure in medieval times. There's a Little Hautbois too, halfway to Buxton, a tiny place that consists of just eight houses, one of which used to be a pub. Formerly, it was important enough to warrant its own church. The church has all but disappeared today but traces of its foundations can apparently still be seen in the grounds of Little Hautbois Hall.

A riverside walk

An enjoyable **circular walk** from Coltishall is to follow the footpath along the north bank of the River Bure through woodland as far as Little Hautbois, where you can cross the bridge to the south bank and cross fields via Hall Farm back to Horstead and Coltishall. A lengthier alternative is to continue northwest from Little Hautbois towards Lamas and Buxton, then return along the river path on the south bank as far as Little Hautbois bridge before taking the route described above.

Kings Head 26 Wroxham Rd ☎ 01603 737426. A 17th-century inn, close to the river and popular with the passing boat-trade, that serves bar meals and has real ales on tap.

Recruiting Sergeant Norwich Rd, Horstead ☎ 01603 737077 ᵺ www.recruitingsergeant.co.uk. In the village of Horstead, next door to Coltishall; the pub menu here makes use of Swannington Farm meat and local seasonal vegetables. Real ales include Adnams, Greene King and Woodforde's.

⑯ Wroxham and Hoveton

These two villages are practically joined at the hip – or rather, at the bridge. Many people, especially visitors, tend to refer to the whole settlement as Wroxham, much to the annoyance of Hovetonites. Effectively, for those who come here to hire a boat, lick an ice cream or shop at Roys, the business end of the village is immediately north of Wroxham Bridge – in Hoveton.

Wroxham (I have lapsed already – it should actually be Hoveton) is famous for two things: as the epicentre of the **broads cruiser hire trade** and self-appointed 'Capital of The Broads', and for **Roys**, the 'world's biggest village store', a local enterprise that is ubiquitous hereabouts. Ask any local, 'Where's Roys?' and they will know what you mean, although they might be incredulous that you need to ask. They'll point you towards Roys supermarket, anyway. 'Roys' was founded back in 1899 by two brothers, Arnold and Alfred Roy, to meet the needs of holidaymakers visiting the Norfolk Broads. Now it has branches throughout Norfolk and, to its credit, prides itself on selling locally sourced produce. Roys of Wroxham is well known throughout Norfolk but, technically, as all of the Roys commercial property lies north of the bridge, it really ought to be called 'Roys of Hoveton'.

Hoveton is anything but a typical sleepy Norfolk village. Once you cross the narrow bridge over the River Bure you'll find the place heaving with people in the summer. However, even if you do not wish to step out onto a motor cruiser here, it's still a good place to rent a canoe and paddle upstream. Canoeing downstream, alongside a flotilla of inexpertly, and sometimes erratically, piloted hire-boats on their way to Wroxham Broad is not everybody's idea of fun but to strike out north along the River Bure towards Belaugh and Coltishall is well worth doing. Canadian canoes can be hired from **Barnes Brinkcraft** at Riverside Road (01603 782625 or 782333; www.barnesbrinkcraft.co.uk).

Hoveton Hall Gardens (01603 782558; www.hovetonhallgardens.co.uk), popular for their azalea and rhododendron displays in late spring, are also close by, but probably more of interest to children is **BeWILDerwood** (01603 783900; www.bewilderwood.co.uk) a little way along the A1062 Horning Road, which describes itself as a 'curious treehouse adventure park'. Certainly, it's designed to exercise and stimulate the mind as much as the body. It's a magical place for children – forest folk like Mildred, the vegetarian Crocklebog who lives in Scary Lake, and the Twiggles, litter-hating goblin-like figures, are BeWILDerwood residents, as is a giant spider called Thornyclod.

BeWILDerwood's environmental pedigree is certainly impressive too. The treehouses, ropewalks and boardwalks are all built from sustainable wood, while the 50 acres of marshland and woodland that make up the site are entirely pesticide-free, guaranteeing that no harmful chemicals leak into the broads. If that were not enough, some 14,000 broad-leaved trees have been planted since the park's creation and the food on site is mainly locally sourced and organic. BeWILDerwood won the British Guild of Travel Writers (www.bgtw.org) award for best new UK tourism project in 2008; as Jane Anderson, who nominated the park for the award, attests it 'harks back to a pre-playstation, pre-mobile, pre-iPod era' even if its creator Tom Blofield does admit to having been partly inspired by the 1990s computer game Myst. BeWILDerwood is open year-round and under-threes go free. Bikes are available to rent at the **Norfolk Broads Cycling Centre** in the car park (07887 480331; www.norfolk broadscycling.co.uk) which also provides useful free cycling maps.

A couple of miles north of Hoveton along Tunstead Road, **Wroxham Barns** (01603 614619; www.wroxham-barns.co.uk) is a range of 18th-century barns and farm buildings that have been converted into craft workshops. Here, you'll find such things as woodturning, pottery and stained glass, all made on site with the finished goods being sold from the workshops. Several enterprises sell local produce, such as the **Norfolk Cider Company** (01683 784876; www.norfolkcider.co.uk), which makes both cider and apple juice and stages occasional demonstrations using antique apple pressing equipment. In 2009, **Uncle Stuart's Micro-brewery** set up for business here to brew and sell its own 'brewed-on-site' ales. Animal-loving children are well catered for as well, with a **Junior Farm** that provides opportunity for children to get up close to animals in a farmyard setting, offering activities like feeding rabbits and goats and grooming ponies.

Barton Broad, Hickling Broad and around

⑰ Horning

Heading east from Hoveton along the A1062 the first place that you come to is Horning, which, from a boating point of view, lies downstream along the River Bure beyond **Wroxham Broad**, **Hoveton Great Broad** and **Hoveton Little Broad**. Horning functions a little like a mini version of Wroxham. Firmly given over to the hire cruiser trade, it's all Edwardian thatch roofs and mock Tudor cottages that, depending on your taste, can be just the wrong side of quaint. Useful – indeed, invaluable – for cyclists and walkers is the seasonal **passenger ferry** next to the Ferry Inn pub that crosses the river here, avoiding all those twisting road miles involved in crossing the River Bure at Wroxham Bridge. In a car, of course, you have no choice.

From Horning, the River Bure meanders east through the Bure Marshes, with channels connecting it with Cockshoot Broad and Ranworth Broad, both ripe for exploration by curious boatmen.

A Broadland water trail

Taking me out on the *Electric Eel* at How Hill in late May, Paul, the boatman, gave me the low-down on traditional Broadland ways and how, with encouragement from the Broads Authority, some aspects of the traditional economy are currently being revived. After gliding past a kingfisher's nest in the bank where, perfectly on cue, such a bird darted past us like a rocket-propelled jewel, Paul pointed out a couple of small windmills next to the water where the sails had been removed. 'Do you see what they've done there?' he asked, just a little exasperated. 'Would that be anything to do with Health and Safety?' I ventured. 'Yes, absolutely right. They said they were a hazard for walkers. Can you believe it? They're nine foot above the ground for heaven's sake.'

We soon turned off the River Ant down a narrow tributary to leave the diesel-engine throb of the motor boats far behind. This really was another world, a minimalist landscape of reed, water and a blue slice of sky. Reed has been harvested for centuries in the region for use as thatch but the industry went into decline back in the Victorian period when the railways made cheap pan-tiles and slate available to all. Nowadays, thatch is back in fashion, and there's considerable demand for reed harvested in the Norfolk Broads, as well as the sedge that is used to 'top' the thatch. Reed harvesting is clearly not an easy job. 'You need to be a special character to be a reed cutter,' said Paul, 'It's hard, laborious work and, in the winter when you have to do the cutting, it's freezing cold too. The sedge has to be cut in the summer months and that's just the opposite: there's mosquitoes to bother you and your hands get cut up from gathering the sedge.'

Although reed-cutting is clearly no career for lonely, work-shy rheumatics, there is enough demand for the Norfolk product that the Broads Authority have been training up the young and willing over the past few years and employment has been created for at least a dozen local cutters. There is no question about quality according to Paul. 'Polish reed is a bit cheaper but it doesn't last anywhere near as long. Most thatchers reckon that Norfolk reed lasts for anything between eighty and a hundred years.'

After an hour of squeezing through narrow, reed-fringed channels, we head back to How Hill Staithe. On the way, we stop off at Reedham Broad, a recently reclaimed body of water that has resident bitterns and summer-breeding marsh harriers – a pair of which were quartering the reeds on the other side of the water, painstakingly searching for voles and mice. 'This was a reclaimed meadow with cows on it just thirty years ago but the Broads Authority have encouraged it to revert back to nature. It's manmade, I suppose, but then so are all the broads.'

⑱ Ludham, How Hill and around

The next village reached by taking the road is Ludham, a pleasant, typical Broads village that does not sit on the river itself but just to the north of it.

The village clusters around a crossroads with a pub and a church, and a road opposite the pub leads south past attractive houses with large gardens fronting on to **Womack Water**, a tributary of the River Thurne that serves as a staithe for boats. If you visit on Ludham Open Gardens Day, held every other year in June, you will get the chance to see some of these gardens. Horsefen Road, which leads south along the eastern bank of Womack Water, is similar, with some thatch-roofed barns, the parish staithe and a couple of boatyards. A staithe along here serves as headquarters for the Norfolk Wherry Trust (www.wherryalbion.com) where the wherry *Albion* is moored when it is not out on charter. Given so many water's-edge back gardens, it is perfectly possible for many Ludham residents to visit each other by boat, as I am sure some of them do.

The River Ant joins the Bure just south of Ludham and, a little way along this, **How Hill** rises above the river with its gardens, woodland and manicured lawns. Lest this sound too dramatic, I should add that How Hill, whilst undoubtedly the highest point for miles around, still only manages to reach about 40 feet above sea level. It is a hill, nevertheless – a welcome meniscus in this overwhelmingly two-dimensional landscape.

How Hill House is a residential Broads Study Centre that hosts courses and conferences and is not usually open to the public, although holiday courses and special events are organised by the How Hill Trust (01692 678555; www.how-hill.org.uk). A narrow road with passing places leads up from a junction just before Ludham and there is a free car park on the left just before the main building. The large meadow here – Fisherman's Field – is a popular spot for locals to take picnics, play cricket and fly kites. A track leads across this down to **Toad Hole Cottage**, a small marshman's cottage containing an information centre. A **wildlife walking trail** starts from here, but even better is the **water trail** that lasts for about an hour and makes use of the *Electric Eel* electric boat. The boat only takes six passengers and so it is usually best to book in advance at Toad Hole Cottage. It leaves every hour on the hour between 11am and 3pm on weekends, bank holidays, Easter week and half terms in April, May and October, and daily between 10am and 5pm from June to September.

Alfresco Tea Rooms Norwich Rd ☎01692 678384. Opposite Ludham's St Catherine's Church, this is a fine place for afternoon tea. They source food from within a 12-mile radius wherever possible, with honey coming from How Hill, meat from Ludham and bread from Norwich's Linzers bakery. There's an indoor tearoom and even a small, 'alfresco' element – two tables outside in the back yard.

⑲ Barton Broad

The **River Ant** twists north past How Hill to open into Barton Broad, one of the finest and most unspoiled of all these bodies of water. Barton Broad is the second largest body of water in the broads system and is managed as a nature reserve by the Norfolk Wildlife Trust. Hemmed in by reed-beds and swampy stands of alder, the broad is barely approachable by road and the only meaningful way to visit – other than walking along the short boardwalk – is by canoe or boat.

If you don't have your own boat or dinghy, there is a lot to be said for taking an organised trip on the *Ra*, a solar-powered boat that is usually moored at Gay's Staithe at the western end of the broad near Neatishead. An excellent **boardwalk** starts from the car park near the staithe too. To reach it, you first need to make a short half-mile walk along a footpath and lane to arrive at the start. The trail soon splits into two: one direction leads to a viewing point that looks over the southern edge of the broad, while the other takes a short circular course through the alder carr. It's very green and humid here, with warblers warbling in the trees, dragonflies hawking the moist air and yellow irises pushing up through the sedge. Watch out for mosquitoes though; they can sometimes be a nuisance on warm, still days.

A decade or so ago, Barton Broad was heavily polluted with nutrients from agricultural and sewage run-off but the multi-million-pound **Clear Water Project** has improved the water quality dramatically, even to the point of attracting otters back to the area. Back in the 1960s, the water here was a toxic chemical soup of phosphates (from sewage) and nitrates (from farms). Now, with investment from bodies such as the Millennium Fund and, fittingly, some detergent manufacturers, there has been a dramatic transformation. This is mainly thanks to painstaking suction dredging that has removed the nutrient-rich mud at the bottom of the broad and its channels. Although otters are present, you are far more likely to see herons, grebes, terns and a variety of ducks. Swallowtail butterflies are relatively common at the right time of year – between May and July – too. The waters of Barton Broad host an open regatta each August Bank Holiday organised by the Norfolk Punt Club, and the broad is also used by the Nancy Oldfield Trust to provide sailing and canoeing access for the disabled.

Barton Broad by solar power

The solar-powered *Ra* was built in Germany using stainless steel and teak, and is the first of its type in the UK. Mike Spires, a part-time skipper of the boat, told me, 'It's got 16 batteries and 14 solar panels altogether, so it can keep going even on cloudy days'. Happily, there was little cloud cover on the day we sailed out from Gay's Staithe near Neatishead. As we progressed around the south end of the broad, enjoying the sight of candy-striped grebe chicks riding on their parents' backs, Mike pointed out a narrow channel leading off to the east. 'That's called Ice House Reach. There used to be an icehouse just down there. Ice was collected from the broad and stored there before it was transported all the way down to Yarmouth by wherry.' Close to the mouth of the channel was a small, nondescript island. 'You might not believe it looking at it now but that's known as Pleasure Hill Island. People came to have picnics there and it even used to have a bandstand. They even held dances on it.' The island eventually disappeared: a modern counterpart was built after dredging, although it looks too small to be hosting dances at any time in the near future.

Cruising up to the northern end of the broads where the River Ant makes its entrance, we turned our attention to the water lilies dotting the water's surface. 'They're a really good sign of clean water. Yellow water lily needs good water quality; white needs even better. What's remarkable is that they can lie dormant for years. Water lilies weren't here at all during the 1960s and 70s, when it was like a pea soup here. As soon as the water quality got better they started to appear again, growing from tubers that had lain dormant in the mud at the bottom for decades.'

The Broads, as everyone now knows, are a manmade environment, but it's easy to overlook the way that they have been altered to fit in with man's changing needs over the years. According to Mike, the River Ant did not originally pass through Barton Broad but passed just to the east of it. Irish workmen known as navigators were employed to cut a channel through to the broad so that wherries could be used to transport goods. 'Irish navvies did a lot of work in the Broads. They dug the channel here back in 1729 and there is even a Paddy's Lane in Barton Turf in memory of them.'

An excellent way to explore the broad is to hire a **canoe** for the day from Wayford Bridge (Bank Dayboat, 01692 582457). To canoe south along the River Ant, cross Barton Broad, head up Lime Kiln Dyke to moor and visit Neatishead and perhaps have lunch before returning north, will probably take the best part of a day. It's a fairly energetic outing but, at the end of such a day, you will have better memories and a far more intimate impression of the Broads than will those who have chugged through them in a cruiser.

Barton Broad has three villages that just about touch it – **Irstead**, **Barton Turf** and **Neatishead** – none of which could be described as a metropolis, although Neatishead does have a pub, a shop and a restaurant. Barton Turf has an interesting church with fine paintings on its rood screen but no other facilities whatsoever. Such a distinct lack of facilities may, in fact, represent a temptation for those in search of peace and quiet. A friend of mine who moved to Neatishead from London a dozen or so years ago told me, 'I've got used to living there; I've become a country boy now. Neatishead's got most things we need, like a pub and a restaurant. It's a lovely place to live. Every Saturday morning, we take the children for a walk along the boardwalk at Barton Broad and if we want a taste of big city lights then we just drive into Wroxham and go shopping at Roys. I hardly ever go into Norwich these days, let alone London.'

The stretch of the bank between Barton Turf and Neatishead is known locally as 'Millionaires' Row'. The posh, two-storey boathouses at the water's edge are just the icing on the cake, belonging as they do to large private houses in sumptuous surroundings set well back from the water. Barton Hall on the edge of Barton Turf village is where Lord Nelson's sister once lived and it is claimed that Nelson learned to sail on Barton Broad, presumably when he wasn't doing the same thing in Brancaster Staithe harbour.

Although it is hard to reach Barton Broad using public transport – Smallburgh or Stalham being about as close as you can get – the whole area west of Barton Broad makes for marvellous cycling territory. With a bike, you might also wish to venture south of Neatishead to **Alderfen Broad**, another NWT reserve just outside **Irstead Street** – it's a decent circular walk too, starting in Neatishead. How Hill lies just across the marsh to the east but there is no direct way to reach it on either land or water.

White Horse Inn Neatishead ☎ 01692 630828. An old-fashioned village pub serving decent Adnams and generous portions of pub grub.

⑳ St Benet's Abbey

This atmospheric ruin was built on land granted by King Canute around 1020, probably on the site of a 9th-century pre-Viking hermitage. It's something of a rarity in having a pre-Norman origin and also for managing to survive the Dissolution. It did this by agreeing to a crafty swap of lands belonging to the Diocese of Norwich. The Bishop of Norwich continues to hold the role of abbot here and, once a year on the first day of August, he arrives by wherry to preach an annual service at the site. The gatehouse contains a windmill, squeezed within its walls, that was put up by a local farmer at the turn of the 19th century. A more recent addition is the oak altar cross made from wood given by the Royal Sandringham estate. The Norwich School artist, John Sell Cotman, made a painting of the abbey in the middle of the 19th century, when it looked much as it does today, albeit with sails still present on the windmill. You can see this in Norwich Castle Museum in addition to another splendid painting of it by Henry Bright.

With a mysterious profile that combines these ecclesiastical and vernacular traditions, St Benet's Abbey is at its best viewed from the banks of the river at dusk, when long shadows help to enhance the numinous atmosphere. For those lacking river transport, a visit to the site requires a detour south from the main road at Ludham – an easy cycle ride. The farm track that leads down to the abbey goes past a farmyard that has an enormous high midden of used car tyres of all shapes and sizes. So, if you were curious as to the fate of all the old tyres in Norfolk, now you know.

㉑ Woodbastwick

South of the River Bure, there is a minor road that runs more or less parallel to the river and the A1062 beyond, which connects several villages on the southern fringe of the broads that stretch east of Wroxham. **Salhouse** village lies some distance from the broad of the same name – and its station lies even further away and is pretty useless for waterside exploration. **Woodbastwick**, the next village to the east, with a good pub and brewery, is an altogether better bet. Just

Black sails in the sunset – the Norfolk Wherry

Undoubtedly the most iconic craft on the Broads system, the Norfolk Wherry evolved as a cargo boat based upon the design of the earlier Norfolk Keel, a square-rigged, clinker-built vessel. Norfolk Keels started to vanish from service around 1800 and were succeeded by wherries that could be sailed using a smaller crew. The typical wherry is a shallow-bottomed, double-ended, single-sail boat fitted with a gaff rig; its sail is black as a result of weatherproofing with tar and fish oil. The tall mast was fitted with a counterweight so that it could be lowered to pass under bridges. Most wherries were capable of transporting around 25 tons of goods, which they would carry from boats anchored off the coast at Great Yarmouth or Lowestoft upriver through the broads system. Although once a common sight, they were in steep decline by the 1940s as cargo became increasingly transported by road and rail.

Eight wherries survive in Norfolk today, one of which spent 40 years in Paris as a houseboat before its return to the Broads in 2005. A few have been lovingly restored in recent years. The 60-foot *Albion*, probably the best known, was originally used to haul coal between Bungay and Lowestoft. This vessel has had a colourful, if chequered, career: sinking near Great Yarmouth in 1929, to be raised three days later, and then losing her mast, in 1931. Today, *Albion* is based at Womack Water near Ludham and has been maintained by the Norfolk Wherry Trust (www.wherryalbion.com) since 1949. The craft may be chartered with a skipper and mate for groups of up to 12 people, while members of the Trust have the opportunity to go on pleasure cruises several times a year at a reduced rate. In summer they hold open days when you can meet the crew and look around the boat for free.

As I was shown round the *Albion*, what impressed me most was learning that the 40-ton boat, and other wherries like it, were sailed using just a two-man crew. 'Man beyond the village to the east, the road splits and a track leads down to the Bure where there is a seasonal foot (and cycle) ferry across the river to Horning. There's parking here too, along with a nature trail through the reed beds. If you cross the river here you may perceive a noticeable drop in tranquillity as you step off at Horning, not that that the village is particularly raucous or anything – it's just a lot busier than Woodbastwick.

Woodforde's Brewery (www.woodfordes.co.uk) next door to the Fur and Feather Inn runs occasional brewery tours that must be booked in advance (01603 722218). They have a shop and visitor centre too where, as well as bottles and beer-boxes, you can buy souvenirs that range from key rings to T-shirts.

Fur and Feather Inn Slad Lane ✆ 01603 720003
🕾 www.thefurandfeatherinn.co.uk. A very popular thatched pub with a fireplace and newspapers but no pool table or juke box. The food is hearty English – steak-

and boy, or man and wife, there was just two to sail it', I was told. 'And if they didn't sail, they didn't get paid.' What goods did the wherry carry? 'It carried anything that needed to be carried – coal, bricks, flour, grain – and in the winter when there was ice on the broad it might carry ice down to Yarmouth too. This one worked mostly on the southern system – you know, on the Waveney – but it got about quite a bit.' Standing on the deck you can't help but be impressed by the enormous tree-trunk of a mast that stands proud of the deck. 'They lowered that while they were in motion as they approached the bridges. They were so good at doing it that they didn't even need to slow down.' Below decks, things are pretty cramped and you soon learn that the 'business end' of the boat – the storage area – is, in fact, most of the boat, and there is little space for frivolities like comfort. The sharp end has a tiny cabin called a 'cuddy' where there are two narrow bunks separated by a cast-iron stove – cramped but endearingly cosy.

Another wherry, the *Maud*, was moored in the next staithe, a slightly larger, 42-ton vessel. The skipper on board had sailed wherries in his youth, as had his father and grandfather before him. Massive rope-tying hands seemed to be part of the family inheritance. 'My dad used to carry a chain through the streets of Yarmouth on his way to the boat. He used to throw it in the water to slow it down.' The *Maud* worked right up until her demise in 1965 when she was sunk at Ranworth Broad as protection for the narrow spit of land separating it from Malthouse Broad. She was moved in 1976 to another part of the broad before being resunk. The boat was eventually rescued from the mud to be slowly and painstakingly restored by Vincent and Linda Pargeter between 1981 and 1999. Now she is back on the water once more – a floating museum piece with far more history in her timbers than the photographic display in the hold could possibly hope to relate.

and-kidney pudding, corned beef hash and the like – while the beer is excellent, and so it should be with the Woodforde's brewery right next door. Woodforde's ales tend to find their way into most of the meat dishes too. Local suppliers are used wherever possible, such as Coxford's butchers in Aylsham.

㉒ Ranworth

Ranworth is a charming, dinky little village right next to Malthouse Broad, little brother of neighbouring Ranworth Broad. Ranworth's **St Helen's Church** is well worth a visit, not simply because it has some of best screen paintings in the county and a beautifully illuminated antiphoner (service book) on display, but because it has a feature that offers something that geology does not in this neck of the woods – elevation. A steep, tightly curving staircase leads up 89 steps to the roof of the church tower. It's very narrow so try to avoid two-way traffic if at all possible. The view is undoubtedly worth the climb: the broad and river are laid out in front of you and Broadland comes alive and suddenly means a lot more than just blue and green shading on a map. From here, as well Ranworth and Malthouse Broads immediately below, you can see the Bure and Ant rivers, How Hill, the wind turbines near Happisburgh and even the coast at Yarmouth. On a really clear day, Norwich Cathedral spire is said to be visible.

Ranworth Broad is a Norfolk Wildlife Trust (NWT) reserve of some importance, with a visitor centre, boardwalk and child-friendly nature trail along with the usual range of Broadland wildlife: plentiful wildfowl in the winter months and dragonflies and swallowtails in summer. There's also an enormous roost of cormorants, one of the largest inland roosts in the country. During World War II, a number of wherries met their fate in the water here, by design rather than by accident, sunk to obstruct enemy hydroplanes attempting to land here. More wherries were sunk in the post-war years to prevent erosion of the broad's banks. Indeed, this is where the wherry *Maud*, now happily afloat again, was dredged up from in the early 1980s.

The **boardwalk** to the NWT visitor centre leads from the car park opposite The Maltsters pub, turning a corner past private moorings and continuing a little along the road before it leads into woodland. A magnificent, and very ancient, oak tree stands near the entrance of the boardwalk, which continues through alder carr (see page 71) until you reach the thatched Visitor Centre close to where Maltsters and Ranworth Broad meet. There's an observation point here and fantastic views over the broad and back to Ranworth church.

Ranworth Church Coffee Shop and Visitor Centre St Helen's Church
☎ 01603 270340. Where better to enjoy tea and a cake than in the shadow of the church tower that you have just climbed? Church volunteers run the café – it's cheap and cheerful and you know your money is going to a good cause. Open mid-March to the end of October and weekend afternoons year-round, it has a garden for outdoor seating in summer or tables inside for cooler weather.

㉓ South Walsham and South Walsham Broad

A mile or two south of Ranworth, **South Walsham** sits astride the old Norwich to Acle road. The village is a quiet, rural place, with a pub, a post office and some modern housing tucked away behind the old. There used to be two pubs here but one has gone the way of several in the county and been reincarnated as a Chinese restaurant. Presumably they've found that supplying dim sum in a small Norfolk village is more profitable than pulling pints.

The village is home to the lovely **Fairhaven Woodland and Water Garden** (01603 270683; www.fairhavengarden.co.uk), which comprises over 50 hectares of mature oak woodland, and shady bluebell and candelabra primula-carpeted glades divided by waterways with footbridges stretching across them. I once inadvertently dropped a telephoto lens into the water whilst crossing a bridge here. I managed to retrieve it from the mud, but it was never the same again: every image I've taken since has a little speck of South Walsham silt floating in the frame. Moral: do not try to change lenses when crossing water.

The gardens lead down to privately owned South Walsham Broad from where it is possible to take a short boat trip out onto the broad, or a longer one across the broad and along Fleet Dike to get a view of St Benet's Abbey. The gardens are probably at their best in late spring when the naturalised candelabra primula and rhododendrons are at their prime, but every season has its charms, even winter. The Fairhaven Garden Trust has been run as a charity since 1975 and all gardening is done entirely organically using just leaf mould and compost as fertiliser. Both the trust office and the tearoom are managed in a sustainable manner too.

Just north of the village, **South Walsham Broad** is linked to the River Bure by way of Fleet Dike. There's a footpath that leads past a boatyard all the way along the dike from a car park, and if you fancy making a **circular walk** from here it is quite a long six miles or so via the river and Upton Fen before you return to your starting point. There are no viable short cuts, but it is rewarding and varied, if you are up to it.

From the car park, walk past the boatyard along Fleet Dike, where there are usually a number of hire boats moored up. As you approach the confluence with the River Bure, you cannot help but see the iconic form of St Benet's Abbey ahead on the opposite bank; in fact, you will see it before you see the river itself. The path turns east and along the river, where there will be ditches full of reed and marshy grazing to your right and broads cruisers – and if you are lucky, possibly a wherry – plying the river to your left. Here and there, you'll pass clumps of gnarled old willows. In early summer, there'll be sedge warblers singing in the reeds, dragonflies darting through the air and tortoiseshell, and perhaps even swallowtail, butterflies flapping around.

As the river curves southeast past a drainage pump, continue until it curves the other way and you can see a concrete farm track striking off south across the marshes. Follow this for some way as it zigzags across the marshes away from the river and you will eventually emerge at the far eastern end of the boggy woodland that surrounds Upton Broad. Although the zigzags might persuade you that you are heading the wrong way, don't be tempted to deviate across the marshes until you reach this point: I tried to once and ended up walking through Norfolk's largest nettle colony... in shorts – not to be recommended! A footpath leads from the farm track through a corner of the Upton Fen woods before reaching a road. Walk west through Cargate Green and then take another footpath on the southern flank of the woods until you pass a large modern farm, Holly Farm, where there is a fishing pond.

The entrance to Upton Broad and Marshes NWT reserve is just down from here along Low Road, an important wetland site with rare dragonflies and butterflies like swallowtail and white admiral as well as many scarce water plants. It's a good place to see water voles too, with a waymarked trail and boardwalk for visitors. Back on the road, head across the T-junction to Pilson Green then turn right along the edge of a field where the houses start. Turn right when you reach the road and continue north along it a little way before taking another footpath that leads west after Town House Farm. This will take you back to the South Walsham Broad car park.

The Ship Inn 18 The Street ☎ 10603 270049 🖰 www.theshipsouthwalsham.co.uk. Now a gastro pub, The Ship has a lunchtime and evening menu that mostly features traditional dishes that make use of locally sourced ingredients like Brancaster mussels. Adnams and Woodforde's ales are served on draught and daily specials are available.

㉔ Hickling Broad

Hickling Broad, the largest in all the system, is the classic Norfolk broad, with blue water, golden reed beds and white-sailed yachts bobbing on the water. It's off limits to power craft, which is a blessing, and with a good footpath around its southern side – in actual fact, the Weavers' Way – it is almost as enjoyable for walkers as it is for sailors. The birdwatching is excellent: you can often see marsh harriers hawking the reed beds here, and hear sedge and Cetti's warblers exploding with song within them. In summer, at certain times at least, swallowtail butterflies are just part of the scenery. Like Barton Broad, Hickling Broad is a nature reserve under the jurisdiction of the Norfolk Wildlife Trust, which has a visitor centre (open April to September) and bird observation hides here. A water trail takes visitors by boat across the broad to visit the Tree Tower, a raised observation deck only accessible by the water trail, from where you can get a magnificent view over the broad to the North Sea coast beyond.

Early summer, when the swallowtails and dragonflies are out and about, is perhaps the perfect time to be here but even winter is good if you are wrapped up against the wind that blows straight from the North Sea (it is no coincidence that both sailors and wind-surfers favour this broad). In winter, there is a daily **raptor roost** at Stubb Mill in the middle of the marshes just north of the broad, where you can witness birds of prey flying in to roost at dusk. This can be spectacular at times, with combinations of marsh and hen harriers, merlins, cranes and pink-footed geese. To visit, it is necessary to park at the NWT car park and walk half a mile or so to the viewing area.

Hickling village, just to the north of the broad, is a pleasant enough place to stop for refreshment. The village is split neatly into two parts – **Hickling Heath** and **Hickling Green** – with the former being of most interest to sailors because it is closer to the staithe. The former pub here, the Pleasure Boat Inn, right by the staithe (see box below), used to serve the wherry trade. A young Prince Charles spent a night here back in 1961 when his shooting party could not make it back to base. Seemingly, he was told off by the landlady for making too much noise whilst having a pillow fight. Hickling Green is mainly residential but has its own local, the Greyhound Inn. St Mary's Church, which lies a little way north of Hickling Green, has the curiosity of a horse-drawn hearse inside.

Visiting Hickling Broad without a car is a challenge but far from impossible. Hickling village has bus services from Great Yarmouth and North Walsham, from where it is easy to connect to Norwich and Cromer.

South of Hickling Broad, straddling the busy A149, is **Potter Heigham**, a village resolutely geared to the boat hire trade. The village is best known in these parts for two things: its **medieval bridge**, under which many an inexperienced skipper has come a cropper, and Lathams, a super-cheap discount store. The bridge dates back to 1385 and has a very low arch that can cause headaches (quite literally) to novice sailors. Fortunately, there is a bridge pilot to help boats safely through. There are dozens of waterside bungalows along the River Thurne here; one of them, downstream from the bridge, known as the 'Dutch Tutch' or 'Helter-skelter House', is fabricated from the top of a helter-skelter that used to grace Britannia Pier at Great Yarmouth and was the first residential building on this stretch of the river.

Greyhound Inn The Green, Hickling ☎ 01692 598306 ⌂ www.greyhoundinn.com. A 17th-century brick-and-flint local pub that uses local produce.

A couple of Norfolk terms

carr A carr refers to a boggy wooded area that represents an intermediate stage between a fen or bog and dry woodland. Carrs are typically characterised by alder, willow and sallow trees, which have high tolerance of waterlogged conditions.

staithe This term, used throughout east and northeast England, comes from an Old Norse word for harbour or landing place and usually refers to a narrow manmade channel where boats were landed and unloaded of goods. Norfolk staithes are often used as moorings today.

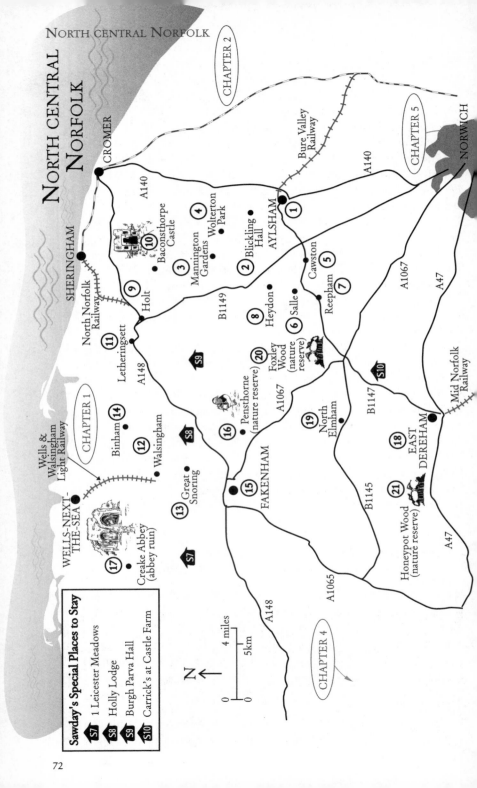

NORTH CENTRAL NORFOLK

North Central Norfolk

North central Norfolk

CHAPTER 2

CHAPTER 5

NORWICH

CROMER

Bure Valley Railway

A140

A140

Baconsthorpe Castle

(10)

(4)

Wolterton Park

Mannington Gardens

(3)

(2)

Blickling Hall

AYLSHAM

(1)

SHERINGHAM

North Norfolk Railway

(9)

Holt

Cawston

(5)

Reepham

(7)

A1067

A47

(11)

Letheringsett

A148

B1149

(8)

Heydon

Salle

(6)

(20)

Foxley Wood (nature reserve)

S9

CHAPTER 1

Wells & Walsingham Light Railway

(14)

Binham

Walsingham

(12)

S8

(16)

Pensthorne (nature reserve)

A1067

(19)

North Elmham

B1147

S10

Mid Norfolk Railway

WELLS-NEXT-THE-SEA

(17)

Creake Abbey (abbey ruin)

S7

(13)

Great Snoring

(15)

FAKENHAM

(18)

EAST DEREHAM

(21)

Honeypot Wood (nature reserve)

B1145

A47

A1065

A148

CHAPTER 4

Sawday's Special Places to Stay

S7	1 Leicester Meadows
S8	Holly Lodge
S9	Burgh Parva Hall
S10	Carrick's at Castle Farm

N

0   4 miles

0   5km

3. NORTH CENTRAL NORFOLK

Norfolk's wool country that once was – this chapter covers the north coast hinterland and the gently undulating landscape of what is sometimes cheekily referred to as 'upland Norfolk'. It's a region of small, solid Georgian towns and massive wool-trade churches, grand estates and country houses: an enclosed landscape with lighter soils and fewer hedgerows than further south. The area is bounded, more or less, by the market towns of Aylsham, Holt, Fakenham and East Dereham, although there will inevitably be the odd diversion. The main rivers here are the Wensum and Bure, which slowly converge as you head east across the county to combine at Breydon Water outside Great Yarmouth.

Visitors tend rush through this part of the county en route to the Norfolk coast, which is a pity because there's plenty of interest here. And it's true to say that you'll find more of the traditional spirit of north Norfolk *away* from the coast than at it. Holt is close enough to the fashionable north coast to have its own claim as an alternative base for visiting that region, a reality reflected in its range of smart shops and places to eat. Aylsham is more overlooked, despite the fact that the presence of Blickling Hall just down the road brings in quite a few visitors. This is a shame as, for my money, it's just as attractive as Holt. Fakenham and East Dereham are a little more humdrum, but both pleasant enough market towns with their own merits.

There are some highly appealing villages. Reepham and Cawston have imposing churches, while Salle is just an imposing church without a village. North Elmham has a Norman chapel and the site of East Anglia's former Saxon cathedral, while Little Walsingham has very much a living pilgrimage tradition. Tucked away in between are sleepy estate villages like Heydon and even sleepier ones like, dare I say it, Great Snoring.

Getting around

This is straightforward enough: there are good roads to Aylsham and Fakenham from Norwich. The main road to Holt branches off the Norwich to Cromer road at Norwich Airport and, once through a rather dreary commuter village, it's a nice drive through intermittent woodland and rolling farmland to reach the market town. East Dereham lies just of the A47 dual carriageway that links Norwich with King's Lynn. Away from these main roads, things are much, much quieter and you would get far more out of the experience by being on a bike.

Public transport

The public transport network is reasonably good, with plenty of **buses** between Norwich and Aylsham, Fakenham and East Dereham, although Holt is better connected with the coast than it is with the Norfolk capital. The fast, regular X1 service that links Great Yarmouth, Norwich, East Dereham and King's Lynn is ever useful, as is the X29 that runs between Norwich and Fakenham. If you want to travel between towns within in the area, like Aylsham and Holt for example, it's more problematic and will require a little more judicious juggling with connections. If you are not too averse to computers, scrutinising www.travelineeastanglia.org.uk usually pays dividends.

Two short **railway** lines may also be of limited use: the Wells & Walsingham Light Railway (01328 711630; www.wellswalsinghamrailway.co.uk) between April and November, and the Mid-Norfolk Railway (01362 690633; www.mnr.org.uk), between East Dereham and Wymondham from March to October.

Cycling

Exploring by bike is idyllic along the back roads of north central Norfolk, and areas like the quiet lanes around Heydon, Reepham and Salle are perfect for casual exploration, with plenty of alluring churches to investigate, strategic well-placed pubs for refreshment and some great views.

The **Marriott's Way** is an excellent off-road path along a disused railway track running between Norwich and Aylsham along a curving route that takes in Reepham and Cawston. The Way, one of the longest stretches of disused railway paths in the country, follows the River Wensum west out of Norwich before curving northwards at Lenwade. It's not exclusively meant for cyclists: it's

A Norfolk cycling odyssey

Sheila Rattray is a rare and unusual woman – in the very best sense. Having retired from her hospital job four years ago, Sheila, a mother of five grown-up children, decided that she needed to keep herself fit now that she would no longer be cycling the seven miles a day that she used to cover between her Norwich home and place of work. She resolved to make up the missing miles by making forays into the Norfolk countryside on her bike. The long-term aim was to visit all the Norfolk villages marked on her road map – effectively, all of them.

As she began to find her outings more and more enjoyable, she upped the ante from 35 to 50 miles a week, then finally to 50 in winter, 100 in summer. Sheila is strict with herself: if she hasn't reached her quota by the end of the week she will make a special expedition just to complete it, even if the weather's bad. She has her own set of rules too. All the journeys have to begin and end at her Norwich home. So far, she has visited every village within 20–25 miles of Norwich and quite a few beyond. The region far to the west around King's Lynn presents a problem though, as it's so distant from Norwich. When I suggested that she take her bike on the Cambridge train out to Thetford or Lakenheath, she baulked slightly, 'No, I think that would be a bit like cheating. I have decided that it all has to be done from home.'

used by all sorts – leisure cyclists, Norwich commuters, dog-walkers and so on – and you really don't need a mountain bike as the surface is mostly pretty smooth, compacted sand or gravel, although it does get rougher after Whitwell. Indeed, the surface of this track was the subject of some controversy in its early days when its compacted sand was found to cause staining. One irate dog-walker complained of her pooch turning irreversibly orange as a result, and for a while the route become known to Norfolk County Hall insiders as 'the Tango trail'. If you think the Marriott's Way as a whole seems improbably curved for a railway track then you are quite right: the 180-degree Themelthorpe Curve that leads to Reepham was the sharpest bend in all of Britain's railway network. It was constructed in 1960 for moving freight, mainly concrete, from Lenwade but didn't stay in service for long as it was closed down in 1985.

Walking

This isn't vintage walking territory, but you can find plenty of pleasant enough options for casual wandering, with numerous circular walks possible around the small market towns. The 1:25,000 OS Explorer maps 238 and 251 pretty well cover it.

Probably the most rewarding terrain lies in places like Hockering and Foxley – both of which have gorgeous ancient tracts of woodland – or in open parkland of great **estates**, of which Blickling Park, Wolterton Park and Holt Country Park fit the bill nicely, with walks that take in lakes, pasture, woodland

Sheila clearly loves her cycling. Early on in her born-again cyclist career, she cycled all the way from Norwich to Montrose, the place of her birth, in Scotland. More recently, she continued that journey even further north, cycling from Montrose to Orkney and Shetland in quite awful weather. Sheila's probably happiest on her day trips in Norfolk though. 'I really like those roads that don't have white lines down them – the wee ones with grass in the middle and sand at the edge. I like all the wee flowers at the wayside too. Last year, I saw the biggest bank of cowslips I'd ever seen in my life – somewhere near Fundenhall. I enjoy looking at the stock in the fields; it reminds me of growing up on a cattle farm in Aberdeenshire. I love to see the rivers too – especially when they flood – and the wee thatched houses in the villages.'

Sheila's preparation for an excursion is minimal to say the least. 'I don't take food – I'll maybe get something from a farm shop and I like an ice cream sometimes too.' She doesn't take a map either. 'I'll follow the signposts and ask for directions. Talking to people, that's the thing – they're usually really friendly when they find out what I'm up to. I do like getting a bit lost too.'

Looking at the map she showed me, covered in felt-tip marks showing where she had been, I noticed that there were no marks south of the Waveney. Perhaps, she didn't bother recording these. 'Och no, I've never crossed into Suffolk, if it's not Norfolk it doesn't get cycled.'

and sweeping views. You could also try sections of the Mariott's Way (see Cycling, page 74), or the Weavers' Way and Bure Valley Walk that both terminate in Aylsham, or the Nar Valley Way from Beetley, near Gressenhall, north of East Dereham, to Castle Acre and beyond.

Aylsham and northwards

① Aylsham

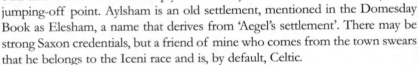

In many ways, Aylsham is the archetypal Norfolk market town. Sitting squarely between Norwich and the coast at Cromer, it is distant enough from both to have an independent life of its own and is far more than simply a dormitory town or coastal jumping-off point. Aylsham is an old settlement, mentioned in the Domesday Book as Elesham, a name that derives from 'Aegel's settlement'. There may be strong Saxon credentials, but a friend of mine who comes from the town swears that he belongs to the Iceni race and is, by default, Celtic.

Like Worstead, Aylsham was once a weaving town, in this case one that specialised in linen. Powerful medieval nobleman John of Gaunt became lord of the manor here in 1372, which meant, rather curiously in geographical terms, that the town became part of the Duchy of Lancaster. Although John of Gaunt appears on horseback on the town's sign, it is unlikely that he ever actually set foot here in real life. The town's **market** originated in 1519 thanks to a charter from Henry VIII. The small market square remains the heart and soul of the town today and the oldest building around it is the Black Boys Inn that has stood on the same site since the mid 17th century. There used to be a Black Boys pub in Norwich's Pottergate too but this was re-named some years ago in a nod to political correctness (casual racism and pub signs are not such strange bedfellows when you consider the number of Saracen's Heads and Turk's Heads found throughout the country that glorify the prejudices of the Crusades). The Black Boys would have always been the town's most prominent hostelry, serving as a coaching inn on the Cromer to Norwich run. Daniel Defoe is said to have stayed here – there again he did visit pretty well everywhere in the region.

There's a twice-weekly market in the square and a **farmers' market** on the morning of the first and third Saturday of the month. Equally well known, within the county at least, are the **Monday sales auctions**. Years ago, the Monday auctions used to bring all manner of old boys to town to buy and sell agricultural paraphernalia to each other. You could buy house-clearance rubbish for next to nothing. These days, it's quite a bit posher, with antique dealers perusing the items on offer. There's even a separate artworks sale that attracts national dealers.

Proud to be Slow

Aylsham has admirable green credentials. It proudly became plastic-bag-free in 2008 and even the new Tesco supermarket, opened in July of that year, claims to be the 'world's greenest supermarket' constructed as it was from sustainable materials such as recyclable plastic. In recognition of Aylsham's enviable quality of life and very liveable nature, the town successfully became Norfolk's first **Cittaslow** ('Slow Town') in 2004, the second town to do so in the country (Diss joined shortly after). Originating in Italy, the concept of a Cittaslow town is that of a community that relishes good food, a relaxed living and working environment and a high quality of life above more mundane concerns like the availability of supermarkets and car parks. In Norfolk, both Diss and Aylsham have managed to fulfil these criteria with consummate ease, although both certainly have supermarkets and parking too. Aylsham had to change very little to become a fully-fledged member as it already quite effortlessly ticked all the right boxes. This is easy to believe: Aylsham has always been 'slow', although perhaps 'laid back' is a more fitting description for the town as it hurtles snail-like into the 21st century.

Aylsham's Slow Town standing is closely linked to its Slow Food credentials. **Slow Food Aylsham** (www.slowfoodaylsham.org.uk) was formed in 2004 in anticipation of its coming Cittaslow status. Slow Food Aylsham actively supports local food producers and retailers and does its best to encourage people to shop locally. According to Slow Food 'convivium' leader Liz Jones, Aylsham sees itself as an 'unpretentious foodie town', and for a small town of just 6,000 to boast three butcher's shops, two greengrocers, two fishmongers, several cafés and a fortnightly farmers' market this seems a reasonable description. There's a food festival held in October that promotes local food businesses in addition to highlighting the benefits of slow food to both local environment and economy.

Just north of the market square you'll find the church of **St Michael and All Angels**, where the landscape gardener Humphry Repton, who lived nearby at Sustead, lies buried in the graveyard. Repton's tomb has the following inscription, which celebrates the very essence of impermanence and the cycle of life, and perhaps anticipates the Slow way of thinking with its eco-centric, altruistic outlook:

> 'Not like Egyptian tyrants consecrate,
> Unmixed with others shall my dust remain;
> But mould'ring, blending, melting into earth,
> Mine shall give form and colour to the rose;
> And while its vivid blossoms cheer mankind,
> Its perfumed odours shall ascend to heaven.'

The town is small enough to walk around in half an hour or so and my recommendation, after the market square and church, is to wander down towards the watermill at Burgh-next-Aylsham a little further downstream along the River Bure. Surprisingly perhaps, the section of the Bure that runs through the town was not navigable until the 18th century and, even then, wherries from the coast would struggle to reach the staithe. You can reach Burgh-next-Aylsham by following the Bure Valley Walk from the Bure Valley Railway Station, where there's a tourist information centre. The railway is a good way to arrive here if you're coming from Wroxham and The Broads (see page 41). Heading southeast alongside the railway, turn left after about a mile and a half just before Brampton when you reach a small stream marked on maps as The Mermaid.

At **Erpingham**, just north of Aylsham, **Alby Crafts** (01263 761590; www.albycrafts.co.uk) is a craft centre set in two courtyards of converted brick-and-flint farm buildings. Here, there's a range of shops and galleries as well as working studios where woodturning, stained-glass making and sculpture take place, plus a tea room and gardens

Black Boys Hotel Market Place, Aylsham ☎ 01263 732122
🌐 www.blackboyshotel.co.uk. Right on the market square, this long-standing hotel and restaurant serves a fairly traditional English menu that includes local produce such as aged English beef from Swannington Farm.
G F White Traditional Butchers 16 Red Lion St, Aylsham ☎ 01263 732264
🌐 www.whitesbutchers.co.uk. An award-winning traditional family butcher specialising in meat, game and poultry. Many products are prepared to traditional family recipes and they will prepare meat to order.

② Blickling Hall, ③ Mannington Gardens and ④ Wolterton Park

A short way north of Aylsham, Blickling Hall (01263 738030; www.national trust.org.uk) is one of England's most prestigious country estates and has been in the care of the National Trust since 1940. Anne Boleyn may well have been born here, although there seems to be some uncertainty, but the building that you see standing today dates from after her time, the 1620s, and is a superb example of Jacobean architecture. The house attracts a large number of visitors, as do the formal gardens, but what cheapskates like myself often prefer is simply to walk (for free) the miles of footpaths that run through the estate. All manner of possible walks start either from near to the entrance or, further away, from the car park at Itteringham Common. Approaching the park from the Great Wood to the west allows for super views across oak-studded parkland to the lake and Blickling Hall beyond. You should also definitely check out 'The Pyramid', marked on most maps as a mausoleum. This is actually both of those things: a 45-foot high, pyramid-shaped mausoleum that holds the grave of John, the 2nd Earl of Buckinghamshire, who died in 1793. It's all rather esoteric and Egyptian in character, and really quite a bizarre sight tucked away in this corridor of conifers, and missed by a surprising number of visitors.

While you're here, you might want to call in at **Samphire** (01263 734464; www.samphireshop.co.uk) in the Estate Barn next door to the Buckinghamshire Arms close to the Blickling Hall entrance. Samphire is a food shop with a difference, with all its products locally sourced from small-scale suppliers. Being on first-name terms with their suppliers means that they can be confident that the rare-breed meats, organic pork and poultry sold here have high standards of animal welfare. There's also bread from North Elmham Bakery and vegetables from local growers. The pork pies come very highly rated.

Not as well known but well worth a visit, nearby **Mannington Gardens** and **Wolterton Park** (01263 584175 or 768444; www.manningtongardens.co.uk) both belong to the Walpole family. Mannington Hall is not open to the public except by special appointment but its gardens are open in summer and make for pleasant walking. Wolterton Park, landscaped by Humphry Repton, is open year-round and has walks of varying length along a good network of public rights of way and permissive paths. There's the ruin of a round-tower church close to the car park and the hall itself is also open for tours each Friday in summer. **Barker**  **Organics** (01263 768966) run the walled garden belonging to the hall as an organic smallholding and have a few organic open days each year.

><><><

S₽ Buckinghamshire Arms Blickling ✆ 01263 732133. A Jacobean Inn, owned by the National Trust, in a similar style to the hall, close to the estate entrance. There's a pleasant outdoor garden for al fresco drinking and dining in summer.

S₽ Saracen's Head Wolterton ✆ 01263 768909 🖰 www.saracenshead-norfolk.co.uk. Tucked away on a quiet lane close to the Wolterton estate, this isolated country inn serves up local produce like venison, rabbit, mussels and crab in a convivial bar with a wood-burner.

S⑨ Walpole Arms The Common, Itteringham ☎ 01263 587258
☝ www.thewalpolearms.co.uk. The daily chalkboard here boasts an adventurous,
seasonal menu that brims with local produce like Cromer crab and venison from
the Gunton estate. You can eat either in the bar or in the stylish dining room.
There's an excellent wine-list and Adnams and Woodforde's ales on tap too.

West of Aylsham

West of Aylsham, the villages of **Reepham** and **Cawston** both have
impressive, beautiful churches, while the massive wool church at **Salle** more or
less stands on its own. Heydon is a handsome estate village. Reepham, Cawston
and Salle all lie in close proximity to each other, which makes their oversized
churches all the more remarkable.

⑤ Cawston

Cawston is a largish but compact village with a fascinating church and a rather
good café that is popular with cyclists, in what is excellent cycling territory – the
Marriott's Way goes right past the village and the local back roads are heaven-
sent for those on two wheels.

The village's **St Agnes Church** is a marvel, certainly one of the most
interesting in the county. Even before you enter, you encounter
some fearful gargoyles on the parapets and a splendid green
man and a dragon in the spandrels above the west door. Inside,
there's a double hammerbeam roof strewn with huge angels, a
rare 15th-century rood screen and wooden box pews. The local
gentry had the comfy box pews while the hoi-polloi had to fend
for themselves. The class system was as rife in church on Sundays as
it was for the rest of the week outside. A friend from the village told me this is
where the expression 'go to the wall' comes from. 'If you didn't have a family
pew in the church, you would have to "go to the wall". You'd have to stand up
at the side for the service'. The stained glass is gorgeous but even better is the
rood screen, created around 1460 and with about 20 paintings by Flemish artists
– a series of saints, famous and less well known, including St John the
Evangelist, St Jude and St Matthew (who wears glasses to read his book).

Cawston is also home to **Broadland Wineries** (01603 872474;
www.broadland-wineries.com), a business that established itself here 40 years
ago. The BRC and Organic accredited wines are not grape-based but are British
fruit and country wines made from fruit like blackcurrants and elderflower.

All Things Nice 9 High St ☎ 01603 871246. A popular, family-run café, deli and
patisserie, selling produce from local suppliers.

⑥ Salle

There is not much to Salle village, a couple of miles west of Cawston, apart from a few cottages and a well-used cricket pitch. John Betjeman is reported to have said that, church-wise, you are either a Cawston or a Salle man. Really though, both have their charms. The spandrels above the door of **St Peter and St Paul's church** here have no green man but, instead, a pair of scale-covered angels.

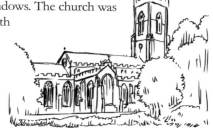

Inside, there's a real sense of space, accentuated perhaps by the absence of stained glass in many of the windows. The church was in a terrible state at the end of the 19th century but restoration finally came with funds provided by Duleep Singh (the last Maharajah of Punjab) of the Elveden Estate (see page 188). The repairs followed William Morris's philosophy of sensitive restoration as opposed to the more typical Gothic makeover fashionable at the time.

As a result, there is almost nothing Victorian to be seen here. What you will see is an enormously tall wooden font cover, supported by a sort of winch system, which dates from the 15th century, and distant angels and bosses high in the roof beams that retain some of their original medieval paint. If you want to see some bosses close up, go through the door at the northwest corner near the font where you'll find a narrow staircase leading up to a Lady Chapel, which has some wonderfully quirky bosses in the vaulted ceiling.

What I find most touching about the place are the carvings in the 15th-century misericord seats that have a variety of faces, some benevolent, some quite threatening. One looks like a tempestuous Greek god; another, a gentle monk, his head polished from hands gripping on to him over the centuries. The best are two facing corner stalls that depict two monks deep in conversation, their faces pure medieval but also somehow quite contemporary.

⑦ Reepham

The largest of this trio, just south of Salle, Reepham is a small town with a fine market place that has the King's Arms, a 17th-century coaching inn, on one side, and what was once a brewery, the Old Brewery House Hotel, on the other. A market takes place here every Wednesday.

Reepham is rare in having three churches (one of which is ruined), side by side and sharing the same churchyard – reputedly one of only two places in Europe like this. St Mary's Church is joined to Whitwell St Michael by a vestry corridor, while the third church belonging to Hackford parish burned down in the 16th century to leave just a fragment of wall. This unusual state of affairs features on the town sign that also shows the three sisters who were supposedly responsible for building all three churches – complete nonsense of course as they were built over a much longer period. The three-in-one churchyard actually came about by all three churches being built on the intersecting point of the respective parish boundaries of Reepham, Hackford and Whitwell.

The town instigated a **summer festival** in August 2008 that featured arts, music, comedy and crafts. Its 2009 successor was hailed as a great success and hopefully this will prove to be an ongoing annual tradition.

At Salle Moor Hall Farm between Salle and Reepham, **Salle Hall Organics** (✆ 01603 879406 🌐 www.salleorganics.co.uk) have a great range of fresh and flavoursome fruit and veg on sale from their farm shop in part of a converted 16th-century barn.

Kings Arms Market Place ✆ 01603 870345. A 17th-century former coaching inn with Adnams and Woodfordes ales and a reasonable bar menu.

⑧ Heydon

North of Salle, Heydon Hall lies at the centre of a leafy estate of pasture and parkland. Over the years, the tiny estate village of Heydon, with its wide green and Earle Arms pub, has become well known, locally at least, as a popular focus for weekend outings. If anywhere in Norfolk deserves the accolade of 'hidden village', this does. Heydon became Norfolk's first conservation area back in 1971 and has won a couple of Best Kept Village awards.

Part of the explanation for the village's pristine status comes from the fact that there is no through road. You arrive at the village green by the pub, tearoom and well and that's about as far as you can go on wheels. The estate's rented cottages that surround the green have attracted quite a bohemian community over the years and, in many ways, the whole village is something of a Victorian throwback. There's also a slightly feudal feel to the place, as everything in the village, including the pub, tearoom, smithy and all the houses, is owned by the Bulwer Long family who have lived in the hall since 1640. This timeless quality has not gone completely unnoticed and Heydon's village green is the sort of place beloved of movie location scouts – it has certainly featured in more than a film or two. If you remove the cars from the scene, there is nothing whatsoever to give the game away that Queen Victoria is no longer on the throne. The commemorative well in her name that dates from 1887 is, in fact, the village's most recent structure.

Earle Arms The Street ✆ 01263 587376. With Adnams ales, a good selection of wines and decent pub grub, this pub on the green is very popular at weekend lunchtimes.

Village Tea Room The Street ✆ 01263 587211

🌐 www.heydonvillageteashop.co.uk. A cosy village tearoom filled with china knick-knacks that serves light lunches, snacks and cream teas. Be aware of the 15-minute 'last orders' before closing, as they seem rather strict about this.

A short Heydon walk

With a lovely green, a pub and a tearoom, Heydon is a good place to use as the focus of a walk or a cycle ride. A good option for a short, two-mile walk along a rectangle of tracks and lanes is to wander past the church and the gatehouse of Heydon Hall, turning left along a broad track and past a meadow before entering some woodland. You'll soon pass a house tucked away in the trees to the right, fork left along a path across Old Common to a minor road where you should turn left and continue south to reach a junction with a bigger road. Turn left and then left again and you will find yourself back at the village green. Cyclists who want to venture a little further could make a three-cornered circuit through Reepham, Cawston and Heydon, taking in Salle along the way, using a combination of farm tracks, minor roads and a section of the Marriott's Way.

Holt and around

⑨ Holt

Better known to visitors to the county than Aylsham, Holt seems a more cosmopolitan sort of place. Standing en route to Norfolk's prestigious north coast, it is an old market town that has found renewed life. Like Aylsham, it is solidly Georgian, but there's a confidence and sassiness here too that comes from its proximity to places like Blakeney and Cley-next-the-Sea.

As with many market towns, a devastating fire wrecked the town in the past: almost all its buildings were reduced to ash on 1 May 1708. The subsequent rebuild has resulted in a handsome Georgian centre, although one survivor is Gresham's School, Norfolk's most prestigious public school dating from 1555, which brings a certain amount of gravitas to the community.

The town centre is certainly attractive, with elegant colour-washed frontages and a handful of narrow lanes running off the high street. What becomes immediately apparent is the staggering number of **shops** and services for such a small place; not just along the main streets but also set back from the High Street in a procession of courtyards – Feather's Yard, Old Stable Yard and the largest, Apple Yard, which has the excellent Holt Bookshop (01263 715858; www.holtbookshoponline.co.uk). Two more lie just off Albert Street – Lees Yard and Chapel Yard. In addition to the newsagents, chip shops and greengrocers that you might expect in a small Norfolk town, there are also a surprising number of clothes shops, galleries, bakeries, kitchen shops and antiquarian bookshops. I really cannot think of anywhere of similar size where you would find quite so many cafés and tearooms – not in East Anglia anyway – and where else would you find five – yes, *five* – estate agents hugger-mugger, side by side in the market place? Unless you are planning on buying a property here, you will probably find the **tourist information centre** (0871 200 3071) of far more use. It is on the Market Place next door to the Bircham Gallery.

If Harrods were to open up a branch in Norfolk, they would probably put it here, but actually there is no need as Holt already has a pretty close equivalent in **Bakers & Larners** (8–12 Market Place ✆ 01263 712244 🖰 www.bakersandlarners.co.uk), a smart department store with an exceptionally well-stocked and rather luxurious food hall that claims 125 varieties of cheese. There's also a wine department that has a bewilderingly wide choice of varieties and vintages.

Great to be Green (9 Chapel Yard, Albert St ✆ 01263 711733) is, as its name suggests, a home and garden shop in which everything is either British Made or Fair Trade, while Bird Ventures next door (✆ 01263 710203 🖰 www.birdventures.co.uk) is a wildlife shop for those who want to provide for the wildlife in their garden.

Byfords 1–3 Shirehall Plain ✆ 01263 711400 🖰 www.byfords.org.uk. An all-day brasserie and deli that also functions as a 'posh B&B', Byfords is a Holt institution with superb homemade food and snacks, and especially fine cakes and puddings.

S◗ The Hunny Bell The Green, Hunworth NR24 2AA ✆ 01263 712300 🖰 www.thehunnybell.co.uk. A few miles south of Holt towards Melton Constable, this upmarket eatery sits by a lovely village green in the Glaven Valley. Food is fresh, imaginative and locally sourced and offerings include King's Lynn brown shrimps, Brancaster mussels and Norfolk Wherry beer-battered cod. The bread is homemade and the beer supplied by Wolf's Norfolk ales.

Owl Tea Room and Bakery White Lion St ✆ 01263 313232. On the corner of White Lion Street and Church Street, this busy place that has claims as Norfolk's Oldest Tea Rooms serves light lunches, snacks and afternoon tea in cosy rooms behind the bakery and also in the small garden. The 'Please switch off your mobile phone' signs make for pleasant respite.

⑩ Baconsthorpe Castle

The main reason for coming to the out-of-the-way village of Baconsthorpe is for a look at Baconsthorpe Castle , which lies some way from the village along rutted farm tracks. The castle is really more of a fortified manor than anything else. Henry Heydon started construction in 1486 and the Heydon family lived here for almost 200 years, expanding their property as their family wealth grew. It fell into ruin in the mid 17th century when the Heydon fortune went into decline and the family were obliged to take a sledge hammer to their property and sell it off for use as building materials. The outer gatehouse, a later addition, has survived better than most, and this alone continued to be occupied until 1920 when one of its towers collapsed. It must have been an odd and slightly creepy place to live, so far from anywhere else other than the farm next door. With jackdaws noisily swirling around in the trees above the moat, it remains a lonely, atmospherically mysterious spot today.

Half of the fun is getting here, which from any direction requires venturing along twisting country roads before striking out on farm tracks for the last mile or so. If you come from the south, you'll pass first through Plumstead, which just about typifies the rural landscape around these parts: a narrow sandy road and rolling fields; round bales of hay rising over a farmyard wall; an isolated phone box next to an overgrown churchyard; boxes of tomatoes and marrows for sale outside cottage doors. Cycle here and you will appreciate it even more, or you could drive here and then do a circular walk on arrival. There are even occasional Sanders buses to the village from Holt and Sheringham. The sign in the car park has some good walking suggestions including a circuit that takes in Hempstead and Baconsthorpe via Becket's Farm and Ash Tree Farm, with the opportunity for a drink or snack at the Hare & Hounds in Baconsthorpe village.

⑪ Letheringsett

Take the Fakenham road from Holt and you soon reach Letheringsett on the River Glaven, with a pub on the west side of the river and a watermill on the east. **Letheringsett Watermill** (01263 713153; www.letheringsettwater

mill.co.uk) sits behind a large millpond, a constant source of power for this, the only working watermill in the county. It's a solid, four-storey building with a shop on the ground floor that sells a variety of flours from the mill in addition to a range of whole foods. For £3, you can visit the working parts of the mill and there are working demonstrations of the milling process from time to time.

The present mill dates from 1802, although one stood on the same site at the time of the Domesday Book. The mill was converted to diesel power in the 1940s but was reconverted to waterpower in 1984. Mike Thurwell, who started restoring it in 1987, had absolutely no experience of milling at all when he took the place on but today it's a highly successful enterprise. 'I can't keep up with demand,' he told me. 'We produce about 3½ tons a week at the moment but we could easily get rid of eight tons. We've just got two new millstones from Holland made from German quartz – they cost £3,500 each – but I don't know how good they are yet as I'm still running them in.' Running in new stones means that the flour produced needs to be sent off for inspection until it is declared fit for human consumption. 'The test flour can be used for pigs as they don't mind a bit of grit in their diet.' Different millstones are used to produce different grades of flour. 'The French burr stones we use to make white flour, and we use the Derbyshire for wholemeal. With the new stones up and running we should be able to increase production up to about seven tons of flour a week.' Did the mill ever run dry? Was there ever a danger of power failure? 'You're joking,' says Mike dismissively. 'There's a million gallons of water out there in the millpond. Every bit of water in the river goes past this mill.'

Walsingham to Fakenham

⑫ Walsingham and ⑬ Great Snoring

'England's Nazareth', it likes to call itself, although 'Norfolk's Lourdes' might be equally appropriate. Walsingham is actually two adjoining villages, Little Walsingham and Great Walsingham, and in true Norfolk topsy-turvy style, Little Walsingham is the larger of the pair.

The village has long been famous as one of Britain's foremost pilgrimage centres, a tradition that began just before the Norman Conquest in 1061 when a Saxon noblewoman had a vision of the Virgin Mary here. A wooden replica of the house of the Holy Family in Nazareth was constructed and an Augustinian priory founded in the 12th century to enclose the chapel. This set the ball rolling for what would become an important European pilgrimage tradition which continued until the time of Henry VIII when the shrine and priory were destroyed as part of the Dissolution, despite the fact that the monarch had made his way here from Cambridge in his youth. The pilgrimage was re-established at the end of the 19th century and has gone from strength to strength ever since.

Both Catholic and Anglican **pilgrimages** are held here. The largest annual event, the Anglican National Pilgrimage, takes place here each Whitsun, when there is usually a good deal of heckling from hard-line Protestant pickets who view the proceedings as shameless popery. Numerous other pilgrimages happen throughout the year and the quaint narrow streets of Little Walsingham are sporadically busy almost year-round. Summer attracts quite a number of non-pilgrim visitors too. Whatever your take on religion, Walsingham is certainly an attractive place that has not allowed itself to become too fazed by centuries of Marian mayhem. In fact, it is probably its very status as a pilgrimage centre that has, by and large, kept the village so untainted by modern development.

It's an interesting place to wander and reflect on what has or hasn't changed over the centuries. Today's pilgrims mostly come by coach or car and are generally better-scrubbed and less disease-laden than those who would have gravitated here in medieval times. No doubt the charlatans, quacks and dodgy corrupt monks who would have preyed on hapless pilgrims are thinner on the ground too. In terms of buildings, all that is left of the original Augustinian priory is a large arched window that stands in the abbey gardens, a Norman gateway and two wishing wells. You must pay to enter the abbey gardens and pass through the tourist office by the 'pump' to do so. The **pump**, in fact a 16th-century octagonal pump-house with an iron brazier on top, has pride of place in Common Place, the square that is Walsingham's's heart, with the tourist office, Shirehall and Bull pub all surrounding it.

The **Shirehall Museum** (01328 820510) served as a hostel in the 16th century but was converted into the Shirehall at the end of the 18th century. The courtroom is now part of the museum, which gives a good overview of the village's history as a pilgrimage site. The **High Street**, a very pretty street composed almost entirely of timbered houses, leads off Common Place. Along here, you'll find a few gift shops, the evocatively eroded Norman gate of the priory, a crocodile or two of pilgrims in season, and splendidly old-fashioned tearooms like The Swallows and The Old Bakehouse. The gift shop on the corner has such a large choice of jam and candles that you could almost imagine this becoming a place of pilgrimage in its own right.

A couple of miles south along a narrow road at **Houghton St Giles** you'll come to the **Slipper Chapel**, a restored 14th-century building that houses the contemporary Catholic shrine. This has long been considered the last staging point along the pilgrimage route to Walsingham and the done thing, for the pious at least, was to remove footwear here and continue the last stretch into Walsingham barefoot. Numerous kings have performed this act of piety in the past, even Henry VIII, although few do it today. While the hardcore devout may be thinner on the ground these days, they are certainly still out there. A few years ago, I remember seeing a man hauling an enormous cross along the hard shoulder of the Fakenham road just outside Norwich. Quite obviously, he was Walsingham-bound. The only concession that this modern pilgrim had made to ease his tough journey was to affix a little wheel to the bottom of his cross to make hauling slightly easier.

The gloss put on the area by its religious connections makes it easy to overlook the loveliness of the valley of the River Stiffkey hereabouts. From the Slipper Chapel, you can cross a ford to reach tiny Houghton St Giles and then continue up what seems like a surprisingly steep hill to reach Great Snoring. Stop halfway along just before Canister Hall Farm and you'll be rewarded by what I think is one of the choicest views in north Norfolk, looking west over the valley and the folded hills beyond – a scene that presents perfect counter evidence for use in any 'it's all flat' debate. **Great Snoring** isn't dull but it is certainly sleepy, almost somnolent. It's actually quite a charming little village tucked into a fold of a gently sloping land. **Little Snoring**, close to the A148, is a little more wide-awake and, somewhat contrarily, quite a bit larger than its neighbour. Here, the rather unusual church of **St Andrew** is set slightly back from the village on a sloping site. The church has a round tower that has a windmill-like cap and what look to be dormer windows, but the really odd thing about the tower is that it is detached from the main body of the church, which is of a later build. The suggestion is that there may originally have been two Gothic churches side by side on this site although no one seems to know for sure. There used to be an airfield beyond Church Farm next to the church that was a base for Mosquito and Lancaster bombers during World War II, commemorated by plaques in the church and a Mosquito and propeller on the village sign.

Bull Inn 8 Common Place, Little Walsingham ☎ 01328 820333. Decent Adnams beer and reasonable pub grub at lunchtime but not evenings.

Green Man Inn Holt Rd, Little Snoring ☎ 01328 878350. On the A148, this has a decent range of bar food and Adnams and guest real ales.

Old Bakehouse Tea Room 33 High St, Little Walsingham ☎ 01328 820454. One of several old-fashioned tea rooms in the village.

⑭ Binham

Turn right off the A148 just beyond Letheringsett and head due west and you pass through a landscape of big fields and small villages – Saxlingham, Field Dalling, Binham. It is well worth stopping at **Binham** to see the remains of **St Mary's Priory**, all the more remarkable because, although the rest of the priory lies in ruins, its church has been patched up and had its aisles removed to become the village parish church.

In a landscape of flint and brick, churches made of stone are rare indeed and this one is a monastic ghost that looks all the more odd for the ornate windows of its facade being blocked up with workaday brick. An architectural historian might talk excitedly of the priory's west window being the earliest example of Decorated tracery in England but you really do need to know this in order to appreciate just how atmospheric it all is.

Apart from the stone used for the church, the rest of Binham village is made almost entirely of flint – the extensive farm buildings, the cattle yard walls, the village cottages. You would be hard-pushed to find a flintier place, making the finely dressed imported stone of the priory church seem all the more precious as a result. With Blakeney port just down the road in one direction and the pilgrimage centre of Walsingham in the other, Binham with its priory must have been a bustling place back in the medieval period. Today, the village is the very antithesis of 'bustling', but guided tours of the church and monastery take place between May and September at 2.30 on Sunday and Tuesday afternoons.

⑮ Fakenham and ⑯ Pensthorpe

A medium-sized market town on the River Wensum, Fakenham is more of a place to shop and do business than go out of your way to see. I feel a bit sorry for poor Fakenham as the town seems never to have fully recovered from being described in the *Daily Telegraph* as 'one of the most boring places on earth' a decade or so ago. While it's not the most dynamic of towns, I could think of hundreds more places where I would rather not be. Its centre has a modestly attractive Georgian square that hosts a weekly market on Thursday mornings and a **farmers' market** on the fourth Saturday morning of each month. There's also a town race course, the only other one in the county besides Great Yarmouth. Above all though, you also really have to warm to a town that has taken the trouble of opening its very own **Museum of Gas and Local History**

(01328 863507; www.fakenhamgasmuseum.com), which celebrates the former **gas works** that produced the town's gas supply between 1846 and 1965.

Pensthorpe (01328 851465; www.pensthorpe.com), just outside the town, is the biggest local draw, a nature reserve with a large collection of waterfowl in natural surroundings. With a wide range of habitats, plenty of wild birds turn up too – 171 species recorded in total. The BBC television natural history show *Springwatch* broadcasts from here, which is quite a feather in the cap for the place if you'll pardon the (bird) pun. As well as gardens and wildflower meadows for adults to enjoy, there are plenty of activities for children like pond dipping and bug walks.

The Bull Inn 41 Bridge St, Fakenham ☎ 01328 853410 🖥 www.thefakenhambull.co.uk. This handy freehouse offers straightforward bar meals and five real ales on tap.

⑰ Creake Abbey

Northwest of Fakenham towards Burnham Market and the coast beyond are the twin villages of **South Creake** and **North Creake**, both quiet, pleasant villages with greens, duck ponds and neat flint cottages. Just beyond North Creake you'll find the ruins of **Creake Abbey**, originally an almshouse founded by the Augustinian order which attained abbey status in 1231. Fire and the Black Death in the 15th century, and Henry VIII in the 16th, all contributed to the abbey's downfall and what remains is an evocative ruin in the keep of English Heritage. **Creake Abbey Studios** (07801 418907; www.creakeabbey studios.co.uk) is right next door, a craft and arts centre with galleries and a café in a set of converted farm buildings. There's a **farmers' market** held here on the morning of the first Saturday of each month except January, and an apple fair in October.

The Ostrich 1 Fakenham Rd, South Creake ☎ 01328 823320. A bustling 17th-century inn with a good bar menu and Adnams and Woodforde's ales on handpump.

East Dereham and around

⑱ East Dereham

So where is *West* Dereham, you might ask? Out in the Fens in the middle of nowhere is the answer, so just plain 'Dereham' will do. If you made a cardboard cut-out of Norfolk and looked for the central point from which to suspend it, you would probably find it passes close to Dereham – it doesn't get much more mid-Norfolk than this.

Although it is not immediately obvious, East Dereham's quite an ancient place. The churchyard of St Nicholas has **Withburga's Well** named after a daughter of the 7th-century Saxon monarch King Anna (yes, king!) who founded a convent here. Withburga's shrine became famous for its miracles until AD984 when the Abbot and monks from the monastery at Ely came trophy hunting and made off with her remains into the mists of the Fens. The well is said to be filled from a spring that erupted from beneath Withburga's empty grave. The town has a few literary connections too: George Borrow was born at the outskirts of the town at Dumpling Green, just a few years after William Cowper died here; there's a shrine to the latter in the church.

There's nothing to see of Dereham's Saxon past, and little of the medieval other than the church. What greets the eye is mostly the rebuild that followed post-Tudor fires, although there is a row of 16th-century cottages near the church known as **Bonner's Cottages** that have Suffolk-style pargetting. Their name comes from Bishop Bonner, who lived here as a curate before his stint as Bishop of London. Bonner was anything but a kind and gentle soul: as an enthusiastic foot soldier of 'Bloody' Queen Mary's excesses, he sent many a Protestant heretic to a fiery death.

The most enjoyable way to arrive here is by train on the **Mid-Norfolk Railway** (01362 690633; www.mnr.org.uk) from Wymondham (see page 135). You could buy a return ticket from Wymondham or, alternatively, just a single to here, continuing your journey by bus – there are frequent services east and west to Norwich, Swaffham and King's Lynn. Dereham station is something of a throwback to the 1950s and has quite a nice café, so if you don't want to bother going into town and you could easily while away half an hour or so here whilst waiting for the return train.

For a thorough exposition of Norfolk social and agricultural history, a visit to the village of Gressenhall is in order. **Gressenhall Farm and Workhouse** (01362 860563; www.museums.norfolk.gov.uk) is a combined museum and farm set in 50 acres of countryside a few miles north of Dereham. The approach is hands-on: while the 18th-century workhouse seems to ooze despair from the very fabric of the building, much of the history is told through the recorded lives of inmates. The punishment cell may be rather sobering but there are fun activities too – for children, at least – like dressing up in Victorian clothes and cart rides. The collections gallery has all manner of fascinating artefacts including a hurdy-gurdy and a portable Turkish bath. As well as family events during school holidays, the museum stages special events days such as a Norfolk History Fair and Apple Day in October. For walkers, the Nar Valley Way begins (or ends) at the museum.

⑲ North Elmham

A little way north of Gressenhall, you come to North Elmham, a large, rather sprawling village that was once connected to Dereham and Fakenham by the Mid-Norfolk railway. Plans are afoot to extend the Wymondham to Dereham Mid-Norfolk line as far as North Elmham, or rather reinstate it; for the time being though, the village has a Railway pub, a station road and even a station building but no railway.

North Elmham was the site of the Bishopric of East Anglia until 1075, but of the Saxon cathedral that stood here, virtually no trace remains. What you will find instead are the flinty remains of a Norman church built by Herbert de Losinga alongside the earthworks of a 14th-century castle built by Henry le Despencer, a later Bishop of Norwich. The ruins occupy a pretty spot at the edge of the village surrounded by old chestnut trees.

The Railway Station Rd ☎ 01362 668300. Solid home-cooked pub food and a good selection of Norfolk ales in a cosy environment with sofas and an open fire.

⑳ Foxley Wood and ㉑ Honeypot Wood

Norfolk has some wonderful tracts of ancient woodland and two of these lie quite close to Dereham. The Norfolk Wildlife Trust manages Foxley and Honeypot woods, which are fine reminders of what much of central Norfolk must once have been like before widespread agriculture took hold. It is tempting to think of woods like these as truly wild places left over from the last ice age but, really, they are not. They have been rigorously managed over the centuries, albeit in a sustainable way. These days, of course, there is little demand for woodland products like hazel wands but the ancient art of coppicing is still practised, creating the dappled conditions needed for what have become quite scarce plants like primroses, cowslips and early purple orchids.

These woodlands are all good for butterflies and birds and, in springtime especially, for idyllic walks along the grassy rides. Northeast of East Dereham, just beyond Foxley and Bawdeswell (which are on the A1067), **Foxley Wood** is Norfolk's largest remaining ancient woodland. It was intensively coppiced in medieval times and, as well as hazel, it yielded other woodland products such as tree bark used in the tanning industry. The bluebells are so well known locally that the woodland rides can get almost busy at bluebell time (late April–early May). Several waymarked trails penetrate the heart of the wood. Their margins are sometimes boggy following prolonged wet weather but if you stick to the central part of the ride it's usually not too wet underfoot. Four miles west of East Dereham and just north of Wendling, **Honeypot Wood** is smaller and takes its name from a nearby medieval sewage dump or 'honey pit' – a euphemism if ever there was one. Like Foxley Wood, it is at its very best in spring when enough light filters through the canopy to allow woodland plants like twayblades, wood anemones and, of course, bluebells to flourish.

Mermaid Inn Church St, Elsing ☎ 01362 637640 ◌ www.elsingmermaidinn.co.uk. In a village northeast of Dereham and a few miles from Foxley Wood, this 15th-century country inn has home-cooked food and a choice of real ales.

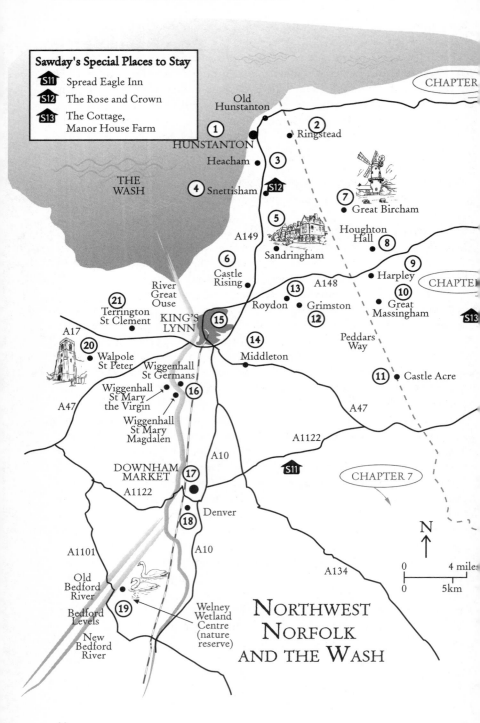

Sawday's Special Places to Stay

S11 Spread Eagle Inn

S12 The Rose and Crown

S13 The Cottage, Manor House Farm

CHAPTER

Old Hunstanton

① HUNSTANTON

② Ringstead

Heacham ③

④ Snettisham S12

THE WASH

⑤

⑦ Great Bircham

A149

Sandringham

Houghton Hall ⑧

⑥ Castle Rising

River Great Ouse

② Terrington St Clement

KING'S LYNN ⑮

⑬

A148

Roydon ⑫ Grimston

⑨ Harpley CHAPTER

⑩ Great Massingham

S13

A17

⑳ Walpole St Peter

Wiggenhall St Germans

Wiggenhall St Mary the Virgin ⑯

⑭ Middleton

Peddars Way

⑪ Castle Acre

Wiggenhall St Mary Magdalen

A47

A47

A1122

A10

DOWNHAM MARKET ⑰

A1122

Denver

⑱

S11

CHAPTER 7

N

A1101

Old Bedford River

Bedford Levels

⑲

New Bedford River

Welney Wetland Centre (nature reserve)

NORTHWEST NORFOLK AND THE WASH

A134

0   4 miles

0   5km

4. NORTHWEST NORFOLK AND THE WASH

As you head west along the north Norfolk coast, it turns south just before the resort of **Hunstanton** and with a change of direction, comes a change of character. Instead of vast expanses of salt marshes, pebble cottages and silted medieval harbours we find ourselves in a zone of sandy beaches and low dunes, stone-banded cliffs and low chalk ridges inland. The coast runs down as far as **King's Lynn**, which once had a far more important place in the scheme of things than it has today but, there again, so did Norfolk as a whole.

It may seem strange to witness the sun setting out to sea – this is *East Anglia* after all. But the realisation that **the Wash** is just a rather wide inlet will come when, in fine weather, you see the wind turbines on the far Lincolnshire shore, or, on a very clear day, catch a glimpse of the 'Boston Stump', the improbably tall tower of Boston's St Botolph's church. The Wash's beaches attract both holidaymakers and wildfowl, with buckets, spades and suntan oil out in force at Snettisham in the summer months, and geese, ducks and waders feasting on the tidal mudflats and sandbanks offshore in winter.

Inland from the coast it is a different picture, with low chalk hills, quietly attractive chalk-built villages like **Ringstead** and lush pasture with scattered patches of woodland. Further inland still and you edge into the light soils of what's sometimes termed as High Norfolk – the agricultural landscape of north Norfolk enclosure, with its hedgerows and woodland copses. The slow pace of life here quickens only marginally in its urban centres, old-fashioned market towns like **Swaffham** and **Downham Market** that lie on the edge of this region and give way to **Breckland** and **The Fens** respectively. On the whole though, smaller villages like Great Bircham and Great Massingham, both far from 'great', are generally more typical of this ultra-rural corner of the county. This is estate country too, with **Sandringham**, the Royal family's country retreat, being the prime example. The hall at **Houghton** is even more impressive and one of the finest country houses in East Anglia.

King's Lynn, once a thriving port, is central to the area and although it may seem unprepossessing in many ways, has a concentration of intriguing distractions centred around its historic core. South and west of here lie the spectacularly contour-free, drained arable region of **the Fens**, often associated with Norfolk but really far more typical of Cambridgeshire and south Lincolnshire than Norfolk as a whole. The Fens are not to everyone's taste, but have huge wide skies and distant horizons that are unsullied by anything as presumptuous as a hill or contour. Lines of straight poplars stretch into the distance like a French impressionist painting; pylons recede to vanishing point – you can almost sense the curvature of the earth.

The **Peddars Way** runs as straight as an arrow through this whole area, beginning uncertainly – or rather, ill-defined – in the heathland at Knettishall near Thetford but gaining confidence, and a more obvious surface, as it progresses through **Castle Acre** across the heathland and chalk ridges of west Norfolk to terminate at Holme-next-the-Sea. Such a linear, determined route suggests a Roman origin, and it was constructed as a military thoroughfare in their campaign to pacify Norfolk's warring Iceni tribes. When the Romans finally removed their sandals from these shores and high-tailed it back to Rome in time for the fall of their empire, the route came into its own as a thoroughfare for peddlers, thieves, drovers and pilgrims. So Norfolk's answer to the *Life of Brian* line, 'What have the Romans ever done for us?', could well be 'The Peddars Way'.

Getting around

Public transport

Geographically west Norfolk is somewhat out on a limb and this isolation is reflected in its **train** connections. Rail services connect King's Lynn with Cambridge and London but there's no direct service to Norwich. Hunstanton has not been part of the railway network since 1969.

By **bus**, the situation is slightly better but by no means marvellous. The exemplary Coasthopper service along Norfolk's north coast runs as far as Hunstanton, from where good connections south to King's Lynn call at villages along the A149 – Heacham, Snettisham, Dersingham and Castle Rising. The X1, a direct, and reasonably quick, bus service runs between Norwich and King's Lynn calling at East Dereham and Swaffham *en route*. **Norfolk Green** (www.norfolkgreen.co.uk), the same company that runs the Coasthopper route, has services running east from King's Lynn to the north coast and larger villages like Great Massingham but unfortunately some of the smaller villages, especially those in The Fens, are harder to reach.

Cycling

Cycling is enjoyable in much of this region, if you keep off major roads like the A149, and avoid the A47 and A17 trunk roads at all costs. The terrain is varied and rewarding, and the hills are gentle. Best of all, is to take advantage of those sections of the **Peddars Way** which, doubling as a bridleway, can be used by mountain or hybrid bikes. The track is fine for mountain and touring bikes but sleek racers with tyres the width of a coin will not do well here.

Walking

Some of the best **walking** in the area is along stretches of the valley of the **River Nar**, a lovely chalk stream that has been designated an SSSI (Site of Special Scientific Interest) along its entire length. The river flows through Castle

Acre, West Acre and Narborough, and any of these is a decent base for setting off for a circular walk.

The **Nar Valley Way** runs 34 miles from the Gressenhall Farm and Workhouse (see page 90) all the way to King's Lynn. This links with both the Peddars Way at Castle Acre and the Wash Coast Path at King's Lynn. The Nar Valley Group of Parishes have produced a useful leaflet, *Footsteps through Time: Walks in the Nar Valley*, that outlines five circular walks starting in Narborough, Castle Acre or West Acre. You should be able to find the leaflet at tourist centres.

Close to Kings Lynn, **Roydon Common** offers a bracing walk well away from habitation, and **Ringstead Downs** near Hunstanton is another good choice for short, leisurely strolls. To get close up to **the Wash**, explore the Peter Scott Walk, which runs a very tranquil ten miles along the sea bank from King's Lynn to the mouth of the Nene at Sutton Bridge in Lincolnshire (the great naturalist after which it's named lived in a lighthouse on the east bank of the Nene), with choice coastal and fenland views and some excellent bird-watching opportunities.

Tourist information

Downham Market The Priory Centre, Priory Rd ☎ 01366 383287.
Hunstanton The Green ☎ 01485 532610.
King's Lynn The Customs House, Purfleet Quay ☎ 01553 763044.
Fens Tourism 🖱 www.visitthefens.co.uk.
Visit West Norfolk 🖱 www.west-norfolk.gov.uk.

The northwest corner: Hunstanton to Castle Rising

① Hunstanton

Rather like a smaller version of Cromer, Hunstanton –'Hunston' if you live there, 'Sunny Hunny' if you take to the beach – is a seaside resort that came to prominence during the Victorian railway age. It has a somewhat different appearance and atmosphere to its north Norfolk competitor though as, among the mock Tudor of its seafront hotels, others are built of warm red **carrstone**, the tough red limestone that gives character to this part of the county. Living in east Norfolk as I do, you become so used to seeing only flint or brick used for domestic architecture that this corner of the county can almost seem like alien territory. But no, this is still Norfolk: the air, the accents, the pace of things – these are all constants. Norfolk is a wide county and Norwich and Great Yarmouth lie so far to the east that many people who live around here hardly ever travel there; instead, they look to King's Lynn or Cambridge for their ration of big city lights.

There are traces of Neolithic settlement in the area, but the town you see today is the result of planned development by Henry Styleman Le Strange of Hunstanton Hall in the mid 1840s, who encouraged investment in the railway line between the town and King's Lynn in an attempt to attract visitors to its fine sandy beaches. The venture was a success and well-to-do Victorians came in droves, even the Prince of Wales, later to be Edward VII, who stayed here whilst recovering from typhoid (perhaps his other favourite, Cromer, was considered a bit too fast-paced for this purpose).

Hunstanton is pleasant enough, with a promenade, beach and sloping central green, but for my money, its greatest attraction lies north of the modern town centre in Old Hunstanton, where the gorgeous **banded cliffs** are made of layers of red limestone ('red chalk') with a white chalk layer on top. The cliffs – a perfect geology textbook illustration – are framed by a foreground of chalky sand and green, seaweed-covered rocks. With the setting sun lighting up the cliffs as it lowers across the Wash, and a painterly combination of red, white, green and blue, this is the sort of place that landscape photographers get excited about.

Old Hunstanton, which is little more than an estate village that has become a suburb of the larger town, has the remains – little more than an arch – of **St Edmund's Chapel**. This dates from 1272 and is reputed to have been built on the very spot where the saint landed when he arrived from Germany to become King of East Anglia. It's pleasant to stroll along the top of cliffs here, past the pitch and putt course, the ruined chapel and a disused white lighthouse towards the glitzier side of town. Better still though, is to go one way along the beach, admiring the candy-striped cliffs, and return via the clifftop walk.

><><><

Hunstanton seems to have a dearth of decent, traditional pubs. Your best bet is probably the Ancient Mariner or, better still, make your way out to The Gintrap in Ringstead.

Ancient Mariner Inn Golf Course Rd ☎ 01485 534411. A stone's throw from the dunes behind Old Hunstanton beach, this unpretentious village pub has Adnams and guest beers on tap and good, honest bar meals.

Caley Hall Hotel ☎ 01485 533486 🖰 www.caleyhallhotel.co.uk. This converted 17th-century manor house in Old Hunstanton, originally part of the Le Strange estate, has a recently refurbished restaurant that utilises local produce as much as possible.

Golden Lion Hotel The Green ☎ 01485 532688. Hunstanton's oldest building with a view west over the sea. This dates from 1846 and originally stood on its own on top of the cliffs and was nicknamed 'Le Strange's Folly'. These days, it's a hotel with a restaurant and two bars serving cask ales.

THE NORTHWEST CORNER: HUNSTANTON TO CASTLE RISING

② Ringstead

A small, attractive village of whitewashed cottages just inland from the coast, and on the route of the Peddars Way, Ringstead is chocolate-box pretty, has a lovely pub and is a good starting point for leisurely walks along the valley of the Ringstead Downs immediately west of the village. The village's original church, St Peter's, is now long gone as a place of worship but its Norman round tower still remains to the south of the village.

Ringstead Downs

These are hardly the South Downs, but there are some similarities. Unimproved chalk grassland such as this is rare in Norfolk. Ringstead Downs is a short stretch of dry glacial valley, a far northern extension of the same chalk strata that make up the Chilterns and Cambridgeshire's Gog Magog Hills. The chalky soil ensures plenty of wild flowers that are rarely found elsewhere in the region, as well as a good show of butterfly species like Brown Argus and warblers in summer. On a sunny day, the gentle slopes here provide an ideal setting for a leisurely picnic, with butterflies fluttering by, the contented buzz of bees and the scent of thyme creating as much a sense of bucolic well-being as a 1970s shampoo advert.

Courtyard Farm, just east of Ringstead village, which Lord Peter Melchett farms according to organic principles, has a farm shop that is open between 12.00 and 15.00 on Wednesdays to sell its own organic produce. The contact is Lucy at the farm's Bunkhouse Barn (☎01485 525251).

SP Gin Trap Inn High St ☎01485 525264 ✍ www.gintrapinn.co.uk. The Gin Trap dates to 1667, although the conservatory dining room is a far more recent addition. The friendly, oak-beamed bar has real ales such as Adnams and Woodforde's and a crackling fire, while the comforting food on offer in either the bar or the restaurant is mostly locally sourced, with beef and pork from nearby Courtyard Farm and oysters from Thornham.

③ Heacham

Heacham, just south of Hunstanton on the coast, has a beach but is best known for something else – **lavender**. In summer, coach-loads come from afar to view the bushes in their mauve, serried ranks. On a warm sunny day, the aromatic oils released from the plants permeate the air so much that the whole area is redolent of a National Trust gift shop. Lavender garden and distillery tours are available at **Caley Mill Farm**, headquarters of Norfolk Lavender Ltd (01485 570384; www.norfolk-lavender.co.uk), where a tea room and gift shop sell all manner of lavender products. The company was founded in 1932 and lavender has been grown around Caley Mill since 1936. Henry Head, who has worked here for over thirty years, told me a little about the company. 'Here at Norfolk Lavender

we've kept alive the great tradition of English lavender growing – for 60 years we were the only significant growers in the country. Caley Mill was a Victorian water mill built in 1837 but now it's our headquarters and we've got shops, a tearoom and plant centre here, as well as our new Rare Breeds Animal centre.' I asked him why this part of west Norfolk is so suitable for lavender growing. It is, after all, a plant that has its natural home on sun-baked Mediterranean hillsides. 'With one exception, all the varieties that we grow here were developed by us for their suitability for the local conditions. The locality is ideal: there's plenty of sunshine, free-draining soils and not too much rain.'

The village also has a curious association with **Pocahontas** and the village sign depicts the celebrated Powhatan Indian princess. Pocahontas married an English Virginian settler, John Rolfe, in 1614 and the two of them travelled to England together in 1616. At first, the couple spent some time in the capital, delighting the London set, but later moved on to live at Rolfe's country house at **Heacham Hall** for a while. The pair attempted to return to Virginia in 1617 but Pocahontas fell ill with smallpox before they had even left English waters. She was taken ashore before she died, to be buried at Gravesend. Many descendants of the Rolfe family lie buried at **Heacham Church**, a 12th-century building of Norman origin that is said to have the oldest church bell in East Anglia.

Now converted to holiday accommodation, Heacham's erstwhile **railway station** used to serve the now defunct King's Lynn to Hunstanton line, which operated for just over a hundred years between 1866 and 1969, when Norfolk was much better connected by rail than it is today.

The Cottage Pantry 28 High St ☎ 01485 572220. A cosy and convenient place for tea, a snack or light meal.

Fox and Hounds 22 Station Rd ☎ 01485 570345
🖰 www.foxandhoundsheacham.co.uk. The website of this atmospheric place suggests that you can either bring your granny or come on your own. This depends partly on your granny's liking for real ale as the pub has its own Fox brewery (🖰 www.foxbrewery.co.uk) on the premises that produces no fewer than nine different ales – some traditional, like Heacham Gold; some less so, like Da Krai with lemongrass. The brewery's ales feature prominently in the pub's cooking too, which cuts down food miles quite admirably.

④ Snettisham

The beach here is enormous – wide and spacious – but the village is just as well known for its RSPB reserve. Both lie away from the village, around two miles to the west. There has been an important carrstone quarry here for centuries and much of the stone that you see in walls around this part of the county probably originates from here.

The Snettisham area has clearly been settled for millennia: a great hoard of treasure trove was discovered close to the village – 75 complete golden torcs (solid gold neck rings that must have been almost too heavy to wear) and even more fragmentary ones that date from the 1st century AD, as well as a great deal of Romano-British jewellery, all now at the British Museum.

Snettisham's **St Mary's Church**, with its tall 14th-century spire, has been raved about by architectural writers Nikolaus Pevsner and Simon Jenkins for its west window, with its complex, lace-like tracery. The east and south windows were replaced after having been bombed by a Zeppelin in 1915 – the very first air attack on an English church, a unique honour of sorts.

At the shoreline, the tide can go out for miles here, leaving a vast area of mud and sand, ideal for feeding birds and games of cricket. Naturally, birds have the advantage of being able to fly away if cut off by rapidly incoming tides; strolling humans do not have this facility. The **RSPB reserve** (01485 542689; www.rspb.org.uk.) here really comes into its own during the autumn and winter months when high tides push tens of thousands of waders up on to the shoreline. The higher the tide, the easier it is to see the birds. Low tides require telescopes and an aptitude for identifying indeterminate blobs in the distant mud. Be aware that is a long walk from the RSPB car park to the reserve, but there's plenty to look for in the reeds along the way. The nearest bus stop for both beach and reserve is on the A149 at the Beach Road junction.

Snettisham Park Farm (01485 542425; www.snettishampark.co.uk), with its entrance close to the church on the Bircham road, is a working farm that offers hands-on activities likely to appeal to children. Animals include what you would normally expect on a farm, plus deer and, even more exotically, llamas. Deer safaris feature a 45-minute commentated tractor and trailer ride, and there are a number of farm trails.

S **Rose and Crown** Old Church Rd ☎ 01485 541382
🍴 www.roseandcrownsnettisham.co.uk. A whitewashed 14th-century inn with roses around the door; what could be more quintessentially English? Inside, it is a warren of rooms with log fires and low ceilings. The imaginative menu mixes tradition with the exotic but always sources locally where possible. It's just as much a pub as a restaurant too, with a good choice of real ales in the bar.

⑤ Sandringham

Following the A149 south from Snettisham, **Dersingham** is the next village you will come across, although it is not so special, with plenty of modern housing development. The village adjoins the **Sandringham Estate** (01553 612908; www.sandringhamestate.co.uk), with **Sandringham House** set in 60 acres of landscaped, wooded gardens, and best known as the place where the Queen eats

her Christmas turkey before watching herself on TV. Queen Victoria's son, Edward the Prince of Wales, first came across the country house and estate here in 1861 and snapped them up them forthwith (he rejected Houghton Hall, which was also offered for purchase). The Prince rebuilt the main residence to his own tastes in 1870 and landscaped the grounds, adding a ballroom later on, which sees use today as the venue for estate workers' Christmas parties. The author John Seymour describes the house as 'very ugly – like a huge and grandiose Victorian seaside hotel', but he does have a point as, scaled down in size, it wouldn't look too out of place sitting above the promenade in Cromer. Anyway, you can make up your own mind if you choose to visit. The wooded grounds are, indisputably, quite lovely.

For devotees of local vernacular style, the 16th-century church of **St Mary Magdalene** is widely considered one of the very best carrstone buildings in existence. This is, of course, where the Royal Family comes to worship at Christmas and so you have probably glimpsed it already on television. The estate's museum has a large and rather bizarre collection of royal vehicles and some of the gifts given to the Royal Family over the years. The gift shop sells all manner of royal memorabilia but the **estate farm shop** is perhaps more appealing, with local cheese, estate-produced rare-breed organic meat and a large selections of jams and chutneys.

Discounted admission prices to the estate are on offer to those who choose to arrive by public transport. The Coasthopper bus provides a regular service to the visitor centre, as does the Coastliner service from King's Lynn. The Sustrans National Cycle Route 1 passes nearby.

⑥ Castle Rising

Between Dersingham and King's Lynn, Castle Rising village is attractive in its own right. There's **St Lawrence's Church** with its Norman and Early-English features and the Hospital of the Holy and Undivided Trinity opposite but what most come to see is the village's mighty **Norman castle**. This impressive and seemingly impregnable ruin, owned by English Heritage, has a typical Norman square keep similar to Norwich Castle's; it peeps over the top of the huge oval defensive earthworks that surround it. Ruins of a Saxon and Norman chapel lie partly buried in the earthworks' north side. The earthworks are believed to predate the castle and may be Roman or earlier.

Edward III made use of the castle to banish his mother Isabella, the 'She-wolf of France', after she had colluded with her lover in the death of her husband, Edward II, reputedly by a grisly method that required the unorthodox use of fire-stoking equipment. The means of this brutal murder is most likely pure myth, however, and some accounts even suggest that Edward II escaped to live in exile. For Isabella, it was a relatively liberal banishment, more a kind of voluntary house arrest, as she continued to move around the country relatively freely and did not go mad in her confinement as is sometimes alleged. Later occupants of the castle included the Black Prince and Richard II, and later still, Henry VIII, who sold it to the Howard family.

Opposite the church, the red-brick **Hospital of the Holy and Undivided Trinity**, also known as the Howard Bede House, is effectively an almshouse founded by Henry Howard, the Earl of Northampton, in 1614. It continues to house a dozen elderly ladies to this day who, following the statute set down by Henry Howard, must 'be able to read, single, 56 at least, no common beggar, harlot, scold, drunkard, haunter of taverns, inns or alehouses' – tough conditions indeed, especially the alehouse requirement. Once a year, in thanksgiving to their founder, the Howard Bede women march to church as a group wearing Jacobean costume and conical headgear. Who said tradition was dead?

East from Sandringham and Castle Rising

⑦ Great Bircham

East of Dersingham, just beyond the route of the Peddars Way, and south of the village of **Docking**, lies Great Bircham with one of the best-preserved windmills in Norfolk. Like the village of Docking, this sits on a hill. Great Bircham is one of three villages within the parish of Bircham: just north is Bircham Newton and to the east is Bircham Tofts. **Great Bircham Windmill** (01485 578393; www.birchamwindmill.co.uk), just west of the village, has changed hands quite a number of times since it was first built in 1846. Originally located on land belonging to the Houghton estate, it was purchased in a derelict state by the Royal Sandringham estate in 1939 before being sold on to a private owner in 1976. A thorough restoration project began in 1977, and by 1981 its four sails were back in place. The fully restored mill stands an impressive five storeys tall and has a cottage and long-established bakery attached, where bread is still baked today.

The mill, bakery and tearoom are open every day for visitors during normal working hours from April to September. Special events and craft courses are put on from time to time, with regular courses that teach arcane crafts like walking-stick carving and wool-spinning. The tearooms on the site of the old granary specialise in cream teas, so after indulging in one of these here you might need the mill's cycle hire facility. There is also a campsite.

Kings Head Hotel ☏ 01485 578 265 🖰 www.the-kings-head-bircham.co.uk. This small hotel is a listed 19th-century coach house with a thoroughly modernised interior. The restaurant overlooks a sheltered courtyard, and the modern bar has a selection of four real ales.

Houghton and Harpley

Minor roads south and southwest of Great Bircham lead to the south entrance of Houghton Hall at New Houghton where you enter the estate's vast array of woodland and the deer park with an unusual herd of white fallow deer. This part of west Norfolk has been the seat of the Walpole family since the 14th century and the present incumbents, Lord and Lady Cholmondeley, are direct descendants of this long line.

⑧ *Houghton Hall*

Houghton Hall (01485 528569; www.houghtonhall.com), in early 18th-century Palladian style, is Norfolk's largest country house, and both house and estate reflect the flamboyant tastes of Norfolk 'new money' some three centuries ago. Planning regulations were less proscriptive in those days, and **Sir Robert Walpole**, England's first Prime Minister, who built the house in the 1720s, saw fit to pull down the nearby village of Houghton (which, with a mention in the Domesday Book, had been around since at least 1086), on purely aesthetic grounds as he claimed it spoiled his view. Houghton's Early-English 13th-century village church of St Martin, however, was left well alone. So the unsightly villagers were moved to a new village, New Houghton, immediately south of the estate.

No expense was spared with the new hall: rather than use Norfolk brick, Walpole opted to build in Yorkshire stone, and the interior was sumptuously furnished and decorated with Old Masters. These are no longer at Houghton Hall as its paintings were sold to Catherine the Great, the Czarina of Russia, by Sir Robert's dissolute grandson, George, the third Earl of Orford, in order to pay off debts. His collection ended up in the Hermitage in St Petersburg, where they remain to this day.

The house, museum and gardens are open to the public between Easter and the end of September.

⑨ *Harpley*

South of the Houghton Estate, the small village of Harpley is unremarkable, but it does boast a decent pub and a slightly shabby but highly atmospheric church. **St Lawrence's Church** is a curious musty place of decorated Gothic. The ridge of the roof is studded with angels with folded wings and the benches inside have carvings of all manner of wild animals – monkeys, bears and even mythical creatures – in addition to a pleasing carving of St James the pilgrim with his staff, satchel and shell.

A walk from Harpley

You might want to try a **circular walk** from the village that uses the Peddars Way for some of the way. Leave the pub and turn left then take the footpath that leads down a track on the other side of the road heading southwest. This meanders across fields to reach the Peddars Way at Clarke's Farm. Walk north along the Way, dipping down to cross the A148 and pass Harpley Dams Cottages before gently climbing up

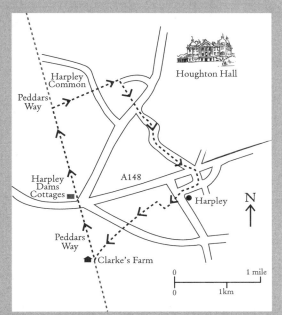

Harpley Common

Peddars Way

Houghton Hall

Harpley Dams Cottages

A148

Harpley

Peddars Way

Clarke's Farm

N

0   1 mile
0   1km

towards Harpley Common. This is quite a remote stretch of the Peddars Way, with wide horizons and huge skies; sufficiently tranquil that all you will probably hear is the clattering song of a skylark and perhaps the distant drone of a tractor. The Way is a grassy track here, uneven in places but rarely waterlogged. You might notice some old marl pits in the fields around here: 18th-century diggings in which the extracted clay or 'marl' was spread on fields to improve the light soils. Some of the pits are marked by small clumps of trees, while others that have gone under the plough are just irregular depressions. After a couple of miles heading north along the Way, you'll reach a bridleway that slopes away to the east. Take this and follow it as it dips and rises again to curve around the southern limit of the Houghton Estate before crossing a minor road past a field barn to climb very gently back to Harpley.

Rose and Crown Nethergate St, Harpley ☎ 01485 520577. An intimate village pub with well-kept ale and good, unpretentious food.

⑩ Great Massingham

Not far from Houghton Hall and the village of Harpley, and just south of its sister community of Little Massingham, Great Massingham is a very pretty village of 18th- and 19th-century cottages set against an impressively large and carefully mown green studded with daisies. The village has several ponds that originally were probably fish ponds for the village's former 11th-century Augustinian priory that today lies in ruins. It is possible that the village is actually much older than this and dates from as far back as the 5th century when the area was settled by a

group of Angles and Saxons in the wake of the Roman withdrawal. The leader of this group may have been Maesron and the settlers known as Maersings, hence the village becoming Maersingham and later, Massingham.

Mad Dog Lane, which leads from the village past council houses to the Peddars Way, does not appear to have any dogs – mad or otherwise – prowling along it but it would be interesting to know how this name came about. Perhaps the deranged animal escaped from nearby Kennel Farm? Given its sizeable ponds, ducks rather than dogs tend to sum up the character of the village – a detail that has not gone unnoticed by the local hostelry.

A small, private airfield just east of the village saw service as an RAF bomber base during World War II. Robert Walpole, the first English Prime Minister, was educated in the village and appears on the village sign alongside a monk, an RAF bomber, a sheep and a tractor. Curiously, no ducks are represented.

⑪ Castle Acre

Conveniently straddling the route of the Peddars Way, Castle Acre makes a welcome stopover for hikers, but is well worth a visit even for those not inexorably striding towards Holme-next-the-Sea (where the Peddars Way ends). The village does contain, of course, a castle – an early Norman one in this case – but not that much survives other than its sprawling earthworks and a gateway. Far more impressive are the Norman ruins of **Castle Acre Priory**, founded just after the conquest in 1090, a highly atmospheric place to wander, especially late in the day with the sun low in the western sky. It may seem just like any other Norfolk village today but, left to your own devices, it is still possible to get an inkling as to just how important Castle Acre was back in the Norman period.

The village sits on a low chalk hill above the River Nar, a compact place of flint-and-brick houses that take up the space of what would have been the outer bailey of the castle on the hill. The village's flint 16th-century gatehouse would have been the bailey gate. The priory is a little lower down to the east, in fields beside the River Nar's north bank. Founded by William de Warenne, son-in-law of William the Conqueror, the abbey was set up as a daughter priory of St Pancras at Lewes in Sussex, which in turn reported to the Cluniac Priory in Burgundy. The original priory was built within the walls of the castle but this proved too small and the monastery was soon moved to its current location. As is often the way with medieval religious orders, the priory went on to have a colourful and sometimes notorious life, with considerable friction between the Cluniac mother house and various English kings, notably the early Edwards, resulting in the priory being considered 'alien' and therefore heavily taxed. Not all medieval monks led blameless lives: in 1351, some of those at the priory were accused of 'living as vagabonds in secular habit' and the king felt it necessary to send his Serjeant-at-Arms to make arrests. Castle Acre Priory eventually became naturalised in 1373 and subsequently lost its connection with its French motherhouse.

Lying close to the route of pilgrimage to Walsingham, the priory set itself up in competition by selling indulgences to penitents on the first two days of August each year. The priory already had its very own relic, the arm of St Philip, but this did not turn out to be a particularly big crowd-puller; in fact, it only earned ten shillings from its exhibition during the whole of 1533. With the advent of the Dissolution, the priory changed ownership swiftly several times over, passing through the hands of Thomas Howard the Duke of Norfolk, Elizabeth I, Thomas Gresham and eventually, the Coke family. It is now owned by English Heritage.

In the village itself, both **The Ostrich Inn** (✆ 01760 755398) and **The Albert Victor** (✆ 01760 755213) in Stocks Green are decent enough places for a drink or a meal. Both have outdoor beer gardens. **Church Gate Tearooms** (✆ 01760 755551) and **Barnfield's Tearooms** (✆ 01760 755577), also on Stocks Green, are convenient places for coffee and snacks.

The George and Dragon Newton, Castle Acre PE32 2BX ✆ 01760 755046 ✆ www.newtongeorge.co.uk. Just outside Castle Acre, this 17th-century inn offers old-fashioned comfort (and wireless internet), home-cooked local produce and a selection of real ales. The pub hosts occasional folk and jazz evenings. It also offers local gardeners the opportunity of exchanging surplus produce for meal credits – a fantastic idea.

⑫ Grimston and ⑬ Roydon

The road (Lynn Lane) that leads from Great Massingham to King's Lynn via **Grimston** and **Roydon** is vastly more pleasurably than the frenetic, speed-crazed A47 trunk road further to the south. It is wider than it appears on the map and surprisingly quiet, striking west across the lonely country of Grimston Heath. The road ranges relatively high for Norfolk but seems higher, almost as if it were upland country somewhere else in Britain. Grimston is a carrstone village without any great incentive for travellers to stop, as is Roydon, but shortly after the village is an off-road parking place to the left from where you can make an exploration of Roydon Common.

Roydon Common is a large area of heathland, looked after by the Norfolk Wildlife Trust, where heather thrives and sheep safely graze. The sheep, along with some ponies, are a fairly recent introduction as part of a management scheme to keep the habitat intact. A rough path leads towards an odd-looking isolated tower on a low hill. The tower is marked on the OS map as being among the conifers of Grimston Warren but the trees shown on the map have since been felled. 'Warren' is certainly right, as there is plenty of evidence of rabbits here. Occasional lapwings and curlews fly up from the heather, and hen harriers are not uncommon in winter. What is odd about this large area of heathland, just a stone's throw from the Wash, is how alien it seems to most of the rest of Norfolk. The view is impressive, with gentle valleys and plantations stretching in the distance and barely a village or church tower in sight. It might even be Exmoor or one of the flatter parts of the Pennines but just over the brow of the hill to the west is industrial King's Lynn, Norfolk's third largest town.

Much of the terrain around here, like Snettisham to the north, is one of old and new carrstone quarries, the disused quarries returning to heathland if left to their own devices long enough. A little south of here, just across the B1145, you'll find evidence of another type of mineral extraction – sand – although not just any old sand but the finest and purest variety used for glassmaking. If you head into King's Lynn from here, along the B1145, you'll pass a swanky country park with sailing club and golf course at the smart dormitory village of **Leziate**.

South of Leziate, just across the disused railway line, a large neo-gothic castellated mansion hides behind high walls. This is Middleton Towers, a moated medieval house that is pure Gormenghast and looks unlikely to welcome strangers. The house was originally a 14th-century fortified manor house, founded by the Scales family on a large, moated platform. Not much remains of the original today but a bridleway leads off the road into woods just south of the complex if you would like a closer look. In the early post-war years, Middleton Towers hosted speedway races and celebrities like George Formby were invited to open the proceedings. These days, it is clear that whatever goes on there is very much a private affair.

⑭ Middleton

A little further south, in the village of Middleton itself, are the remains of **Middleton Castle**, an 11th-century motte-and-bailey fortress, now reduced to the appearance of a large green molehill. Further south still, another four miles or so, you'll find what's left of **Wormegay Castle**, another fortified motte-and-bailey castle that began life as a Saxon manorial complex. West of here, all roads lead to that west Norfolk metropolis – King's Lynn.

The Dabbling Duck 11 Abbey Rd, Great Massingham ☎ 01485 520827 ⏚ www.thedabblingduck.co.uk. Formerly the Rose & Crown, the Dabbling Duck stands on the village green in full view of a duck pond with its residents doing just that. The food on offer includes seafood from the north Norfolk coast and sirloin steaks from the Holkham Estate. Adnams and Woodforde's beers are served straight from the barrel.

⑮ King's Lynn

Everyone driving into Norfolk from the Midlands or the North catches a glimpse of King's Lynn's outer reaches as they negotiate the huge roundabout on the A47. To be honest, it is not a wholly prepossessing sight: an industrial landscape of grain mills, pylons and a tall tinned-soup factory that bears the legend, 'Campbells'. Just west of the roundabout is a vast paper-recycling plant built of low, square blocks that themselves could even be made up of lofty blocks of old newspapers. With food processing still the biggest employer here, King's Lynn can, at first glance, appear to be a frozen-fish-finger wasteland – the natural domain of Captain Birdseye. Having said that, it is best that you put all your prejudices to one side, for the time being at least, as King's Lynn really does have quite a lot to offer, especially for those with an interest in maritime history.

Still Norfolk's third largest town, King's Lynn has an important place in both Norfolk and English history. Its rich architectural heritage hints at its hugely eminent status as a port in former times and it still has the scent of distant shores in its nostrils and the dirt of sea trade under its fingernails.

Historic Lynn

King's Lynn was England's third biggest port in the 14th century, the medieval period's equivalent of what Liverpool was in Victorian times, and as a member of the Hanseatic League between the 14th and 17th centuries, it looked east to trading partners in northern Europe and the Baltic as far as modern-day Estonia. Plain old 'Lynn' became King's Lynn (or Lynn Regis) when the town became royal property following Henry VIII's dissolution of the monasteries and it was a royalist stronghold during the civil war a century later. In the aftermath of Norfolk's wool production years, grain exports became increasingly important from the 17th century onwards.

The railway came to the town in 1847, providing an easy London connection and with Sandringham coming to prominence in the later years of the 19th century the town regained some of the prosperity lost during the previous one. The modern town underwent considerable decline in the 1980s and in 1987 became, somewhat notoriously, the first place in the UK to introduce CCTV as a means of monitoring the activity of town centre ne'er-do wells. Despite its position in the far west of the county, the language on the street remains firmly Norfolk, with none of the East Midlands cadences found a little further west in the Lincolnshire Fens. Portuguese and Polish are also widely spoken.

The beauty of King's Lynn as a place to visit is that its historic core is small and easy to walk around. In a half-day you could see most of the major sights and get a feel for the place; a full day is a better option though. The town's most iconic building is its elegant square **Custom House**, built in 1683 by the local architect Henry Bell and which now serves as the town's **tourist office**. The helpful staff here can suggest a walking route that takes in all the main places of interest.

The customs house is on **Purfleet Dock**, the original harbour inlet along South Quay. Standing at the Custom House, you should notice immediately the figure of a sailor in tricorn hat clutching a sea-chart and looking out across the River Ouse. This being Norfolk, it is reasonable to assume that it's a likeness of Nelson but no, this is the town's own son, George Vancouver, a sea captain credited with the discovery of the long-searched-for North West Passage and who went on to give his name to Canada's Pacific coast city. A decorative brass compass set into the concrete at the end of the dock associates various maritime aspirations with compass points – northwest is whaling, northeast is trade (and so on) – and has a roll-call of Norfolk mariners around it including Captain Vancouver, Captain John Smith and, of course, Admiral Nelson.

Old King's Lynn certainly has plenty to see: the arcaded terrace of Hanseatic buildings – the only ones in the country – plenty of cobbled lanes and handsome Georgian merchants' houses. Town centre life revolves chiefly around two squares, **Saturday Market Place** and **Tuesday Market Place**, which both do exactly what they say on the tin. Tuesday Market Place is the more northerly of the two, just a block in from the Great Ouse River. The **Corn Exchange** here has an impressive front to it although the rest of it is modern and undistinguished. King Street running south has the **Arts Centre**, a restored 15th-century **guildhall**, and just beyond it a narrow alleyway, Ferry Lane, which leads to the dock for the pedestrian **ferry** across the river to West Lynn.

South of the Customs House is a warren of narrow streets filled with an impressive array of Tudor, Jacobean and Flemish houses, courtyards, warehouses and cottages. Most notable are **St Margaret's House**, a row of restored Hanseatic warehouses that date from 1475, but there's plenty of interest at every corner.

Saturday Market Place has the enormous **St Margaret's Church**, which dates from 1101 and dominates the small square. It has twin towers, one of them much rebuilt after it crashed dramatically onto the nave during a storm in 1741. The south tower sports an odd-looking clock. Odd-looking that is until you realise that it gives you the time of the high tide and the phase of the moon. I am no expert on high tides but currently it does not seem to be very accurate, so do not set your watch or launch your boat by it. Directly opposite, the chequerboard stone-and-flint **Town Hall**, or Guildhall of the Holy Trinity, which stands next to the Old Gaol House, looks at first to be of a single build but the original building, dating back to Tudor times, was enlarged considerably by the town's fathers in the Georgian period. I was lucky enough to be given a tour by a friendly curator, who, dying to show someone around, explained the development of the building to me in detail. He walked me through to the paintings in the Georgian annex where there was a portrait of Nelson looking boyish and approachable, despite the sea battle raging in the background. 'This was painted six months after his death,' the curator informed me. 'He looks well, doesn't he, all things considered?' It was apparently a copy of a popular portrait around at the time. We moved on to a portrait of George Vancouver, King's Lynn's own son. 'You know, you used to be able to see his old house in the town centre. There was a plaque and everything. Well, that was until the 1960s when the planners knocked the old buildings down to put up a shopping precinct. They've knocked that down too now.'

Just east of the town hall is a small park that has an isolated tower with an arch beneath – **Greyfriars Tower** – all that remains of a friary established in the 13th century by Fransciscan monks. The southeast corner of the park has the **town library**, an Edwardian gothic fantasy in brick and carrstone. Further east again is a much larger park with a Georgian Walk and the **Red Mount Chapel**, which, along with **South Gate** on London Road, dates from the time of the 15th-century fortifications of the town.

I find the most rewarding activity in King's Lynn is to take a leisurely amble along South Quay and try to rekindle the atmosphere at the height of its maritime trade. There are a couple of decent museums to investigate too. The **Town House Museum of Lynn Life** (46 Queen St; 01553 773450) paints a touching picture the town's social history, with plenty of activities for children, and the recently expanded **True's Yard Fishing Heritage Museum** (North St; 01553 770479; www.truesyard.co.uk) explores the town's maritime past. Pride of place must go, however, to **Lynn Museum** (Market St; 01553 775001), which has the reconstructed Seahenge display (see page 37).

The Peter Scott Walk

If you're hankering after a long coastal walk along The Wash, you might consider doing the **Peter Scott Walk** that leads west into Lincolnshire from King's Lynn. The walk begins at West Lynn, easily reached by regular passenger ferry from South Quay. The path leads north along the River Great Ouse as far as The Wash before skirting the south shore as far as the River Nene where twin lighthouses flank the river's outfall. Sutton Bridge, in Lincolnshire, lies about three miles inland from here. The walk is around ten miles in total but if you are depending on public transport you still have to get to and from the end/start point at the mouth of the Nene. One solution might be to take a bus to Sutton and then a taxi to the picnic place at East Bank. You could then walk east to West Lynn, taking the ferry to King's Lynn at the end of your walk.

Green Quay South Quay ☎ 01553 818500 🖰 www.thegreenquay.co.uk. This converted 16th-century warehouse, home of the Green Quay Wash Discovery Centre, is a fine place to recuperate with coffee and cake.

Wenns 9–10 Saturday Market Place ☎ 0871 917 0007. A cosy real-ale pub just up from the Town Hall and St Margaret's Church.

West into Fenland

Heading west from King's Lynn, you experience a sudden and quite dramatic change of scenery. Instead of leafy hedgerows, scattered woodland and softly undulating valleys, there are wide expanses of black soil, scattered rambling farmsteads with ugly modern barns and occasional villages that have a more insular feel than further east.

Those travelling into East Anglia for the first time may assume that all Norfolk looks like this. It doesn't, of course – it is a misleading preface to what comes later with the slightly more undulating charms of High Norfolk – but at least a quarter of the county does consist of the Fens, even if a quarter of Norfolk's population most certainly does not live here. This is definitely the most overlooked part of the county (for good reason, you might say). But despite its relentless flatness and uncompromising scenery, Norfolk's Fenland has more to offer other than just celery, fertile soil and easy cycling: there are a couple of quite extraordinary **churches**, spectacular winter assemblies of swans and wildfowl at places like **Welney**, and the comfortable market town of **Downham Market**.

⑯ The Wiggenhalls

South of King's Lynn, strung along the course of the Great Ouse River, are four villages prefixed Wiggenhall, each differentiated from the others by the name of its church: Wiggenhall St Mary Magdalen, Wiggenhall St Mary the Virgin, Wiggenhall St Peter and Wiggenhall St Germans. Strictly speaking, these are not of the Fens but in the **Norfolk Marshlands** – slightly higher land that has been inhabited for millennia. All four villages are pre-Norman, Saxon settlements with a timeless charm about them that is hard to find in the Fens proper. They also have some quite remarkable churches.

Of the four Wiggenhalls, **Wiggenhall St Mary Magdalen** has for me the most distinguished church. This lofty 15th-century building is a fine exemplar of medieval balance and proportion, with a plethora of medieval stained glass and fine carved benches. Earnest hagiographers may be interested to note that the church has a gallery featuring some obscure saints who have spectacularly failed to become household names: St Leger, St Callistus, St Britus... the list goes on.

St Germaine's church at **Wiggenhall St Germans** has an altogether different appeal. Here it is the woodwork that attracts attention, with resplendent poppies carved in the bench-ends along with a variety of animated human figures that include musicians, drunks, various sinners and courting couples. All of the Seven Deadly Sins are represented: Avarice clutches bags of money; Anger wields a sword; Lust, my favourite (carving that is, not necessarily the sin), is represented by a loving couple standing in the jaws of a giant fish, presumably the mouth of Hell.

Two river walks around the Wiggenhalls

A recommended and easy three-mile walk from **Wiggenhall St Mary Magdalen** crosses **Magdalen Bridge** (note this is the Magdalen Bridge by the village, not to be confused with another of the same name near Lordsbridge a mile or so northwest) and heads north along the east bank of the Great Ouse River, past tiny **Wiggenhall St Peter** and its handsome roofless church to **Wiggenhall St Germans**, probably the most picturesque of all the four villages. The river has always been the life-blood of the village and, for centuries, this has been a favoured mooring place for Fen boatmen on their way to King's Lynn – a factor that explains why such a small place used to have three thriving pubs. Today it just has the Crown & Anchor. Return along the west bank.

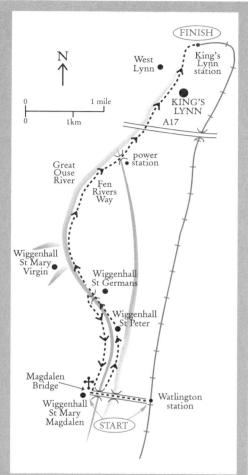

Another possibility, and an enjoyable eight-mile walk, is to approach the Wiggenhalls by **train** from King's Lynn. The starting point in this case would be **Watlington station**, which lies at the halfway point on the train line between King's Lynn and Downham Market. From the station, head west to the metal bridge over the Relief Channel and then cross Magdalen Bridge just beyond it. After crossing the Great Ouse to have a look at St Mary Magdalen church, re-cross the river and follow the signposted Fen Rivers Way north all the way to King's Lynn, passing Wiggenhall St Peter, Wiggenhall St Germans and the power station at Eau Brink Cut along the way. The Fen Rivers Way terminates at Green Quay where you'll find a very welcome café and visitor centre.

Crown and Anchor 16 Lynn Rd, Wiggenhall St Germans ☎ 01553 617340. A Greene King pub close to the church, with outside tables by the river.

⑰ Downham Market

Downham Market stands at the eastern edge of the Fens, with the Great Ouse River and manmade New Bedford Drain running alongside each other west of the town centre. As with many other places in west Norfolk, the predominant building material here is carrstone, which gives the buildings a warm and mellow look. The town's most iconic sight is probably its **clock tower**, a fancy Victorian cast-iron structure that is central to the market place. In medieval times, the town was well known for its butter market and horse fair. It has had a handful of famous visitors over the centuries: Nelson came here to go to school and Charles I stayed (or rather, hid dressed as a clergyman) for a night after fleeing the Battle of Naseby during the civil war. The town was once an important river port but the arrival of the railway soon took away much of this trade following the construction of the Riley Channel, which succeeded in carrying the waters of the Cut-Off Channel to the main channel of the Great Ouse at King's Lynn.

Crown Hotel 12 Bridge St, Downham Market ✆ 01366 382322. This 17th-century coaching inn with a selection of real ales and decent pub grub is a handy central choice.

⑱ Denver

Just a couple of miles south of Downham Market, Denver is a relatively new village that dates from the time of the construction of the first **Denver Sluice** in 1651. The brains behind this project was Cornelius Vermuyden, a Dutch engineer commissioned to drain some of vast acreage of wetlands owned by the Duke of Bedford. The original drainage cut is no longer there but the so-called Old Sluice, which serves the same function as the original, dates from 1834, while the newer Great Denver Sluice was created in 1964. The wetland area between these two channels, generally referred to as the Ouse Washes, is allowed to flood in winter in order to keep the surrounding fields drained and as a result creates a vitally important winter habitat for wildfowl.

If you visit in summer, you'll probably find more of interest at **Denver Windmill** (01366 384009; www.denvermill.co.uk), which was re-opened after careful restoration in 2000. Built in 1835, the mill saw service grinding flour for over a hundred years until lightning struck its sails in 1941. It has a visitor centre, a tearoom and a bakery.

Jenyns Arms 1 Sluice Bank, Denver ✆ 01366 383366. With a large dining conservatory, reasonable pub fare and Sunday roasts, this is handily placed for a visit to the mill.

⑲ Welney Wetland Centre

Welney, a small village sitting on the Norfolk bank of Hundred Foot Bank, one of the Fens' prime manmade water courses, is home to the splendid **Welney Wetland Centre** (01353 860711; www.wwt.org.uk/welney) run by the Wildfowl and Wetlands Trust. This nature reserve has plenty of interest throughout the seasons but really comes into its own in the winter months when vast numbers of wild swans – both whooper and Bewick's – gather on the **Ouse Marshes** here to feed and avoid the far harsher conditions in Siberia and Iceland. One of the joys of watching wild swans here is the centre's heated observatory, which gives visitors a birder's eye view of proceedings whilst they languish in relative comfort – a far cry from shivering with a telescope outside at the mercy of the elements. The **swan feeds**, in particular, are quite spectacular, with the birds gracefully thrashing about for grain right beneath your comfortably warm nose. Children and adults tend to love this, even those not normally bowled over by natural history close up in the flesh. Feeds take place between the end of October and the middle of March around midday and just before sunset. Another feed takes place at around 18.30 by floodlight and this is usually the best attended, in bird terms, as many swans fly in to the lagoon to roost after dusk. For all the feeding times, it is best to arrive half an hour before.

The **visitor centre** has all the right-on environmental credentials: loos that flush with rainwater, solar-power-produced electricity, geothermal heating and reed-bed wastewater cleansing – plus a decent café, a gift-shop and a pond room with giant-sized models of creatures found on the reserve. In the warmer months, there are summer walks around the reserve and children can try pond-dipping.

⑳ Walpole St Peter

The Walpoles – there are three of them – are unexciting dormitory villages filled with modern bungalow estates: here in deepest Fenland, it seems that even houses do not dare raise their heads above the parapet of what most of us regard as sea-level. How odd then that one of Norfolk's very finest churches can be found here, way out west in the agribusiness shabbiness of the Fens, far from the action and as close to Leicester as it is to Norwich. **St Peter's Church** in Walpole St Peter (obviously) is a worthy rival to that of Terrington St Clement; it's a magnificent and very large parish church that is sometimes referred to as the 'Queen of the Marshland'.

㉑ Terrington St Clement

The A17 west of King's Lynn is not a road one drives along for pleasure, and **Terrington St Clement** itself, a large and not particularly attractive village, has little to warrant a detour were it not for its magnificent parish church often dubbed 'the Cathedral of the Marshland'. **St Clement's Church** is a massive 14th-century masterpiece with impressive buttresses and a detached tower.

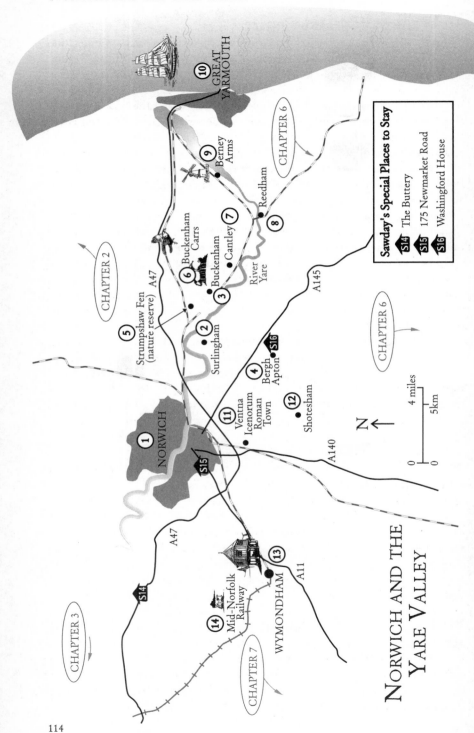

Sawday's Special Places to Stay

S14 The Buttery
S15 175 Newmarket Road
S16 Washingford House

GREAT YARMOUTH

⑩

⑨ Berney Arms

Reedham

⑧

CHAPTER 6

Buckenham Carrs

⑥ Buckenham
⑦ Cantley

③
River Yare

Strumpshaw Fen (nature reserve)

A47

CHAPTER 2

⑤

② Surlingham

A145

CHAPTER 6

④ Bergh Apton S16

⑫ Shotesham

⑪ Ventna Icenorum Roman Town

① NORWICH

S15

N

4 miles
5km

0
0

A140

A47

Mid-Norfolk Railway

S14

⑬

WYMONDHAM
A11

⑭

CHAPTER 3

CHAPTER 7

NORWICH AND THE YARE VALLEY

5. NORWICH AND THE YARE VALLEY

T his area comes as something of a catch-all, a means of including parts of east and south Norfolk that don't conveniently fit in elsewhere. The River Yare that flows from central Norfolk to Great Yarmouth is perhaps an obvious point of focus: a natural conduit for river trade between Norwich and the coast. This same river also connects with the Broads at Breydon Water, and even has a couple of important minor broads of its own at Surlingham and Rockland. If the Yare Valley is a convenient means of incorporating uncooperative slices of east Norfolk, then the valley of the River Tas can be brought in to do the same for south Norfolk. The modest River Tas, which joins the Yare just south of Norwich (having quietly meandered up from south Norfolk), has nothing of the importance of the Yare, but it does link a number of villages south of Norwich that are worth a visit.

The key focus for both these rivers is Norwich, a place of such importance that in a book like this it is almost tempting to ignore it in case it takes over the text completely. I will aim for the middle way of brevity. It is probably true to say that Slow philosophy has its heart in the villages and market towns rather than cities, but Norwich is hardly your average city. At the other end of the River Yare stands Great Yarmouth, a large, slightly threadbare sort of place that some might prefer to avoid. It, too, has its own story to tell. The River Tas has no such urban centres, just a few likable villages strung along minor roads in pretty rolling south Norfolk countryside. There's some interesting history and unsung places half-hidden away here in what is effectively Norwich's commuter belt.

The rivers

The River Yare is the main focus though. As Norfolk's broadest river it was a vital waterway for trade until quite recently and remains an important area for wildlife, with the whole of its floodplain, as far as Norwich itself, lying under the aegis of the Broads Authority. It's a formidable barrier too that, strikingly, has only one crossing place between Norwich and Yarmouth. The nature writer Mark Cocker, himself a resident of the Yare Valley, points out in his fascinating book *Crow Country* that communities that can quite clearly see each other on either side of the river usually have absolutely no contact with each other, as such contact would require a massive detour. How different from the situation along the River Waveney (see *Chapter 6*) where villages on both the Norfolk and Suffolk banks visit each other's market places (and supermarkets) without a second thought. It would make more sense in a way if Norfolk north of the Yare were deemed a different county to that south of the river. Those living in Langley Green south of the Yare tend to be more interested in getting into

Norwich at weekends than they are curious about what happens in Cantley, north of the river, whose lights they can see at night.

Getting around

Travelling along the Yare Valley is easy enough, as long as you don't want to cross the river. The A47 runs between Norwich and Great Yarmouth, north of the River Yare, a dual carriageway for part of the way. This continues as the southern bypass at Norwich and links to the A11 south before continuing west to East Dereham and King's Lynn. The section between Acle and Great Yarmouth is a straight-as-a-die single carriageway across a wind-blown, windmill-studded marshland, and notorious for speed merchants and accidents. Heading south, the A140, an old Roman road, runs more or less parallel to the spidery course of the River Tas, to eventually cross the River Waveney near Diss.

Buses and trains

Public transport is better than average. A regular **bus service** connects Norwich with Great Yarmouth, while the services that link Norwich with Thetford, Diss and Beccles also pass through south Norfolk towns and villages like Loddon, Long Stratton, Wymondham and Attleborough. The fastest east–west service is the ever-useful X1 that plies between Lowestoft and King's Lynn via Great Yarmouth, Norwich and Swaffham. There are more local services too, like the 001 Norwich to Surlingham service and the 570 Norwich to Haddiscoe route that goes via Bergh Apton. Traveline (0870 6082608; www.traveline.org.uk) has specific details of routes and timetables.

For **train travel**, the Wherry Line (08457 484950; www.wherry lines.org.uk) is invaluable, with regular trains between Norwich, Great Yarmouth and Lowestoft that usefully stop at places like Buckenham, Acle, Reedham and Berney Arms, which are ideal starting points for walks. Some of the stations like Berney Arms are request stops only, and only a limited number of trains will stop at them, so it is best to study the timetable closely. The National Express Norwich to Peterborough train service has stops at Wymondham and Attleborough.

Cycling

Cycling, as elsewhere in the region, is fine as long as you keep well away from the main roads. Fortunately, there are sufficient minor roads that getting around is reasonable. Some of the narrow lanes close to the river on either bank are a real pleasure, although you need to be ever vigilant of absent-minded locals and Norwich commuters speeding home in their 4x4s. Sustrans National Cycle Network route 1 (Harwich to Hull; www.sustrans.org.uk) passes through this area, coming up from the Waveney Valley to Loddon and then following minor roads through villages south of the Yare on its way into Norwich. Part of the Wherryman's Way (see below) is also suitable for cyclists.

Walking

There's plenty of scope for enjoyable waterside **walking**, particularly east of Rockland Broad from where a riverside path goes all the way to Breydon Water. There's the same on the opposite bank from Buckenham eastwards and the northern bank has the distinct advantage that there are a couple of useful railway stations along the way that avoid the necessity of doubling back. With a car, circular walks are feasible if you are willing to combine stretches of riverside with paths across marshes and some road walking.

The area's two long-distance trails deserve a look, if only in part, as they lead through some of the most attractive stretches of the river valleys. The **Wherryman's Way** follows the River Yare from Norwich to Great Yarmouth by way of a 35-mile route that takes in historic sites and wildlife areas. The route follows the south bank of the River Yare to Hardley, loops around the River Chet to Loddon then, crossing the river at its only ferry point at Reedham, continues along the north bank of the river to Breydon Water and Great Yarmouth. A booklet, available free from tourist information centres or direct from Norfolk County Council (01603 223317), details a dozen circular walks along the way. The same walks can also be downloaded from www.wherrymansway.net. The last stretch of the Wherryman's Way between Reedham and Great Yarmouth lies conveniently close to the Wherry Line stations of Reedham and Berney Arms, and so lends itself easily to combined rail and foot outings. A good option is to take the train to the Berney Arms request stop then walk either west to Reedham or east to Great Yarmouth and pick up a return train.

Other long-distance trails are **Boudica's Way**, a 40-mile route connecting Diss to Norwich that meanders through a number of south Norfolk villages along the way, and the **Tas Valley Way**, a 25-mile walk from Eaton, just southwest of Norwich to Attleborough. A further route developed in recent years by South Norfolk Council is **Kett's Country**, a 21-mile walk between Cringleford and Wymondham. Details and maps of all of these can be obtained from South Norfolk Council at their Swan Lane, Long Stratton office (01508 533945) or downloaded from www.south-norfolk.gov.uk.

Tourist information

Great Yarmouth Maritime House, 25 Marine Parade ☎ 01493 846346
🖰 www.great-yarmouth.co.uk.
Loddon The Old Town Hall, 1 Bridge St ☎ 01508 521028
🖰 www.south-norfolk.gov.uk (seasonal).
Norwich The Forum, Millennium Plain ☎ 01603 213999 🖰 www.visitnorwich.co.uk.
Wymondham Market Cross, Market Place ☎ 01953 604721 (seasonal).

① Norwich

*'A fine old city, perhaps the most curious specimen
at present extant of the genuine old English town.'*
George Borrow *Lavengro*

As the city sign tells you as you drive in, Norwich is a fine
city. Former Norwich City goalkeeper Robert Green once
dubbed Norwich 'a city the size of a town with a village mentality',
which can be seen as both criticism and praise depending on your viewpoint.
The general image is that of a city out on a limb that is out of step with modern
times; a place of gauche, unfashionable attitudes and a dodgy football team;
Alan Partridge, Delia Smith, parochialism, mustard, banking and insurance.

Naturally enough, the reality is somewhat different: Alan Partridge is a
fictitious character (although there really is a Radio Norwich these days), Delia
Smith lives in Suffolk despite her regular outings to Carrow Road, and Norwich
Union have re-branded as Aviva and outsourced to Sheffield and India.
Contrary to expectations, the city is increasingly cosmopolitan, has a thriving
university and is one of the fastest growing cities in England. Simply put,
Norwich punches well above its weight.

Norwich is a very liveable sort of place. Where I live, close to the city wall, just
south of the centre but well outside the fashionable 'Golden Triangle' beloved
of university lecturers and media folk, is a case in point. Within five minutes'
walk from my house are two independent cafés, half a dozen decent pubs and
a couple of really good ones. It's a five-minute walk to the bus station, and ten
minutes to one of the oldest permanent food markets in the country; fifteen
minutes' walk to a thriving arts centre and twenty to a fantastic independent
cinema. There's a 'real meat' butcher's just up the road too, and on Fridays
mornings a mobile fish van comes from Lowestoft with fish so fresh that it is
almost still twitching. The fishmonger gives me the news from the coast – what
the fishing's like at Lowestoft, whether the boats are going out to sea or not. It
is good to have this sort of connectedness in an urban environment, as Norwich
is just about big enough to forget sometimes that you are living in the middle of
a mainly rural region. If this sounds a little smug, then there are a few pitfalls
too: traffic noise and fumes, and the perception by metropolitan types that you
reside in some dull and decidedly unfashionable backwater.

The story goes that Norwich has a pub for every day of the year and a church
for every week. Not quite right – there were actually 700 pubs in the city in
medieval times, 363 in 1905 (within the city walls) and around 140 in the whole
of Norwich today – but it does give a ball-park figure. As elsewhere in the
country, pubs seem to be closing for business almost every week and of the
city's surviving 31 medieval churches, two-thirds lie empty or find modern use
as puppet theatres, art studios, or even pregnancy crisis centres. That is still a lot
of churches for a city of just 130,000... and plenty of pubs.

A potted history

Back in the late 11th century, Norwich was England's second largest city. It had existed as a large Saxon town before the conquest but the arrival of the Normans brought the cathedral, castle and a large increase in population. As it was an important weaving centre, Flemish and Walloon migrants came from across the North Sea in the 16th century to join the throng, to be followed later by French Huguenots. Norwich has always been demonstrably tolerant of 'strangers' and even sometimes radical in outlook, with a strong working-class tradition.

To see Norwich simply as a quaint cathedral city is misleading; as well as medieval streets and cosy Anglo-Saxon provincialism there are also the usual urban problems. True, the centre has cobbled streets, 12th-century walls and Tudor buildings, but beyond this lie grids of Victorian terraces, large council estates (some of Britain's very first council estates – Mile Cross and Larkman – were constructed here in the late 1920s) and sprawling suburbs. The city was bombed quite badly in World War II, especially in April 1942 as part of the so-called Baedeker Raids, in which the popular tourist guide was used to select targets of cultural rather than strategic importance.

The city centre

Plenty of guidebooks will give you the nitty-gritty background – the churches, historic buildings etc. Instead I've picked a few favourite places.

The castle, museums and cathedral

The first places that most guidebooks mention are the castle and cathedral, both Norman in origin and both worthy of your time. **Norwich Castle** stands on a hill above the city centre, its Norman keep a serious square building that serves as the city's historical museum these days: Norwich Castle Museum & Art Gallery (01603 493625; www.museums.norfolk.gov.uk). A sign at the entrance tells the story of Robert Kett, a yeoman farmer who led a peasants' revolt in 1549 and, after camping out on Mousehold Heath with thousands of followers, was finally defeated by government troops. It is probably significant that it took 400 years before he attained local hero status and received a plaque to his memory. As the sign tells you, Kett was hanged at the castle, although it does not mention that he was hanged alive in chains to suffer a slow, cruel death. Norwich Castle once featured in *Monty Python's Flying Circus* as the setting for a particularly silly sketch in which medieval soldiers hurled themselves from battlements, but whenever I see the castle walls, I just think of poor Robert Kett.

Inside the Castle Museum, there's the usual dungeon display to frighten sensitive souls, as well as galleries devoted to archaeology and natural history. An interesting room devoted to the Iceni-Roman conflict in East Anglia has, as well as displays of Iceni bling – huge gold torcs – from the Snettisham Treasure, a virtual Roman chariot ride to delight children. Probably most distinctive though, is the museum's fine art collection. Several rooms are devoted to works of the **Norwich School**, with a wealth of paintings by artists such as John Crome, Joseph Stannard and John Sell Cotman. My personal favourites are the watercolours by John Sell Cotman that make use of an exquisite blue and gold palette. *St Benet's Abbey* (1831) looks as if it is almost floating on the water. Give or take a few Broads cruisers, the scene looks much the same today (see page 65). The Castle Museum has a very sensible 'Pop in for a £1' policy, which allows visits between 12.00 and 13.00 (during school term), or the hour before closing, for just £1.

On the subject of museums, there are a couple of others that are worth an hour of anyone's time. **Strangers' Hall** (01603 667229), at Charing Cross in the shadow of St Gregory's Church, is an interesting social history museum in a delightful Tudor building. Just above it, on Colegate, is St John Maddermarket, another recycled medieval church that has long functioned as a tiny independent theatre. There's a good small museum dedicated to the Norwich shoe and textile industry at **The Bridewell** (01603 629127) in Bridewell Alley. St Andrew's Church next door is second only to St Peter Mancroft in size and has a 15th-century window that shows the Devil dancing with a bishop on a chessboard.

Any decent guidebook will tell you that work started on **Norwich Cathedral** in 1086 at the behest of Bishop Herbert Losinga, so I won't elaborate. It is a magnificent Gothic building, with the second-highest spire in Britain, but I like the small details best. Take a peek at the intricately carved wooden bosses in the cloisters and you will find some that go well beyond the usual themes of the Life of Christ and the Apocalypse, and some which are downright rude.

Another part of the inner city frequently included on city tours, and for good reason, is **King Street**, southeast of the castle mound, which has a wealth of Tudor buildings, tiny courtyards and, best of all, **Dragon Hall** (01603 663922; www.dragonhall.org), an impressive medieval merchant's hall. The neighbourhood has been tidied up in recent years but it has always been interesting even back in the days when it was better known as the city's red-light district (the Wensum River and its sailors being just a stone's throw away).

There are plenty of interesting nooks and crannies around here, so simply delving and wandering at will is probably the best policy. Further on from Dragon Hall there's Wensum Lodge, an adult education centre. The bar here, **Jurnet's Bar**, is worth a look – and a drink if it's open – as it is in the crypt-like basement of a medieval Jewish merchant's house.

Immediately over the river is **Riverside**, a stretch of new entertainment development that, to put it mildly, is 'lively' at weekends. Prince of Wales Road, the thoroughfare that leads down across the river to the railway station, sees a great deal of pre-nightclub carousing on Friday and Saturday nights. All cities have similar areas, of course, but Prince of Wales Road is best avoided on weekend nights unless you are under 25 and full of cheap booze. A taxi driver once remarked, 'It's like Beirut out there', as we drove slowly along it trying to avoid the lurching bodies. I felt it necessary to mention that I had been to Beirut and compared with this it was actually rather nice.

The Lanes and market

Norwich Lanes is a recent re-branding of the city centre's narrow medieval streets. This complex of streets, lanes and alleyways, designated 'the independent shopping and lifestyle quarter' (www.norwichlanes.co.uk), connect three parallel streets north of Norwich Market and Guildhall: St Giles Street, Pottergate and St Benedict's Street, with Norwich Castle, St Andrew's Hall, St Benedict's Church (just a tower since 1944) and St Giles Church all standing as corner pieces. There are plenty of independent shops, cafes and yet more churches within, as well as Jarrold's elegant department store and the pedestrian thoroughfare of London Street with its shops, buskers and *Big Issue* sellers.

Connecting Castle Street and Gentleman's Walk in front of the market, **Royal Arcade** is the delightful Edwardian passageway with a charming Art Nouveau entrance and lamps. It's said there was a 'ghost shop' down here, one that mysteriously appeared and disappeared from time to time. Alongside a decent café and jewellery, toy and fudge sellers is the famous **Colman's Mustard Shop** (01603 627889; www.colmansmustardshop.com), which is as much a museum as a place to buy jars of Norwich's favourite mouth-searing paste.

Norwich Market has operated continuously in the same spot since Norman times (the earlier Saxon market was down at Tombland but was moved when the Normans began to build the cathedral). It's a six-day-a-week affair (closed Sunday) – the largest daily open market in Britain – that sells all manner of local fruit, vegetables, meat and fish as well as clothes and household goods. There's a place to get keys cut and shoes mended while you wait, and a chip stall that comes highly rated by Norwich residents judging by its never-ending queue. The mushy-pea stall here has been in business for 60 years, with the same family running it all that time. A few years ago the market complex was expensively revamped after much deliberation and not a little controversy. The old market had uneven floors and narrow alleyways but the new stalls are a little smaller than those that stood before and haven't gone down too well with some stallholders and shoppers – a textbook example of a committee coming up with a compromise that, ultimately, nobody really seems to like.

City Hall looms above the market, a long, brick 1930s building with rampant lions at its steps that look decidedly Babylonian. The design was apparently based upon that of Stockholm Town Hall but the large square clock tower, seen from all over the city, always puts me in mind of a Marrakech minaret. I am more taken with the two buildings that stand opposite each other just to the south. **St Peter Mancroft Church** has dominated the marketplace since the mid 15-th-century, a wonderful Perpendicular building with a hammerbeam roof that is filled with light – my favourite Norwich church and I am sure I am not alone in this. The church contains the grave of Sir Thomas Browne (1605–82), a Norwich-based medical man and all-round polymath famous for the books *Urn Burial* and *Religio Medici* (W G Sebald devotes half a chapter to him in *Rings of Saturn*). A statue of him contemplating a piece of urn is just across the way in front of Next. There is also a large modernist 'brain' sculpture – in the spirit of Browne's intellectual pursuits, perhaps, but not without its critics.

A car park and lacklustre library used to stand opposite St Peter Mancroft but this burned down in 1994 – public records and hardback thrillers are highly combustible. The void has been filled by **The Forum** (www.theforumnorwich.co.uk), a bold Millennium Commission project that has been an enormous success. The Forum is a large glass-fronted complex in the shape of a horseshoe that contains the Norfolk & Norwich Millennium Library, the regional BBC studios, a café, a restaurant and tourist information. There's a large internal foyer area for exhibitions and performances, and occasional farmers' markets and craft stalls. How a building made of glass, tubular steel and brick can fit so well into such a tight space in a medieval city is remarkable. Part of this may be down to the longer-than-standard handmade bricks used in the horseshoe walls, the same as in the city hall opposite. Between The Forum and St Peter Mancroft is a paved plaza with amphitheatre-like steps that provide a ready venue for street theatre events and for an ice skating rink in winter. It's always busy and, whether by accident or design, seems to provide what the Italians term 'a convivial space', a natural relaxed focus for the city centre.

In addition to the castle and cathedral, the place most often mentioned on tourist trawls through the city is **Elm Hill**, a cobbled street that descends down to Wensum Street from behind St Andrew's Hall. There's no longer an elm here but I do remember the one that used to stand here and the valiant efforts made to save it once it had become infected with that arboreal plague, Dutch elm disease. Elm Hill has galleries, a café or two and a couple of quirky shops, and by the time you reach the bottom you are very close to Fye Bridge and the River Wensum – the part of Norwich locals refer to as 'Norwich over the Water'.

Norwich churches

Norwich has so many churches that it is easy to overdo it and see too many in too short a time. Ecclesiastical architecture needs plenty of time for digestion. A personal choice would be the aforementioned St Peter Mancroft, Norwich Cathedral, naturally, and perhaps the tiny **Shrine Church of St Julian**, just off King Street. St Julian's is actually a reconstruction – the original was bombed during World War II – but it still has a story to tell. This was the site where Julian of Norwich, a 14th-century mystic anchoress, built a cell for herself and turned her back on the world to write *Revelations of Divine Love*, the first work to be written by a woman in English.

I'm fond too of **St Benedict's Street** with its five decommissioned churches strung along its length like ports of call on a spiritual pub crawl. Closest to Grapes Hill with its flinty scraps of city wall is **St Benedict's Church**, now just a freestanding round tower thanks to a World War II bombing raid. A little further on, opposite the Ten Bells pub, is St Swithin's, which has long served as the venue for the **Norwich Arts Centre**, a wonderful institution that puts on a broad range of concerts and events.

A little further still is **St Margaret's** and then my namesake **St Laurence's**, which in medieval times would have had direct access via steps to the River Wensum below. If you take at close look at its western wall from the delightfully named St Lawrence Little Steps (note the spelling; people get my name wrong too), you should be able to make out a stone carving showing St Laurence's martyrdom on a hot iron grill. Reportedly crying out to his tormentors, 'Turn me over I'm done on this side', he has become the patron saint of both cooks and comedians. The church serves as a craft market today. One of the stallholders told me that some of those who use the place sense a none-too-pleasant atmosphere in the western end of the church, 'There's a very strange feel to it – really quite evil. We all think it. There's a door there and I was thinking of having a look to see what was behind it. Then I just thought to myself, "No, I really don't think so"'. Further on at Charing Cross, the junction of St Benedict's with Westlegate, stands **St Gregory's Church**. All this – five redundant churches – within a five-minute, 400-metre walk.

Nonconformist Norwich

Norwich has more than just medieval churches, of course; and the churches built in more recent centuries have not been solely Anglican either. Roman Catholics have their own **pro-cathedral of St John the Baptist**, a massive Victorian Gothic edifice, at the top of Earlham Road, with The Tuns, a genuine (rather than faux-Paddy) Irish pub, conveniently opposite. As a centre of nonconformity, there have been all sorts of congregations worshipping in the city. The 18th-century **Octagon Chapel** on Colegate, built by Thomas Ivory, the same architect who built the splendid Georgian Assembly Rooms on Rampant Horse Street, is highly unusual and indeed octagonal. Originally built by Presbyterians, it became Unitarian in the 19th century.

There's also a marvellous curio in the form of the nonconformist **Rosary Road Cemetery** just east of Thorpe railway station, where the same nonconformist worshippers often ended up, as well as quite a few railway workers from the nearby station. This is a delightful place to wander in peace and quiet, listening to birdsong and examining gravestones. Surprisingly, this is the earliest nonconformist cemetery in England, and older than any of the larger London equivalents. In earlier times, resolute nonconformists often met grisly deaths at the hands of the orthodoxy. The site of the **Lollard's Pit** just across Riverside Road from Bishop's Bridge is testament to this, although only a commemorative plate remains today. As George Borrow remarks in *Lavengro*, 'It has had its martyrs, the venerable old town'.

Modernist Norwich

If modern architecture floats your boat, you might want to make a pilgrimage west of the city to my alma mater, the University of East Anglia, where you'll find the **Sainsbury Centre for Visual Arts**, an aircraft hangar of a building designed by Sir Norman Foster when he was still relatively unknown. Whatever your view is of the building's aesthetic appeal – I doubt if Prince Charles is an admirer – it certainly works well as a gallery for the arts and, as well as the permanent collection, hosts frequent special exhibitions by prestigious artists. The Sainsbury Centre and 'ziggurats' of the university buildings look down on a tree-lined manmade lake, usually referred to as UEA Broad, which has matured nicely since it was first created out of a gravel pit in the mid 1970s and now has a wealth of wildlife in and around its waters. It's a favourite spot for anglers, local joggers and dog-walkers.

North of UEA Broad, behind woodland and parallel to Bluebell Lane, a footpath takes you past a series of meadows filled with rescue horses of all shapes and sizes: tiny Shetland ponies, standard-size horses, donkeys, even a mule. The kind chap who rescues and nurtures these unfortunate beasts told me 'We get a lot of them from the continent, Italy especially. It costs a lot to ship them over here but it's worth it.' On regular walks here, it is heart-warming to see what were once sorry animals slowly regain their fettle with time. The place made the local news a while ago when a Shetland pony shared the same field as an old mare. To everyone's surprise, the pair produced a foal together in defiance of the assumption that the stallion was too short and the mare, too old.

Green Norwich

Norwich is by any standards a green city, and I'm not referring to its many parks and open spaces like Chapelfield Gardens within the city walls and Mousehold Heath, beyond. In 2006, the city was voted England's greenest city, having the highest concentration of eco-friendly businesses in the country. This is probably not unconnected to the fact that the Green Party do so well here that Norwich is frequently mooted as likely to be first place in Britain to return a Green MP to Westminster. The first **Norwich & Norfolk Sustainable Living Festival** was held in the city in 2009, with all manner of exhibitions and events taking place at The Forum and the University of East Anglia. The Forum is also the location for occasional farmers' markets.

As you might expect, the city has a decent number of outlets for locally produced organic produce. **The Green Grocers** (01603 250000; www.thegreengrocers.co.uk) at 2, Earlham House, Earlham Road sells food and drink that is 90% organic and/or locally produced and also has a carbon-neutral project to offset its emissions. This is also the location for the **Golden Triangle Farmers' Market**, which takes place from 10.00 to 15.00 every second Sunday of the month. There's another regular farmers' market on Gentleman's Walk in front of the 'proper' market on the first and third Sundays of the month from 10.00 to 16.00. For meat eaters, **Harvey's Pure Meat** at 63 Grove Road (01603 621908; www.puremeat.org.uk) specialises in organic meat and seasonal game. Anna's Farm Store (01603 665982) at 30 Magdalen Street in the north of the city has all kinds of local organic produce. Of course, **Norwich Market** itself should not be overlooked with its wealth of local produce and excellent fish stalls.

Returning to the sense of green meaning 'foliage', several city gardens are worth a visit. My first choice would be **The Plantation Garden** (01603 811424; www.plantationgarden.co.uk) at 4 Earlham Road, right beside St John's RC Church. This was created a century and a half ago in an abandoned chalk quarry but lay completely forgotten until its rediscovery 25 years ago. Also referred to as 'The Secret Garden' because it really was secret until quite recently, its Gothic fountain, Italianate terrace and woodland walkways have all been lovingly restored, although it is still very much a work in progress. It is open year-round but there's the bonus of tea and cake (£1.50) on summer Sunday afternoons. **The Bishop's Garden** (www.norwich.anglican.org/gardens), open on several days a year, is a delightful swathe of perennial borders hidden away behind 700-year-old walls in the cloistered enclave of Cathedral Close. For a taste of the tropical, Will Giles's **Exotic Garden** (01603 623167; www.exoticgarden.com) at 126 Thorpe Road just goes to show what can be done with a south-facing slope, time, skill and plenty of bubble wrap for winter protection. The garden is open on Sunday afternoons from late June to late October.

Pubs

Norwich is blessed with a superb choice of pubs that range from traditional locals to sophisticated eateries. As well as those listed below, my other favourites for a drink are The Trafford Arms, The Shed, The King's Arms, The Duke of Wellington and The Wig & Pen.

Adam and Eve Bishopsgate ℂ 01603 667423. Splendidly ancient and character-laden hostelry, resplendent with floral tubs and hanging baskets; good-value pubby food.

Ⓢ Fat Cat 49 West End St ℂ 01603 624364. A Victorian corner pub that is real-ale heaven, this has around 30 real ales on offer at any given time. Strictly booze and no food, this traditional pub of the old school is austere, crowded, noisy and very good fun.

Ⓢ Mad Moose Arms 2 Warwick St ℂ 01508 492497. Formerly 'The Warwick' in a previous incarnation, this is now the more relaxed, less polished sister pub to the Wildebeest Arms (see page 134). A good modern pub serving Wolf Ales.

Cafés

Here is just a small sample of personal city-centre favourites:

Café Morello 5 Orford St ℂ 01603 764441.
King of Hearts Café 7–15 Fye Bridge St ℂ 01603 620805.
Little Red Roaster 81B Grove Rd ℂ 01603 624886.
Logans 5 Swan Lane ℂ 01603 764341.
Marmalades 19 Royal Arcade ℂ 01603 767047.
No 33 33 Exchange St ℂ 01603 626097.
Olives 40 Elm Hill ℂ 01603 230500 ⊕ www.olivesnorwich.co.uk.

Along the Yare – south bank

② Surlingham

A few miles east of Norwich, on the south bank of the River Yare, lies the village of Surlingham. The riverside Ferry Boat pub is busy in summer with boat customers but the ferry no longer operates, which is rather a pity. Most people arriving by boat tend just to call in at the pub, or perhaps moor in the broad further on, but there's plenty to see on foot around the village. If you have your own transport, St Mary's Church just west of the village is the best place to park up as you can make an interesting **circular walk** from here that takes in a good variety of scenery within a relatively short distance.

A footpath leads down past ponds and dykes to the river. There are dragonflies a plenty and all those other things that tend to characterise Norfolk's slow-moving waterways – yellow flag irises, reed-mace, ragged robin, the sweet smell of water mint and the occasional splash of a frog. Arriving at the river, you come to a path shaded by willows that continues past reed beds and a bird hide as far as the Ferry House pub. Blackthorn grows plentifully along the path here, which is one of my favourite places to collect sloes (for making sloe gin) on a bright early winter's day when there's a nip in the air. Of course, if you are here earlier in the year then you cannot 'go sloe' as I do. A concrete road leads inland from the pub through a swampy alder carr, at the end of which is a track to the right next to a house with a dovecote. The path leads along the edge of a field and past a rifle range until it passes beneath the remains of St Saviour's, an evocative ruined church, and continues along a track to St Mary's where you started. If you make a short detour to the ruins of St Saviour's you'll come across the graves of local naturalist and writer Ted Ellis (1909–1986) and his wife, Phyllis. The graves are simple, austere even, but it is undeniably a lovely spot for any lifelong lover of nature to rest his bones. Continuing up the track towards St Mary's, the house on the left, just before the church, usually has jars of honey for sale and an honesty box at its gate – this is the home of Orchid Apiaries, which produces several tons of honey annually from Surlingham hives.

Surlingham parish is a large one that extends east of the village to Surlingham Marsh, Surlingham Wood and **Wheatfen Nature Reserve** (01508 538036; www.wheatfen.org), a reserve first established by the naturalist Ted Ellis (see above), who lived in a cottage here for 40 years before his death in 1986. Visitors to the reserve are welcome and there are several trails across marshes and woodland, where you are likely to see (or, more likely, hear) sedge and reed warblers, and perhaps witness marsh harriers gliding overhead. In late May and early June, you might even come across that Broadland speciality, the swallowtail butterfly.

③ Rockland Broad

This lies just south of Wheatfen Nature Reserve, a sheltered body of water connected to the Yare by a dyke. The New Inn pub is on the road next to a footpath that leads around the west side of the broad.

From Claxton, the road more or less follows the course of the river through Langley Green and Langley Street to Hardley Street, all tiny hamlets surrounded by vast marshes. The floodplain of the river is very wide, flat and low here and the marshes extensive. The very mention of Hardley Street puts me in mind of a time 25 years or so ago when I found myself out on the marshes here during a violent thunderstorm. In a vast wet area where everything is at sea-level and with no trees, a soggy man makes a rather good lightning conductor – or so I thought, as I ran back to my car with jagged shafts of electricity fizzing around me. Fortunately, it did not turn out to be the electrifying experience that it might have been and I escaped unscathed. I tend to listen more closely to weather forecasts these days.

New Inn 12 New Inn Hill, Rockland St Mary ☎ 01508 538403. Next to the Rockland Broad staithe, with modern British food.

A circular walk from Rockland Broad

An enjoyable **circular walk** can be made from the New Inn at Rockland Broad, although it's a fair bit longer than the one from Sheringham church. From the pub, where there is a car park over the road, follow the footpath along the staithe and then along the track that leads around the broad. You'll just about be able to see the broad through the trees but, frustratingly, there is no access to it other than by boat. The path continues along a dyke until it reaches the River Yare, where you follow the riverside path until you reach a bridleway heading inland across the marshes from the Beauchamp Arms pub. Turn right at the road through Claxton village and head past Claxton Manor to Claxton Corner, where you continue along a farm track to reach a small wood, from where a footpath crosses the fields back to the road near the New Inn.

④ Bergh Apton

Bergh Apton – that's *Ber*-apton not *Bergh*-apton – is a large, sprawling village south of Rockland St Mary, just the other side of the A146. There's not much of a centre to the village but it's an interesting place to visit if you happen to coincide with the sculpture trail held every three years: this offers the opportunity not only to see works by local sculptors but also to snoop around some rather wonderful village gardens. The village was originally two separate settlements, Apton to the northwest and Bergh to the southeast, which explains its considerable size. Apton's church disappeared long ago and the two parishes were combined so that Bergh's church of St Peter and St Paul might serve both. The **sculpture trail** (www.berghapton.org.uk), held over three weekends in late May and June, has to some extent become a victim of its own success, with several thousands attending in 2005 and 2008. Bicycles are useful as the trail is extensive and requires quite a long afternoon on foot. The next sculpture trail should be in 2011.

Along the Yare – north bank

The north bank of the River Yare has the railway line to Great Yarmouth and so is far more accessible if you want to use public transport. A couple of stops along the line are worth heading for if you are looking for quiet walk or are at all interested in birds and wildlife.

⑤ Strumpshaw Fen

The village of Strumpshaw lies midway between Brundall and Lingwood but Strumpshaw Fen Nature Reserve (www.rspb.org.uk), an extensive wetland reserve run by the RSPB, is actually closer to Brundall. The reserve, which lies just across the river from Wheatfen Reserve and Surlingham Marshes, has all the wetland birds that you might expect plus some others that you might not, with bitterns, harriers, warblers, woodpeckers and numerous waders and ducks all lining up to be seen. It is also a reliable place to see swallowtail butterflies, which in my experience are easiest to spot in late May when they are still a tad sluggish.

The main entrance and visitor centre are a little over a mile from Buckenham station and so this is a possibility if you are arriving by train. You should bear in mind though that only a limited number of trains stop at Buckenham as it is a request stop – four on Sundays, one on Saturdays and none in the week. On a Sunday, you could combine a visit to Strumpshaw with one to Berney Arms and Breydon Water. The rest of the week, you'll have to use Brundall station instead, which requires a slightly longer walk to reach the reserve entrance. Buses 17 and 17a also run hourly between Norwich and Strumpshaw; get off at the stop at the junction of Long Lane and Stone Road, from where it's a ten-minute walk.

⑥ Buckenham Carrs

A large wooded area just east of Buckenham station, **Buckenham Carrs** is in winter home to an enormous rook and jackdaw roost mentioned in the Domesday Book. It's thought there may be as many as 80,000 birds. The roost is the central motif of Mark Cocker's *Crow Country*, which celebrates both crows and the Yare Valley where he lives. The Buckenham roost, which takes place in the winter months, roughly between late October and March, is quite a spectacle to behold, a natural phenomenon that has been taking place long before the fields were ploughed here and the church at Buckenham constructed. Ideally, you'll want a crisp winter's evening with a clear sky and a full moon. The best vantage point is to walk up the narrow road from Buckenham station until you reach a copse on the left with a small ruined brick shelter. You'll see it all from here.

A building of rooks at Buckenham

The performance – if you can call it that – is a slow burn. Just after sunset, groups of rooks, and some jackdaws, fly in to gather on the large ploughed area immediately to the west; others land in the trees that surround it. Some have come quite a long way to be sociable but the crow conversation taking place sounds rather tetchy, all guttural complaining caws.

Momentum slowly builds as more and more groups of birds fly in to land in the field. As the light fades, the noise from the congregation builds louder and eerily expectant: something is clearly about to happen. Eventually, when the darkness is almost complete some sort of signal spurs the birds airborne and the sky blackens with rooks that swirl noisily east to settle in the woods of Buckenham Carrs where they will spend the night together.

It's an astonishing, almost primal, event. One that almost laughs in the face of man's perceived dominion over nature. No collective noun can adequately describe it: a building of rooks, a train of jackdaws. It's less a murder of crows, more a mass execution.

⑦ Cantley and ⑧ Reedham

Working eastwards, the next village along the river is Cantley, best known for its **sugar beet factory** that belches out sickly-smelling smoke in the winter months. Cantley's sugar-beet factory, seen from far and wide, is as much an icon of the River Yare as a Norfolk wherry, and is the magnet for all the lumbering lorries that trundle these roads in winter brimful of knobbly roots.

Reedham, further east, has the only surviving **car and passenger ferry** along the river and consequently is the only point between Norwich and Great Yarmouth where it is possible to cross. The cable ferry, which takes up to three cars at a time, operates year-round. If this service seems a quaint throwback of value only to tourists then consider that crossing the river here can save a round-trip of around 30 miles, so there may be queues in summer. The village, listed as Redaham in the Domesday Book, is thought to have been a Roman military station -- there are fragments of Roman brick in the village's St John the Baptist church – and, as with many other East Anglian locations, Edmund, King of East Anglia, is rumoured to have lived here for a while. As well as having a popular riverside pub, the village is also home to the Humpty Dumpty Brewery (01493 701818; www.humptydumptybrewery.co.uk), which uses locally produced malt and whose Broadland Surprise was voted Champion Beer of Norfolk 2010. Another Humpty Dumpty brew, the aptly named Norfolk Nectar, makes use of local honey. It's a three-and-a-half-mile walk along the riverbank to Berney Arms from here, a worthwhile outing from which you could return by train if you got your timing right. Otherwise, there are easy circular road walks around the village.

The Lord Nelson 38 Riverside ☎ 01493 701548 🖰 www.lordnelsonpub.com. With plain pub grub and seven real ales to choose from, this pub by the water and swing bridge is a convenient stop. The beer festival held here on August Bank Holiday weekends has music by local bands and a perplexing choice of local real ales.

⑨ Berney Arms

Berney Arms must be the oddest railway stop in the country. I use the word 'stop' advisedly, rather than station, as that is all there is to it: a sign and small platform to get off or on the few trains that stop here. It takes its name from a local landowner, Thomas Trench Berney, who in 1844 sold land to the railway company on condition that they built a station and kept it open for perpetuity. The station is unstaffed, of course, and as you might imagine, three and a half miles from the nearest road and right in the heart of the vast spread of Halvergate Marshes, rather isolated.

A walk from Berney Arms

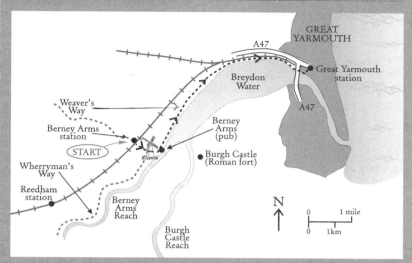

With just two trains a day and five on Sundays, walking is the only thing to do here, unless you want to spend hours waiting on the platform. Fortunately, the walking is very good: the Wherryman's Way runs nearby and you have the choice of going west to Reedham, northwest along the Weavers' Way to Halvergate or east to Great Yarmouth along the shore of Breydon Water. My preferred choice would be the third.

From the station follow the footpath, part of the Weavers' Way, to the river, where there is a drainage windmill. Then head east along the Wherryman's Way to reach the Berney Arms pub, which has Woodforde's ales and a garden right by the water. This is usually open daily in the summer and at weekends in the winter. The trade these days is almost entirely walkers, birdwatchers or boaters – there are several moorings here – but in the past this isolated pub would have had a colourful clientele of wherrymen, wildfowlers, poachers and fishermen. Just after the pub, you arrive at the confluence of the Yare and Waveney and the start of Breydon Water. Look south along the Waveney River and you should be able to make out the outline of Gariannonum/Burgh Castle (see page 164). From here, the Wherryman's Way continues all the way along the north shore of Breydon Water until it reaches Great Yarmouth where it narrows to a channel to flow south into the sea at Gorleston. Great Yarmouth railway station is right by Breydon Bridge at the start of the town.

Breydon Water is a large tidal estuary, a wonderful place for birdwatchers and a great place to walk, although it is quite an austere landscape, especially at low tide when glistening grey mud stretches to the skyline. The sky is often grey too, or that is how it seems to me, as whenever I come here it always seems to be overcast as if there were a perpetual cloud hanging over the place. Winter is peak season here, for birds at least, with tens of thousands of waders, ducks and swans feeding in the mud.

⑩ Great Yarmouth

Not so great these days, some might say. Great
Yarmouth is hardly an obvious Slow destination but
it would be wrong to dismiss it completely. Once, there
was a thriving herring fishing industry here. This faded
out in the early years of the 20th century, by which
time the town had found new fortune as a seaside
resort. The 1970s heralded an era of cheap Mediterranean holidays and many of
the town's former devotees stared to look further afield to destinations like the
Costa Brava instead. Once again, the town's diminishing fortunes were bailed
out by a new source of income; this time, it was North Sea oil and gas.

Great Yarmouth is a town of two halves: an isthmus that shows its seafaring
side along South Quay to the west, and its holiday resort face along the
promenade to the east. Neither half is doing particularly well these days but
both will provide a degree of culture shock if you travel here direct from
somewhere like Southwold, a very different sort of place although just 20 miles
away. Great Yarmouth, the resort is as you might expect: an East Anglian
Blackpool with a pier, sandy beach, deckchairs, buckets and spades – it's
traditional in the sense of being a place where you can still buy sticks of rock,
see a waxworks museum and even have a 'gypsy' woman tell your fortune. The
accents are northern, Midlands or Norfolk, although move a few streets in from
the promenade and you'll hear plenty of Polish and Portuguese instead.

There's still something quintessentially English about Great Yarmouth sea
front, and it's refreshing to discover that not everyone who can afford it has
upped sticks to Benidorm or Corfu. Next to the pier, you might see a large
extended family of Birmingham Indians, as I did one bright August day: mothers
and aunties in glorious saris chatting and devouring chips on the sea wall; teenage
girls texting their friends and giggling; boys playing serious cricket on the sand
with proper stumps and a hard ball. Observing this heart-warming scene from
posters above the pier are Jim Davidson and Roy 'Chubby' Brown, comedians
not known for their love of liberal inclusivity – it all struck a wonderful chord.

Heritage Quarter

Yarmouth's other side can be found in its **Heritage Quarter** along South Quay,
which begins at the bridge and Victorian Town Hall and stretches south along
the River Yare. There will also be the 1930 herring boat *Lydia Eva*, the very last
of the steam drifters, moored at the top of the quay unless it has been moved
to pastures new since I was last there. **Elizabeth House** (01493 855746;
www.museums.norfolk.gov.uk) at 4 South Quay was the home of a Tudor
merchant, while **The Tollhouse** (01493 858900), a little further south and just
inland, dates from the 12th century and was used as a gaol. Some surviving **Row
Houses** (01493 857900; www.english-heritage.org.uk) are open to visitors just
south of here, while back on South Quay at number 26 is **The Nelson
Museum** (01493 850698; www.nelson-museum.co.uk), which is precisely that, a

museum dedicated to the life and times of the Norfolk naval hero. You'll encounter more Row Houses along Nottingham Way near the museum.

If you're not heading straight from there to the Time and Tide Museum (see below), wander further along South Quay towards the 43-metre-high **Nelson Monument** that overlooks the mouth of the river. This is not vintage Norfolk scenery, but interestingly grim, with enormous heaps of metal scrap in yards, closed warehouses, rough-looking pubs and a few dodgy-looking characters. There's a semi-abandoned air to the streets here that reminds me a little of Sheffield's Don Valley in the late 1980s – the ghost of unemployment and vanished industry.

The **Time and Tide Museum** (01493 743930; www.museums.norfolk. gov.uk) on Blackfriars Road, opposite a large chunk of the medieval Town Wall, is rather wonderful and it's worth visiting Yarmouth for this alone. A European Museum of the Year finalist in 2006, it gives a wonderful account of Great Yarmouth life through the ages, particularly its seafaring tradition. It's a hands-on place that children really enjoy and there's plenty of archive film and taped interviews to make the history come alive. 'We're a bit Tardis-like here,' the guide explained, 'but we manage to pack a lot into a small space. The building used to be a herring curing works and a lot of people ask if we pump the smell in for atmosphere. We don't: it's in the fabric of the building itself.' The building really does smell strongly of herrings, which gives you a clue as to the sort of social stigma that the itinerant Scots fisher girls who came 'tae Yarmooth' must have suffered, given that their working days were spent elbow-deep in briny fish. As well as plenty of great displays and nostalgic newsreels of the joys of the herring fishing life ('There's nothing more stately than a shoal of herring coming over the side'), there's a reconstructed 'row' of cottages with tiny, tidy front rooms and piped voices. It is all rather moving, which is surely what any top-notch museum should aspire to be.

Tall Ships in Yarmouth

Great Yarmouth's Maritime Festival (www.maritime-festival.co.uk) in September is a fine reminder of East Anglia's once-glorious seafaring tradition. With majestic tall ships moored on South Quay alongside numerous tents and stalls with a general maritime theme, it draws large crowds of local families, old sailors and curious landlubbers. It's a rare opportunity to poke around a tall ship, talk to experts and hang around with sailors. As well as ships to explore, there are craft stalls, information stands and even displays by Newfoundland rescue dogs, with fried herrings for sale, and salty sea shanties sung by crusty men with pewter tankards in the real ale tent. If you want to buy a ship in a bottle, a piece of seashell sculpture or a Caister Lifeboat sweatshirt, this is definitely the place to be.

Café Cru North Drive ☎ 01493 842000 🖰 www.imperialhotel.co.uk/cafe-cru. Located at the Imperial Hotel, this has a menu offering modern British food.

Gallon Pot Market Place ☎ 01493 842230. Conveniently situated pub near the market for drinks and pub grub.

Mariners Tavern 60 Howard St ☎ 08721 077077. Considered by some locals to be the best real ale pub in town (it won Norfolk CAMRA Branch Pub of the Year in 2010), this has a cosy feel and is reasonably close to the railway station.

Silver Darlings Café Blackfriars Rd. In the courtyard of Time and Tide museum – you don't need a ticket for the café – this is a convenient port of call before or after a museum visit. Good tea and snacks too.

Away from the Yare

⑪ Venta Icenorum and ⑫ Shotesham

The River Tas wiggles its way up from south Norfolk to its confluence with the Yare just outside Norwich. There's a Bronze Age henge marked on maps close to this point, beneath pylons next to the railway tracks and the Norwich inner ring road, but I have never been able to make out more than a few vague bumps in a field – evidently it's a job for a photographer in a helicopter.

Venture a little further south, past Caistor St Edmund, and there's more impressive archaeology in the form of **Venta Icenorum Roman Town**, a rectangle of raised walls and fortifications with traces of Roman brick that once served as the *Civitas* of the Iceni tribe and the most important Roman Centre in East Anglia. Not surprisingly, **Boudica's Way**, a recently created long-distance footpath, passes right by it, although the evidence suggests that the streets and buildings of the town were not constructed until well after Boudica's bloody revolt against Roman rule in AD61.

Away from the river, **Shotesham** is an attractive village set among lush bucolic meadows. A good circular walk from here would be to follow Boudica's Way south to Saxlingham Nethergate, then return to the village via Shotesham Lane and Roger's Lane. On the return leg, you will pass the evocatively ruined church of St Martin alongside its replacement next to Shotesham Old Hall.

⑤ Wildebeest Arms Norwich Rd, Stoke Holy Cross ☎ 01598 492497 🖰 www.thewildebeest.co.uk. Just south of Venta Icenorum. More special inside than out, with a winter fire and an African theme in one long room divided by a central bar: this justifiably popular dining inn serves very good, freshly made food that includes old English favourites.

⑬ Wymondham and ⑭ the Mid-Norfolk Railway

Wedged in between the course of the Yare and Tas rivers southwest of Norwich, just off the A11 dual carriageway, stands the market town of **Wymondham**, a prosperous sort of place that is just far enough away from Norwich to have a life of its own. Wymondham is both well to do and well connected, having a major road running past it, a good bus service and regular train connections to Norwich and Cambridge.

The first thing you need to know is that it's pronounced 'Wind-am' – to say 'Wy-mond-ham' will just induce hilarity in the natives. If you take the B1172 via Hethersett to reach the town, as the bus does, you'll pass **Kett's Oak** by the roadside a mile short of the town's outskirts. The tree is reputed to be that under which Robert Kett, a Wymondham native, gathered supporters and made a rousing speech that set in motion his uprising against the enclosure of common land in 1549. The tree is partially supported by props these days but it still seems to be flourishing enough to produce acorns.

Like many other market towns, much of medieval Wymondham went up in smoke, and, in 1615, a fire started by three gypsies by the name of Flodder gutted many of the town's buildings. The market cross that you see today is an early 17th-century rebuild, as is much of the historic town centre, and it is thanks to the town remaining rather a backwater in the Victorian era that so many old buildings remain today. The 1617 **market cross**, which doubles as the Tourist Information Centre, is probably the town's best-known structure – on stilts to protect valuable documents from floodwater and rats. Live rats used to be nailed to it in order to set an example to fellow vermin but the practice was discontinued in 1902 when a child died as the result of a rat bite.

Wymondham Abbey, or to give it its full name, the Abbey Church of St Mary and St Thomas of Canterbury, is the town's other iconic building, a twin-towered parish church that started life as a Benedictine priory. The monastic buildings were demolished following the Dissolution and the church was partially destroyed, but a visit by Elizabeth I in 1573 ensured that some repairs were made. It is the two towers that make the church such a distinctive local landmark. The eastern octagonal tower is older, part of the original Norman abbey church, while the square western tower dates from 1448 and once had Robert Kett's brother, William, hung in chains from it and left to rot. Looking at the interior, it is hard to imagine such cruel events ever taking place here, as the hammerbeam roof bristles with benign wooden angels beaming goodwill down onto the congregation.

Walk towards the River Tiffey from the abbey and cross it and you'll arrive at a railway line and the station – well, platform – of the **Mid-Norfolk Railway** (www.mnr.org.uk). At weekends, and some Wednesdays, between April and October two or three trains a day run in either direction between here and East

Dereham. Enthusiastic volunteers ensure that the trains always run on time and it's a highly enjoyable excursion, especially if you manage to get on one of the steam trains. En route, you'll pass through some forgotten little outposts of central Norfolk like Thuxton and Yaxham, where you can get off if you like and have a walk. East Dereham is the terminus for the time being, but plans are afoot for the line to be restored as far as North Elmham.

Wymondham's other railway station – the proper one, if you like – has regular trains in both directions to Norwich and Cambridge but the station is worth a visit in its own right for its **'Brief Encounter'** refreshment room, which cleverly manages to fuse cinematic romance with railway memorabilia. It has two separate dining areas, one of which has railway-carriage-style seating. There are also enough railway memorabilia spread about to make bona fide trainspotters think they have died and gone to heaven.

Further down the A11 at Besthorpe near **Attleborough**, you'll find the award-winning Wolf Brewery (www.wolfbrewery.com), whose founder Wolf Witham was the driving force behind the Reindeer, one of the first brew pubs to open in Norwich back in the 1980s. There's a shop at the brewery and pre-booked tours are possible for groups of eight or more.

Brief Encounter Restaurant Wymondham Station ☎ 01953 606433 🖰 www.wymondham-station.com. Morning coffee, afternoon teas, light lunches and weekend evening meals served in nostalgic, railway-centred surroundings.
Green Dragon 6 Church St ☎ 01953 607907 🖰 www.greendragon-pub.co.uk. A handsome 16th-century inn serving home-cooked English food with an emphasis on local produce. Cask-conditioned ales and an extensive wine list.

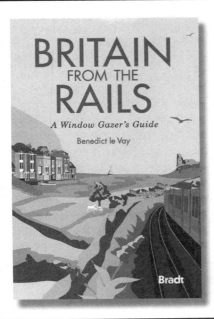

137

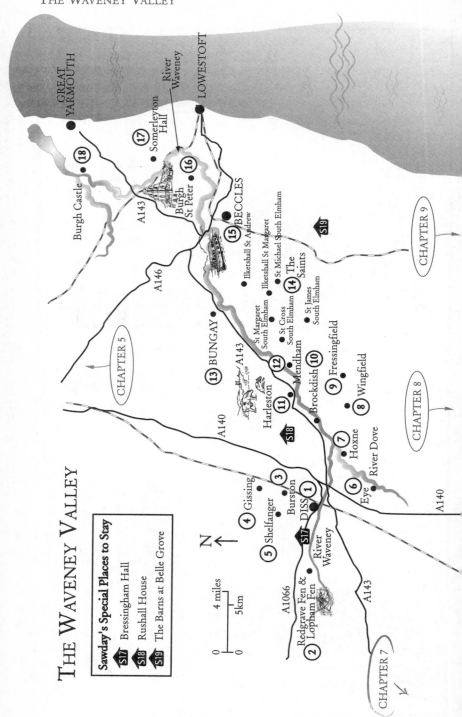

THE WAVENEY VALLEY

Sawday's Special Places to Stay

S17 Bressingham Hall
S18 Rushall House
S19 The Barns at Belle Grove

GREAT YARMOUTH

Burgh Castle

River Waveney

Somerleyton Hall

LOWESTOFT

17

18

A143

Burgh St Peter

16

A146

BECCLES

15

Ilketshall St Andrew

Ilketshall St Margaret

St Michael South Elmham

14 The Saints

St Margaret South Elmham

St Cross South Elmham

St James South Elmham

CHAPTER 9

S19

BUNGAY

13

A143

Mendham

12

Brockdish

10

Fressingfield

9

Wingfield

8

Harleston

11

S18

A140

Hoxne

7

River Dove

A140

CHAPTER 5

CHAPTER 8

Gissing

4

Shelfanger

5

Burston

3

DISS

1

S17

Eye

6

Redgrave Fen & Lopham Fen

2

A1066

River Waveney

A143

CHAPTER 7

N

4 miles

5km

0

0

138

6. THE WAVENEY VALLEY

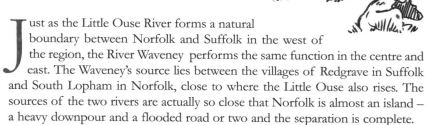

'Were I in my castle
Upon the River Waveney
I wouldne give a button
For the King of Cockney.'
Hugh 'the Bold' Bigod, 1173

Just as the Little Ouse River forms a natural boundary between Norfolk and Suffolk in the west of the region, the River Waveney performs the same function in the centre and east. The Waveney's source lies between the villages of Redgrave in Suffolk and South Lopham in Norfolk, close to where the Little Ouse also rises. The sources of the two rivers are actually so close that Norfolk is almost an island – a heavy downpour and a flooded road or two and the separation is complete.

From its humble origins in Redgrave Fen, the Waveney flows east through the small towns of Diss (Norfolk), Bungay and Beccles (Suffolk) before looping north around Lowestoft to join the River Yare at Breydon Water and eventually go to sea at Great Yarmouth. East of Bungay, the river lies within the boundary of the Broads Authority and the river is connected to Oulton Broad just west of Lowestoft by a manmade channel, Oulton Dyke.

All this talk of rivers and county boundaries might suggest that the Waveney forms some sort of impenetrable barrier. Far from it: the river is more of a conduit than anything, a far cry from the situation with the Yare to the north where the river represents a real physical obstacle. The Waveney, in contrast, has plenty of bridges spanning it, especially in its western reaches. The Waveney Valley may not be much of a valley in physical terms – it's hardly Kashmir – but it does have a personality all of its own that seems quite separate from the rest of Norfolk and Suffolk. Teenagers along the Waveney Valley may display keen allegiances to either Norwich City or Ipswich Town but that is about as far as it goes. The birdsong in the hedgerows sounds pretty much the same on either bank.

So what characterises the Waveney Valley? It's a sense of cosy isolation, where south Norfolk eases into the clay country of north Suffolk, where there are fewer big estates, and more commons, ancient hedgerows and moated farmhouses; more meandering tracks that seem to follow every field boundary before ending up nowhere in particular. There has probably been less change over the past fifty years in this region than anywhere else in southern England. While the attractions of north Norfolk have undoubtedly lured numerous outsiders, down-sizers and weekenders over the years, the Waveney Valley has a different kind of draw. Those that have settled here have tended to become more integrated into the existing community. It has long attracted artists, writers and craftsmen and there was a noticeable, if small-scale, invasion of folk escaping the city for something simpler and more wholesome back in the 1970s – they are mostly still here. The writer Roger Deakin (1943–2006), who lived in Mellis near Diss and single-handedly rebuilt a semi-derelict, cruck-built house before settling down to write, was one of these. He describes this influx in his book *Wildwood*.

The arty side

A surprising number of artists work from the towns and villages of the valley: for the three weekends in July of the annual **Harleston and Waveney Arts Trail** (www.hwat.org.uk) you can visit them in their studios. Constable and Gainsborough may have immortalised the Stour Valley further south on the Essex border but that just happened to be where they lived. It might just as easily have been the Waveney Valley. To quote author and pioneer of sustainable living John Seymour: 'If John Constable had been born at Harleston, instead of at East Bergholt, we would have processions of motor coaches along the Waveney instead of along the Stour'. As for present-day local artists, perhaps the recently deceased Mary Newcomb (1922–2008) is the most representative for her innocent, yet evocative, vignettes of country life – not exclusively featuring the Waveney Valley but certainly evoking its spirit.

Several well-known writers are or have been based in the valley too. The aforementioned Roger Deakin chronicled the changes of the season in *Notes from Walnut Tree Farm* and to a lesser extent in *Wildwood*, while nature writer Richard Mabey has more recently moved to the area and his Waveney Valley home features prominently in his book *Nature Cure*. Louis 'Captain Corelli's Mandolin' de Bernières has settled near Bungay, and W G Sebald in *The Rings of Saturn*, his meandering introspective walk through a rather sombre Suffolk, spends enough time in the Waveney Valley to be quite spectacularly rude about a small hotel in Harleston.

It's easy to get carried away of course. Like everywhere else, there's an element of reactionary nimbyism here on occasion – the greatest fears seemingly being the provision of caravan sites for travellers and wind-farms – but overall, it's pretty welcoming and lacking the self-satisfaction sometimes found in more high-profile parts of the region. The key words here are probably 'self-contained' and 'authentic': real places with real shops serving real people. I begin by looking at Diss, the urban centre for the west of the valley, which exemplifies this outlook perfectly. As Britain's third appointed **'cittaslow'** (Slow Town), it is a town that perfectly encapsulates the Waveney Valley's distinctive atmosphere and human pace of life. Diss and Beccles are about as urban as it gets here, which may give you some idea as to what to expect.

Getting around

Making your way along the Waveney Valley is easy enough. The main towns and villages are linked by the A143 that runs from Bury St Edmunds to Great

Yarmouth. From its Suffolk beginning, the road crosses the county boundary at Diss and continues along the Norfolk side of the river as it heads towards the coast, apart from a brief detour into Bungay on the Suffolk bank. For motorists, it's a convenient way of speeding east or west but the minor roads that thread through the valley are infinitely more enjoyable. Thankfully – and sensibly – the buses that run along the valley avoid the A143 for the most part, preferring to detour through the villages where most of their passengers are.

Public transport

This could be better; there again, it could be worse. Diss has a regular **train** service to Norwich, as it lies on the main Norwich–London line. Regular trains also run between Norwich and Lowestoft. **Bus** transport is somewhat restricted but reasonable enough in daylight hours, with buses running along most of the length of the valley. The Anglian Bus (01502 711109; www.anglianbus.co.uk) 580 service runs hourly between Beccles and Diss via Bungay and Harleston during working hours, Monday to Saturday (excluding bank holidays), as does the 581 between Beccles and Great Yarmouth. The Norwich to Halesworth Anglian Bus service 588 connects Norwich to Bungay with hourly buses during working hours, Monday to Saturday, and with a two-hourly service on Sundays and bank holidays. Simonds Bus service 1 also connects Norwich and Diss around four times a day, but not on Sundays.

Cycling

If you want to make use of muscle power alone, there is plenty of potential for cycling in the Waveney Valley, although you will want to avoid the A143 wherever possible. Otherwise, there are lots of quiet country roads and tracks to explore. If needs be, you can hire a bike at Bungay at Outney Meadow Caravan Park and at Burgh St Peter in the Waveney Valley Centre (see canoeing below).

By water

Transport by **boat** is an option east of Geldeston, which is the limit of navigation for motor boats. Day boats are for hire at Beccles, Burgh St Peter and Oulton Broad and there is scope for **canoeing** too, although the river is noticeably tidal east of Beccles. A stretch for canoeing recommended by the Upper Waveney Valley Project is 20-mile section of the river between Brockdish, west of Harleston, and Ellingham Weir, east of Bungay. Canoe hire is possible at Bungay at Outney Meadow Caravan Park (01986 892338; www.outneymeadow.co.uk), Geldeston at Rowan Craft (01508 518208; www.rowancraft.com) and Burgh St Peter at the Waveney Valley Centre (01502 677343; www.waveneyrivercentre.co.uk). Contact the Waveney Valley Canoe Club (www.waveneyvalleycanoeclub.co.uk) for further advice.

Family canoeing capers

Poppy Mathews

We are Poppy, John, Jamie (15) and Izzy (12) and we all enjoy canoeing. The Broads are very busy with cruisers throughout the summer, and we were keen to see if it was possible to hire Canadian canoes from the commercial boatyards and still find quiet places to paddle. In early June, John and I caught the train to Wroxham then walked through the moored yachts, gleaming in the early summer sunshine, until we found a little wooden shed that advertised canoe hire.

After paying our £20 for three hours, we set off, paddling rather nervously past the shiny hulls towering over us in the marina until we got out into the river. We went under a couple of bridges thronging with shoppers and cars, then upstream into what quickly became an oasis of quiet and calmness. For half of our allotted time we paddled quite steadily, interested in how far we could go without killing ourselves, but also wanting to appreciate the glorious day around us. After a quick stop for lunch, we turned around and headed back, noticing that it was quite a bit harder going back against the wind – or maybe we were just getting tired! In total, we paddled about five miles in three hours.

It was a really lovely afternoon and we decided that we should do it again sometime, next time with the kids. Fast forward to the summer hols and, with packed lunch and swimming things, we caught the bus from Norwich to Bungay on the River Waveney. We had phoned ahead and booked two canoes, so knew we had a great day ahead of us. After a quick chat about who was going with whom, we were off on our second canoe adventure of the summer. Jamie and Izzy led the way downstream, negotiating a couple of low bridges before we got out into open countryside where the river meandered elegantly through meadows with grazing cows.

The river is quite shallow and we played a game of trying to hit patches of reed growing in the water with the canoe. Much enjoyment was had with lots of shrieking and laughing; not so good if any of your party was trying to spot water voles as John was. Nevertheless, it was great fun.

There was a spot of portaging to do before reaching a mill pool overhung by willows, where we had a quick sandwich and a swim before heading back. We paddled back upstream past the launching place, with the river becoming much narrower and windy with overhanging branches. This was exciting and we felt as if we were paddling through mangroves! Early morning or evening canoeists have often seen otters in this stretch. We weren't lucky in this respect but were compensated with fine views of kingfishers flashing along the river and diving to catch fish. All in all, canoeing as a family was less tranquil than being on our own but it was more fun and we will certainly be doing it again.

Walking

There is some absolutely lovely walking to be had, particularly by the river. Most villages lie close enough to one another for decent circular walks to be possible and with such quiet back roads even road walking is a pleasure. The **Angles Way** long-distance route threads its way along the valley between Breckland and Lowestoft; eastwards from Beccles it follows the river bank – the best option is to walk the nine miles from there to Oulton Broad South station and get the train back to Beccles.

Tourist information

Beccles The Quay, Fen Lane ✆ 01502 713196.
Diss Mere's Mouth, Mere St ✆ 01379 650523.
Harleston Tourist information Point, 8 Exchange St ✆ 01379 851917.
Broads website ⌂ www.broads-authority.gov.uk.
East of England Tourism (⌂ www.eet.org.uk) is in the process of producing a series of guides to sustainable tourism in the region. These will aim to reduce car dependency and encourage visitors to experience the local area. Currently, there are guides to **Bungay**, **Loddon** and **Somerleyton and Oulton Broad** available but look out for further coverage in the future as a total of 50 will be published between 2010 and 2013.

Diss and around

① Diss

Diss is very much a town of two halves. The modern part of the town, east of the centre close to the A140, with its supermarkets, swimming pool, fitness centre and railway station, is pretty undistinguished and could be almost anywhere: passing through it on the way to the bus station by the park does not prepare you for what is to come. The bus station – just a small bus park with a shelter – lies on Park Road, a busy thoroughfare that has lorries thundering along it shaking the leaves from the trees. But cross the road into the park and walk past a pavilion down to the water and historic Diss will suddenly unveil itself in front of you – a far more appealing prospect.

Old Diss centres around a body of water, **The Mere**, a six-acre, spring-fed lake that gives the town its name, as *dice* in Anglo-Saxon means 'standing water' or words to that effect. Diss folk claim that this glacial remnant is at least 60 feet deep, with about 20 feet of water and 40 feet of mud, so it is not a place to drop your keys. The common theory is that it was formed when the underlying chalk bedrock collapsed, an altogether more plausible theory than it being the mouth of an extinct volcano, as a few Diss residents still believe. The Mere was badly polluted in the 19th century, with high mercury levels brought about by local hatters and dyers making use of its water. Bizarrely, it was also around this time that The Mere was stocked with eels, which, according to some accounts, threw themselves from the water at every opportunity such was the level of pollution. Thankfully, it's clean enough to swim in these days, although this is expressly forbidden. Global warming being what it is, it is unlikely that there will ever be a repeat of the winter cricket matches and ice carnivals that were held on its frozen waters in the early 19th century.

A waterside path leads from the southern shore to what is usually referred to as **The Mere's Mouth**, where there is an information centre and the Diss Publishers Bookshop and Café, which as well as a selection of local books has café tables by the water. Quite likely, there will also be someone selling ice creams from the back of a Morris Traveller. It's a place to feed the ducks, lick an ice cream and have a 'mardle' (Norfolk-speak for leisurely chat) on market days. Formerly, this was the only part of The Mere that provided open access to the public, although now there is access to all of the southern side from the park where Diss's rebellious youth flaunt authority by riding their bikes in a no-cycling area – that's about as lawless as it gets. These days, there's an electric fountain in the middle of The Mere that spouts like a mini Jet d'Eau on Lake Geneva.

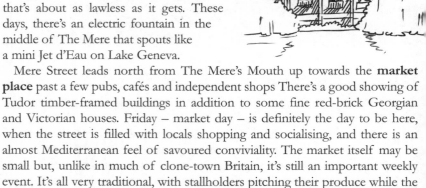

Mere Street leads north from The Mere's Mouth up towards the **market place** past a few pubs, cafés and independent shops There's a good showing of Tudor timber-framed buildings in addition to some fine red-brick Georgian and Victorian houses. Friday – market day – is definitely the day to be here, when the street is filled with locals shopping and socialising, and there is an almost Mediterranean feel of savoured conviviality. The market itself may be small but, unlike in much of clone-town Britain, it's still an important weekly event. It's all very traditional, with stallholders pitching their produce while the market-day chip van does good business, with an ever-lengthening queue of hungry locals queuing for a large portion served in recycled squares of the *Daily Express* for just 80p.

As well as the weekly event, there's a **farmers' market** held here on the second Saturday of each month. For those looking for a regular local supplier, **Desmond Duncan's Organic Boxes** (01379 652101; www.organicsfor all.co.uk) can provide boxes packed full of organic fruit and vegetables, delivered free to addresses in Suffolk and the Norwich area.

Diss Museum (01379 650618), located in a small building right at the top of the market place, is a community museum run by enthusiastic volunteers. When I visited, there was a Tom Paine display that celebrated his bicentennial, although it was unclear if this would remain on display for good (Paine was born in Thetford in 1732; see page 182; he worked as a stay-maker in Diss for a short period before finally leaving Norfolk). Either way, there are plenty of interesting artefacts and archive photographs. There's a decent selection of second-hand books too: for 50p, I came away clutching a history of Diss Town FC and subsequently discovered that 7 May 1994 was the club's greatest hour: they beat Taunton FC 2–1 in extra time at Wembley to win the FA Vase – real 'Roy of the Rovers' stuff. Chatting with the volunteer on duty, I learned a little about local rivalries in this border town. 'They're a funny lot over there in Suffolk but it's mostly good-natured banter between us,' she said. 'Mind you, there's some old boys at The Cock at Fair Green who'll tell you about how they used to keep a close eye on those that came over the Palgrave bridge. There are all sorts of stories about how some used to lie in wait to attack Suffolk men coming over.' We got talking about Fair Green itself – the meadow on the edge of town that was once the setting for medieval fairs and which is still used today for special events. 'If there is one thing that would make Diss people revolt it would be to try to develop Fair Green for new housing. It's an absolute no-no – the people would be up in arms.'

St Mary's Church dominates the market place, a fine 13th-century building in the Decorated style with a peaceful churchyard that has benches for market-day chip-eaters, town philosophers and courting couples. If you have an interest in folklore, you might like to seek out the rather owl-like green man grimacing above the south porch. The church's most famous rector was John Skelton, who was rector here from 1504 until his death in 1529. Skelton, who had earlier served as tutor to the young Henry VIII and had been Poet Laureate of both Oxford and Cambridge universities, remains firmly in the number one place of the town's most illustrious citizens. A later Poet Laureate, John Betjeman, was another admirer of the town. The church puts on free monthly lunchtime concerts in summer and has a few stalls selling local produce at its church hall on Friday mornings..

If you continue along Mount Street from St Mary's you'll find more handsome Georgian houses lining a quiet street. If, instead, you head west along St Nicholas Street then you'll come to the **Corn Hall**, which like most such buildings in these parts is in the mid-19th-century neoclassical style. The days of cereal wheeling and dealing may be past but it is still an active place, with regular concerts and plays. **Cobb's Yard** and **Norfolk House Yard** on the same street have a number of tempting independent shops and cafés that include Frederick's Fine Foods delicatessen and an old-fashioned sweet shop, appropriately called The Sweetie Shop, that has numerous jars of sticky confections and, rather improbably, sugar-free chocolate. (Walking through the market place I had heard two teenage girls say, 'Let's go straight to the Sweetie Shop' before putting a spurt on up the hill.) There's also a wholefood shop, Natural Foodstore, as well as Amandines Café.

Slow Diss

Diss, along with Aylsham, bears the distinction of being one of two Norfolk towns that belong to the **Cittaslow** movement. Diss became a Cittaslow in 2006 and its sense of community is actively promoted by **Diss Community Partnership**. Having helped Diss gain its Cittaslow status, the partnership has gone on to establish a film festival and a local history and art festival in the town, as well as setting up **Taste of Diss**, a festival of local food held in July, and **Dissit**, a literature festival. The Cittaslow Centre has also devised a **Snail Trail** to the town for visitors, which covers many of the landmarks mentioned here. The Cittaslow Centre at 7 Cobbs Yard (www.cittaslowdiss.co.uk) has a community shop and gallery.

Fair Green is set apart from the rest of the old town but worth a detour. You can reach it by walking west along Park Road from the bus station and turning left at the roundabout. Once you round the corner, the contrast is extreme. Gone are the noisy lorries thundering along Park Road; you suddenly find yourself next to an idyllic village green with a cafe, a pub and a restaurant clustered around its eastern end. The trestle tables on the green itself are certainly inviting, the perfect place to sit whilst enjoying an early evening pint at The Cock, but if you keep going, you'll soon reach the bridge across the River Waveney, little more than a weed-strewn stream at this point. The green, which is surrounded by highly attractive 16th- and 17th-century houses, was granted a charter for a fair in 1185 and must have presented quite a sight back in the days when bear baiting and cock fighting were regarded as quite ordinary pursuits. The Cock Inn no doubt gets its name from such activities, as do many other 'Cock' pubs in the region. The fair was finally closed by Parliament in 1872, ostensibly because of its reputation for 'disorderly behaviour'.

If you are just looking for a coffee and a snack, there are a couple of options along Mere Road. **Diss Publishers Bookshop and Café** has some tables outside overlooking The Mere, as does **Mere Moments** further up. The options listed below are a little further away from the centre but really not that far.

Angel Café Fair Green ☎ 01379 640353 ✎ www.theangelcafe.co.uk. With a banner of 'heavenly food at down-to-earth prices', the Angel café serves up organic meals and snacks, with plenty of vegetarian options. It's also good for espresso coffee, homemade cakes and desserts.

Cock Inn Lower Denmark St, Fair Green ☎ 01379 643633
✎ www.cockinndiss.co.uk. With a decent selection of real ales, a short but varied menu and a great view over the green, this is a sound choice. Live music events on some nights.

Fayre View Restaurant 65 Lower Denmark St, Fair Green ☎ 01379 644684

🖰 www.fayreview.co.uk. In a pink 16th-century building that was once a post office, this smart bistro offers fixed-price lunch and dinner menus.

② Redgrave and Lopham Fen

West of Diss, the Waveney begins as a tiny trickle at Redgrave and Lopham Fen, very close to where the Little Ouse also rises. Dig a ditch between them and you have an island – Norfolk! The Fen, which covers 125 hectares and is the largest surviving area of river valley fen in England, has been managed by the Suffolk Wildlife Trust for the past 50 years (although it straddles both counties) and has an impressive cluster of designations as a wetland of national and international importance. It is also one of only two sites in the country that has native **fen raft spiders**, as well as being a prime habitat for dragonflies and butterflies, mammals like otters and pipistrelle bats, and a recorded 96 bird species.

Like the Norfolk Broads, the fen was traditionally used for reed and sedge cutting for thatching, as well as cattle grazing at its drier margins. Part of the Suffolk Wildlife Trust's management strategy is to use Hebridean sheep and Polish Konik ponies to control the vegetation. The black Hebridean sheep look strangely at home grazing here, as do the small grey ponies that thrive in the wet conditions. These all add to its atmosphere as quite a primeval place and the presence of the semi-aquatic raft spiders certainly fits in with this image. Arachnophobes should probably be aware that the fen raft spider is one of Britain's largest, although even here they are pretty scarce. There's a visitor centre (Low Common Road, South Lopham; 01379 688333) run by the Suffolk Wildlife Trust, and three dedicated nature trails.

If you come here, you can take a look at either or both of **South Lopham** and **Redgrave** villages. Both are pleasant places that have exactly what you expect: a pub, a church and (for the time being, anyway) a post office. Take your pick – Norfolk or Suffolk. Redgrave is slightly closer; South Lopham has the larger, older church with what Simon Jenkins describes as Norfolk's best Norman tower.

Blooming Bressingham

If you're a steam-engine fanatic, you might also be interested in the collection at **Bressingham Gardens** (01379 688585; www.bressingham.co.uk) on the road to Diss, which has endless rainbow beds of hardy perennials as well as a large collection of steam engines, a fire museum and a 800-metre-long light railway. Alan Bloom, who must have felt a calling given his surname, created the gardens in 1961, and grandson Jason, who manages the nursery over the road, has kept up the family tradition.

③ Burston

The village of Burston, a couple of miles north of Diss, is famous for its **Burston Strike School** and its teachers, Tom and Kitty Higdon, who kept the school going from 1914 until just after Tom Higdon's death in 1939 (see box). This was the longest strike in British history and a textbook case of Norfolk's radical tradition that often has the working man standing up to overbearing authority. Today, the school is a museum (01379 741565) and a rallying point for the old guard of the political Left on the first weekend in September. Politics aside, there's a **farmers' market** held in the village between 9am and noon on the first Saturday of each month at BOCM Paul's Pavilion, Mill Road.

The strike school **museum** is what most come to see. There's a fascinating photographic display and selection of newspaper cuttings, and an information booklet that has the picture of a Norfolk pig with the words: 'You may push me, You may shuv, But I'm hanged if I'll be druv, From Burston', which says all there is to say.

The **annual rally** takes place on the first Sunday in September. It's a colourful, upbeat affair with bunting and trades union banners alongside stalls selling snacks and the collected works of V I Lenin. Proceedings get fully under way after a march 'around the candlestick' that replicates the route taken by the schoolchildren on 1 April 1914. Then there are a few speeches and music. I have been here a few times but individual rallies tend to blur into each another. I clearly remember seeing Dennis Skinner with shirt unbuttoned to his waist making a stirring, and very funny, speech on one occasion, and Tony Benn recounting the famous words of Thomas Paine from *Rights of Man:* 'My country is the world, my religion is to do good.' Attendance has fluctuated in recent years but the 90th anniversary in 2007 enjoyed the best turnout for ages.

The Higdons lie buried side by side in the churchyard of **St Mary's**, which lost its tower back in the 18th century and was unceremoniously patched up with red brick. Now the church functions partially as a sort of school hall and is usually kept locked. It would be interesting to know what the Reverend Elland, the Higdons' nemesis, would make of this were he alive.

Burston Crown Mill Rd ✆ 01379 741257 🖰 www.burstoncrown.com. An old redbrick building with wooden beams, an open fireplace and a rock 'n roll chef (apparently he cooked for U2 and Bruce Springsteen in the past). Local produce is used wherever possible for both the bar menu and the à la carte, and there are four real ales to choose from and a decent wine list.

The Burston Strike School

'The labourer must henceforth take his place industrially socially and politically with the best and foremost of the land.'
Tom Higdon, 1917

In brief, the story goes that Tom and Kitty Higdon were appointed as teachers at Burston School in 1911 after previously working for nine years at Wood Dalling in north Norfolk. The Higdons, who were Christian socialists, had complained about the poor conditions at the Dalling school and the frequent interruption of the children's education when recruited for farm work. Many of the farmers employing the children were also school managers and tensions mounted as a result of this, particularly as the Higdons had also encouraged local farm labourers to join trades unions. When matters came to a head, the Higdons were given the simple choice of dismissal or removal to a different school.

The couple were transferred to Burston, where they found conditions much the same: their complaints to the school managers, the chairman of whom was the local rector, created tensions here too. The pair were dismissed on fabricated charges of pupil abuse on April Fool's Day 1914 and, following their dismissal, 66 of the school's 72 pupils marched along Burston's 'candlestick' (a circular route around the village) carrying placards that bore messages like 'We Want Our Teachers Back'. Many parents refused to send their children to the official council school and, as a result, a separate 'strike' school was established.

The Burston Strike School, as it came to be known, began as little more than a tent on the village green but later moved to a carpenter's shop in the village. There was considerable intimidation by local employers against the rebel parents and many workers were sacked or evicted from their tied cottages. The village rector, the Reverend Charles Tucker Eland, who firmly believed that labourers should know their place in the social order, also went as far as evicting poor families from church land. Fortunately, the labour shortage created by the onset of World War I worked to the advantage of the labourers. Money was raised by labour organisations such as the Agricultural Labourers' Union and the Railwaymen and, by 1917, there were sufficient funds to build a new schoolhouse. Both Sylvia Pankhurst and George Lansbury attended the opening ceremony in that same year. The school ran until 1939 when Tom Higdon died and the same modest building serves today as a museum of the strike school's history. There has been a rally organised by the TGWU held annually in the village since 1984, the 70th anniversary of the school's founding.

④ Gissing and ⑤ Shelfanger

Heading north from Burston, the next village is **Gissing**, which also has a **St Mary's Church**, this one with a Saxon round tower and Norman doorway. There's an old hall with a medieval moat here, and a modern water tower too – both south Norfolk specialities. To the west, **Shelfanger** has its **Lammas Meadows**, which stand on the side of the road to Diss forming a tract of land attached to several farms. These are a relic of a medieval open field system of farming and, according to tradition, cannot be cropped, although the various owners are permitted to cut hay after Lammas Day (1 August). I recall seeing them carpeted with wild orchids in early summer twenty or so years ago.

⑥ Eye

Just south of Diss, Eye is a quiet, self-contained little market town just south of the River Waveney in Suffolk. It actually lies on the west bank of the River Dove, a tributary of the Waveney, and is home to a church tower that the architectural writer Nikolaus Pevsner deemed 'one of the wonders of Suffolk'. The church in question is that of **St Peter and St Paul** and its 101-foot-high tower is remarkable for the flint flushwork on its west side. The church stands beneath a Norman **castle mound**, which is now all mound and no castle but gives quite a view of the town nevertheless. The town clings tightly to the base of this: a small maze of streets and ancient houses dominated by the brick-and-flint panel Victorian **Town Hall** with its ornate clock-tower. The town's Guildhall stands beside the church, an impressive Tudor building

The town gets its curious name from an Old English word for 'island', and when it was first settled it probably was almost entirely surrounded by water and marshland associated with the River Dove: the surrounding area still sometimes floods.

Eye Castle was constructed in the years that immediately followed the Norman Conquest and a Benedictine Priory was founded shortly after in the town in 1086–87. Hugh Bigod, the 1st Earl of Norfolk, attacked the castle in 1173 during the rebellion against Henry II and it never really recovered, although its prison continued in use as late as the 17th century. You can climb up to the castle mound by following the signs from the car park at Buckshorn Lane. The path takes you through a small estate of modern wedge-shaped Toblerone-like houses, across a meadow and up some steps to the top. At the top, there used to stand a building known as **Kerrison's Folly**, constructed in the mid-19th century by General Sir Edward Kerrison, reputedly as a home for the batman who had served him at the Battle of Waterloo. Part of the folly was used as a museum in the early years of the 20th century but there are just

Alastair Sawday's

Special Places to Stay

We have been building our collection of Special Places to Stay since 1994 and are delighted to dish up a small selection for you here.

How do we choose our Special Places?

It's simple. There are no rules, no boxes to tick. We choose places that we like and are fiercely subjective in our choices. We also recognise that one person's idea of special is not necessarily someone else's so there is a huge variety of places and prices on our website and in our books. Those who are familiar with our Special Places series know that we look for comfort, originality and authenticity and reject the insincere, the anonymous and the banal.

Inspections

We visit every place to get a feel for how it ticks. We don't take a clipboard and we don't have a list of what is acceptable and what is not. Instead, we chat with the owner or manager and then look carefully and sensitively round the house. It's all very informal, but it gives us an excellent idea of who would enjoy staying there. Once chosen, properties are re-inspected every few years to keep things fresh and accurate. In between inspections we rely on feedback from our army of readers, as well as from staff members who are encouraged to visit properties across the series. This feedback is invaluable to us and we always follow up on comments, so do let us know how you get on in these places. You can do this and find out more about each of those Special Places at **www.sawdays.co.uk**.

Disclaimer

We make no claims to pure objectivity in choosing our Special Places. They are here because we like them. Our opinions and tastes are ours alone; we hope you will share them. We have done our utmost to get our facts right but apologise unreservedly for any mistakes that may have crept in.

You should know that we don't check such things as fire alarms, swimming pool security or any other regulations with which owners of properties receiving paying guests should comply. This is the responsibility of the owners.

We hope you enjoy your stay with our owners, all of whom can deepen your understanding and experience of Norfolk & Suffolk.

S1 Gin Trap Inn

S2 Rose Cottage

An actor and a lawyer run this old English Inn. Steve and Cindy left London for the quiet life and haven't stopped since. A smart whitewashed exterior gives way to a beamed locals' bar, a crackling fire and the original dining room in Farrow & Ball hues. Upstairs, are three delightful bedrooms in smart country style. Two have big bathrooms with claw-foot baths and separate showers, all come with timber frames, cushioned window seats and the odd chandelier. Come down for delicious food: Norfolk mussels, local sausages, poached winter fruits. You're on the Peddars Way, Sandringham is close and fabulous sandy beaches beckon.

In the most sought-after village in North Norfolk is the sweetest terraced cottage – stylishly decorated inside and out. Mary Kemp is a cookery writer – hence the super kitchen and shelves of cookery books. The front door leads into the living room with big blue sofas, a basket of logs, magazines, board games and paintings aplenty. Bedrooms are fresh and cottage-cosy; the bathroom – small but spotless – is downstairs. Sun yourself in the furnished courtyard garden... all this in the middle of Burnham Market, bustling with boutiques, galleries and delis, and whose Goose Beck runs charmingly down the centre of the green.

Steve Knowles & Cindy Cook
6 High Street, Hunstanton, Norfolk PE36 5JU
- £78–£140. Singles from £49.
- 3 doubles.
- Lunch from £7.
- À la carte dinner from £20.
- 01485 525264
- www.gintrapinn.co.uk

Mary Kemp
Front Street,
Burnham Market, Norfolk PE31 8EJ
- £400–£750 per week.
- Cottage for 4.
- Self-catering.
- 01953 717670
- www.northnorfolkcottage.com

The oak four-poster – a beauty – came with the house. Part of the building (1400) is the oldest in Wells; in those days, the merchant could bring his boats up to the door. Liz and Dennis know the history, and happily share it. Inside is warm, friendly, inviting: the mahogany shines, the bathrooms sparkle, there are papers for breakfast, books to borrow and pretty sash windows overlooking salt marshes. As for Wells, it is on the famous Coastal Path, has a quay bustling with sailing boats and 16 miles of sands. Birdwatch by day, dine out at night – easy when you're in the centre. Breakfasts are a treat.

A listed former laundry, the old Wash House matches the neighbouring fishermen's cottages: flint-faced and quaint. But step inside to another world: an uncluttered, slate-floored space, with leather sofas, heated floors and, above, skylights with remote-control blinds. Oak beams divide the snazzy open plan kitchen and the sitting area from the flint-walled master bedroom, upstairs is another simpler bedroom. There's no garden, but there is a table and chairs in the shared courtyard. You're close to the path that snakes along the coast, so walking is exceptional and birdlife abounds. You may even spot seals offshore.

Elizabeth & Dennis Woods
47 Freeman Street,
Wells-next-the-Sea, Norfolk NR23 1BQ
- From £70. Singles £45.
- 2: 1 four-poster, 1 double.
- Pubs/restaurants 300 yds.
- 01328 711877
- www.the-merchants-house.co.uk

Frenesi Ewing
Loades Yard,
Blakeney, Norfolk NR25 7NA
- £445-£615 per week.
- Cottage for 2-3.
- Self-catering.
- 0845 658 6655
- www.thewashhouse.co.uk

📷 S5 Manor Farmhouse

A family buzz and candlelight in the farmhouse where you eat, peace in the 17th-century barn where you stay. All rooms lead off its charming, stylish, vaulted sitting room with cosy winter fire. You have a four-poster and a tiny shower on the ground floor, then two narrow staircases to two beautifully-dressed bedrooms upstairs – small, quirky, fun, with a tucked-up-in-the-roof feel. Come for a sunny courtyard garden, billiards in the stable, fresh flowers, lovely hosts, gorgeous food – and you may come and go as you please. Great value, a perfect rural retreat.

David & Rosie Eldridge
Happisburgh, Norfolk NR12 0SA
- From £50. Singles from £40.
- 3: 1 double, 1 twin/double, 1 four-poster.
- Dinner, 3 courses, £17.50. BYO.
  Pubs 1 mile.
- 01692 651262
- www.northnorfolk.co.uk/manorbarn

📷 S6 Manor House

Sally looks after you beautifully in this elegant house on the edge of Halvergate marshes. Excellent walking – the Weavers Way runs past the farmhouse door – and there is good birdwatching; spot pink-footed geese in winter. Your sitting room is an open landing outside the bedroom with comfortable chairs, TV, books, guides and fresh flowers. Bedrooms are traditional and spotless with soft colours, splashes of colour from cushions and curtains and touches of luxury; mattresses are firm, bathrooms sparkle. Breakfast bacon and sausages are from the farm shop – wonderful – and jams and marmalades are homemade.

Sally More
Tunstall Road, Norwich, Norfolk NR13 3PS
- £80-£90. Singles £40.
- 2: 1 double with separate bath;
  1 twin sharing bath (let to same party only).
- Packed lunch £6.50. Pub 3 miles.
- 01493 700279
- www.manorhousenorfolk.co.uk

📷 1 Leicester Meadows

Up among 13 acres of wild meadow and woodland – not another building in sight. It's all so relaxed and unhurried: barn owls roosting in the outhouse, hens strutting the garden, geese pottering up from the pond. The 19th-century cottages, once the home of workers on the Holkham estate, have been imaginatively restored and enlarged. (Bob was an architect, Sara an art teacher; both are immensely friendly and helpful.) Polished wood and old brick are topped with bright rugs; paintings and ceramics engage the eye; steep stairs take you up to the bedrooms – one large, contemporary and elegant, the other cosy and fun.

Bob & Sara Freakley
South Creake,
Fakenham, Norfolk NR21 9NZ
- From £65. Singles from £45.
- 2: 1 double; 1 double with separate bath.
- Supper from £15. Pub 1 mile.
- 01328 823533
- www.leicestermeadows.com

📷 Holly Lodge

The whole place radiates a lavish attention to detail, from the spoilingly comfortable beds to the complimentary bottle of wine. It's perfect for those who love their privacy: these three snug guest 'cottages' have their own entrances as well as smart iron bedsteads and rugs on stone tiles, neat little shower rooms and tapestry-seat chairs, and books, music and TVs. Enjoy the Mediterranean garden with pond and decking in summer, the handsome conservatory and the utter peace. Your hosts are delightful: ex restaurateur Jeremy who cooks enthusiastically, ethically and with panache, and Canadian-raised Gill.

Jeremy Bolam
Thursford Green, Norfolk NR21 0AS
- £90-£120. Singles £70-£100.
- 3 cottages for 2.
- Dinner, 3 courses with wine, £19.50.
  Pubs/restaurants 1 mile.
- 01328 878465
- www.hollylodgeguesthouse.co.uk

🏠 S9 Burgh Parva Hall

🏠 S10 Carrick's at Castle Farm

Sunlight bathes the Norfolk longhouse on summer afternoons; the welcome from the Heals is as warm. The listed house is all that remains of the old village of Burgh Parva, deserted after the Great Plague. It's a handsome house and warmly inviting... old furniture, rugs, books, pictures and Magnet the terrier-daschund. Large guest bedrooms face the sunsets and the garden annexe makes a sweet hideaway, especially in the summer. Breakfast eggs are from the garden hens, vegetables are home-grown, fish comes fresh from Holt and the game may have been shot by William. Settle down by the fire and tuck in.

A comfortable, and jolly, mix of farmhouse B&B – rare-breed cattle, tractors, a large, warm-bricked house – and a rather swish interior. Both Jean and John are passionate about conservation and the protection of wildlife, and here you have absolute quiet for birdwatching, fishing, shooting or walking; recover in the drawing room with its books and lovely river views from long windows. Bedrooms are large, light and well thought-out with great bathrooms and binoculars, food is home grown or local, and there is coffee and cake, or wine, when you arrive. The pretty garden leads down to the River Wensum and a footpath.

Judy & William Heal
Melton Constable, Norfolk NR24 2PU
- £60-£80. Singles from £35.
- 3: 1 double, 1 twin;
  1 twin with separate bath.
- Dinner £22. BYO.
  Pub/restaurant 4 miles.
- 01263 862569

Jean Wright
Castle Farm, Dereham, Norfolk NR20 4JT
- From £85. Singles £55.
- 4: 2 doubles; 1 double, 1 twin each
  with separate bath (let to same party only).
- Dinner, 3 courses, £20. BYO. Pub 0.5 miles.
- 01362 638302
- www.carricksatcastlefarm.co.uk

S11 Spread Eagle Inn

Martin and Lori's traditional coaching inn stands in a peaceful estate village in open country. The old stables, forge and carriage house next door have been converted into stylish rooms that keep some original features, including the suite's splendid brick forge. Bathrooms have 'Norfolk Natural Soap', there are roll-away beds for children (under 12s stay free in the parents' room) and every room has a terrace. In the terracotta-walled bar, bag a table by the wood-burner or head for the carpeted dining room with its high-backed leather chairs, colourful murals and modern British food sourced from Norfolk produce.

Martin & Lori Halpin
Church Road, King's Lynn, Norfolk PE33 9GF
- From £70.
- 5: 4 doubles, 1 twin.
- Main courses £14.95-£19.95; bar meals (lunch) £4.95-£10.95; Sunday roast £8.95.
- 01366 347995
- www.spreadeaglenorfolk.co.uk

S12 The Rose & Crown

Roses round the door and twisting passages within, it is gloriously English. Holkham sausages, mash and onion gravy for the traditionalists; plaice with kale and salsa verde, and white chocolate and coconut brûlée for the more adventurous. A flurry of rather stylish bedrooms, the quietest in the extension off the courtyard, come in pale blue tones and have a beachy feel. But the Rose and Crown is still proud to be a pub: fine beers on hand pump, low ceilings, uneven floors, old beams and log fires and a walled garden which used to be the village bowling green. It's great value and the north-coast beaches are stupendous.

Anthony & Jeannette Goodrich
Old Church Road,
King's Lynn, Norfolk PE31 7LX
- £90-£110. Singles £70-£90.
- 16 twins/doubles.
- Main courses £8.50-£14.50.
- 01485 541382
- www.roseandcrownsnettisham.co.uk

🏠 S13 Manor House Farm

In the private stable wing and next-door cottage of this traditional Norfolk farmhouse, surrounded by four acres of lovingly tended gardens, are beautiful fresh rooms with wildly comfortable beds and a sitting room for guests; expect antiques, colourful rugs and fresh flowers. Breakfast, served in the elegant dining room of the main house, is home-grown and delicious: fruit, eggs from the Welsummer hens, and bacon and sausages from their own happy pigs. Libby and Robin have won conservation awards for the farm – and the glorious north Norfolk coast is 20 minutes away.

Elisabeth Ellis
Wellingham, King's Lynn, Norfolk PE32 2TH
- £90–£100.
  Singles £50–£65.
- 2: 1 double, 1 twin/double.
- Restaurant 1.5 miles.
- 01328 838227
- www.manor-house-farm.co.uk

🏠 S14 The Buttery

Down a farm track, a treasure: a thatch-and-flint octagonal dairy house perfectly restored by local craftsmen and as neat as a new pin. You get a jacuzzi bath, a little kitchen and a fridge stocked with delicious bacon and ground coffee so you can breakfast when you want – and take it onto the sun terrace in good weather. The sitting room is terracotta-tiled and has a music system, a warming fire and a sofabed for those who don't want to tackle the steep wooden stairs to the snuggly mezzanine bedroom. You may walk from the door into parkland and woods, or try your hand at tennis or fishing.

Deborah Meynell
Berry Hall, Norwich, Norfolk NR9 5AX
- £80–£95.
- Cottage: 1 double, sitting room
  & small kitchen.
- Pub 10-minute walk.
- 01603 880541
- www.thebuttery.thesiliconworkshop.com

📷 175 Newmarket Road

📷 Washingford House

You can walk to the centre of town, but this Edwardian villa is rather grandly set back from the road in its large garden with mature shrubs and trees. Sit quietly in the guest sitting room with local art, books and papers to read; there's a sunny conservatory with bright sofas overlooking a well-tended garden and a heated indoor pool. Charming Dawn gives you extremely elegant, well-dressed bedrooms with an interesting mix of modern and antique furniture, sumptuous linen and quiet views; bathrooms are large, warm and well lit. Breakfast is generous and there's lots to explore on the doorstep.

Dawn & Peter Thompson
Norwich, Norfolk NR4 6AP
- From £75.
  Singles £35-£50.
- 3 doubles.
- Pubs 0.25 miles.
- 01603 506160
- www.bedandbreakfastinnorwich.co.uk

Tall octagonal chimney stacks and a Georgian façade give the house a stately air. In fact, it's the friendliest of places to stay and Paris gives you a delicious, locally sourced breakfast including plenty of fresh fruit. The house, originally Tudor, is a delightful mix of old and new. Large light-filled bedrooms have loads of good books and views over the four-acre garden, a favourite haunt for local birds. Bergh Apton is a conservation village seven miles from Norwich and you are in the heart of it; perfect for cycling and the twelve Wherryman's Way circular walks are close by.

Paris & Nigel Back
Cookes Road, Norwich, Norfolk NR15 1AA
- £65-£75. Singles £35-£45.
- 2: 1 twin/double;
  1 single with separate bath.
- Pubs/restaurants 4-6 miles.
- 01508 550924
- www.washingford.com

🏠 Bressingham Hall

Past the famous steam museum and onto the mansion house, built in 1780 for the Squire of Bressingham. It's a handsome house with high ceilings, light-filled rooms and large sash windows with sensational garden views. All is deeply old-fashioned but that is part of the charm. You breakfast in a sunny, east-facing room on Grandad's rhubarb baked with brown sugar, locally cured bacon and local farm eggs. There's a sitting room with an open log fire and views, bedrooms are large and filled with books, magazines and easy chairs, bathrooms are clean and adequate, and Ian is delightful.

Ian Tilden
Bressingham,
Diss, Norfolk IP22 2AA
- £80. Singles £55.
  Entry to gardens & steam museum included.
- 3: 1 double, 1 twin, 1 family room.
- Pub/restaurant 0.25 miles.
- 01379 687243
- www.bressinghamgardens.com

🏠 Rushall House

Plenty of treats to be had in this light and bright Victorian rectory: blue-shelled eggs for breakfast, homemade cake for tea, and radios, books and sofas in the double bedrooms. The wood-burner warm sitting room is classically decorated with a contemporary touch, airy bedrooms have pale walls, rich fabrics and a grand mix of colours and textiles (Jane's vintage furniture and fabrics are for sale in the courtyard studio). Walk or cycle after breakfast – it's good flat countryside and there are plenty of restorative pubs. Jane and Martin are relaxed hosts, and children will love collecting the eggs.

Martin Hubner & Jane Gardiner
Dickleburgh Road, Diss, Norfolk IP21 4RX
- From £65. Singles £40.
- 3: 1 double;
  1 double, 1 twin sharing bath/shower.
- Dinner £23. BYO.
  Pubs/restaurants 0.5-3 miles.
- 01379 741557
- www.rushallhouse.co.uk

S19 The Barns at Belle Grove

Within handsome oak barns Jo and Nick have laid out the treasure from their eastern travels. From a romantic gatehouse to a granary hideaway – each has its own charm and sun-catching garden. Rich red sofas, rugs and massive fireplaces, carved bedheads with fine linen, thick white towels and glittering tiles. Nick is a talented builder and recycles everything: beams and bricks, troughs and tractors; his solar panels feed the underfloor heating. If you catch the local travel bug, nearby Halesworth has brilliant butchers and grocers, and the sea at Southwold is a few miles away. You can even hire the owners' beach hut.

Jo Jordan & Nick Fisher
Belle Grove Farm,
Halesworth, Suffolk IP19 8QU
- £475-£1,225 per week.
- Cottages for 2-6.
- Self-catering.
- 01986 873124
- www.bellegrovebarns.com

S20 Strattons

Nowhere is perfect, but Strattons comes close. It's one of the country's most eco-friendly hotels and if you arrive by public transport, you get a 10% discount on B&B. Silky bantams strut on the lawn, inside is crammed with mosaics and murals and marble busts: Les and Vanessa met at art school. It is an informal bohemian country-house bolthole of French inspiration in a small market town. Bedrooms are exquisite, food in the candlelit restaurant is wonderful and almost all organic, perhaps nettle and barley broth, leg of Papworth lamb, rhubarb and ginger crème brûlée. Unmissable.

Vanessa & Les Scott
4 Ash Close, Swaffham, Norfolk PE37 7NH
- £150-£175. Suites & apartments £200-£225. Singles from £120.
- 14: 6 doubles, 1 twin/double, 5 suites, 2 apts.
- Lunch from £10.
- À la carte dinner, 3 courses, £35-£40.
- 01760 723845
- www.strattonshotel.com

🏠 College Farm   🏠 The Manse

Lavender has done B&B for years and looks after her stupendous listed house single-handedly. Over afternoon tea, she tells colourful stories of the house and her family's local history: from 1349 until the Dissolution of the Monasteries the house was a college of priests and there's stunning Jacobean panelling in the dining room. Bedrooms are big and lived-in, two of the bathrooms are tiny, all have lovely views over the garden with its pingos (ice age ponds). Come for history and architecture and friendly Lavender, and breakfast from the farm shop down the road.

Unmissable in its coat of rich red paint, the beamed, 16th-century Manse overlooks a historic village green. The owners will present you with a superb breakfast each day, plus homemade cakes or scones for tea, and a fresh posy of garden flowers. Robin, ex diplomatic service, has a passion for opera; Bridget organises the church choir. The guest quarters are completely private and deliciously cosy; there are polished antiques, fine porcelain and a wood-burning stove, a rose-tumbled garden for breakfast on fine days, and a chivalrous black labrador called Tristan, always happy to take guests for a walk.

Lavender Garnier
Thompson, Thetford, Norfolk IP24 1QG
- From £60. Singles £30.
- 3: 1 twin, 1 twin/double;
  1 double with separate bath.
  Extra shower available.
- Afternoon tea included. Pub 1 mile.
- 01953 483318

Bridget & Robin Oaten
The Green,
Hartest, Suffolk IP29 4DH
- From £70.
  Singles from £40.
- 1 twin/double & sitting room.
- Pub/restaurant 2-minute walk.
- 01284 830226

S23 The Old Manse Barn

A large, lush loft apartment in sleepy Suffolk; this living/eating/sleeping space of blond wood, white walls and big windows has an urban feel yet overlooks glorious countryside. Secluded from the main house, in a timber-clad barn, the style is thrillingly modern: leather sofas, glass dining table, stainless steel kitchenette. Floor lights dance off the walls, CD surround-sound creates mood and you can watch the stars from your bed. Homemade granola, local bread and ham in the fridge – breakfast when you like. There's peace for romance, solitude for work, a garden to sit in and friendly Sue to suggest the best pubs.

Sue & Ian Jones
Chapel Road,
Bury St Edmunds, Suffolk IP30 0HE
- From £70.
- Apartment: 1 double & kitchenette.
- Pubs within walking distance.
- 01284 828120
- www.theoldmansebarn.co.uk

S24 Milden Hall

Over five generations of Hawkins have lived in this seemingly grand 16th-century hall farmhouse with its smooth wooden floors, enormous windows and vast fireplaces. Bedrooms range from big to huge, are elegantly old-fashioned and filled with interesting tapestries, wall hangings and lovely furniture; it's a bit of a trek to the loo from the family room so you need to be nimble. Juliet is a passionate conservationist, full of ideas for making the most of the surrounding countryside, on foot or by bicycle. Expect delicious home-grown bacon, sausages, bantam eggs and fruit compotes for breakfast.

Juliet & Christopher Hawkins
Milden, Lavenham, Suffolk CO10 9NY
- £60–£90. Singles from £40.
- 3: 2 twins, 1 family room, sharing bathroom.
- Occasional light supper £15. BYO.
  Pubs/restaurants 2-3 miles.
- 01787 247235
- www.thehall-milden.co.uk

🏠S25 Gilly Parva, Gillyflower

You are in Constable country and the peace is palpable. Wind down the tree-lined lane to the lake: on one side is the family home, on the other is Gilly Parva – a modern, part timber-clad house. Inside, walls are pale yellow and there are stacks of books, magazines and pictures, plus underfloor heating. Your bedroom is separated by a rich turquoise wooden divider and has super views to water and woods. The galley kitchen, separate, is well-equipped. Wander in your part of the garden amongst exotic gums, bamboos and pines and watch mallards, moorhens and herons on the water. Pretty medieval villages and good walks abound.

Sir Martin Berthoud
Stoke by Nayland, Suffolk CO6 4RD
- £300-£400 per week.
- House for 2 plus sofabed.
- Self-catering
- 01206 263237
- web.me.com/martinberthoud1/Site/details.html

🏠S26 Abbey House

A spectacular arrival. Find a handsome, listed, Dutch-gabled house (1846) fronted by an impressive fishpond – the monks ate well here – upon which black swans glide. On land, the peacocks lord it over the chickens. Sue's welcome is warm and easy, her bedrooms simply and comfortably arranged, each with a couple of armchairs and garden or pond views. High ceilings and large windows make for a light, tranquil atmosphere. Settle down in front of the fire in the guest drawing room, or wander out through French windows to the shrub walk. Breakfast sausages and bacon are local; the eggs are from just outside.

Sue Bagnall
Monk Soham, Framlingham, Suffolk IP13 7EN
- £60-£80.
  Singles £30-£40.
- 3: 2 doubles; 1 twin with separate bath.
- Pubs 2.5 miles.
- 01728 685225
- www.abbey-house.net

⌂ Sheep Cottages

Five centuries have passed since this village cottage was built; since then it's housed a baker, cobbler – and probably a wool merchant and his livestock! Now it is a pair of cottages, low-ceilinged and wonderfullly wonky, but admirably done up in a simple and uncluttered style. Bedrooms are charming – an old chair, pine chest, vase of flowers; and comfortable – new mattresses come with honeycomb cotton covers. Bathrooms are light and beamy; kitchens well-organised. Each cottage has its own entrance and south-facing garden; and the village is sweet: an art gallery, a good butcher and a deli that supplies the Royal Family.

Sue Gazzard
Bruisyard Road, Peasenhall, Suffolk IP17 2HP
- Black Sheep £420-£740 per week.
  White Sheep £620-£946 per week.
- Black Sheep for 4. White Sheep for 6.
- Self-catering.
- 0208 692 6069
- www.sheepcottages.co.uk

⌂ Poplar Farm House

Only a few miles from Ipswich but down a green lane, this rambling farm house has a pretty, white-washed porch and higgledy-piggledy roof. All light, elegant and spacious with wonderful flowers, art, sumptuous soft furnishings (made by Sally) and quirky sculptures; expect comfortable beds, laundered linen and smart bathrooms. Sally and linguist Penton are relaxed and humorous; have tasty eggs from their handsome hens, homemade bread, veg from the garden on an artistically laid table. Play tennis, swim, steam in the sauna or book one of Sally's arts and crafts courses, then wander in the woods with friendly collies Shale and Wizard.

Penton Lewis & Sally Sparrow
Poplar Lane, Ipswich, Suffolk IP8 3HL
- From £65. Singles £55.
- 3: 2 doubles, 1 twin with 2 shared bath/shower rooms.
- Dinner, 3 courses, £15-£25. Packed lunch £7. Pub 1 mile.
- 01473 601211
- www.poplarfarmhousesuffolkbb.eu

S29 Arch House

Arch House stands in three acres of garden, meadow and woodland, in easy reach of the sea, Snape Maltings and Minsmere bird reserve. It is also home to the delightful and fun-loving Araminta and Hugh. He, a keen member of the Soil Association, shoots, fishes and grows his own veg; she offers complementary therapies. Both are fabulous cooks and you eat well in the farmhouse kitchen. The décor is traditional, the bedrooms colourful, and the elegant drawing/dining room has a boudoir grand piano. Trout, salmon or game for dinner; at breakfast, eggs from the hens. Wonderful value.

Araminta Stewart & Hugh Peacock
Aldeburgh Road,
Aldringham, Suffolk IP16 4QF
- £55-£70. Singles £35.
- 2: 1 double, 1 twin with separate bath.
- Dinner from £15. BYO. Pub 200 yds.
- 01728 832615
- www.archhouse-aldeburgh.com

S30 The Westleton Crown

This is one of England's oldest coaching inns, with 800 years of continuous service under its belt. Inside, find the best of old and new: Farrow & Ball hues, leather sofas and a tongue-and-groove bar, panelled walls, stripped floors, ancient beams and spindle-back chairs. There are corners to hide in, flames flickering in an open fire, a huge map on the wall for walkers. Fish comes from Lowestoft boats, local butchers provide local meat. Lovely bedrooms are cool lime white with comfy beds dressed in fine cotton. Super bathrooms are fitted out in Fired Earth; the best have claw-foot baths. Aldeburgh and Southwold are close.

Sarah Harrod
The Street, Saxmundham, Suffolk IP17 3AD
- £115-£250. Singles from £90.
- 25: 19 doubles, 2 twins, 3 family rooms, 1 single.
- Lunch & dinner £5-£30.
- 01728 648777
- www.westletoncrown.co.uk

remnants of walls left now – it collapsed in the 1960s. If the story is true, then Kerrison's batman must have enjoyed waking up to a bird's-eye view of the town in his later years. You can enjoy the same perspective by climbing up the enclosed wooden staircase. The interpretive board here has a drawing of what the castle might have looked like in the 16th century when a windmill stood on the top – quite a sight in this land without hills.

Once down from the castle, the town's **Guildhall** is worth a look too: a timbered Tudor building that has the archangel Gabriel carved into one of its corner posts. There's another impressive Tudor building on the corner of Church Street and Buckshorn Lane, close to the Town Hall, currently a pharmacy.

Queens Head 7 Cross St, Eye; ☎01379 870153. This 16th-century inn has decent pub food and is the only survivor of around 15 pubs that served the town just a couple of decades ago.

Diss to Harleston

Take the A143 east of Diss and you'll soon end up in Harleston. It's better to take your time though, and explore the villages and footpaths that lead down to the water meadows. Even the local bus has the good sense to avoid the main road where it can and make a tour through the villages along the way.

⑦ Hoxne

Hoxne (pronounced 'hoxen') is a pretty village just south of 'The Crotch', the confluence of the Waveney and the Dove. The village has some elegant cottages and a nice pub but its real claim to fame is as the place where **St Edmund** was killed by marauding Danes. This may not be true of course – it may well have been elsewhere – but it is Hoxne that has claimed the legend and it has the monument to prove it, so there you are. The legend dictates that St Edmund was taken prisoner here and tied to a nearby oak tree before being shot dead with arrows. A stone monument to him stands in the middle of a field at the spot where an old oak was brought down by lightning in the 19th century. When it was subsequently broken up for timber, the tree apparently revealed a Viking arrowhead. Such history may be rather tangential but it is captivating all the same. Naturally, the tree in question would have to have been at least a thousand years old.

If you walk south along the village's high street past The Swan, you'll soon come to a minor road off to the left. Turn down here and you'll see the stone **Goldbrook Bridge**, under which Edmund was supposedly discovered hiding, his glinting spurs spotted by a young, newly wed couple who snitched to the Danes. St Edmund is said to have put a curse on all newlyweds crossing the bridge so Hoxne is probably not the ideal place for a honeymoon. The bridge makes no claims to be the original: one side bears the legend, 'KING

EDMUND TAKEN PRISONER HERE – AD870' and the other, 'GOLDBROOK BRIDGE – AD1878'. Just over the bridge stands a newish village hall in brick and flint, appropriately called St Edmund's Hall and a rather impressive building as village halls go. The gable wall has a plaque beneath the window that tells of King Edmund being taking prisoner and slain, while the apex has a relief carving that shows Edmund lurking beneath the bridge with sword in hand as Danes cross above him. The car park has an information board with details of a five-mile circular walk that snakes back into Norfolk to take in Billingford windmill. Thoughtfully, perhaps because this is still a pilgrimage site of sorts, there is also a picnic table for weary walkers. If you wish to see the St Edmund monument where the oak tree use to stand, then continue south a little way past some very smart thatched cottages and you'll soon see a sign pointing towards the monument in the middle of a barley field.

Further references to St Edmund can be found in Hoxne's **St Peter and St Paul's Church**, as you might expect. A bench-end shows the saint's head being carried by a wolf, and an oak screen depicting events from his life is reputedly made from the tree that was destroyed by lightning where his monument stands.

Hoxne's history clearly stretches back further than the Saxon time of St Edmund: in 1992, a local man looking for a lost hammer in a nearby field found an enormous hoard of over 15,000 Roman gold and silver coins, jewellery and tableware instead, probably hidden in the turbulent 5th century when Roman rule was breaking down. The Hoxne hoard, the largest ever found of its type in the United Kingdom, is now in safe keeping in the British Museum.

S) Swan Inn Low St ☎ 01379 668275 🖰 www.hoxneswan.co.uk. Built in 1480 by the Bishop of Norwich, this atmospheric listed building is all sloping floors, oak beams and open fires, with a ten-foot-wide inglenook in the main bar. It is very popular at weekends and so it's best to book ahead. Two beer festivals are held each year here, one in May and the other to commemorate St Edmund's Day in November.

⑧ Wingfield

Wynkefelde the Saxon held Honour and Fee
Ere William the Norman came over the sea.

The Wingfields were an old Saxon family who gave their name to Wingfield village itself. Sir John de Wingfield, chief of staff of the Black Prince, founded both Wingfield College and St Andrew's Church in the mid 14th century. Wingfield Castle, which was the seat of the Wingfields and their successors the de la Poles, Earls and Dukes of Suffolk, is now just a ruin next to a farm. **Wingfield College** was partly demolished before being remodelled in a Palladian style in the 18th century. The college's farm buildings now incorporate **Wingfield Barns** (www.wingfieldbarns.com), hosting arts, drama and theatrical events. Wingfield College itself is a private residence but the house and gardens can be visited on pre-booked guided tours (01206 769607; www.wingfield college.com) at roughly monthly intervals from April to September. The collegiate church of **St Andrew** here has the stone tomb of Sir John de Wingfield alongside the wood and alabaster tombs of Michael and John de la Pole and their wives. The church also contains a curious 18th-century wooden sentry box called 'The Hud', which was used outside by priests performing funeral services in inclement weather.

S♥ De la Pole Arms Church Rd ☎ 01379 384545. This free house has Adnams ales, hearty home-cooked British food that uses local produce, and a log fire in winter.

⑨ Fressingfield

East of Wingfield on the Harleston to Framlingham road, a knot of houses cluster around a church at Fressingfield. The village has a tidy prosperous air and two thriving pubs to bear this out – unusual in a place of this size. In warmer weather, there's inevitably a handful of people enjoying a drink at an outside table of the Swan Inn, and a nearly full car park at the rather grander **Fox and Goose Inn** (just up the hill behind the Church of St Peter and St Paul), built in 1509 and formerly serving as the village's guildhall. This Tudor building operates as a popular gastro-pub these days and even in the late 1960s it was famous for its food according to the author John Seymour, who suggested that people came from as far away as Yorkshire 'just for the eating' and recommended booking a day or two ahead. Back in those days, most pubs served just crisps and pickled eggs along with very unreal ale – or scampi and chips if you were lucky – so you have to admire the continuity of tradition here.

The **Church of St Peter and St Paul** is a veritable cathedral to the use of unstained oak, with some marvellous 15th-century bench ends in the form of saints and a hammerbeam roof. There's a fine example of medieval graffiti here too, with the initials 'A P' incised into a bench. This is considered to be the handiwork of Alice de la Pole, granddaughter of the poet Chaucer, who was perhaps the medieval equivalent of a graffiti tagger. All that wood ripe for carving must have been just too much of a temptation and as Duchess of Norfolk she would hardly expect to be punished for her petty act of vandalism.

The church is the venue for a music festival in September, the **Fressingfield Music Festival** (www.fressingfield.suffolk.gov.uk/festivals), that attracts some big names in the world of classical music. The 2009 festival had performances by Julian Lloyd Webber, Emma Kirkby and the Choir of Christ's College, Cambridge.

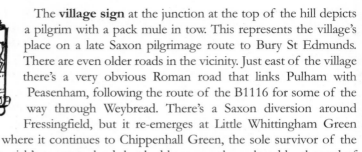

The **village sign** at the junction at the top of the hill depicts a pilgrim with a pack mule in tow. This represents the village's place on a late Saxon pilgrimage route to Bury St Edmunds. There are even older roads in the vicinity. Just east of the village there's a very obvious Roman road that links Pulham with Peasenham, following the route of the B1116 for some of the way through Weybread. There's a Saxon diversion around Fressingfield, but it re-emerges at Little Whittingham Green where it continues to Chippenhall Green, the sole survivor of the parish's common land that had been mostly enclosed by the end of the 18th century. If you take this same old Roman Road north from Fressingfield towards Harleston, you'll pass through **Weybridge** and **Weybread Street**, a linear sprawl of houses with a seemingly endless stretch of 30mph speed limit – imposed perhaps because of the irresistible temptation that dead-straight pieces of road like this offer to speed merchants.

A literary diversion – Herod's Temple in Suffolk

In his rambling masterpiece, *The Rings of Saturn*, W G Sebald describes walking a stretch of Roman road in east Suffolk. Setting out from Yoxford, he walks for four hours across a sparsely populated landscape in which he sees nothing other than harvested cornfields and a sky heavy with clouds (Sebald's landscapes always seem to be strangely devoid of people).

He ends up at a remote moated house where he encounters Thomas Abrams, a remarkable farmer who has been building an accurate scale model of the Temple of Jerusalem for the past twenty years. Sebald describes Abrams as having spent years studying sources as obscure as rare tracts on Roman architecture and the *Mishnah*, the first major work of the rabbinic *Torah*, in order to pursue his obsession. Sebald discovers that Abrams's project has already attracted a number of interested parties: one morning the farmer found that the man who had parked his Rolls Royce in his driveway was none other than Lord Rothschild.

It's a typical tangential Sebald tale – with singular, Sisyphus-like characters turning up in odd places – but who knows what schemes and obsessions are dreamed up in these isolated Suffolk farmsteads? It turns out that Abrams is, in fact, Alec Garrard, a friend of Sebald's, who has subsequently published an illustrated book, *The Splendour of the Temple* in which his 1:100 scale model is used to describe the history and architecture of the temple that existed between 19BC and AD70. Garrard, now approaching 80 years in age, is long retired but still hard at work on his magnificent model. After 30 years and an estimated 33,000 hours of work, he is realistic that the model temple will never be completed in his lifetime.

Suffolk is yet to earn the reputation of Bordeaux or the Napa Valley but it does have a few vineyards where brave English wine growers do their best to conjure the spirit of Bacchus from the heavy clay soil. **Willow House Vineyard** (01379 586868; www.oak-hill.co.uk) in the centre of the village behind the church produces its own Oak Hill Wines named after an 800-year-old oak tree that overlooks the vines, the last vestige of an ancient wood. Four hundred vines were planted here back in 1987 and the vineyard produces three types of white wine – dry, sweet and oaked.

Fox and Goose Inn ☎ 01379 586247 ⌂ www.foxandgoose.net. In a Tudor building that was the former guildhall, this is a very popular place so booking is almost essential; it has two Michelin rosettes. Most produce is sourced within a six-mile radius. The pub has suggestions for a couple of moderate walks in the area before or after a meal here.

Swan Inn ☎ 01379 586280 ⌂ www.fressingfieldswan.co.uk. With outdoor tables overlooking the road and the beck, this has straightforward bar food and a decent selection of real ales.

⑩ Brockdish

Brockdish is a lovely little place in the valley just a few miles shy of Harleston. There's a decent pub here and some good walks: you could follow the Angles Way down to the river and cross to the south bank here, or follow it in the opposite direction where it climbs above the village before leading west towards Diss. The valley here, on the East Anglia scale of things at least, is impressive and the briefest of climbs up out of the village will bring the reward of a view of the watermeadows in the valley bottom that stretch east from here along the Waveney's northern bank. Across the river in Suffolk, there's another short but sharp incline and it's hard to think of anywhere else in the region where you are more aware of actually being in a valley. Granted, it's hardly south Wales but it's impressive after Broadland or the Fens.

Opposite the village pub there's an old chapel and behind this is a sloping meadow that is home to the **Upper Waveney Sculpture Meadow** (01379 668552; www.upperwaveneysculpturemeadow.co.uk). This project was still in its infancy at the time of writing but it will be interesting to see how it develops. The sculpture meadow is the initiative of Christopher Parr and Rebecca Lyne, who live in the village and work collaboratively to create fine art sculpture and distinctive kiln-formed glass. Their aim is to open the meadow to the public on a number of days throughout the year, and include family art days and Fleeting Flames fire-sculpture events in addition to opening for the annual Harleston and Waveney Art Trail. Parr and Lyne acquired the sloping two-acre meadow from a local farmer. Rebecca Lyne told me, 'We thought it would be in keeping with the spirit of the village if we could use the meadow for outdoor sculpture rather than housing development. We'd like to involve the local community as much as possible and that's why we are putting on these family art days.' The family days involve workshops that encourage both children and adults to get creative, with puppet making, body art, sculpture and pottery painting all taking place.

In contrast to the large fields of corn that surround it, the sculpture meadow has been encouraged to revert to its natural state, Although it is pretty much dominated by ragwort for now, other species are slowly starting to establish themselves. 'This was just another arable field ten years ago,' Christopher Parr explained. 'Then it was left to grow uncultivated and the thistles sprang up. We've left some of the ragwort around the edge for cinnabar moths but we want to encourage other wild meadow flowers to grow here. There are already plenty of butterflies. The idea really is for a space that's good for art and for wildlife.' There's a splendid view to be had from the top of the meadow, where you can see the river's watermeadows with their contentedly grazing cattle and the sloping cornfields of Suffolk beyond.

Harleston to Beccles

⑪ Harleston

Harleston is the urban magnet for this stretch of the valley, although 'urban' is probably too big a word for a pleasant little market town. As with many places of this size, medieval fires saw to it that most of the town's earlier thatch and timber frames went up in flames so what remains today is mostly solid Georgian red brick with the odd Tudor survivor. Market day, still important to the town, is on Wednesdays.

Harleston's most conspicuous landmark is the almost minaret-like **clock tower** on the market place that used to belong to St John's Chapel of Ease. The chapel was founded in the 14th century but was in a ruinous state by the 18th. A new church was built on Broad Street to replace it and the old chapel was demolished and replaced with a grocer's shop, which remains there today. As with many agricultural towns in the region, there's a conspicuous Victorian **corn exchange**: a stark white neoclassical building that was opened for commerce in 1849 but which served as a local court in later years. Since its early days, when its walls must have resounded to the bargaining cries of Norfolk farmers, the building has seen use as a skating rink, furniture market, dance hall and even a delicatessen and restaurant. At the time of writing it was up for sale.

The Market Place, which tends to be on the sleepy side apart from Wednesday mornings, has another town landmark: the J D Young Hotel, originally known as **The Magpie Inn** – the original distinctive sign can still be seen – which has served as a coaching inn for centuries. Churchill and Eisenhower are reputed to have met here during World War II, presumably not over a pint. Just across from the hotel is a large Georgian house with two enormous sequoias that look as if they will burst out of the garden like slow-growing triffids in the next century or two. The town's other coaching inn is **The Swan** in The Thoroughfare, which was built by Robert Green, a conspirator in Kett's Rebellion who may have been rewarded with this property for snitching on his colleague – hardly the noblest of ways to get a start in the pub trade.

The Old Market Place, which no longer has a market, has Harleston's oldest building at number 18, an Elizabethan hall house that originally would have been jettied. A handsome, three-storey Georgian building here serves as a café, art gallery and the headquarters of the annual **Harleston and Waveney Art Trail** (01379 855366; www.hwat.org.uk) that takes place over three weekends in June and July and opens up the studios of local artists to visitors. All of the studios are within an eight-mile radius of Harleston and can be visited by bike, car or on foot. If you were wondering why there is no medieval parish church to be found in Harleston, it is because the town shares the same parish as **Redenhall**, which does have a magnificent 15th-century church.

⑫ Mendham

Just across the Waveney from Harleston in Suffolk is the small village of Mendham. This was the birthplace of **Sir Alfred Munnings**, the East Anglian painter of horses and rural scenes and one-time president of the Royal Academy, whose father owned the mill just outside the village. If you approach the village from the south via the Witherdale road, Mendham seems remote despite its proximity to Harleston. The village is set in the river's flood valley amidst lush water meadows and lines of poplars. It's a quiet, dreamy place, with a church and a single pub that is called, appropriately, The Sir Alfred Munnings. The car park opposite the pub has a notice board with a suggested five-mile circular walk – along Sconch Beck to St Cross South Elmham. The Angles Way passes through the village as it crosses into Norfolk and there's a footpath that leads across Mendham Marshes past the ruins of a Cluniac priory.

Alternatively, you could just saunter past the pub down to the river. This is classic Waveney Valley scenery – the sort of thing Munnings might have painted if he had not concentrated on horse fairs or attacking modernism quite so much. It's the kind of landscape that brings reverie. The iron bridge crossing the Waveney seems like a giant staple attaching Norfolk to the Suffolk mainland. Brown cows wandering the meadows contentedly graze and flick flies away, keeping their eyes on a pair of locals fishing beneath the trees and catching nothing. As poplars rustle in the breeze, the very English sound of an accordion drifts down from the Munnings pub. It could almost be the 18th century, if it wasn't for the fishermen's car parked by the road. As I am taking all this in, a man who is clearly the worse for drink ambles down the road towards the bridge. He stumbles exactly halfway across, pauses for a moment, then goes back the way he has come. It is as if he is fearful to place his feet on Norfolk soil, or there is some sort of invisible barrier. Two minutes later, a sleek Jaguar arrives from the north to pick the man up. Then it turns around and ferries him back across the bridge… into Norfolk.

Gurney's Harleston Gallery, 3 The Old Market Place ☎ 01379 855366. On the ground floor of this contemporary art gallery, this airy café-bistro serves excellent coffee, cakes and light meals at very reasonable prices. It is also open on Friday and Saturday evenings, when steaks, seafood and a weekly menu are available.

⑬ Bungay

Your school geography lessons should have taught you that the ideal defensive site is either at the top of a hill or in the meander of a river. This is East Anglia, so the first of these requirements is rather wishful thinking; the second, however, is provided for perfectly at **Bungay** where the River Waveney coils like a flexing eel. It does have a hill of sorts too, and this is the site Hugh Bigod, the 1st Earl of Norfolk, chose for his castle in 1173, on high ground overlooking a meander. Hugh 'the Bold' Bigod was a fierce rival of Henry II (who had made his castle at Orford, see page 249) but was forced to surrender his Bungay fortress to the king as a penalty for aligning himself with an insurrection led by Henry's rebellious sons. If it had succeeded he would have gained custody of Norwich Castle; the words at the start of this chapter record his regrets.

Author John Seymour describes Bungay as 'the most interesting town in the Waveney Valley'. I'm not sure – I might just plump for Diss – but it's certainly a self-contained, likeable place that, with a castle, an independent theatre and a distinctive eccentric character, seems to punch well above its weight for somewhere so small. Over the years, it's been a centre for leather working, boat building and more recently printing but it has always also been an important market town for the region.

As with most small towns in East Anglia, Bungay's heart is its Market Place. Central to this is the octagonal **Butter Cross** that has a lead figure of Justice with her scales on top of its cupola. Like many other settlements where medieval wood and thatch predominated, a serious fire spread through the old town in the late 17th century and Bungay's plentiful Georgian buildings reflect a post-1688 rebuild. There's a pleasing mix of architecture spread throughout the centre but **Bridge Street**, with its colourfully painted houses sloping steeply down towards the river, is particularly attractive. This is a street that seems to happily harbour some of Bungay's undeniable eccentricities too: take a look at the anarchic bric-a-brac shop with its back-yard chicken coops opposite the Chequers pub for a taste of what indifference to convention can do.

Most of what you see now of **Bungay Castle** was actually constructed by Hugh's ancestor Roger Bigod at the end of the 13th century. Today, there are two crumbling towers of the original gatehouse and some outer walls that you can visit and with a bit of luck they will have removed the scaffolding by the time you get here. There's a visitor centre at the entrance, which has a café and tourist information in season. To get a good view across to Earsham on the other side of the Waveney Valley you can climb up **Castle Hills** from the visitor centre. In celebration of its founder, the **Bigod Way** is a ten-mile loop around the town that starts and ends at the castle. It's a lengthy walk that takes four or five hours but there's plenty of historical and wildlife interest along the way.

Although there were said to be five churches in the town in the 11th century, just two survive today: **Holy Trinity** with its Saxon round tower, the oldest complete building in town, and **St Mary's**. St Mary's, now deconsecrated, is famous in these parts for its role in the **Black Shuck legend** (see page 47), when the legendary black dog with fiery eyes ran amuck in the church and killed two worshippers having already caused untold damage at far-off Blythburgh church that same morning of 4 August, 1577. This fanciful tale has long passed into local folklore, although versions of it differ quite widely. According to one account, a woman who went to school in Bungay in the late 19th century remembers Black Shuck as being a cat and recalls children singing the song:

'Scratch cat of Bungay
Hanging on the door
Take a stick and knock it down
And it won't come anymore.'

Whatever his form, puss or pooch, Black Shuck did not leave any evidence of his visit at St Mary's (there are at least putative 'scorch marks' at Blythburgh), although he does put in an appearance on the town's coat of arms. There's also a rather attractive tapestry of Bungay's history hanging in the church with a panel detailing the rampaging dog with the legend, '1577: Black Dog entered during a fearful storm and two men died.'

Bungay is not all about castles and churches. With the River Waveney just a shadow of what it used to be, it is easy to overlook the importance that the river once held for the town. Once the lock at Geldeston was established in the late 17th century, and the river canalised, wherries were able to ship goods up here from the coast. Upper Olland Street in the town centre probably gets its name from a derivation of 'oak lands' and locally plentiful oak would have been used to build wherries in the Staithe area of the town. Indeed, William Brighton, builder of the *Albion* (see page 66), used to work here, while the boat itself used to ply its trade between Bungay Staithe and the coast at Lowestoft. These days, Geldeston is as far as navigation goes for anything larger than a canoe.

All this serious talk of history and tradition is well and good but if you ask a local for an instant word association with Bungay you'll probably end up with 'chicken roundabout'. Bungay's so-called **Chicken Roundabout** is the sort of small town silliness that local newspapers and regional television networks delight in. The roundabout in question is just across the river where the roads to Norwich, Ditchingham and Beccles spin off and, yes, it really does have chickens living on it. The roundabout is so highly thought of in the town that you can even buy books about it, and CD recordings of songs on that theme.

The Chocolate Box shop opposite Butter Cross, as well as having jars of sweets and a good range of Bungay-themed books, coasters and tea towels, also has Chicken Roundabout jigsaws and board games (for 2–4 players) – a niche market if ever there was one. Sadly, the chickens seem to have fled the coop… or gone home to roost – on my last visit, I didn't see a single one.

Foul play at Bungay's Chicken Roundabout

What came first, the chickens or the roundabout? The chickens did, in fact. It is thought that the colony of chickens living in the middle of a roundabout on the A143 just outside Bungay were originally allotment escapees that managed to survive on grain from the nearby maltings. The chickens survived the building of a bypass in 1983 thanks to this grain, but when the maltings went up in flames in 1999 their free food supply vanished. Thankfully, since then they have been kept alive thanks to the efforts of a local character known as the 'chicken man', who makes a two-mile round trip with his wheelbarrow most days just to feed them.

There has been considerable pressure in the past to remove them as these very free-range chickens have been branded a potential danger to traffic by local authorities. Bungay citizens have strongly resisted their removal however, and have signed petitions and even dressed up in chicken costumes to promote their cause. It seemed that the chickens were safe until a sharp decline in their numbers was reported in 2009. Predators such as foxes have been blamed, as has theft by chicken rustlers, but their decline remains something of a mystery and local chicken watchers, if not the chickens themselves, find themselves foxed.

For cycling, the **Godric Way** is a 24-mile route around Bungay that starts and ends at Butter Cross and passes through Ellingham, Broome, Ditchingham, Earsham, Denton, Alburgh, Homersfield, Mettingham and The Saints – all places in which a slow cycle through is worth a dozen drive-bys.

Several cafes and tearooms are dotted around the town centre. The **Buttercross Tea Rooms** (☎ 018986 893002), just down from the Buttercross on Cross Street, is an unfussy but perfectly pleasant place for a snack or coffee, as is the more upmarket **Earsham Street Café** (☎ 01986 893103).

Castle Inn 35 Earsham St ☎ 01986 892283 🖥 www.thecastleinn.net. With an imaginative menu that does its level best to utilise locally sourced food, this is probably Bungay's nicest place to eat. There's also an elegant but cosy bar that serves local cider and ales and a good selection of wines.

Queen's Head Station Rd, Earsham NR35 2TS ☎ 01986 892623. Just west of Bungay in the village of Earsham, this pub has its own real-ale brewery, the Waveney Brewing Company, attached.

⑭ The Saints

South of Bungay on the Suffolk side of the river is a handful of small villages known locally as **'The Saints'**. They are: St Mary South Elmham, St Cross South Elmham, St Margaret South Elmham, St Nicholas South Elmham, St James South Elmham, St Michael South Elmham, St Peter South Elmham, All Saints South Elmham, Ilketshall St Margaret, Ilketshall St John, Ilketshall St Andrew, Ilketshall St Lawrence and All Saints Mettingham. I suppose you might also call them 'The South Elmhams and Ilketshalls', but that does not quite have the same ring to it.

These are medieval parishes that never coalesced to form a city as they did in Norwich. As someone else has remarked, if one of these villages had been a port, a defensive fortress or important market place, then the history of the area might have been quite different and, instead of a clump of tiny villages, we might find a city. But it can seem as if the medieval period has not yet completely passed by in this corner of Suffolk where even Harleston and Bungay can feel a long way off. There are no specific sights here, apart perhaps from South Elmham Minster – the charm of 'The Saints' is, as they say, subtle – but it's an area that rewards relaxed wanderings. It is perhaps worth noting that one of the villages, South Elmham St Michael, is one of only two 'thankful villages' in Suffolk (there are none at all in Norfolk). It is, in other words, a rare village in which all soldiers returned from World War I and has no need of a war memorial.

'The Saints' is definitely an area for cycling. Driving around it in a car, you will inevitably get lost – cars are just too fast for this maze of narrow lanes and confusing signpost. South of the curiously named St Cross South Elmham stands **South Elmham Hall**, a 16th-century farmhouse that these days functions as a place to stay. Just south of the hall, standing alone in a field surrounded by trees, is the evocative ruin of **South Elmham Minster**. The Minster was an Episcopal chapel built for Herbert de Losinga, Bishop of Norwich, who also founded a monastery at North Elmham (in Norfolk) and a smaller one at Hoxne. It has been dated as 11th century, although a Saxon 10th-century tomb slab has been found on the same site and so some place of worship must have existed previously. It's a mysterious place and the hornbeams that surround the ruin provide a wonderful haven for birds. With luck, you may even see hawfinches here, exotic-looking birds that are about the closest thing to a parrot that you can find in Suffolk.

The land beside The Beck, the stream that runs through it, which has buttercup meadows, coppiced elm hedges (kept like this to prevent a return of Dutch elm disease) and ancient hornbeam pollards, was once a medieval deer park. Now it provides grazing for British White cattle – a rare breed – and walks for visitors. The Bateman's Barn Visitor Centre (01986 782526; www.batemansbarn.co.uk) at the hall has information about wildlife walks in the vicinity and a café that opens Thursdays, Fridays, Sundays and bank holidays. The hall and gardens are open for guided walks on Thursdays and some Sundays and bank holidays from the beginning of May until the end of September.

A mile west of Ilketshall St Margaret is **St Peter's Hall**, a 13th-century moated hall that was extended in the 15th century using what is euphemistically known as 'architectural salvage' from nearby Flixton Priory, hence its fine Norman stone. The hall itself is a restaurant today but St Peter's Hall is probably best known for its **St Peter's Brewery** (01986 782322; www.stpetersbrewery.co.uk), established in 1996, that produces tasty, traditionally brewed beers in distinctive oval bottles. Local malts are used for brewing and the water used is drawn from a deep chalk aquifer beneath the ground. The rather medicinal bottle design, which dates back to 1770, helps to create the impression that what you are drinking is actually doing you good – it works for me. The visitors' shop opposite the hall is open every day.

If cider is your thing then you might wish to pay a visit to **The Cider Place** (01986 781353) at Cherry Tree Farm, Ilketshall St Lawrence, which has a wide range of ciders, country wines and meads, and has tastings most days of the week. Keeping with the apple theme, the **Metfield Stores** (01379 586204; www.metfield.org.uk), a community shop in Metfield village, just west of St James South Elmham, specialises in local produce that includes some rare varieties like Darcy Spice. The store celebrates Apple Day (and Apple Week too) each year in October, often with a local nurseryman on hand to dispense advice. The Metfield Stores, which is, in fact, the only shop in the village, is staffed by volunteers and is very active in promoting local suppliers and produce.

SP St Peter's Hall St Peter South Elmham ☎ 01986 782288
🍴 www.stpetershallsuffolk.co.uk. This offers fine dining in a panelled Tudor great hall, with sophisticated English cuisine that makes use of local meat and game. There's also a library bar with ales from St Peter's Brewery.

Beccles and the lower Waveney Valley

East of Geldeston, the river is wide enough for navigation as it meanders north to merge with the River Yare at Breydon Water. This, of course, has considerable effect on the river's character, which morphs from sleepy tranquil backwater to busy thoroughfare within a matter of miles. The county line itself follows the river faithfully until it branches off to the coast near Herringfleet towards a point more or less midway between Great Yarmouth and Lowestoft.

⑮ Beccles

The largest town in the valley, **Beccles** is pleasant enough but a place that most tend to pass through rather than stay in. The town is solidly Georgian as, like elsewhere, its timbered Tudor core was destroyed by a succession of ravaging fires. The river used to have far more significance to town life than it does now, and Beccles was once a  flourishing port with many wherries passing by. Herrings from the coast used to be an important commodity here and, in the medieval period, Beccles annually provided tens of thousands of the fish to the monks at Bury St Edmunds.

Boats still have a part to play, as Beccles is the most southerly point on the Broads system. The river here is not quite as hectic in summer as the Bure and Thurne are to the north but it's busy enough. The actual limit of navigation is at **Geldeston Lock** just west of Beccles, where there is also a decent pub. There's some good walking on the Beccles Marshes close to the town and short **boat trips** can be made on the Edwardian-style *Liana*, which travels to Geldeston or Aldeby according to tides. You can book this at the **Broads Information Centre** at The Quay (01502 713196).

The Bear and Bells 11 Old Market, Beccles ☎ 01502 712291. Pub-restaurant with free-range meat roasts on Sundays.
Beccles Farmers' Market Beccles Heliport ⌖ www.becclesfarmersmarket.co.uk. Has around thirty stalls on the first and third Saturday of the month.

The lower Waveney valley: ⑯ Burgh St Peter, ⑰ Somerleyton Hall and ⑱ Burgh Castle

The Waveney turns back on itself at Oulton Dyke, where there is a channel leading through to Oulton Broad and Lowestoft. To the west of the river, tucked away inland in Norfolk almost equidistant between the Waveney and the Yare, are the somewhat isolated villages of **Wheatacre**, **Aldeby**, where there is a priory, and **Burgh St Peter**.

The last of these has the odd-looking church of **St Mary the Virgin** with its four-section tower shaped like a ziggurat or, as some have fancied, even a collapsible square telescope. The body of the church dates from the 13th century but the tower is a late 18th-century replacement for an earlier one that had collapsed. The tower's curious form is supposed to have been based on a Mesopotamian ziggurat seen by William Boycott, the rector's son, on his travels.

There was, in fact, a whole dynasty of Boycotts serving as rectors at the church for a continuous period of 135 years. It was Captain Charles Cunningham Boycott, the son of the second Boycott rector, who, serving as an Irish estate agent, first introduced the word 'boycott' into the English language when he suffered social ostracism for refusing to reduce rents.

On the Suffolk side of the river, just north of here, there's Somerleyton, home to **Somerleyton Hall** (01502 730224; www.somerleyton.co.uk) with its remodelled Anglo-Italian stately home, walled gardens and Victorian yew-hedge maze planted in 1846. **Fritton Country Park**, along with

Fritton Lake with its lush wooded shoreline and rowing boats for hire, open to the public at Easter and between July and early September, lies just to the north of the estate.

The Angles Way in winter

I did this long-distance walk in midwinter, over eight days of the coldest weather to hit East Anglia so far this millennium. I started each stage from my home in Norwich, using public transport to reach the day's trail head. Some of the bus and train connections were tight but it was all just about feasible – on weekdays at least.

The first section involved a lengthy stretch along the south bank of Breydon Water, always at its best on bright, frosty days when the water sparkles and migrant waders work the mud. The waymarked footpath left the estuary at Burgh Castle to dawdle through the dormitory village of Belton, probably the dullest stretch along the entire route. After skirting a golf course, the Way led across fields to pass the Redwings Animal Sanctuary where I was delighted to see a large number of the eponymous winter thrushes congregating in the paddocks. After passing two charming churches – first, thatched and round-towered Fritton St Edmund's, then Ashby St Mary's, isolated among fields – I arrived at the slightly eccentric estate village of Somerleyton. Next day, I followed the railway line east along the marsh edge to wind up at Oulton village.

The stretch from Oulton Broad to Beccles followed the bank of the Waveney for much of the way – an elemental landscape of water and grazing marsh. Beccles to Earsham came next: hard work on my chosen day because the ground was frozen solid. I slithered my way out of the town, past Roos Hall then through fields that looked down upon the Waveney and picturesquely frozen marshes that, with only the distant thrum of traffic to remind one of the 21st century, resembled a scene from a Constable painting. Emerging at the hamlet of Shipmeadow, I crossed the A143 to

The end of the road, or rather river, comes at Breydon Water where the impressive Roman ruins of **Burgh Castle** (originally known as *Gariannonum*) loom over the confluence of the Yare and Waveney. The castle's crucial strategic position hardly needs mentioning but these massive brick-and-flint fortifications were abandoned at the beginning of the 5th century when the Romans finally thought better of occupying such intractable northern territory. An Irish missionary, Fursey, founded a monastery within the same walls about two centuries later but subsequent attacks by Danish raiders soon encouraged him to decamp to France.

⑤ Duke's Head Slugs Lane, Somerleyton ☏ 01502 730281
🖥 www.somerleyton.co.uk. A 17th-century village inn, now a gastropub, that overlooks the Somerleyton Estate. This has a roaring fire and a cosy bar and dining area serving good seasonal food, real ales and fine wines. There's also a beer garden overlooking the Waveney River.
Wherry Inn 7 The Street, Geldeston ☏ 01508 518371. A traditional pub with a good range of real ales and seasonal menu.

head across fields next to a converted workhouse that was now a desirable residence but which must once have been a miserable place to live. Close to the ruins of Mettingham Castle, I followed a timeless green lane lined with coppiced hazel and, before I knew it, found myself gazing down on Wainford Mill just outside Bungay.

Rather than diverting into Bungay, the Angles Way crosses back into Norfolk here to follow the meander of the river. I took the track through woodland above Ditchingham Lodge and, arriving at Earsham Mill, crossed into Suffolk once more to traverse lush riverside meadows as far as the village of Mendham. After a gentle climb up the north side of the valley I arrived in Harleston. The next leg followed the south bank of the river as far as Brockdish, where the way crossed a bridge back into Norfolk and, after climbing and skirting the village churchyard, I followed another lengthy stretch of green lane and farm tracks across beet fields to end up in Scole.

Arriving at Diss Mere the following day, I found the resident ducks looked rather confused by the frozen state of things. I headed west out of town alongside Roydon Fen to reach the gorse-covered heath of Wortham Lings and eventually arrived at the source of the Waveney (and the Ouse) near Redgrave after a splendid leafy section through the woodland area of the nature reserve.

A final day's walk brought me to Knettishall Heath in Breckland where future options awaited me: the Peddars Way north to Holme-next-the Sea or the Iceni Way to Thetford and Hunstanton. I had walked around 80 miles in total – perhaps more like 90 – and had encountered virtually no-one along the way give or take the odd dog-walker. For those in search of tranquillity and mid-winter exercise, walks like this certainly have plenty to recommend them.

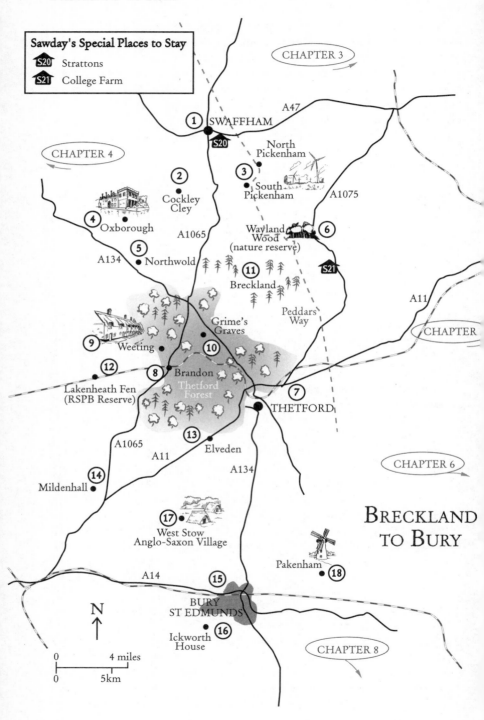

Sawday's Special Places to Stay

S20 Strattons
S21 College Farm

CHAPTER 3

CHAPTER 4

① SWAFFHAM
S20

② North Pickenham
③
South Pickenham
A47
A1075

Cockley Cley

④ Oxborough

A1065
Wayland Wood (nature reserve)
⑥
S21

⑤ Northwold
A134

⑪ Breckland

A11

CHAPTER

Peddars Way

⑨ Weeting
Grime's Graves

⑩

⑧ Brandon
Thetford Forest

⑦ THETFORD

⑫ Lakenheath Fen (RSPB Reserve)

⑬ Elveden

A1065
A11
A134

CHAPTER 6

⑭ Mildenhall

⑰ West Stow Anglo-Saxon Village

Pakenham

BRECKLAND TO BURY

A14
⑮
BURY ST EDMUNDS
⑱

N
↑

0   4 miles
0   5km

⑯ Ickworth House

CHAPTER 8

7. BRECKLAND TO BURY

This chapter covers two regions, Breckland and the western region of Suffolk that lies immediately south of it, and straddles the Norfolk–Suffolk county boundary. The area has just three towns: Swaffham in the north, at the northern edge of Breckland, Thetford right in the middle of it and Bury St Edmunds in Suffolk in the south. All three have historical interest well beyond what one might expect. Thetford was home to the monarchs of East Anglia and the seat of a bishopric; it was also the birthplace of that staunch anti-monarchist Thomas Paine. Swaffham is an old-fashioned market town with a futuristic but very green Ecotech centre. Bury St Edmunds is a place apart, the capital and burial site of the Saxon King Edmund.

The Brecks and Thetford Forest

Although Breckland borders the pancake-flat region of the Fens, it really could not be more different. Breckland, in contrast to the fertile black soil found in the Fens, has light, sandy soil that is far less ideal for intensive farming. The word 'breck' comes from a word that means land that becomes quickly exhausted. It's the closest thing that  Britain has to a desert and this is really not so far-fetched, as the rainfall is the lowest in the country, summer temperatures can be among the highest, and winter frosts, the hardest. The sand that covers the chalk was originally wind-blown, but trees have since been planted to stabilise the soil. Back in the days before such enlightened ideas, when large estates sought to maximise their profits by introducing sheep, the sand blew freely around causing untold damage, depleting thin topsoil in one place and covering up fertile land in another.

Naturally, what is a shortcoming today was actually a boon in the distant past. In Neolithic times, Britain's very first farmers were drawn to the region because Breckland's light soil was easy to work with their limited stone tools, and because there was no dense forest needing to be cleared with nothing other than brute strength and a hand axe. The region had a plentiful supply of flint too, the machine steel of the Neolithic Age.

With careful farming, Breckland became reasonably prosperous and **Thetford**, its capital, became an important regional capital in the Anglo-Saxon period. It was later, in the medieval period, when the real damage was done. Sheep were introduced to the land in large numbers and allowed to roam freely, overgrazing and damaging the soil with their hooves. In north Norfolk, sheep may have brought fortune but here they just heralded disaster. Breckland became increasingly depopulated as a result – the area is still sparsely populated today – and rabbits and pheasants became the land's only bounty.

The vast **Thetford Forest**, flanking the A11 around Thetford itself, is a recent innovation, planted by the Forestry Commission after World War I to provide a strategic reserve of timber. Much of what is not forest goes to make up the **Stanford Battle Area**, established in 1942, where the Army practise manoeuvres and test ordinance. Vast stands of Scots and Corsican pine may be what most people immediately associate with Breckland these days but it is a very recent trend. Step back just a hundred years in time and you would see only sandy heathland, gorse and rabbits – lots of rabbits. It almost goes without saying that this is a part of East Anglia that many speed through without stopping. Consequently, it is not as well known as perhaps it deserves to be. Outside the few towns, Breckland's distinctive habitat is a prized haven for wildlife: it is home to several species of plant, insect, bird and mammal that are found almost nowhere else in the country.

Getting around

Public transport

This is far from wonderful. The main towns, at least, can be reached by bus or train, apart from Swaffham, which no longer has a functioning railway. Thetford stands on the Norwich to Cambridge rail line and has a regular **rail service** to both cities – almost hourly during the day. Bury St Edmunds has rail links to Cambridge too, although no direct service to Norwich: you need to change at Stowmarket. Trains to Ely link with national services north and south.

Bus services run from Norwich to Swaffham and Thetford, and from Cambridge and Ipswich to Bury St Edmunds. There's the useful X1 Excel service run by First, half-hourly through most of the day, that connects Swaffham with King's Lynn and Peterborough to the west and Norwich, Great Yarmouth and Lowestoft to the east. Local services also run from all three main towns to outlying villages. The 200/201 bus service runs between Thetford and Mildenhall, calling at Santon Downham, Brandon and Lakenheath along the way. Several direct bus services run each day between Thetford and Bury St Edmunds but none between Thetford and Swaffham; for this, you will need to travel via King's Lynn, a long detour. Bus routes and times can be checked online at www.travelineeastanglia.org.uk.

Cycling

Given a general lack of traffic and quiet roads, the Brecks have plenty of potential for cycling. Thetford Forest has lots of off-road choices too. For those who want to go farther afield, Sustrans National Cycle Route 13 (www.sustrans.org.uk) connects Thetford and Watton with National Cycle Route 1.

East of England Tourism have devised an interesting twenty-mile **circular route** (with a possible ten-mile short cut), centred on Swaffham, that links the Ecotech wind turbine, Cockley Cley Nature Reserve, Oxburgh Hall and Gooderstone Water Gardens; the route can be downloaded from www.brecks.org.

You can buy a cycling pack that details five **easy routes** in the Brecks suitable for family cycling (£3 from tourist information centres). These tend to be theme-based, for instance a Pingoland Explorer Trail and a Flint-Hunters' Explorer Trail.

Thetford Forest Park has three waymarked forest trails of varying difficulty that start from the High Lodge Forest Centre, where bike hire is also available at Bike Art (01842 810090; www.bike-art.com). Harling Drove is a fairly long easy route through the heart of Thetford Forest that is suitable for both cyclists and walkers.

For more suggestions in the area, the useful website www.peacefulbyways.co.uk has two rides that start in **Swaffham** (plus others from **Castle Acre** and **East Dereham**). One is a flat and easy eight miles while the other is longer at 24 miles and covers slightly more undulating terrain. The shorter route heads southwest to the village of Cockley Cley, then takes a charming pine-lined country road north before turning right to return to Swaffham via the hamlet of Drymere. The longer route is an interesting southwestern circuit that takes in Drymere, Beachamwell, Barton Bendish, Boughton, Oxborough Hall, Gooderstone and Cockley Cley. With so many things to see en route and a couple of decent pubs too, this deserves a slow cycle and savouring it all in full.

Horse riding

There's scope to abandon two wheels for four legs in the region too and the potential for riding is probably the best in East Anglia. Horse riders have free access on all Forestry Commission freehold land. The Peddars Way is bridleway for most of its course, and other possibilities include the Swaffham Bridle Route and the Hockwold-cum-Wilton Bridle Route, details of which can be downloaded from www.countrysideaccess.norfolk.gov.uk.

Walking

Most will probably want to rely on their own two legs though, and there's some excellent walking to be had. The obvious choice for long-distance hikers is, of course, the **Peddars Way**, an ancient, well-publicised National Trail that begins at Knettishall Heath near the Norfolk-Suffolk border and strides irrepressibly north-north-west until it reaches The Wash at Holme-next-the-Sea. It is perfectly feasible to do short sections of this, and some of its most interesting stretches actually lie within the Brecks. The route is waymarked with acorn motifs and very easy to follow, though its sheer straightness can make the going a tad monotonous at times.

Other **long-distance routes** are **St Edmund Way** (Brandon to Flatford via Thetford and Bury St Edmunds – 88 miles), **Iceni Way** (Knettishall Heath to Holme-next-the-Sea via Brandon and the Fens) and **Hereward Way** (Harling Drove to Rutland via Peterborough, Ely and Brandon –110 miles).

You can walk anywhere you like on Forestry Commission land and numerous circular walks are waymarked from all the main parking areas. **Harling Drove**, mentioned, is a good option for a longer, ten-mile walk right through the heart of the forest. Further suggestions for shorter walks are made in the appropriate places in this chapter.

Tourist information

Brecks Tourism Partnership web:www.brecks.org.

Visit Suffolk ⌖ www.visit-suffolk.org.uk.

Brandon Country Park Bury Rd ☎ 01842 814955 ⌖ www.forest-heath.gov.uk.

Bury St Edmunds 6 Angel Hill ☎ 01284 764667 ⌖ www.stedmundsbury.gov.uk.

Swaffham Town Museum, London St, Swaffham ☎ 01760 722255
⌖ www.aroundswaffham.co.uk.

Thetford 2newhorizons Travel Agency, Market Place, Thetford ☎ 01842 751975
⌖ www.explorethetford.co.uk.

Watton The Visitor Centre, Wayland House ☎ 01953 880212
⌖ www.wayland-tourism.org.uk.

Around Swaffham

① Swaffham

Swaffham is something of a perfect example of an old-fashioned market town, with all the necessary ingredients: a market square, handsome Georgian houses, a leisurely rhythm and little evidence of the more boorish trappings of modern life. Sitting midway between King's Lynn and East Dereham, Fakenham and Thetford, it has long served as the regional centre for the farming country hereabouts. It lies within Breckland but only just, located at that region's northern edge. In the 18th and early 19th century the town became a fashionable social centre for the gentry and even became known as the 'Montpelier of England', such was its elegance and the reputation of its healthy, dry air. Wealthy farmers would come here with their families in season for dancing and racing. At some stage in its history, hare-coursing was invented here.

Hallowed be thy Kingdom?

Swaffham became the choice for the setting for the ITV series *Kingdom*, in which the town doubled as the fictional town of Market Shipborough, a TV-town of somewhat idealised Norfolkness where Stephen Fry works as a solicitor and improbable things happen. Serious Norfolk speech aficionados and self-appointed dialect police were a bit put out by the occasional 'ooh arr' West Country accents portrayed on screen but you might well sympathise with the actors, as East Anglian accents are notoriously tricky to emulate. Most Swaffham folk, in fact, are actually quite proud that their town appears regularly on the telly – you can even buy a stick of Market Shipborough rock at the Swaffham tourist office. Whatever the critical acclaim, *Kingdom* has certainly put Swaffham on the map, although not necessarily in the right place, as some disappointed visitors have been known to ask for directions to the beach. It is not here, it's at Holkham, 20 miles away.

William E Johns of *Biggles* fame lived here before World War I. Lottery-winning ex-dustman and 'King of Chavs' Michael Carroll, vilified in the East Anglian media as the 'lotto lout', chose Swaffham as a place to live too, buying a large house here and living the life of a modern-day Roman emperor before his money and luck ran out.

Swaffham life centres around its **market place** where a market is held each Saturday. Author and self-sufficiency pioneer John Seymour claimed it to be 'one of excellent surviving old markets where you can buy a second-hand washing machine, a dozen white rabbits, or a goat'. He was writing back in the late 1960s, and things have changed a little, but not that much – it's still thriving. You might have trouble finding a goat these days but rabbits should not prove too difficult. There's a handsome array of Regency buildings neatly arranged around this commercial wedge with its central **Butter Cross**, a neoclassical dome mounted on pillars, with a statue of the Roman grain goddess Ceres on top, an apposite choice for this arable region. Facing the market place, the Italianate red-brick 1858 **Cornhall** – now the local job centre – has more arable allusions, with a round panel containing a wheat sheaf on its gable. Many of the surrounding buildings are Georgian, the most noteworthy being the 1817 **Assembly Rooms,** home to an indoor market on Fridays with stalls that sell all manner of wholesome homemade goods. Among other less grand but cheerfully quirky buildings are the old post office (now a pet shop), just off the market place on Lynn Street, with its tiny conical tower that serves no obvious useful purpose and handsome Victorian brick lettering above its door.

Swaffham's appeal lies in its detail and mix. Only one of the major supermarkets has a base here and instead you'll find lots of independent shops selling household goods, groceries, hardware and haircuts, while a gentlemen's hairdresser on the square advertises itself with a traditional barber pole and a large wooden sign that takes up half the window stating 'The Town Barber'.

Even the tattoo parlour next to the old post office looks cosy and welcoming, nestled away in a fine Georgian building.

Swaffham's more cosmopolitan than first appears and boasts a Lithuanian shop, Indian and Chinese takeaways and even a Russian restaurant called 'Rasputin's' – 'the first in Norfolk' – a strange name for a place to eat perhaps (but then I do recall seeing a 'Lady Di' restaurant in Azerbaijan).

A short distance from the market place you'll find the 15th-century **Church of St Peter and St Paul** with a splendid hammerbeam roof filled with 88 angels flying in formation. The churchyard itself is a peaceful green haven that seems as if it should belong to a tiny village rather than the centre of a market town. It's worth the teeniest of detours to take a look at the wooden angels inside and perhaps wonder what an untutored medieval peasant might have made of them as he sat there on a Sunday. For a congregation mostly made up farm workers that rarely travelled far beyond the parish of their birth the local church would almost inevitably be the most remarkable sight they would ever witness. The church's wooden benches have medieval carvings that include the so-called **'Swaffham Pedlar'** – the merchant John Chapman, who also features on the well-known Swaffham town sign. The story behind this is that Chapman, following an impulse to seek his fortune in London, is told by a stranger on London Bridge that he should return home and look under a tree there to find his treasure. Eventually he returns home to find a pot of gold in his own garden. Whatever the truth behind this tale, John Chapman was certainly a generous benefactor of the church, most likely just a wealthy merchant who made his money in the time-honoured way.

'The Pedlar of Swaffham' town sign is the handiwork of Harry Carter, former art teacher at Hammond's High School, who is also the talent behind many other north Norfolk carved village signs. Harry Carter's uncle was Howard Carter, the eminent Egyptologist who discovered the tomb of Tutankhamun and, rather fancifully, is rumoured to have died as the result of the boy-king's 'curse'. Harry Carter's sign is at a corner of the market place in a flower bed opposite the old school gates, while an exhibition of Howard Carter's quest in Egypt's Valley of the Kings can be seen in **Swaffham Museum** (01760 721230; www.swaffhammuseum.co.uk), which also doubles as the tourist information office.

Standing outside the door of the museum and looking towards the market place you may suddenly become aware of a large white rotor blade slicing up the air above Ceres on the Butter Cross, an astonishing juxtaposition of classical tradition, medieval commerce and the modern green technology of the **Ecotech Centre** (01760 726100; www.ecotech.org.uk), open on weekdays year-round. Modern credibility came to the town with the establishment of this back in 1998, its unmissably enormous wind turbine looming next to the A47 giving the impression of blowing speeding King's Lynn-bound motorists further westwards. (There's a local joke that the wind turbines in the Wash do their bit to dissipate global warming by cooling the land with their fanning action.) First there was one wind turbine, now there are two, with a further eight in the nearby Peddars Way village of North Pickenham. Both turbines are operated by Ecotricity and together they generate more than three megawatts of power. Turbine tours (£5) can be pre-booked or you can take your chances and just turn up. There is an observation deck below one of the turbines and free entrance to the gardens, café and shop.

Swaffham's market place has several pubs and cafés. By the Butter Cross itself is the **Market Cross Coffee Bar** (☎ 01760 33671) with outdoor tables, while through the arch at the pedestrianised thoroughfare of Plowright Place you will find the **The Teapot Café**, again with both inside and outside tables.

Ceres Book and Coffee Shop 20 London St ☎ 01760 722504. This excellent independent bookshop selling new and second-hand books, maps and guides also serves coffee and homemade cakes in its charming three-table backroom café. It is closed on Wednesdays.

Strattons Hotel Ash Close ☎ 01760 723845 ⊕ www.strattonshotel.com. Just off the market place, this luxurious eco-friendly hotel serves wonderful, totally organic, locally sourced food in its candlelit restaurant. For a real indulgence, sample full afternoon tea here.

② Cockley Cley and around

As you leave Swaffham to the southwest through bungalow-filled outskirts, the Breckland scenery starts quickly to become apparent, with twisted stands of Scots pine shading the verges and large open fields of barley and sugar beet before the forest beyond. The first village you reach is Cockley Cley, a small village that is home to a reconstructed **Iceni Village** (01760 724588; www.icenivillage.com), effectively a small theme park that attempts to replicate an Iron Age village of the kind that the Iceni may have lived in shortly before the Roman invasion. There are severed heads on sticks and a snake pit to create atmosphere, as well as a nature trail and a museum filled with old farm machinery.

Just west of Cockley Cley, **Beachamwell** has the lovely thatched church of St Mary's with its hexagonal Saxon tower. An earthwork just north of the village – the Devil's Dyke – is believed to be a Saxon territorial boundary. Other sections of this turn up elsewhere in southwest Norfolk, such as west of Garboldisham. **Barton Bendish**, a little further west, has two churches, St Mary's and St Andrew's. The parish used to have three, but the church of All Saints was pulled down in the 18th century for material to patch up St Mary's Church and for repairing roads. There seems to be a plethora of St Mary's churches in this part of the county.

Twenty Churchwardens Cockley Cley ☎ 01760721439. Close to All Saints' Church in the village; the name refers to a type of clay pipe rather than the pub's clientele.

This used to be a school and it has only been a pub since 1968. Adnams and other real ales alongside simple, straightforward pub grub.

③ The Pickenhams

Just east of Swaffham, on the route of the Peddars Way and next to the banks of the River Wissey, are North and South Pickenham. **South Pickenham** has All Saints, a lovely little round-tower church with a very rural feel to it. You can find five round towers within a nine-mile radius of here: at South Pickenham, Merton, Watton, Threxton and Rockland. Pickenham Hall is central to the village, a large turn-of-the-century edifice that stands out very much as the local squire's abode.

The restored **St Mary's Church** at nearby **Houghton-on-the-Hill** is little more than a five-minute detour for Peddars Way walkers and a worthy expedition in its own right too. The church has become quite well known for its (probably 10th-century) wall murals, some of the earliest in

A visit to St Mary's, Houghton-on-the-Hill

I walked up here on a hot summer's afternoon to be greeted by Pam, one of Bob Davey's enthusiastic helpers, who showed me around and explained the murals using an artist's impression of what they may have looked like in their original, complete form. Pam pointed out the details on *The Last Judgement* in which the virtuous rose to heaven while sinners had to undergo torment by little red devils. 'The idea was to scare the locals into leading good lives.' The drawings are cartoon-like, not especially skilled but endearing, with figures that have the moonish faces and big eyes of Byzantine frescos. *Adam and Eve in the Garden of Eden* portrays Eve as a much larger figure than Adam, which leads me to mutter something about this being a pre-Renaissance lack of understanding about perspective. 'Yes possibly, but Bob thinks this just may be the way that women were revered back in those times. Most men got killed one way or another when they were still young. Women generally lived longer and were more important than we might give credit for.'

Bob himself came over to speak, a twinkle-eyed octogenarian in a bright yellow shirt and flowing snowy beard. He handed me some leaflets on the church before telling me, 'We haven't had chance to print it yet but this all needs updating a bit I'm afraid. We've got some new dates now and everything's a bit earlier than it says in the booklet.' He went on, 'Originally there was a Roman spa up here – it's a natural aquifer – and there's quite a lot of recycled Roman brick in the nave. There was a wooden church here first that was dedicated to St Felix and we've found some evidence of that. Then they added a flint chancel in the 7th century and a round tower in the 13th century but that fell down, so they put up one of those fashionable square towers instead.'

Europe, but is equally famous for its remarkable restoration story, the work for the most part of just one man. The church has been painstakingly restored thanks to the efforts of Bob Davey, a retired engineer from North Pickenham. He first began work on what was an ivy-covered, semi-derelict ruin back in 1987, when it had been abandoned since the 1930s. By 1993, thanks to Bob's interest and hard work, it had attained grade 1 listed status. This involved far more than simply physical renovation. When he first discovered the church, it was being used for black magic rituals and the Satanist congregation were none too keen on Bob's renewed interest in their ceremonial centre (Satanists had been reported here back in 1968 by a frightened walker who had accidentally stumbled upon them). Almost single-handedly, Bob stood up to what he considered a desecration of the church and continually tried to bar the Satanists entry, despite death threats and curses that were hurled his way. Pragmatically, he did go on to recruit a burly Territorial Army unit to lie in wait for the Satanists one night, and this surprise ambush seemed to drive them away for good, although the threats continued for a while. Since then, the church has been re-blessed and used for occasional non-denominational services – it had never actually been deconsecrated.

Since interest in St Mary's, and especially the wall paintings, has taken off, there has been a constant stream of experts coming to offer their opinions about the church's history. With so many axes to grind, it is hardly surprising that sparks have flown on occasions. Opinions vary but the nave that stands today may be anything between Late Saxon to Early Norman in origin. 'Look at those, they are definitely Saxon windows', Bob asserts defiantly as he points upwards, his face breaking into a wide grin, 'But there are those who'll swear they're not'. As for the murals, estimates range from the 9th to the late 11th century but Bob himself thinks, 'Somewhere around the middle 900s'.

It is undoubtedly a complex sequence, but a church in some form or other has stood here since Anglo-Saxon times. The murals are faded and partial but, having been buried beneath later medieval wall paintings and Victorian plaster for centuries, it is quite remarkable that they have survived at all, especially as they were exposed without a roof for many years. Spend a little time contemplating the paintings and savouring the atmosphere of this remote place and you may feel that you are getting some rare insight to what the world would have looked like to Anglo-Saxons at the dawn of the second millennium. It is certainly a special place.

After being ticked off by Pam for standing too long, and being told to sit down, Bob went on to tell me something of his television appearances – he has become quite a celebrity in the world of church restoration. The BBC had wanted to do a re-enactment of the time when a Satanist tried to run him over with a car. 'They had to do about six takes for that one', he tells me, chuckling mischievously, 'I had to keep jumping out of the way of this car until they got the camera angles right'.

There's no doubt that St Mary's has had more than its fair share of problems over the years. During World War I, a returning Zeppelin dumped its bombs in the churchyard damaging the building and in the 1930s it lost all of its parishioners when the neighbouring village of Houghton was finally deserted. The indignity of Satanistic worship came with the second half of the 20th century, and to cap all of this, thieves stole lead from the newly replaced roof in 2007. For good measure, it is also supposed to be haunted by a couple of Carmelite monks.

Bob – now Bob Davey MBE – still works hard in and around the church despite his advanced years. He has recently created a beautiful garden in what was once an overgrown churchyard. If you want to pay a visit, you can view the interior of the church between 14.00 and 16.00 daily (01760 440470 for group visits or tours at other times). With luck, Bob will tell you all about its history and show with quiet pride his press cuttings and photographs that record several royal visits. He is also extremely proud of the publication that documents how St Mary's was co-winner alongside Windsor Castle of a prestigious RICS (Royal Institution of Chartered Surveyors) Building Conservation Award in 1998.

The hamlet that once stood near here was known as **Houghton Town**, but the church and a few farm buildings are all that now remain. The last villagers left in 1936, evicted by a squire who wanted to turn his arable land over to the more profitable use of shooting for game. The last of the surviving cottages were bulldozed in 1994. Look carefully and you may be able to make out a few bumps in the fields to the north – the ghostly remnants of what was once a community.

North Pickenham, the village to the north, has St Andrew's as its parish church, a much grander affair than little St Mary's. Just west of the village is an old airfield that used to be RAF North Pickenham, which served as an American B-24 Liberator bomber base during World War II. This became a base for nuclear missiles in late 50s and 60s and a focus for early CND protests. The planes and missiles are long gone now and these days the airbase provides the site for a karting circuit, a wind farm and a Bernard Matthews turkey farm, which according to the *Guinness Book of Records* is the world's largest, producing one million birds annually. In his desire for what he sees as a 'sustainable future', Bernard Matthews has put in a proposal for two more turbines on the airfield site. This does rather prompt the question as to exactly what sort of sustainability one million factory-farmed turkeys per annum represents.

Blue Lion Houghton Lane, North Pickenham ☎ 01760 440289
🍺 www.thebluelionpub.co.uk. Popular with Peddars Way trudgers, this village pub has beers from local breweries such as Humpty Dumpty Reedcutter from Reedham and Worth the Wait from nearby Beeston Brewery. There's no food at present, although a restaurant is planned.

④ Oxborough

Oxborough is only a tiny village but it is also the location for **Oxburgh Hall**, a splendid Tudor country house that was the seat of the Bedingfield family and now belongs to the National Trust. Even without the Tudor hall, the village is interesting for the **Church of St John the Evangelist**, with its adjoining Tudor Bedingfield Chapel, endowed by Sir Edmund Bedingfield and containing the terracotta tombs of Sir Edmund and his wife. This was no exercise in humility: terracotta may be commonplace today but it was considered ultra chic in Tudor times. The main church building, which lies just outside the walls of the house, has a rather ruinous demeanour thanks to its spire collapsing in 1948. The nave was ruined by the incident but the chancel, south chapel and north aisle managed to escape damage. When I visited in summer 2009, the church was open but the Bedingfield Chapel was locked. Scaffolding around the tomb indicated that some repair work was being carried out and clearly the worry was that a hapless visitor might be struck by falling masonry.

Oxburgh Hall

This is an undeniably lovely building. Its location is very special too, in fertile farmland on the edge of both the Fens and the Brecks. With turrets and crenellations, intricate brickwork, tall chimneypots and a surrounding moat, it is  pretty much the ideal of the perfect stately home. The Bedingfields built the place in 1482, obtaining a charter for a fortified building from Edward IV, but despite its turrets and crenellations, it has always served as an ancestral home and never as a castle. As both Catholics and royalists in Protestant East Anglia, the Bedingfields tended to find themselves caught between two stones: Rome and the English crown. Their position was precarious, but they managed to survive and even became prosperous once more during the Restoration. The hall passed into the hands of the National Trust in 1952.

Just up the road from Oxborough is the neighbouring village of **Gooderstone** with its Gooderstone Water Gardens (01603 712913; www.gooderstonewatergardens.co.uk), with six acres of ponds, waterways and nature trails connected by footbridges.

Bedingfield Arms Oxborough ℓ 01366 328300. Originally an estate coach house, this pub close to the entrance and car park for Oxburgh Hall has a beer garden for summer drinking and a log fire for cold winter days.

⑤♪ Spread Eagle Inn Church Rd, Barton Bendish ℓ 01366 347995 ⏁ www.spreadeaglenorfolk.co.uk. Serves straightforward bar food and modern British food in the pricier restaurant. Produce is sourced from within Norfolk where possible.

The Breck-Fen border country, and into Breckland proper

Continuing due south from Oxborough you enter a borderland where Breckland meets the Fens. Some have gone so far to describe this as a coastline, which is not so fanciful when you ponder that not so very long ago most of the Fens were underwater. It's a marvellous area, explored by few outsiders, that has all the wide horizons and enormous skies you might expect. Although it's a long way from the traditional notion of 'hilly', it can almost seem as if you can see halfway across England as the land dips down west into Fenland and lays out a tapestry of fields filled with corn, barley and beet. Among a clutch of notable villages here, Northwold is among the finest.

⑤ Northwold

This long linear village comes as an unexpected delight when you first stumble across it after a long, confusing meander south from Oxborough. With bee-buzzing gardens of hollyhocks and roses lining the road, and walls sporting a diverse array of brick, carrstone, chalk and flint, it's a place that might genuinely fit into the clichéd category of 'best-kept secret'. If this were on the north coast it would be full of holiday homes, with a delicatessen and a stream of motorists passing by. Thankfully, it's refreshingly ungentrified – there's just an active pub and a post office/shop – and the road is mercifully quiet.

There's a lovely church here too. **St Andrew's Church** is best known for its Easter Sepulchre in the chancel, largely made from chalk, which has a relief of Roman soldiers skulking in an olive grove. Being chalk, it's soft and was easily damaged by marauding Puritans who came this way in the mid 17th century; nevertheless, it's easy enough to make out the detail. The hammerbeam roof is likely to draw your eyes upwards before you even reach the chancel as it's painted sky blue, as are the pipes of the organ – the same colour as the bunches of delphiniums that filled the church when I visited. There had just been a flower festival to celebrate 900 years of the Ely diocese and the air was redolent with the cloying scent of lilies. 'That'll be quite a job clearing up that lot,' the cheery churchwarden told me. 'There's a wedding coming up so we'll be getting in some fresh blooms.' They do like their flowers in Northwold.

Methwold, the next of these border villages, is quite a bit bigger, almost a small town, and has a church with a steeple that can be seen from afar. Head west from here to Methwold Hythe and then climb up the road south towards Feltwell and you really get off the beaten track with vast views west across the Methwold Dens and south to the giant satellite-tracking 'golf-ball' radomes at RAF Feltwell.

Crown Inn Northwold ☎ 01366 727317. A local pub serving home-cooked food lunchtimes and evenings. Closed Tue.

⑥ Wayland Wood

Just east of the workaday market town of Watton, Wayland Wood is where the nursery tale of *Babes in the Wood* has its origins, based upon a 16th-century legend in which a pair of orphaned children were taken to the wood to be killed by two men in the pay of a wicked uncle who lived at Griston Hall. With a twinge of conscience, one of the hired men decided to kill his accomplice instead and, instead of killing them, left the children to their fate in the wood. The legend has it that the two children, brother and sister, perished and that they still haunt the wood to this day. Fortunately, the printed version, first published as the ballad *The Norfolk Tragedy* by Thomas Millington in Norwich in 1595, has an altogether happier ending in which the siblings find their way home. The village signs of both Watton and nearby Griston contain representations of the 'babes'.

The wood's name seemingly refers to the 'Babes in the Wood' legend, as Wayland is most likely a corruption of 'wailing'. However, rather than the ghostly moans of abandoned children, you are far more likely be soothed by the contented buzzing of bees and chirruping of birds. Wayland Wood is in the hands of the Norfolk Wildlife Trust these days and is a gorgeous place in late spring when the bird cherry is in bloom and the ground is carpeted with bluebells and early purple orchids. This is a real live chunk of rare ancient woodland and the spirit of the wildwood looms large here. Wayland Wood has probably stood since the last ice age; it's a dappled, mysterious place but, unlike some woods that have a slightly dark and foreboding atmosphere, this one feels light and benevolent. Nevertheless, there used to be a large oak tree here, struck by lightning in 1879, that was rumoured to have been the place where the abandoned children died. The wood is far from completely wild but has been carefully managed since time immemorial to yield hazel rods by coppicing. Indeed, it is the long-term practice of coppicing that has enabled such wonderful ground flora to thrive.

As well as Griston Hall, where the wicked uncle is said to have resided, the nearby village of **Griston** is home to Wayland Prison, a category-C establishment that has included Jeffrey Archer and Reggie Kray among its inmates.

Watton's best known sight is probably its 17th-century clock tower, which was put up in 1679 to house a fire warning bell (there had been a serious fire here a few years earlier). There's a market here on Wednesdays that has been taking place in the same spot since the 13th century.

⑦ Thetford

Raced past by motorists on their way up the A11 to Norwich and the coast, and frequently dismissed as a 'London overspill town', Thetford tends to get overlooked. Like King's Lynn and Great Yarmouth, it can seem a bit run down compared with the rest of the county and, true, it does have some large and unlovely housing and industrial estates that were built for an influx of workers from the south in the 1960s. This is just part of the picture though. Thetford was hugely important before the Norman invasion and even held the bishopric of East Anglia before Norwich did. In historical terms, Norwich is still the young pretender. Ignore the lacklustre outskirts and head straight to the centre and you will find some lovely medieval architecture and absorbing history.

Some history

As a strategic crossing point where the Icknield Way crosses the Little Ouse River, Thetford takes its name from the Anglo-Saxon *Theod* ford – people's ford. Whether or not it was the royal seat of Boudica, the Iceni queen, is highly uncertain but it was certainly an important centre during the late Iron Age and early Roman period. In Anglo-Saxon times, when it was sacked on several occasions by invading Danes, Thetford became the home of the East Anglian monarchs and seat of a bishopric. A more peaceful Dane, Canute, made the town his capital too in 1015, half a century before the Norman Conquest, when Bishop Herbert de Losinga's building of a cathedral in Norwich brought about a slight downsizing of what had become the sixth largest city in England. Despite the religious focus being transferred to Norwich, a Cluniac priory was established here in the 12th century that lasted until the Reformation.

Like much of Breckland, Thetford saw a decline in its fortunes in the medieval period when the bulk of the wool trade shifted to north Norfolk where there was better land and closer ports. The town came back into favour in the 1960s when an influx of people from London moved here to work in the newly opened factories. These days, Thetford has a surprisingly large Portuguese population, estimated to constitute around 30% of the town's total. There has been a slow trickle of foreign workers here since the late 1990s when Portuguese migrants started to come to the town to take up low-paid jobs in the agricultural sector. An unpleasant incident occurred in 2004 following the England versus Portugal football match in which England were defeated. Between 100 and 200 drunken England fans rioted and hurled missiles at the town's Portuguese-run Red Lion pub trapping terrified Portugal supporters inside. Generally though, relations are far more cordial and many Portuguese have chosen to settle here long-term, hence the number of Portuguese-language signs on shops, cafés and even hairdressers. It is a similar situation in King's Lynn, Great Yarmouth and, to a lesser extent, East Dereham. Polish is another language you will hear widely spoken around town and keen linguists might detect Russian, Lithuanian and Spanish too.

The bus station is right in the centre next to the Little Ouse River. It's reached by way of the same narrow medieval street that has the Thetford Grammar School, and I am always impressed how bus drivers manage to negotiate the tight bus station exit on leaving without scratching their paintwork. Beyond the lacklustre shopping precinct just across the river from the bus station, the town centre has a good assortment of medieval and Georgian buildings in timber and flint. The best of these is the **Ancient House**, now the Museum of Thetford Life (01842 752599), in White Hart Street, a 15th-century timber-framed building that is also the base for the town's **tourist information centre**. As well as exhibitions on Thomas Paine and Maharajah Duleep Singh, the museum has 4th-century gold and silver jewellery from the so-called Thetford Treasure hoard discovered in 1979: an object lesson to those who think that putting in long hours with a metal detector is inevitably a waste of time.

The stonework of the town's Norman **castle** is long gone but the motte remains to provide a satisfying mound to climb up and get a view over the town. There is rather more to see at the site of the **Cluniac priory** west of the centre by the river. This was founded in 1103–4 by Richard Bigod to become one of the largest and richest priories in East Anglia. The priory was torn down after the Dissolution but there are still some impressive flinty remains and even bits of original tile flooring in places. The towering remains of the arch of the massive Presbytery window are particularly striking.

Nearby, **Thetford Grammar School** dates back to Saxon times, was re-founded in 1566 and is still active today. Its most famous ex-pupil is **Thomas Paine** (1732–1809) – who had the distinction of being involved in both the French Revolution (where he only escaped execution by a whisker) and the American War of Independence; he was one of the original signatories to the Declaration of Independence and invented the term 'United States of America'. Born in the town, he attended the school between 1744 and 1749 before going on to be apprenticed to his father as a corset maker. The part of the school that Paine would have attended serves as the school library today and, although you cannot enter, you can get a look at this through its wrought-iron gate on Bridge Street.

Paine's gilt **statue** by Sir Charles Wheeler, President of the Royal Academy, stands outside the King's House, with the radical thinker clutching a copy of his revolutionary book *Rights of Man* upside down. Why he holds the book upside down is open to some speculation, although it is generally believed that Wheeler did this deliberately as a means of stimulating debate. The statue was erected by an American benefactor, Joseph Lewis, who was shocked to discover that the birthplace of one of the great supporters of American independence did not have a monument to his memory. Naturally, there was some controversy regarding the erection of the statue as Paine was a freethinker and deeply republican. To their credit though, most natives of Thetford have since taken Paine to their hearts and seem happy to celebrate their connection with this extraordinary man. The statue, which may not be to everyone's taste, stands on a plinth that bears the legend: *World Citizen – Englishman by Birth, French Citizen by Decree, American by Adoption.* Tourist Information at the Ancient House can give details of a **Tom Paine Trail** through the town and the occasional guided tours.

Thomas Paine: Corset maker and revolutionary

'My country is the world, my religion is to do good.'
Rights of Man

Chad Goodwin of the Thomas Paine Society, a font of knowledge regarding all things relating to the man, gave a number of walking tours of Paine's Thetford during the bicentennial celebrations of summer 2009. Standing by the statue in front of the Town Council building, he filled us in on some of the detail of his early life before we moved around the corner to White Hart Street where the Ancient House is. 'This used to be the main London to Norwich road and anyone and everyone who came through Thetford would pass this way. Thetford assizes used to be held here each year and this was the next best thing to a public holiday, with all sorts of entertainment going on and, naturally, public hangings. They used to hang somebody for simply stealing a sheep in those days and it was probably partly from seeing the goings on here that Paine started to develop his social conscience and sense of injustice. Thetford was a classic rotten borough and I am sure that later on when Paine wrote about the corruption of the political class he was probably thinking of Thetford. Reading between the lines, I get the impression that he couldn't wait to leave.'

We walked uphill to the Thomas Paine Hotel, where a plaque commemorates Paine. 'This used to be a private residence known as Grey Gables. There are those who think that it is where Paine was born but there's nothing certain about this. It could have been here, or perhaps it was a place called the Wilderness next to St Andrew's church. Unfortunately, there is no record of his birth at all.' Paine spent just a fraction of his early life in Thetford, and returned to the town only on rare occasions to see his mother once he had left it to live in the south of England. 'It's worth noting that Paine left Thetford with its River Ouse, Cluniac monastery and round-tower church to go and settle in Lewes in Sussex, which coincidentally also has a River Ouse, a Cluniac monastery and a round-tower church. You could say this was just coincidence but Paine must have felt quite at home there.'

After receiving an invitation from Benjamin Franklin, Paine crossed the sea to America but he was rarely still for long, frequently flitting across the Channel to France and even crossing the Atlantic a total of five times in his lifetime. He died and was buried at New Rochelle in New York State in 1809. One of his former adversaries, William Cobbett, who had been gradually converted, partially at least, to Paine's cause, turned up ten years later to dig up his bones and bring them back to Britain for a heroic burial that never happened. 'Cobbett carried the bones around with him when he was fighting a by-election at Coventry. This may not have been considered all that bizarre in those days, but it was certainly quite unusual.' By all accounts, Cobbett kept Paine's mortal remains in a box underneath his bed but following his death they disappeared completely, never to be found again.

Tom Paine aside, Thetford has some other interesting associations. Much of the TV series *Dad's Army* was recorded in and around the town, and a Dad's Army tourist trail highlights spots that became the fictitious Sussex town of Walmington-on-Sea. Plans are afoot from the Thetford Society to place a bronze statue of Captain Mainwaring (the Arthur Lowe character) close to the statue of Thomas Paine, in what would indeed be a strange juxtaposition: one wonders what the two characters would have made of each other.

Maharajah Duleep Singh, the former squire of the nearby Elveden Estate (see page 188), has a very fine equestrian statue set among the shady willows of **Butten Island** in the midst of the Little Ouse River. This is a popular pilgrimage place for Sikhs from all over Britain and beyond and you may well find yourself becoming involved in a friendly photo session here.

A Little Ouse walk

Outside the town, some good **walks** are to be had around Thetford. The most obvious route is along the **Little Ouse Path** that links Thetford with Brandon, most of which follows an old towpath. It's about ten miles of easy walking in total and if you are up to this you could walk all the way then catch a bus or train back from Brandon. A slightly shorter, circular option is to walk west and north along the Little Ouse from Thetford, past a tempting picnic spot at Abbey Heath Weir, and through waterside woodland as far as a large factory. Soon after a footbridge over the river you can zigzag south through forest until you reach a waymarked path to the left that should lead you back to the river and a footbridge at Abbey Heath Weir from where you can retrace your steps to Thetford.

Bell Hotel King St ☎ 01842 754 455 ⏚ www.bellhotel-thetford.com. This 15th-century inn, right in the heart of town, was where the *Dad's Army* cast and crew used to stay. The hotel tends to make the most of this association as well as its reputation for being haunted but serves decent enough pub food and Greene King ales.

Tall Orders King St ☎ 01842 766435. Just up from the Bell Hotel along the pedestrianised King Street, this handy café has both indoor seating and tables on the street.

⑧ Brandon

Just over the border into Suffolk, and west of Thetford on the southern bank of the Little Ouse, is Brandon. If the presence of nearby Grimes Graves is not enough to attest that the town was once central to an important **flint industry**, then just take a look at the buildings. The flint trade was big business as far back as the Neolithic period and returned to prominence with the invention of the musket and the need for gun flints. It is interesting to reflect that, given the area's USAF and RAF bases, the war industry has long played a part in the region.

Brandon's flintknappers had their work cut out back in Napoleonic times when the town grew quite prosperous through supplying the essential parts for the British Army's muzzle-loaders. Virtually all the shots fired at Waterloo would have involved Brandon flint to spark them off. The invention of the percussion cap saw the demise of this trade but, according to John Seymour, flintknappers were still active in the town in the 1960s, when he witnessed men in leather aprons chipping away in the back yard of the Flintknappers Arms pub – where else indeed? You can get a good idea of the town's flintknapping past by visiting the **Brandon Heritage Centre** (07882 891022) on George Street.

The Little Ouse River used to be of far more importance here back in the days when Brandon served as the port for nearby Thetford. These days, forestry rules supreme and it is articulated lorries and the A11, not boats and water, that are the means of distribution for Brandon's produce.

Thetford's brews

Not to be outdone by the **Iceni Brewery** (01842 878922; www.icenibrewery.co.uk; tours available by appointment) just up the road at Ickburgh, there's a brewery in Brandon too – **The Brandon Brewery** (01842 878496; www.brandonbrewery.co.uk) – where you can sample the produce and get a tour if you phone in advance. The brewery is doing its bit for the environment in providing a herd of Breckland highland cattle with spent malted barley for an occasional special treat. Apparently the cattle, which it would seem are far more conservation-conscious grazers than sheep, are very fond of the grain – who can blame them? – and can always be tempted back from wild, overgrown areas with generous helpings of the stuff.

Brandon Country Park, a mile or so south of the town, has forest walks, a tree and history trail, an orienteering course and a visitor centre (01842 810185). About the same distance to the east, along the B1107 to Thetford, is the **Thetford Forest and High Lodge Forest Centre** (01842 815434; www.forestry.gov.uk), which offers free entrance to cyclists and walkers arriving without a car. Four waymarked walks of varying length explore the forest area from the visitor centre, and the four cycling routes include a family route as well as more challenging mountain-bike rides. Cycle hire is available from Bike Art (01842 810090). The centre also organises special summer events such as dusk nightjar rambles and moth expeditions.

⑨ Weeting

Weeting is a village just north of Brandon back over the Norfolk border. A NWT **nature reserve** here, just west of the village, is home to a summer population of **stone curlews**, which might be described as the signature bird of the Brecks – a stocky wader that doesn't wade, with thick strong legs and a large, yellow gimlet eye. It looks the kind of exotic thing that you might expect to come across on parched African plains and, indeed, the Senegal thicknee is a very close relation. The Brecks are, after all, the closest thing we have to African savannah, and birds like stone curlews just emphasise this exoticism. The NWT reserve has a visitor centre and hides with wheelchair access open between April and September, the breeding season of the stone curlew. You might also see woodlarks here, another Breckland speciality, as well as wheatears, hobbies and plenty of butterflies. Interestingly rabbits, often vilified for the damage they do to crops, are here actually encouraged to keep the heathland habitat in check and accordingly are fenced in. The prisoners seem content enough – more *Watership Down* than *Colditz*.

The village itself has a round-tower church, **St Mary's**, and a ruined **Norman castle**. It is also home to what is considered to be the longest terrace of **thatched-roof cottages** in England – I counted eight chimney pots in total. Unfortunately, many of the roofs were damaged in a fire in 2007 but they seem to have been neatly repaired to their former reedy glory now. The castle, owned by English Heritage, is not, in fact, a castle at all but a 12th-century fortified **manor house** with a 14th-century moat. On one corner of the moat stands a domed ice-house, previously used to store ice broken from the frozen moat in winter.

⑩ Grime's Graves

Grime's Graves (01842 810656; www.english-heritage.org.uk) lies a little to the east, just off the Mundford road. If the Peddars Way can be described as being a Roman period M1, then Grime's Graves might be seen as being the equivalent of a Neolithic Sheffield. The 'graves' referred to are actually mine shafts and they belong not to Grime but to Grim, a pagan god. Anglo-Saxons probably knew the site as 'the Devil's holes' because any earlier human working of the landscape was usually viewed to be the work of dark forces.

The product here was that Neolithic equivalent of steel – **flint** – the hard, sharp-edge fracturing stone that litters the fields around here. The site consists of a large complex of flint mineshafts that were worked for at least a millennium from around 3000BC – and probably for much longer, as flint was always inexpensive by comparison with metal. Even after hand axes had long disappeared from the craftsman's and farmer's toolkit, they were still in demand for building and later for the firing mechanism for muskets (see page 184).

The complex is certainly impressive on the ground but aerial photographs give an even more compelling view of this dimpled landscape of over 400 filled-in shafts covering an area of 37 hectares. Thirty or so pits have been excavated to date and you can actually go down one of them, the only place in the country where you can do this. By descending the ladder and peering into the extremely low-roofed galleries you really get a feel for what life must have been like working on the Neolithic flint-face. Bear in mind that Neolithic miners had only red-deer antlers available for picks. Excavation has revealed that, for each pit examined to date, an average of 142 antler picks has been found. Interestingly, about 10% of these were left-handed. A herd of at least a hundred red deer would have been necessary to provide an adequate supply of antlers for excavation.

Duke of Wellington Thetford Rd, Brandon ✆ 01842 810219
🖰 www.thedukebrandon.co.uk. Nothing fancy, just a beer garden, bar snacks and three real ales. Karaoke optional.

⑪ The Breckland heaths

Just north of Thetford is the vast expanse of heathland occupied by the **Stanford Military Training Area** marked on OS maps somewhat alarmingly as 'Danger Area'. For obvious reasons, you are not allowed to go here, although limited access is permitted for walkers passing through on the Peddars Way that runs across its eastern edge. It is a shame in a way because, apart from the odd tank and artillery unit, this is mostly unspoiled heathland with all its usual attendant wildlife. Naturally, the very fact that the public are not permitted to trample across the area means that it is pretty good for wildlife anyway, at least those species that are able to tolerate the odd exploding shell and spurt of mortar fire.

In my capacity as a surveyor of historic farm buildings 20 years or so ago, I did manage to visit the area once with a military escort. There used to be a number of farms dotting the area and we were interested in taking a look. Unfortunately, the army had used most of the buildings for target practice and so there wasn't very much to see, but it was good at least to witness what a wild and unspoiled area this was. The area continues to be used for military training of all sorts and in recent years a facsimile Afghan village has been constructed for training purposes. This comes complete with flat-roofed adobe houses, a mosque and a street market. The roles of Afghan villagers, friend and foe alike, are played by injured Gurkhas. How much useful preparation this gives for subsequent operations in Helmand Province is uncertain. As civilians, we will never get to know just how authentic this faux Afghan enclave is but it's certainly a surreal notion to think that the equivalent of a Taliban theme park lies hidden out here in the Brecks.

With all this talk of where you *cannot* go, it is important to identify where you can. A couple of places on the fringes of the battle area give an authentic flavour of true Breckland heath. **East Wretham Heath**, off the A1075 and belonging to the Norfolk Wildlife Trust (NWT), has old pine woodland and grass heathland on what used to be an airfield. It also has a couple of meres (small lakes) that fluctuate depending on groundwater levels and recent rainfall. **Brettenham Heath**, nearby, has acid heath but no public access although you can view it from the Peddars Way. Of more interest to most and a great place for walking is **Thompson Common** on the eastern fringe of the battle area.

This NWT wetland area is best known for its three hundred or so pingo ponds that were created during the last glacial period. The pingos, which provide habitat for rare water plants, dragonflies and damselflies (and mosquitoes!), were formed here around 10,000 years ago. At least, that is the theory: I know of one geologist who maintains that they are more probably the result of ordinance testing on the battle area. For walkers, the **Great Eastern Pingo Trail** is a circular track that follows part of the Peddars Way and runs for around eight miles taking in both Thompson and Stow Bedon commons and heathland at Great Hockham and Breckles. Access to the trail is from a car park on the A1075 Watton to Great Hockham road. There's a shorter alternative route too that cuts through woodland at Stow Heath and a short 'access for all' trail from the car park. The Peddars Way stretch of the trail goes right past **Thompson Water**, a shallow manmade lake created by damming the River Wissey in the 19th century, which is an excellent place to see grebes and reed warblers in summer and wildfowl in winter. As it's the only sizeable piece of water for miles around, even ospreys sometimes turn up here on passage.

Chequers Inn Griston Rd, Thompson ☏ 01953 483360
🖥 www.thompsonchequers.co.uk. This 17th-century thatched inn opposite the village cricket pitch has seen service as a manor court, doctor's surgery and meeting room in the past. Today it's a village pub convenient for the Great Eastern Pingo Trail. There's decent pub grub too and a reasonable range of real ales.

⑫ Lakenheath Fen RSPB Reserve

This recently created RSPB Reserve (01842 863400; www.rspb.org.uk) lies nearby, between Lakenheath and Hockwold cum Wilton and accessible from a railway station on the Norwich to Cambridge line. The reserve has a wonderful array of birdlife that includes honey buzzard, hobbies, bittern and that most exotic of birds, the golden oriole. Cranes have bred here recently too – the first time in 400 years in the region – and it's also a good place to see cuckoos, which are commonly heard but generally hard to see. The reserve, created from 740 acres of carrot field just over a decade ago, has reverted into a typical fen landscape of reed beds and grazing marshes. There's a visitor centre and toilet facilities, and a number of guided walks and child-friendly events are put on throughout the year.

A number of **trains** on the Norwich–Cambridge line stop here at Lakenheath station at weekends, one each way on Saturdays, three each way on Sundays. It's a request stop so you'll need to tell the conductor in advance and flag down the appropriate approaching train when leaving. A footpath links the station with the RSPB visitor centre and there's a convenient cycle link to the Hereward Way. Getting here in the week without a car is more problematic as the nearest working station is Brandon nearly five miles away. The on-demand Brecks Bus (01842 816170) can be used to reach the reserve from Brandon or Thetford but you need to book it the day before.

Speaking of **golden orioles**, I recall that it used to be possible to see these gorgeous, rather exotic birds swooping across the Cambridge train line somewhere in this vicinity. This was back in the days when they bred in the poplar plantations that lined the tracks. I never did see them from the train but I did once travel to the plantation with birder friends, where we were charmed by the birds' fluting calls and astonished to discover that a brilliant yellow-and-black colour scheme is actually good camouflage for the dappled light of poplars. The trees eventually disappeared as they ended up – quite literally – as matchwood. It's good to know that the birds are back.

Lakenheath itself is dominated by RAF Lakenheath, the home of the largest US Air Force fighter base in Britain. The village that gives the base its name has the medieval church of St Mary's, which has wall paintings of St Edmund and, like Mildenhall, still bears scars from the Civil War with its vandalised corbel angels. Life was evidently tough for angels in the mid 17th century in northwest Suffolk.

⑬ Elveden

Situated astride a busy road just beyond the Little Ouse in Suffolk, to most people this is little more than a sign on the A11 and an inconvenient bottleneck for traffic. It used to be an accident black spot too before traffic-calming measures were introduced. Some will tell you that there have been more people killed on the A11 since World War II than there are names on the obelisk-like war memorial south of the village.

Elveden is a small estate village centred upon Elveden Hall, a somewhat bizarre private residence. The estate (www.elveden.com), which has the largest arable farm in the country, is in the possession of the Earl of Iveagh but the hall itself was emptied of its contents in 1984 and stands empty.

Elveden Hall is best known as the home of **Maharajah Duleep Singh**, a deposed Sikh prince from the Punjab who was exiled to England for his part in the Sikh Wars during Queen Victoria's reign. The Maharajah purchased the estate in 1863 and refurbished the Georgian hall in lavish Moghul style using Italian craftsmen – a North Indian tradition apparently. He also built an aviary where he kept exotic birds and in an unselfconscious effort to outdo the English squirearchy he took up the habits of English country life with a passion, leading parties that shot thousands of pheasants on his estate on an almost daily basis. Naturally, if you have a 17,000-acre estate and a vast private fortune, you can do that sort of thing without worrying too much about the cost of it all. The Maharajah was always keen to impress the inhabitants of his adopted home and tended not to do things by halves. He was even good enough to hand over the Koh-i-Noor diamond to Queen Victoria and to cheerfully convert to the Anglican Church such was his willingness to fit in. An equestrian statue of the Maharajah stands in Thetford and, although he died in Paris in 1893, his surprisingly modest grave lies in the churchyard of Elveden's St Andrew and St Patrick church.

Elveden Hall passed into the hands of the Guinness family after Duleep Singh's death and the first Earl of Iveagh went even further, building a new wing and adding a replica Taj Mahal to the complex. If the hall sounds as if it would make a perfect **film set** then you are quite right as, since its interior was emptied in 1984, Elveden Hall has been used as a location for films such as *Tomb Raider*, the Bond movie *The Living Daylights* and Stanley Kubrick's *Eyes Wide Shut*. The bad news is that the hall is not open to the public. You might try getting a job as a film extra here, as a friend of mine did on *Eyes Wide Shut*. He reports that he didn't see much of the interior but did learn that Tom Cruise was unable to find any suitable accommodation in the area and had to be helicoptered in each day from afar for filming. You can just about get a glimpse of the hall from the rear of the village churchyard and make out its green dome.

St Andrew and St Patrick's Church

A bit of a Victorian-Edwardian Gothic extravaganza this one; with a double apse, a long cloister that connects a priest door to the bell tower and some lovely modern stained glass windows that include a memorial window to Maharajah Duleep Singh. He transformed the original Victorian church of St Andrew on taking over the estate, ploughing money into it for its beautification. When the estate passed into the hands of the Guinness family, the first Earl Iveagh built an entirely new church alongside that effectively created a south aisle. Naturally, in the turn-of-the-century world of the landed gentry, church attendance was compulsory for all estate workers, even non-conformists (the Guinness family did not employ Catholics). The church is kept firmly locked against vandals these days but appointments to look inside can be made by phoning Mr and Mrs Ede at 01842 890607.

Alfresco Courtyard Elveden Estate ☎ 01842 898068 🖰 www.elveden.com. An outdoor café and restaurant (with seats inside for less clement weather) set in a stable courtyard surrounded by estate shops. Snacks, light bites and main courses using meat from the estate. The estate shop has a delicatessen that sells estate game and venison and over 20 varieties of British cheese.

⑭ Mildenhall

I have passed through this town numerous times on the coach trip between Norwich and London. To be honest, it always felt like a bit of an unnecessary detour. Mildenhall has long been an air-force service town – a large RAF airbase just up the road is used by the US Air Force – and the town seems resolutely focused on performing this function. Historically though, Mildenhall was important as a market town long before man took to the skies, and it was also the place where a large Roman hoard – the Mildenhall Treasure, now kept in the British Museum in London – was discovered in 1945.

Connoisseurs of medieval church architecture will want to check out **St Mary's Church**, which has one of the largest porches in Suffolk and a splendid hammerbeam roof of carved angels – some of them plucking lutes – that are said to be riddled with shot left by trigger-happy puritans during the Reformation.

Bury St Edmunds and around

⑮ Bury St Edmunds

One of several jewels in Suffolk's crown and, according to the 19th-century writer William Cobbett, 'the nicest little town in the world', Bury St Edmunds has received much admiration over the years for its special character and, as well as Cobbett, has been lauded by other literary luminaries such as Charles Dickens and Daniel Defoe. Even the name, Bury St Edmunds, has a timeless, quintessentially English appeal that something more humdrum like Ipswich struggles to achieve. Much of the town's history is encapsulated in its very name: St Edmund, that sainted hero of the Anglo-Saxons, was, in fact, buried here and his subsequent canonisation brought almost cult-like status... and pilgrims. Bury St Edmunds is a place of great historical interest, of course, but its one-time draw as a medieval pilgrimage centre is just part of the picture.

A wolf, a corpse, pilgrims and witches

Edmund came to East Anglia from Germany in the mid 9th century to become the King of East Anglia, the last Saxon king before Danish and Norman rule. The Danes, always keen to have things their own way, tortured and killed Edmund in 870 because of his refusal to disavow Christianity. The story goes that his head went missing after his death until it was discovered 40 days later lying between the protective paws of a wolf (a wolf is represented on the town crest in remembrance of this). Once his head had been seamlessly reunited with its body, Edmund's corpse was buried at a place called Haegelisdun – possibly modern-day Hoxne – but was dug up 30 years later to be taken to the monastery of Beodricsworth, which later became known as St Edmundsbury in his honour.

In 1032, the monastery was granted abbey status by the Christian Dane, King

Bury remains affluent and well-to-do today and, even without its St Edmund connections, the town has an undeniable appeal with its unhurried, old-fashioned pace and rich array of Georgian and Victorian architecture. It is quite a mysterious place too, filled with architectural nooks and crannies and occasional murky historical cul-de-sacs.

If you arrive by car and park at the old cattle market, the first thing you'll come to is the spanking new shopping centre, The Arc, opened in 2009, which has a futuristic Debenhams store that looks a little like a cut-price version of Birmingham's silver-buttoned Selfridge's. It is a bold design that may not be to everyone's taste but keep going past the glitzy new shops and you'll soon arrive at the **Butter Market** and neoclassical **Corn Hall**. The rectangular square around the Corn Hall is filled with traders and shoppers on Wednesday and Saturday market days and is the best place in town to buy fresh fruit and vegetables. Beyond this along Abbeygate Street lie the Abbey Gardens and Cathedral on Angel Hill. The helpful **tourist office** opposite the gardens next to the Scandinavia Café can help with recommendations and orientation.

St Edmund's Abbey is little more than an appealing ruin these days, having been destroyed at the time of the Dissolution, but the pleasant **Abbey Gardens**, created in 1831 with flowerbeds and ornamental trees, provide a restful space to wander in and contemplate the time when the site may have been the East Anglian equivalent of Glastonbury. The ornamental beds are lovingly tended and are some of the most colourful plantings I have ever seen – even on a cloudy day you might require a pair of sunglasses. The River Lark flows through the gardens – a river

Canute, and St Edmundsbury Abbey became an important place of pilgrimage following Edmund's canonisation. St Edmund was the patron saint of England for many years but somewhere along the line he was replaced by St George, a historical figure who, if truth be told, may be little more than a myth and has more connections with Turkey and Palestine than with England.

The Normans enlarged the abbey church and the surrounding town, Bury St Edmunds, developed around it to become a prosperous trade and weaving centre. In the 17th century, the town found fame as a centre for its witch trials, in particular that of the year 1645, in which the self-proclaimed Witchfinder General, Matthew Hopkins, saw to it that 18 people were executed in a single day. Bury's prosperity continued through to the 18th century, although the town failed to be caught up in the industrial revolution in the same way that Ipswich did in the Victorian age.

as picturesque as its name suggests. A momentous historical event took place at the abbey here in 1214 on St Edmund's feast day when a gathering of barons and the Archbishop of Canterbury swore on St Edmund's shrine that they would force wayward King John to accept the Charter of Liberties, a document that led the way to the creation of the Magna Carta. **St Edmundsbury Cathedral**, with its intricate, angel-bedecked hammerbeam roof, started life in the 15th century as the Church of St James and was only granted cathedral status in 1914 – to form one of a trio of cathedrals in East Anglia alongside Norwich and Ely. In keeping with the myth of the protective wolf, the Bishop's throne has details of wolves guarding St Edmund. The cathedral was extended in the 1960s and commemorated with a fanfare specially composed by Benjamin Britten. A Gothic-style tower was added as part of a millennium project and opened to great fanfare in 2005.

St Mary's, the sister parish church just to the south, with another hammerbeam roof, poppy-head pews and 11 pairs of flying angels, is even finer according to the discerning eye of Simon Jenkins, who describes St Mary's as being 'left like Cinderella up the road, rather forlorn'. The church's stained glass is probably its most immediately striking feature, especially the west window, which is the largest in any English parish church and was paid for by local landowners in thanks for a bumper harvest in 1854. The chancel arch has a window in the form of a pilgrim's badge that shows Edmund being killed with arrows.

Modern-day, secular Bury St Edmunds owes as much to brewing as to anything else and the **Greene King Brewery** has stood in the town since 1799. There's a museum and a shop on site, and brewery tours can be arranged (01284 714 297). The brewery is also the landlord of what claims to be Britain's smallest pub, **The Nutshell**, just off the market place on The Traverse close to the Victorian Corn Hall. There's a dessicated cat hanging from the ceiling here that was found bricked up behind a wall during building repairs. It's a black cat but certainly not a very lucky one. I will admit to initially being sceptical about the pub's claim to be the smallest in the country. I remember The Vine in Norwich also being rather 'bijou' (as an estate agent might put it) but The Vine, a tiny Thai restaurant these days, is a veritable coaching inn in comparison with the Nutshell. The Greene King Brewery, which did admirably to maintain its real ale business through the lean times of the 1970s, has grown in recent years to become the largest British-owned brewery in the country. However it has its critics for its active acquisition policy of taking over smaller breweries and their pub estates, ironically resulting in less choice of real ales for the consumer.

If small breweries are your preference then you might be better off seeking out Greene King's only local competitor, **The Old Cannon Brewery**, opened only about ten years ago, which has a range of its own ales like Gunners Daughter. The Victorian building that houses the brewery-pub was the home of an earlier Canon Brewery that closed during World War I.

Returning from thoughts of beer to architecture once more, the **Moyse's Hall Museum** (01284 757160) at the top of Butter Market is widely believed to be one of the oldest stone-built domestic buildings in the country. Built sometime around the end of the 12th century, it is something of a mystery why it was constructed of imported flint and limestone rather than the cheaper and far more readily available wood normally used. It was probably done as a show of wealth, and quite a lavish one when you think that materials had to be brought from quarries far away. It's a museum today, with interesting Bronze Age, Anglo-Saxon and Roman exhibits, but has served as a prison, a police station and a workhouse in the past.

The town has a fair number of literary connections. I have already mentioned William Cobbett but **Daniel Defoe** was another visitor, who stayed here at the Cupola House, a former 17th-century inn on The Traverse. **Charles Dickens**, too, spent time at the ivy-covered Angel Hotel and even gave it a mention in *Pickwick Papers*. This Georgian landmark has had more recent celebrities staying there too, most notably Angelina Jolie, who used the hotel as her base whilst filming *Tomb Raider*.

Another well-known Bury St Edmunds landmark that is considerably less refined (although you cannot say the same thing about its product) is the BSC **sugar beet factory** on the A14. This is the biggest of its type in the country and in season – around mid-winter – is the destination for hundreds of clanking lorries delivering beet from the frozen fields of west Suffolk and beyond. Sugar beet is hardly the most beautiful of crops and neither is the machinery of its processing. So, if you detect a slightly cloying smell in the air during your visit then this is its source (if you can detect hops or malt then that is the Greene King Brewery, of course). In fairness, the factory, which has its own power station on site supplying local homes, is a town icon in its own way, a reminder that for all its quaint museum-piece qualities and rarefied medieval atmosphere, this is a major market town in agribusiness country.

Angel Hotel 3 Angel Hill ☎ 01284 714000 🖰 www.theangel.co.uk. The recently revamped bar and restaurant at this Bury institution serves food created from local ingredients that include venison from the Elveden estate. Very reasonable prices considering the quality.

Barwells 39 Abbeygate St ☎ 01284 754084 🖰 www.barwellsfood.com. Apart from the market, another good option for food shopping: a long-standing, family-run food and wine shop that has a tantalising selection of pies, meats, game and gourmet products to choose from. All produce is free range and sourced from farms that meet strict criteria of animal husbandry and natural diets.

Harriet's Tearoom 57 Cornhill ℂ 01284 756256. A good choice for afternoon tea, with old-fashioned service and surroundings.

The Nutshell 17 The Traverse ℂ 01284 764867. You may well be tempted to have a drink in what the Guinness Book of Records claims to be the smallest pub in Britain. There's a choice of Green King ales of course, but no food – it's far too small to have a dining area or even much elbow space.

ⓢ Old Cannon Brewery 86 Cannon St ℂ 01284 768769. A Victorian brewhouse-pub with excellent beer and modern pub food, a five-minute walk from the centre.

⑯ Ickworth House

Amidst sugar beet fields a few miles outside Bury in the village of Horringer, Ickworth House (01284 735 270) is an extraordinary rotunda of a house that is now in the ownership of the National Trust. It was built at the beginning of the 19th century by the fourth Earl of Bristol and Bishop of Derry as a storehouse for his art collection; but some of the intended works of art never arrived because they were taken by Napoleon. Notwithstanding this setback, a collection was amassed that includes Gainsborough, Titian and Hogarth paintings as well as a vast array of Regency furniture. The surrounding park, open throughout the year, was landscaped by Capability Brown, and there is also an Italian-style garden.

ⓢ Beehive The Street, Horringer IP29 5SN ℂ 01284 735260. This modernised yet higgledy-piggledy pub of low beams and flagstone floors is in the village of Horringer, close to Ickworth House, three miles southwest of Bury St Edmunds. There's a beehive out front just in case you were in any doubt. The Beehive has Greene King ales on hand pump and daily specials on offer that might include cured meats, homemade pork, apple and leek sausages or braised oxtail. It is always buzzing at weekends, so it's best to book.

⑰ West Stow Anglo-Saxon Village

Excavations here in the 1960s revealed the remains of the buildings from an Anglo-Saxon settlement as well as a cemetery with over one hundred graves. A

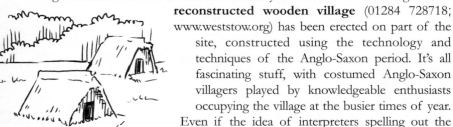

reconstructed wooden village (01284 728718; www.weststow.org) has been erected on part of the site, constructed using the technology and techniques of the Anglo-Saxon period. It's all fascinating stuff, with costumed Anglo-Saxon villagers played by knowledgeable enthusiasts occupying the village at the busier times of year. Even if the idea of interpreters spelling out the history for you is anathema, it is undeniably a great hands-on way for children to learn about the past. Numerous special re-enactment activities in summer are mostly geared towards children, along with demonstrations for all ages of Anglo-Saxon pursuits like fletching and flintknapping.

West Stow Country Park beyond the car park, visitor centre and village, with its mixture of heath and woodland, is a good place for a picnic or a walk along the River Lark.

⑱ Pakenham

Just four miles northeast of Bury, Pakenham glows with pride in being the last parish in England to have a windmill and a watermill both working. The 2003 village sign will remind you of this just in case you weren't aware. There's even a book, *Pakenham – Village of Two Mills* by N R Whitwell, which you can read in full on the village website (www.pakenham-village.co.uk) if your eyes are up to it. The **windmill**, which is black-tarred and dates from 1830, was still in use up to the 1950s. It underwent full refurbishment of its sails in 2000 but, although the sails still turn, it no longer grinds. In contrast, the **watermill** (01284 724075 or 01359 232025; www.pakenhamwatermill.co.uk), a gleaming white building built in 1814, is still fully functional; it's open for visitors at weekend and bank holiday afternoons, and on Thursdays, between Easter and the end of September. The watermill holds milling demonstrations on the first Thursday of the month and you can buy stone-ground wholemeal flower from the mill shop and numerous farmers' markets and food halls in the area. There's also a tearoom.

The village, which has plenty of pretty thatch, also has an unusual cruciform church and the Fox Inn (01359 230347) in the main street if you find yourself in need of sustenance.

⨯⨯⨯⨯

The Six Bells Inn The Green, Bardwell IP31 1AW ☎ 01359 250820
🖥 www.sixbellsbardwell.co.uk. A former *Dad's Army* haunt, this 16th-century country inn in Bardwell village, just north of the A143 Bury to Diss road, featured in the television series and there's a photograph of the cast in the bar. Closed at lunchtimes.

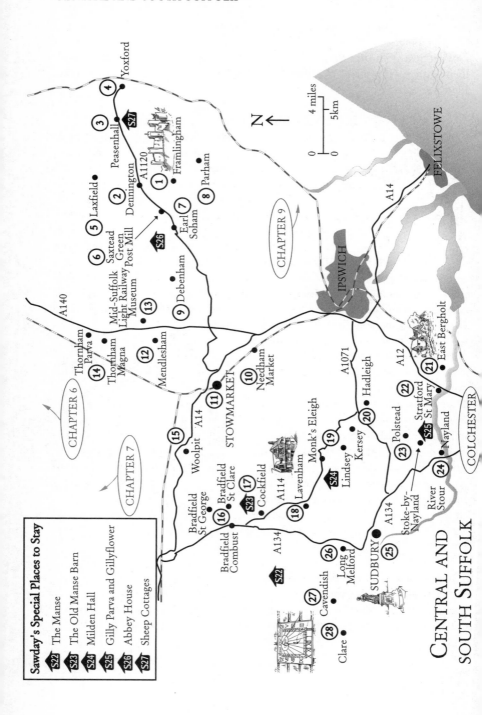

N ←

0 — 4 miles
0 — 5km

Yoxford

④ ⑤ Yoxford

③ S27 Peasenhall

② Laxfield ⑤ Dennington

A1120 Framlingham ①

⑦ Parham ⑧

Saxtead Green Post Mill S26

Mid-Suffolk Light Railway Museum ⑥ Earl Soham

Debenham ⑨ ⑬

A140 ⑬

CHAPTER 9

IPSWICH

A14

FELIXSTOWE

Thornham Parva ⑭
Thornham Magna

Mendlesham ⑫

CHAPTER 6

CHAPTER 7

A14 Woolpit ⑮

STOWMARKET ⑪

Needham Market ⑩

A1071 Hadleigh

A12

East Bergholt

S25 ㉑

㉒ Stratford St Mary

Monk's Eleigh

Bradfield St George ⑯
Bradfield St Clare ⑰
S23 Cockfield

Lavenham S24 ⑲ Lindsey Kersey ⑳ Polstead
Stoke-by-Nayland ㉓
Nayland ㉔

River Stour

COLCHESTER

Bradfield Combust

A134 ㉖ Long Melford

SUDBURY ㉕

S22 ㉗ Cavendish

㉘ Clare

Sawday's Special Places to Stay

S22 The Manse
S23 The Old Manse Barn
S24 Milden Hall
S25 Gilly Parva and Gillyflower
S26 Abbey House
S27 Sheep Cottages

CENTRAL AND SOUTH SUFFOLK

8. Central and south Suffolk

This chapter combines the 'High Suffolk' plateau that rises south of the Waveney Valley with the Suffolk side of the Stour Valley (from East Bergholt and the Stour estuary in the east as far as Clare in the west) that stretches along the Suffolk–Essex border to the south. Let's not get too carried away with the words 'high' or 'plateau' though – as you might expect for East Anglia, it's pretty modest stuff.

'High Suffolk' may be overstating it a bit but compared with the rest of the county it is just that: a rolling plateau of arable farmland interspersed with villages and small market towns. A hundred years ago, this area was almost entirely devoted to agriculture and most of the land is still used for arable crops, although these days most local inhabitants are involved in pursuits other than farming. Despite the vast seas of golden wheat that turn some of these settlements into virtual islands in August, farming involves a very small workforce these days: agriculture may well be big business, but is no longer a big employer. Nevertheless, the towns and villages of this area retain plenty of connections with the soil, as do the people, and although village daily life may no longer revolve around the changing seasons, it still takes notice of them.

In the south of the county, the Stour Valley is still very much a rural idyll, as the Stour babbles its way through fields of contented cattle and past improbably perfect-looking villages. A chocolate-box scene as painted by John Constable – and it was… many times over. It is not so much that Constable was a great painter – although he undoubtedly was – but *what* he painted. Though the heathy character of Constable's Suffolk has disappeared, the subject matter of many of his works is still easily identifiable almost two centuries later. This gives all of us a warm, fuzzy sense of continuity and tradition, and delights even those who do not normally have much time for paintings. Most of all, it somehow encapsulates the essence of rural England. The irony is that many who live here among the Stour Valley's timber-framed splendours are also those that have the most tenuous connections to the area – a classic incomers versus disgruntled locals dilemma. London and the Home Counties are sometimes just a little too close for comfort and the goose that laid the golden egg is in danger of being flattened beneath the wheels of a commuting 4x4. In the old days, geese would walk all the way to London from the area. There again, it was always just a one-way trip.

Getting around

It's easy enough in a car. The main roads are the A12 and A14, both of which lead roughly north to south on either side of Ipswich. The A1120 is the major east-to-west route through central Suffolk and road-signs identify this as a tourist route as it passes close to bone fide tourist draws like the British Bird of Prey Centre at Stonham Aspel, Saxtead Green Post Mill and Framlingham Castle.

Public transport

Central Suffolk tends to be best connected by public transport with Ipswich, the county's largest town, which isn't particularly central itself. The market towns of Stowmarket, Halesworth and Sudbury are minor transport hubs and have reasonable **bus** links with outlying villages, although many routes require going in and out of Ipswich. Suffolk County Council produces booklets of bus timetables centred on towns like Saxmundham and Debenham that helpfully combine all the various routes in each locality and come in useful for planning. These are widely available in shops, pubs and tourist centres and can also be downloaded from the website: www.suffolkonboard.com.

The East Suffolk **train** line, connecting Lowestoft with Ipswich, has stops at Halesworth, Darsham, Saxmundham and Wickham Market along the way. For the Stour Valley, the most useful stop is at Manningtree, which although lying just within Essex is close to East Bergholt, Flatford Mill and the long-distance Stour Valley Path. Manningtree lies on the main Norwich–Ipswich–London line and usually has trains every hour during the day. As always, www.travelineeastanglia.org.uk is a useful resource for journey planning for both buses and trains.

Cycling

Cycling is good in parts, especially away from the A1120. The A12 and A14 are to be avoided for obvious reasons. **National Cycle Route 1** and North Sea Cycle Route (www.sustrans.org) pass right through the locale from Hadleigh in the Stour Valley via Ipswich and Woodbridge through Framlingham and Halesworth to Beccles in the Waveney Valley, while National Cycle Route 51 crosses the county from Ipswich to Bury St Edmunds. The 75-mile circular **Heart of Suffolk Cycle Route** loops through Debenham, Framlingham, Halesworth and the Waveney Valley. In the Stour Valley is part of the **National Byway** (www.nationalbyway.org), still in development in the region, running from Sudbury along the river west. Another option is the 70-mile **Painters' Trail** (www.dedhamvalestourvalley.org), which tours Constable Country in Dedham Vale. A reasonable number of connected bridleways can be used for off-road cycling too.

Escorted tours of the area are offered by Suffolk Cycling Adventures at Benhall near Saxmundham (01728 602338 evenings; www.suffolk cyclingadventures.co.uk) who have itineraries both in central Suffolk and the

Suffolk coast. **Cycle hire** is available at Alton Reservoir, Stutton, near Ipswich (01473 328873), Bicycle Doctor and Hire Service in Ipswich (01473 259853) and Byways Bicycles at Darsham near Saxmundham (01728 668764). Cycle4hire.com (01379 678711; www.cycle4hire.com), based in Eye, can deliver hire bicycles to holiday accommodation in the central Suffolk area.

Walking

Pick your way around carefully and you'll find some worthwhile walking, especially along river banks. The **Gipping Valley River Path** follows the route of the old canal towpath between Stowmarket and Ipswich. The Dedham Vale AONB and Stour Valley Project (www.dedhamvalestourvalley.org) gives a good selection of suggestions for walks in the Stour Valley area and has free downloadable guides on its website. One long-distance footpath passes through the area: the 60-mile **Stour Valley Path**, part of the European Path E2, begins at Cattawade near Manningtree in Essex and loosely follows the River Stour valley west through Sudbury to eventually reach Newmarket. John Harris's Walking in Suffolk website (www.walkinginsuffolk.co.uk) features a wealth of links to downloadable maps and walk guides.

The Thornham Estate is large enough for half a day's walking, with a good network of publicly accessible paths.

Tourist information

East Bergholt Flatford, Flatford Lane, East Bergholt ☎ 01206 299460.
Lavenham Lady St, Lavenham ☎ 01787 248207.
Ipswich St Stephen's Church, St Stephens Lane, Ipswich ☎ 01473 258070.
Stowmarket Museum of East Anglian Life ☎ 01449 676800.
Sudbury Town Hall, Market Hill ☎ 01787 881320.
Woodbridge Station Buildings ☎ 01394 382240.
Dedham AONB and Stour Valley Project ⌖ www.dedhamvalestourvalley.org.
Mid Suffolk District Council ⌖ www.midsuffolk.gov.uk.

Framlingham and around

① Framlingham

'Fram', as most people tend to call it, is a lovely little market town that still functions in the way that a market town is supposed to, providing services to the villages that surround it. Voted the most desirable place to live in England a few years back by *Country Life* magazine, you might think that this would be a rather smug place, but not at all. Framlingham really does not need to try too hard and so it doesn't – the town just goes about its business in the knowledge that while life may be pretty good here it is best not to shout about it too much.

What I find most appealing is that, unlike many other places of a similar size, the town still seems to have a strong sense of community. It's old-fashioned in an unselfconscious way and quite remarkably self-contained for a town of only around 3,000 souls. This is mainly the result of its serving a large rural hinterland, and local village folk, when not scurrying off to Ipswich or the new Waitrose at Saxmundham, will probably choose to come here to do their shopping and pay their bills. Despite all of this, it has more of the character of a big village than a small town. Framlingham certainly embodies the spirit of Slow, although I doubt if many town residents have yet heard of the Cittaslow movement.

On top of all those virtues, the town has a couple of splendid sights – a well-preserved castle, the largest in the county, and a beautiful medieval church. Coming along the road from the direction of Dennington, the first thing you will see of the town as you round the bend at Church Farm will be the mock Gothic spires of Framlingham College, a large independent school. Arriving from the opposite direction, from Parham, is a little less auspicious, as you will pass a batch of warehouses and grain silos as you enter the town. Keep going though and you'll soon reach the **market square** with the church and castle positioned above it: on Tuesday market day most of the space is filled by stalls selling meat, bread, fruit and veg, clothes and bric-a-brac. The Crown Hotel dominates the east side of the square and seems so firmly established that you might think that the square grew up around it – it didn't, though. There's a delightfully quirky second-hand bookshop on the south side next door to an Indian restaurant, a café and a deli. The square's west side has the Dancing Goat café. Walk uphill and you'll soon arrive at the church and castle.

St Michael the Archangel

This church contains the **family tombs** of the Howards, Dukes of Norfolk, who used to own the castle. After the Dissolution of Thetford Priory (see page 181), Thomas Howard, the third Duke of Norfolk, rebuilt the chancel here as the new resting place for his family's bones. Thomas Howard was a lucky man as far as timing went. Uncle of both the wives Henry VIII had executed, Anne Boleyn and Catherine Howard, he continually plotted to gain influence through serving up his more desirable female relatives for the king's attention, and was himself eventually condemned to death, but this was commuted to imprisonment when Henry died on the day before the sentence was due to be carried out. His tomb, the most impressive of the group here, dates from 1554, the year before his son upped sticks and moved in with his new wife's family at Arundel in Sussex. Two kneeling, praying effigies sporting Elizabethan ruffs and neat beards guard the tomb on one side – these are his sons – while his daughters pray together above his head. Henry Fitzroy, a bastard son of Henry VIII, who died aged just 17, has a tomb with a frieze of reliefs from Genesis that was probably once part of Thetford Priory. Another tomb in black marble flanked by angels honours Robert Hitchham, the man who bought the manors of Framlingham and Saxtead from Theophilus, the second Duke of Norfolk, and constructed the poorhouse in Framlingham Castle.

There's more to St Michael's than just tombs, spectacular though they may be. Jean Coles, a Fram resident who used sometimes to work as a guide in the church, drew my attention towards some of its other treasures. 'When I used to show visitors around I would always show them the tombs first because they are my favourites too. But then I would point them towards *The Glory* – it's a real focal point for the church.' *The Glory* is, in fact, a painting that sits in the reredos above the high altar: a bright, mysterious work that has concentric rings of light glowing mystically from its centre, rather like the background for one of William Blake's Old Testament pieces. 'It's a bit of a mystery, that picture. No-one knows who painted it, although we think it dates from the 18th century. It has got the letters 'IHS' in the middle of it and I'm told that signifies the name of Jesus.'

The other treasure is the church's **organ**, just one of three built by the craftsman Thomas Thamar that managed to survive the English Civil War – Oliver Cromwell had a bit of a grudge against ornate instruments like this apparently. 'It was originally made in 1674 for Pembroke College, Cambridge,' Jean told me. 'But they gave it to the church in 1708 when they wanted to get something a bit more up to date for their chapel at the college. The case is even older, from 1630 or even earlier, and that actually has the arms of Pembroke College on it. We get organists coming from all over the country to play it – they really love its sound. They have to book it well in advance, of course, and they are only allowed half an hour each.' Prospective organists might be humbled by knowing who has sat on the bench before them: Felix Mendelssohn is believed to have given lessons on this very same organ on his regular visits from London.

Framlingham Castle

Owned by English Heritage, Framlingham Castle lies just beyond the church on top of the hill, a domineering presence with a dozen hollow towers, a deep dry moat and sturdy, well-

preserved battlements. It's a very special place for a walk around the walls, taking in the views of the village and the mere. Although fortifications existed here in Saxon times, the present castle dates from the 12th century, the work of Roger Bigod, the second Earl of Norfolk. Generations of Howards, whose graves lie in the church, were later incumbents of the castle before their move south to Arundel in 1555. More famously, Mary Tudor mustered her supporters and proclaimed herself Queen while staying here in 1553. Her successor, Elizabeth I, subsequently made use of it as a prison for luckless priests before Pembroke College, Cambridge, took it over and built a poorhouse within its walls that remained in use until 1839. It now serves as a visitor centre and has a display that tells of the various struggles in the castle's history.

The castle has seen varied use in recent years, and periodically hosts summer music festivals like Folk at Fram and Jazz at Fram. For children there's a specially devised audio tour and a set of giant games. William A Dutt writes of rather more vigorous activity taking place within its walls back in 1744, when John Slack the Norfolk champion pugilist fought the Suffolk champion John Smith and won. John Slack went on to meet John James in Broughton, London – they all seem to be called 'John' – and defeated the London champion in less than four minutes.

Just beneath the castle is **Framlingham Mere**, a 33-acre lake that used to be much deeper than it is today and is currently leased to Suffolk Wildlife Trust as a nature reserve for birds and water plants. Looking at the rather puny River Ore that flows into the lake, it seems hard to believe that this same river once brought ships from the coast. The Caen and Northamptonshire stone used for constructing the castle would have come by this route.

A stroll from Framlingham

A short, two-mile **circular walk** begins near the castle. This is a good way to see the castle from a variety of different viewpoints and it also gives a flavour of the surrounding countryside. You follow the path down to the mere from the Castle Inn and enter the Suffolk Wildlife Trust reserve then follow the circular nature trail as far as the footbridge over the River Ore. Leave the trail here and cross the river and follow the left bank to a second footbridge before turning right onto New Road. After about 500 yards, the road turns right at Great Lodge Farm; continue another 200 yards until you reach a footpath to the right. Follow this south along a field edge until you reach another footpath branching left. Take this path, crossing another footbridge, until you reach the B1120 Badingham road, where you turn right and follow Castle Street back to the start.

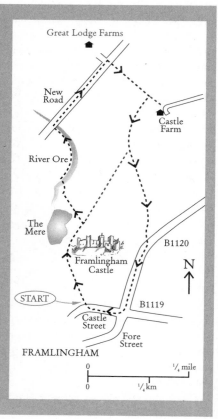

Just outside the town along the Badingham road is the **Shawsgate Vineyard** (01728 723232; www.shawsgate.co.uk), which produces dry and medium sweet whites along with two reds. They also have some small-batch vintage wines and at the time of writing were working on a sparkling product. There's a shop, and Wednesday 90-minute evening tours of the vineyard and production facilities can be pre-booked between May and mid-September by telephoning 01728 724060. You can do a self-guided tour too – the shop will provide a vineyard map and information sheet. Experience Days give tours and tasting on most Saturdays and some Fridays between May and August.

Of the few cafés around the market square, the **Dancing Goat** (☎ 01728 621434) is as convenient as any, with good coffee and some sunny outdoor tables.

Crown Hotel Market Sq ☎ 01728 723521 🖥 www.framlinghamcrown.co.uk. This long-established hotel on the market square has a lunch and evening menu that often features local produce like Blythburgh pork and Southwold fish.

⑤ Station Hotel Station Rd ☎ 01728 723455 🖥 www.thestationhotel.net. There's no longer a station here, nor a functioning 'hotel', but this shabby-chic establishment has been running as a pub since the 1950s. The Station serves imaginative food with a Mediterranean twist in a comfortable, homely setting and makes full use of locally sourced ingredients. There's a good selection of wines to choose from as well as tasty ales from the nearby Earl Soham brewery.

② Dennington

Dennington, on the A1120 north of Framlingham, has all the essential ingredients: a good pub, an interesting parish church and a post office. In fact, the village has what is possibly the oldest post office in the country, which is no mean feat considering the widespread closures of country post offices over the last decade or two. It may be just coincidence but neighbouring Framlingham is also supposed to have two of the country's oldest pillar-boxes, making this area a veritable Shangri-La for postal history anoraks. Most come to see the parish church though, or to have Sunday lunch in the pub.

The church of **St Mary the Virgin** is highly rated by those who make it their business to comment on such matters. It stands out from the crowd thanks to two unique features: a wooden pyx canopy over the altar, and the representation of a sciapod carved onto one of the bench-ends. A sciapod is a mythological desert creature that uses its one enormous foot to shade itself from the sun, an appendage that no doubt comes in useful for leaping too. Mentioned by Pliny in his writings, this is the sole English representation of this curious creature. Other bench-ends represent creatures that are altogether more commonplace, although not in Suffolk – pelicans, tortoises, lions and even a giraffe with a twisted neck. The pyx, which is one of only four in England, is rather like a hanging spire and was used for storing the sacrament back in Catholic times. There are also some rather beautiful, and somewhat spooky, tombs belonging to the Bardolph family, delicately carved from ghostly alabaster and beautifully preserved.

③ Peasenhall

This village lies further east along the A1120, a little beyond Badingham. The dead-straight stretch of road offers some lovely views southeast over the wheat fields towards the coast and even without consulting the map you can sense that this was once a Roman route. Peasenhall is a pretty village with a good smattering of Suffolk pink wash and neat thatched roofs. The village derives its name from 'Pisenhalla' meaning 'a valley where peas grow'. On the back of this somewhat tenuous connection, the village has instigated its very own Pea Festival. The second Peasenhall Pea Festival took place in July 2009 and included such leguminous events as The World Pea Podding Championships, the East Anglian Pea Throwing Championships and the Great Pea Draw. No doubt, it is an admirably green event – you certainly get the impression that it does not take itself too seriously and that proceedings are pea- rather than po-faced.

There's no longer a pub in the village, but **Weavers** is a good tearoom and **Emmett's of Peasenhall** (☎ 01728 660250 🖰 www.emmettsham.co.uk), an old-fashioned food store and smokehouse, is highly regarded for its sweet-cured hams and bacon made from free-range Suffolk pork. The shop also has a small café with a real Italian espresso machine.

⑤ Sibton White Horse Halesworth Rd, Sibton IP17 2JJ ☎ 01728 660337 🖰 www.sibtonwhitehorseinn.co.uk. A traditional village pub, just a mile from Peasenhall, that serves local, seasonal food, excellent real ales and a broad selection of wines.
Weavers Tea Room 2 The Knoll ☎ 01728 660548. A popular and cosy village café that can provide cream teas and good-value three-course lunches.

④ Yoxford

Continuing east along the A1120 from Peasenhall, you pass through Sibton, virtually next door, before arriving at Yoxford. The village hugs the road as far as the junction with the A12 but it is still a rather quiet place nevertheless. With an eclectic mix of building styles that blend attractively, the village has the face of something of an artistic centre, with a number of art shops and galleries alongside a couple of antique businesses. There's a small arts festival held here in August – the box office is the village's Griffin pub.

Holding a strategic location at the junction of two main roads, Yoxford was an important coach stop on the London-to-Yarmouth run in the days before steam power. You can see clear evidence of this at the church where a tall iron signpost points in three directions: Framlingham (10 miles), Yarmouth (30), London (93). The signpost stands tall for a reason – for coachmen to read from their high perch. When the railways came to the area in the 19th century, the village was promoted as a tourist attraction for well-to-do urbanites. 'Yoxford: The Garden of Suffolk' became the catchword, referring to the village's location between three country estates. This 'garden' label was hyped by newspaper journalists and also by some interested parties in the village wishing to cash in on the act. William A Dutt, writing in 1901, was clearly not impressed: 'It may be that injudicious advertisement has had something to do with the district's flattering designation, and that if we had never heard of "Poppyland", Yoxford would have remained unknown and its mediocre charms unproclaimed.' This seems a little harsh, as it is quite a handsome village, with some lovely parkland close to hand.

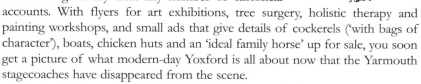

Looking at adverts in the window of Horne's store on the main road probably tells you more about life in the village today than any number of historical accounts. With flyers for art exhibitions, tree surgery, holistic therapy and painting workshops, and small ads that give details of cockerels ('with bags of character'), boats, chicken huts and an 'ideal family horse' up for sale, you soon get a picture of what modern-day Yoxford is all about now that the Yarmouth stagecoaches have disappeared from the scene.

The Cockfield estate lies just behind the village – the former family home of the Blois family who give their name to one of the village pubs. **Cockfield Hall** served as a high-class prison for Lady Catherine Grey, sister of Lady Jane Grey, in 1567 but she died soon after arrival and was buried in her own private chapel in the village's St Peter's Church. The hall, an impressive 16th-century brick building, has a rooftop forest of tall chimneys and crow-step gables. It is visible from the A12 but you can get a much closer look by following the footpath through the gatehouse that lies just beyond Horne's store opposite the church. Follow the footpath for a short while through a dark wood with ancient yews and, after a small footbridge, the wood opens onto open parkland and a clear view of the hall with its large complex of stables and coach-houses all bearing similar architectural detail.

On my last visit, the gatehouse was covered in scaffolding and builders were hard at work at the hall. 'They sold it off a couple of years ago,' a worker told me. 'I think the plan is to do it up and then put it up for hire.' He pointed out the fancy brickwork on the façade behind Horne's. 'That bit's not actually part of the estate. I think it was just added in the same style as the rest of the buildings so that wedding parties would be impressed when they arrived at the entrance to the hall.'

⑤ Laxfield

Laxfield is a couple of miles north of Dennington on the Stradbroke to Haesworth road. Its 16th-century timbered **Guildhall**, across the road from All Saints' Church, has a small museum devoted to local history. This is the village that William 'Smasher' Dowsing, the puritan iconoclast, hailed from. Dowsing's handiwork extended through much of Suffolk, such was his distaste for religious ornament and what he considered 'superstitious pictures'. There's still a Dowsing Farm in the parish. Religious fervour seems to be a tradition in Laxfield, as a century before Dowsing's church-smashing antics, a village man named John Noyes was burned at the stake here for his opposition to the Catholic faith, a brave if foolhardy stance to have during the reign of ex-Framlingham Castle resident, Queen 'Bloody' Mary. In fairness to the villagers, Noyes neighbours all dowsed their fires on the day in protest… well, all but one.

S9 The King's Head Gorams Mill Lane ☎ 01986 798395 ☝ www.laxfield-kingshead.co.uk. Known to all and sundry – well locals at least – as 'The Low House', this is an authentic old-school Suffolk country pub with low ceilings, settles, tiny rooms and narrow passageways. There's no bar as such, just a tap room that serves Adnams ales straight from the barrel. A blackboard menu flags up tasty, rustic, homemade dishes and in summer you might find performing Morris dancers or a horse and trap parked outside.

⑥ Saxtead Green Post Mill

Back on the A1120 and a little way west, Saxtead Green, 2½ miles northwest of Framlingham, has a working **post mill** owned by English Heritage (01728 685789). This is a fine example of the type of Suffolk mill in which the whole body revolves on its base. It dates from 1796 but was completely rebuilt in 1854 following wind damage, then resurrected yet again between 1957 and 1960. The Saxtead Green post mill also appears on the sign of the 17th-century Greene King pub, The Old Mill House (01728 685064) just east of the mill. Another post mill survives in the village of Framsden, further west along the A1120 and south at the B1077.

If you look in the porch of the 15th-century towerless All Saints' Church in Saxtead village you'll see a set of stocks and a whipping post. The stocks bear the none-too-gentle warning to 'Fear God and Honour the King', which is hardly what one might call a progressive attitude.

⑦ Earl Soham

Earl Soham lies a mile or two further west, at a point where the A1120 once again regresses to its original Roman form of an unstinting straight line. It's a sprawling, laid-back place with nice old cottages set back from the road. The village is home to the **Earl Soham Brewery** (01728 684097; www.earlsohambrewery.co.uk), which started life in an old chicken shed at the village's Victoria pub but now brews in an old forge building opposite the village green. The brewery produces a cross-section of ales that give fellow producers Adnams and Greene King a run for their money and range from Victoria, a light 'session beer', to Jolabrug, a stronger, Christmas-only 'Yule Brew'.

S♥ Victoria The Street ☎ 01728 685758. Close to the Earl Soham Brewery, this whitewashed local on the village green serves up hearty pub food and its very own excellent ESB Victoria Ale.

The real-life Akenfield

Back in 1969, author Ronald Blythe published *Akenfield: Portrait of an English Village*, a classic account of Suffolk country life. The book was an evocative portrait of a rural community told through the eyes of its members, and described a farming economy that had not long made the transition from horses to tractors. *Akenfield* was an immediate best seller that single-handedly took responsibility for disabusing city dwellers of some of the romantic notions they might have held about country life. *Akenfield* told it as it was: funny in parts but also gritty and unflinching, it spoke of almost unimaginable poverty and the hardship of rural working-class life from the Victorian era up until the 1930s.

There is no such real place as Akenfield, of course, but it isn't too difficult to deduce that the name is an amalgam of two Suffolk villages – Akenham, just north of Ipswich, and Charsfield close to Wickham Market. Indeed, Charsfield was where Ronald Blyth had carried out a series of interviews with locals in the summer and autumn of 1967 prior to writing his book. He spoke to young and old alike, documenting both the frustrations of youth and the bittersweet memories of senior villagers who were still able to remember events that seemed to belong to another age – picking stones by hand from fields and sewing children into their winter underwear.

The book was turned into a film in 1974. Rather than use professional actors, authentic Suffolk villagers were used instead, a move that angered Equity, the actors' union. The Equity problem was circumvented by doing away with a formal script and having the characters improvising all of their dialogue based upon Blythe's 20-page 'transcript'. It was a neat solution – using locals rather than trained actors ensured authenticity. Ronald Blythe, a lay preacher in real life, played the village vicar. The film was shot over the period of a year in order to reflect the changing seasons, and at weekends only, so that village actors could attend to their usual professions during the week. Once again, the village of Charsfield had a part to play and this was one of several villages in the Wickham Market area, south of the River Deben, that was used as a filming location. Hoo, Debach, Monewden, Dallinghoo, Letheringham and Pettistree were the others. Like the book before it, the film was also highly acclaimed for its rural realism, and it was watched by 13 million viewers on its first television showing – quite an achievement for a film with no cast, no stars and no formal script.

⑧ Parham

Head south along the B1116 from Framlingham and you soon arrive in **Parham**, a village that gave its name to a World War II US Air Force bomber airbase located between the village and its neighbour, Great Glemham. The airfield has the **Parham Airfield Museum** (01728 621373; www.parham airfieldmuseum.co.uk) that stands as a tribute to the 390th Bomb Group that was based here. Between 1943 and 1945, over three hundred bombing missions were flown from the base using B-17 'Flying Fortresses', and the bandleader Glenn Miller performed in a hangar here in 1944. The museum has fairly limited opening hours – mostly Wednesdays and Sundays in summer – so check first if you want to visit. Currently there are proposals for a wind farm on the airfield – Suffolk's first onshore wind farm – with plans for six turbines. Not surprisingly, this is stirring something of a local storm.

A wonderful late-15th-century timber-framed fortified manor house lies close to the village: **Moat Hall** is now part of a farm but used to be the residence of the Uffords, the former earls of Suffolk, and later the Lords Willoughby. You can walk up here along a footpath from the village church of St Mary the Virgin and enjoy some sweeping views along the way.

West of Earl Soham to Stowmarket

Continue west along the A1120 from Earl Soham and you'll soon arrive at Peats Corner, a junction where the B1077 leads south to Framsden, with a recently reconstructed post mill, and past Helmingham Park to Otley, where you'll see a splendid 15th-century moated manor house, rather like the one at Parham. **Otley Hall** (01473 890264; www.otleyhall.co.uk) is open for pre-booked group visits and for individuals as part of the Invitation to View scheme (www.invitationto view.co.uk), with about seven dates available each year. The 10-acre gardens at the hall, which contain historically accurate recreations that include an orchard, herber, knot garden and nuttery, are worth a look in their own right and are open to the public every Wednesday afternoon during the summer months. The extensive gardens at **Helmingham Hall** (www.helmingham.com) are also open to the public in summer and the 400-acre park has herds of both red and fallow deer.

⑨ Debenham

Debenham comes as a surprise from whatever direction you approach. It stands amidst an enormous prairie of golden wheat that seems to stretch almost as far as the horizon – quite a contrast to the softer, wooded parkland further to the east around Yoxford. It's a peach of a village with something of the Lavenham about it, although far less of the touristiness. Its buildings range from magpie-timbered Tudor to Suffolk pink to solid Georgian brick, while the High Street has some charming gardens open to the street, where roses and hollyhocks reach for the sky in a clash of pinks. Scattered among some pricey-looking Tudor

properties are a handful of old-fashioned shops that seem little changed from the 1950s, as well as a clutch of antique shops, galleries and gift shops. The Red Lion on the High Street is a 15th-century jettied building that once served as a guildhall; although it still has its sign, it no longer functions as an inn. Elsewhere, the most substantial medieval buildings on the High Street are The Old House at number 23, which incorporates both of its former neighbours 21 and 25, and number 37, a 16th-century jettied building.

The River Deben rises nearby to give Debenham its name and, known as The Butts, runs as a prolonged ford through the village with the claim that it is the longest of its kind in Britain. The extensive tracts of arable land that surround the town are a relatively new thing: historical accounts suggest that most of the surrounding land was pasture in the 18th century but hedges were enthusiastically grubbed up and trees felled later in that century to make way for cereals. Now the heavy, but highly fertile, clay soils produce exceptionally high yields of wheat and barley. If anywhere in the region deserves the epithet 'Suffolk's bread basket', it is probably here.

The Cyder House at Aspall Hall just north of Debenham (www.aspall.co.uk) has been producing its own Aspall apple juice, cyder and organic cyder vinegar since 1728 so the Chevallier family who have run the place for eight generations should know a thing or two about what to do with apples. Aspall cyder is made only from freshly pressed apples and the notion of stretching fermentations by eking them out with concentrates is anathema. A surprising variety of apple types are used for cyder making: dessert apples such as Cox or Blenheim Orange for sweetness, cookers like Bramley for aroma and acidity, and a mixture of bittersweet apples that might include varieties like Médaille d'Or and Kingston Black to provide perfume, depth and body. So why 'cyder' and not 'cider', you might ask? Why a 'y', not an 'i'? Well, an earlier member of the Chevallier dynasty, John Barrington ('JB') Chevallier (1857–1940), was the first to spell it this way in the 1920s as he considered it indicative of the style he was producing at the time. In respect to their forbear, this distinctive spelling has been adhered to ever since.

It's not all about alcohol – there's organic vinegar and apple juice too. Aspall apple juice is cold-pressed from a mash made from pre-blended apples that hail from most of the country's prime apple locations – Cambridgeshire, Kent and the Wye Valley. Cox and Bramley form the base and these are supplemented by varieties such as Egremont Russett, Discovery and Crispin to achieve the right balance of flavour and acidity.

Garden of Deben – Florist and Café 6 High St, Debenham ℂ 01728 860190. A posh florist that doubles as a café serving light lunches, cakes and organic ice cream.
Teapot Pottery and Café Low Rd, Debenham ℂ 01728 860475. There's a small, cosy tearoom ensconced within this ceramic teapot emporium.

⑩ Needham Market

A small town just southeast of Stowmarket, Needham Market's pride and joy is its Church of St John the Baptist which has a quite astonishing double hammerbeam roof that has been described as 'the culminating acheivement of the English carpenter'; certainly Pevsner waxed lyrical about it in his *Buildings of England: Suffolk*, saying 'the eye scarcely believes what it sees, and has a hard if worthwhile job in working out how this unique effect could be attained'.

Wool combing became big business here in the 15th and 16th centuries until the arrival of the plague in the 1660s. Chains were fixed at either end of the village to prevent the disease spreading to other communities – a noble gesture that wiped out two-thirds of the town's population. Chainhouse Road in the town commemorates this event, as does another road known as The Causeway, a more palatable variant of 'the corpseway' that was used to move plague victims out of town for burial at the church in nearby Barking.

Meanwhile the River Gipping, which flows to the east, makes a rewarding strolling ground. The river was navigable in the medieval period and was used to bring stone for the building of the abbey at Bury St Edmunds. Then in the late 18th century, the river was canalised and a series of 15 locks were set up between Needham Market and Ipswich so that barges could navigate between Stowmarket and the coast. The towpath of what became known as The Stowmarket Navigation is still in place today and you can walk all the way to Ipswich from here, or even better, from Stowmarket. The **Gipping Valley River Path** is a 17-mile walk if done in its entirety from Stowmarket railway station to Ipswich docks, an interesting and peaceful route past locks and old watermills. It's a long way but the beauty of it is that both ends can be easily reached by train. Indeed, the Norwich–Ipswich–London railway line runs parallel to the canal for much of the way.

A **farmers' market** takes place in Needham Market between 9.00 and 13.00 on the third Saturday of each month.

⑪ Stowmarket

Central Suffolk's largest settlement, in truth Stowmarket is little more than a pleasant market town (with a market on Thursday and Saturday), but what is really special here is the **Museum of East Anglian Life** (014449 612229; www.eastanglianlife.org.uk), on a 75-acre site close to the town centre. The museum, or MEAL as it likes to call itself, wonderfully encapsulates all things rural East Anglia, with a range of reconstructed old buildings giving a historic perspective on traditional East Anglian life. These include windpumps and watermills. You'll see displays of local trades and crafts like brewing and rope-making as well as agricultural machinery and a collection of rare-breed animals such as Red Poll cattle and Suffolk Punch horses. MEAL stages special children's activity days in summer that include egg hunts, pond dipping and Victorian days. For adults, an annual CAMRA beer festival takes place in the museum's Abbot's Hall barn each year with a heady choice of East Anglian real ales and ciders. A traditional music day takes place in July, and in past years the museum has also staged a gypsy arts festival with international artists.

North of Stowmarket towards Diss

⑫ Mendlesham

Mendlesham is well known locally for its cloud-scraping TV and radio mast, an ugly beacon for miles around, but there's more to the village than just towering steel. The church of **St Mary** is large for a village of this size and highly unusual in being the last surviving Anglo-Catholic parish church in the county, where Mass is celebrated daily and the biggest event in the religious calendar is the Feast of the Assumption. Not surprisingly, the airy interior is filled with candles, icons, several altars and the persistent whiff of incense. For those with more interest in cudgel-wielding than Catholic ceremony, there's also a fine and fierce woodwose (see page 248) in the northern porch, and a village armoury in the room above it that contains armour dating from between the 15th and 17th centuries that was kept for use by villagers in the event of an insurrection. You're supposed to have an appointment to view the armoury, but you might just get lucky.

In the village itself, by the village sign, a **preaching stone** is said to have been used as a platform by mendicant friars in the 14th century and later by followers of the preacher John Wesley in the 18th. No doubt, it has also been put to use on occasion by the odd reveller delivering an opinionated rant on his or her way home from the village pub.

⑬ The Mid-Suffolk Light Railway Museum

Wetheringsett is Mendlesham's neighbour just across the A140. This is the home of the Mid-Suffolk Light Railway Museum (www.mslr.org.uk), at the village's former Brockford station (there used to be a stop at Mendlesham too). The MSLR, or 'Middy' as it was known, was inaugurated in 1904 and had ten stations along a line that transported passengers between Haughley, north of Stowmarket, and Laxfield. Closure eventually came in 1951, by which time almost all of the passengers were children on their way to and from school. The museum was set up in 1990 and has displays of artefacts, photographs and rolling stock. It's open on Sundays and bank holidays from Easter until the end of September, and also on Wednesdays in August.

⑭ The Thornham Estate and Thornham Parva

A little further north and you reach the villages of **Thornham Magna** and **Thornham Parva** just west of the A140. Thornham Hall sits between the two villages, the original hall having been demolished in the 1950s, and the Thornham Estate offers 12 miles of waymarked walks through parkland, woods and farmland and water meadows known as **Thornham Walks** (01379 788700; www.thornham.org.uk), with maps available for £1 from the information board at the main car park. Thornham Walks also incorporate a Victorian **walled garden** that can be reached by a surfaced path from the car park suitable for wheelchairs and pushchairs.

For those wanting more than informal self-guided strolls, Thornham Walks' staff are able to organise bespoke guided walks and environmental activities for groups and even 'environmental birthday parties'. With so much management work and maintenance needing to be done, volunteers are always welcome. Helen Sibley, one of two staff members who manage access to the walks, told me, 'We rely heavily on volunteer help. We have a regular volunteer day on the last Sunday of every month and every Tuesday, plus we have a team of probationers who work here once every other week and on Sundays. The Walks always require more volunteers and no experience is needed, just enthusiasm.' Helen went on to explain how the Thornham Walks came into being. 'The late Lord Henniker retired from the diplomatic service and became involved with a variety of grant-making trusts, helping people living in deprived areas of London. He and his wife retired to Thornham Magna in the 1970s, where there was a shortage of both local jobs and affordable housing, and together they began a programme of diversification of the Thornham Estate in order to try to alleviate some of these problems. Redundant farm buildings were turned into reasonably priced workshops for small businesses, others into offices and some into houses. The Estate had few rights of way at the time and the Hennikers were determined to open it up to the public. Twelve miles of waymarked walks were created and these became known as Thornham Walks, which are now enjoyed by thousands of visitors each year. Lord Henniker's final project was the derelict Walled Garden. The walls were restored and the garden was planted as a walled orchard with extensive glass houses.' The Walled Garden now serves as a centre for people with disabilities to learn horticultural skills.

Special events take place throughout the year at the Thornham Walks, such as dawn chorus birdsong walks, butterfly walks and fungi forages, also guided walks in the Upper Waveney Valley and Mid Suffolk. Some events, like scarecrow building and pond dipping, are specifically geared towards children's interests.

As its Latin suffix suggests, **Thornham Parva** is the smaller of the twin villages. 'Little thorny village' has very few houses but it does have a remarkable thatched Saxon church, **St Mary's**, which is famous not so much for its tiny size, its thatched roof or circular Saxon window, but for its famous 14th-century retable (altarpiece) – the largest surviving example from the medieval period – which managed to outlive the iconoclast reformers of the 16th century by hiding away, more or less forgotten, in a stable. Lord Henniker of Thornham Hall rediscovered the work in a pile of wood in 1927 and presented it to St Mary's Church where his brother was parson. The altarpiece, now lovingly restored by a Cambridge University team, dates from around 1300 and shows strong

Dominican influence with representations of eight saints witnessing the Crucifixion, one of whom, to give it noteworthy East Anglian context, is local hero St Edmund. The Musée de Cluny in Paris has another piece that would once have belonged alongside this, but the two sections became separated at the time of Henry VIII's Dissolution. The pronounced Dominican style suggests that both pieces originated from Thetford Friary, a 13th-century Dominican stronghold that has since disappeared and now lies under the foundations of Thetford Grammar School (see page 181). Stepping out of the church, you might want to take a look at the churchyard, which holds the grave of Sir Basil Spence, the architect of Coventry Cathedral.

Fleece Inn Front St, Mendlesham ☎01449 766511. A 16th-century beamed pub with floors sloping every which way. Greene King ales and decent pub grub.
Forge Tearooms Thornham Walks ☎01379 783035. Close to the beginning of the walks, near the car park.
Four Horseshoes Wickham Rd, Thornham Magna ☎01379 678777. An attractive thatched building with plenty of exposed woodwork, this dining pub serves traditional English favourites and European dishes along with a decent choice of real ales.
Old Coach House Thormham Estate ☎01379 783373
🖰 www.thornhamcoachhouse.co.uk. In a converted coachhouse on the Thornham Estate, this is open between 10.00 and 15.00, Thu to Sun, for light lunches, coffee and cakes, with roast lunches on Sun.

Between Stowmarket, Bury St Edmunds and Hadleigh

⑮ Woolpit

The name Woolpit is a bit of an odd one, and nothing to do with the wool trade. It first appeared in a document in 1005, long before the wool trade started to flourish in the region. One suggestion is that it may derive from the Old English *wulf pytt* (a pit for trapping wolves).

Woolpit was a place of pilgrimage in the medieval period, with pilgrims coming to pay their respects to the Shrine of Our Lady of Woolpit that was probably housed in what is now the vestry of the village's Church of St Mary – there's still a well called Our Lady's Well in a field just northeast of the church. The early 16th century and the Dissolution brought an end to the pilgrimage trade, so the village shifted its economy to the more prosaic pursuit of manufacturing bricks. Woolpit's first brick kilns and pits were recorded in 1574, and by the 18th century, a large number of villagers were employed in three pits here. This brick industry's unique selling point was that it produced a very distinctive and elegant type of brick known as 'Woolpit white'. Many of the village's buildings are built of these 'whites' but many thousands more – millions probably – left the village to be shipped to provide fancy brickwork elsewhere. The local clay is not exactly white but it is paler than usual, and the subsequent pale brick became highly sought after and widely used locally. It is even rumoured that Woolpit whites were used in the construction of George Washington's first White House. You can browse a permanent display on Woolpit brickmaking in the village's small **Woolpit and District Museum** (01359 240822; www.woolpit.org/museum).

As Hilary Bradt attests (see box below), Woolpit's **Church of St Mary** really is quite exceptional. Its double hammerbeam roof has a whole squadron of angels, and there's also a magnificent Tudor eagle lectern and what writer Simon Jenkins describes as 'a church within a church' – a sumptuous two-storey porch. The spire, with its flying buttresses, is a Victorian replacement.

Swan Inn The Street, Woolpit ☎ 01359 240482 www.woolpitswan.co.uk. A traditional 15th-century coaching inn in the centre of the village that serves local ales and daily specials.

A church walk in central Suffolk

Before settling down to write this guide's companion Slow Devon & Exmoor, *Hilary Bradt spent a considerable amount of time sniffing out Suffolk churches on an epic Land's-End-to-Lowestoft bus journey, together with Janice Booth whose* Green Children of Woolpit *box is on page 215. Here's a brief description of how they spent their day in the Woolpit area.*

'We'd already done a wonderful church walk near Bury. Then it was our last day, with some final churches to visit and footpaths to walk. We'd selected Beyton, Hessett and Woolpit, linked by lanes and paths. All were special: Beyton for its round tower and carved pew-ends, Hessett for its wonderful 14th-century murals showing the seven deadly sins and tradesmen's tools (a warning not to work on Sundays) and Woolpit – wonderful Woolpit – which was so crammed with angels you felt the whole church might take to the wing. We sat on a bench at the village pump and waited for the bus for Stowmarket. The sun was warm, there were no cars, few people and even the pub was sleeping. At that moment, I would have been happy to travel this way for ever, just catching the next bus to wherever I fancied. The feeling didn't last, however. By the time we reached Diss, having stopped to explore Eye, we'd seen the last bus of the day leave for Beccles without us.'

The Green Children of Woolpit

Janice Booth

A wrought-iron sign in Woolpit village centre shows a wolf, a church and two children. The wolf and the church are easy to interpret, but the children are part of a more curious tale.

Sometime in the mid 12th century, so the story goes, harvesters found two frightened children crying in a field: a girl of about ten years old and a boy who was younger. They wore strange clothes, spoke in an unknown language and their skins were green. Although clearly famished, initially they refused all food – until offered some raw beans. They seized on these with great delight and tried to open the stalks, thinking that was where the beans lay. When villagers split the pods and gave them the beans inside, they ate them greedily.

They were taken to the home of the knight Sir Richard de Calne, who cared for them. Gradually their green colour faded. The boy was always sickly and soon died, but the girl survived to normal adulthood and eventually married. When she had learned enough English, she explained their origins: she and her brother had come from a land of perpetual twilight, where the sun never shone and the people (Christians) were green. Far away across a broad river, they could see another land that glowed with light, but their people did not travel there. In one version of the legend, she claims they were swept up by a whirlwind; in another, she and her brother wandered into a cave, mysteriously drawn by the distant sound of bells, when they were tending the family's sheep, and after many days lost in the dark passages they emerged at Woolpit.

The main sources of the legend are Ralph, Abbot of Coggeshall, and William Newburg, both contemporary chroniclers probably born within a decade or so of the alleged event but writing about it some years after. It's not impossible that one copied details from the other. The words they put into the mouth of the girl are improbably complex for a child who knew no English before she was ten; but both claim that the children spoke a strange language, and were green. The colour might perhaps be explained by vividly green clothing – its vegetable dye could have run and stained their skin – and/or the sickly pallor of anaemia. As for the language, could they somehow have come from across the English Channel? Or, language apart, were they linked to the old legend of the Norfolk man who was appointed guardian to his wealthy brother's two children, whom he then tried to murder in order to gain their inheritance? Having failed, he later abandoned them in Wayland Wood (see page 179) near Thetford and they're said to be the original 'Babes in the Wood'. Choose your own theory!

A similar event allegedly occurred seven centuries later, in Spain, but descriptions of it are suspiciously like those of the Woolpit tale.

The legend is well covered on www.anomalyinfo.com, among other websites.

⑯ The Bradfields

Further west and closer to Bury St Edmunds, the Bradfields consist of three pretty villages: **Bradfield St George**, **Bradfield St Clare** and **Bradfield Combust**. All are sprawling parishes with narrow, twisting lanes that lend themselves perfectly to bicycle outings. Bradfield St Clare is another candidate for the actual site of St Edmund's martyrdom, although it is best not to mention this to anyone in Hoxne (see page 151). The parish of Bradfield St George is the setting for *Corduroy* by the Suffolk country writer Adrian Bell (father of journalist Martin Bell) who named it Benfield St George in his semi-fictional account of Suffolk rural life. 'Corduroy' is quite an apt term to describe the gentle green furrows and folds of this landscape in spring.

Bradfield Woods (01449 737996; www.suffolkwildlife.co.uk) nearby, close to Felsham Hall, has been coppiced traditionally since the 13th century. These woods once belonged to the Abbey of St Edmundsbury but these days are managed as a nature reserve by the Suffolk Wildlife Trust. As with most ancient woodland, it is a wonderful refuge for wildlife, with a broad variety of plants, plenty of migrant songbirds like garden warblers and blackcaps, and woodland mammals such as stoats and badgers. Spring is probably the perfect time to visit when the coppiced areas are awash with flowers like early purple orchid and wild garlic, and the newly arrived birds are in full song. The chances of hearing nightingales singing are very good at this time of year even though their numbers have declined in recent years. Three coloured trails lead along the rides – you can pick up a trail guide from the visitor centre or by the notice board.

Fox and Hounds Felsham Rd, Bradfield St George IP30 0AB ☎ 01284 386379. A Victorian pub with a dining area and an above average selection of Suffolk real ales.

⑰ Cockfield

South of the Bradfields, just off the Bury to Sudbury road, Cockfield is a scattered village composed of nine small hamlets widely spread out around the central village of Cockfield with its 14th-century St Peter's Church. Each of the hamlets takes its name from the green that it lies next to – Colchester Green, Buttons Green and so on. One of the hamlets, Parsonage Green, has a literary connection as Robert Louis Stevenson wrote *Treasure Island* whilst staying at Old Rectory here.

As elsewhere in the less populated parts of Norfolk and Suffolk, ghosts of the recent past lurk here in the form of a disused US Air Force airfield from World War II. Lavenham airfield close to Smithwood Green was the base of the 487th Bomb Group from 1944 to 45 and B24 Liberators and B17 Flying Fortresses rumbled out of here on their way to bombing targets in Germany. Part of the airfield taxiway now serves as a public footpath. With scattered greens, moated farmhouses and gently undulating terrain, this is a marvellous area to spend awhile exploring on foot, although Lavenham just down the road to the south might prove to be just too much of a temptation.

Three Horseshoes Stow's Hill, Cockfield IP30 0JB ☎ 01284 828177. A long, thatched 14th-century building with exposed beams and a crown-post roof that is one of the oldest pubs in Suffolk; Mauldons and Greene King ales.

⑱ Lavenham

The cherry liqueur in the Suffolk assortment box, Lavenham is the village that has showed up on a thousand calendars, jigsaws and chocolate boxes. With wobbly timber-framed cottages, flower-bedecked gardens and thatch galore it's even more overwhelmingly gorgeous than the many lovely villages that grace the Stour Valley just south of here. Its beauty makes it almost unreal: the only things that do not seem to be half-timbered are the smart cars lining the cobbles – although you might see the odd Morris Traveller doing its best to complement the vernacular. Like a very rich, celebratory meal, too much exposure might induce a little artery thickening but as a once-in-a-while experience Lavenham is unparalleled – just don't try to build a bungalow here, or open a kebab shop.

Lavenham grew fat and rich on the medieval wool trade and by the early 16th century had become the 14th-wealthiest town in the country, paying more tax than York or Lincoln. Prosperous merchants invested their fortunes in real estate and what would have been considered very desirable properties for the time. Then as now, close-studded timbers spoke of affluence, albeit for rather different reasons; living in a plastered cage of medieval woodwork did not come cheap. A decline in the town's fortunes came with the 16th century, thanks to undercutting by newly arrived Dutch weavers from Colchester, but it was this decline and the transferral of the weaving industry elsewhere that have managed to keep Lavenham so beautifully preserved. If it had had access to the new-fangled waterpower used in the west and northwest of England, or had been near a coalfield, its buildings would very likely never have survived so intact.

With an astonishing total of 361 listed buildings in the village, there is little point in my directing you to more than one or two: you can just potter around the rest at will. Although they've been meticulously restored, it seems remarkable that some of the timber-framed buildings are actually still standing given the eccentric tilt to the horizontal that some of them have. Some of the wobbliest houses, like the almost cartoon-like 'Cordwainers', can be seen at the corner of the High Street and Market Lane.

The all-white and quite spectacular **Guildhall** dominates the market square across from The Angel pub. This was the headquarters of the town's powerful Guild of Corpus Christi, and it's a hugely impressive 16th- and 17th-century building that is whitewashed all over, beams and all. The square itself has some

very fine Georgian houses to complement the Tudor and if you look down the steep street alongside The Angel, you'll see the lush folds of the valleys beyond.

The town's church of **St Peter and St Paul** is, as you might expect, large and exceptionally grand. It was rebuilt in the late 15th century by a consortium of local families, who were no doubt willingly converting their wool-wealth into what might be termed 'medieval fire-insurance' – a generous gift to God to avert any possibility of a fiery afterlife. The flint tower seems enormous, 140 feet high and visible for miles, while the interior is lavish, with a chantry dedicated to St Catherine and St Blaise, who, martyred by being 'combed to death' by the emperor Diocletian, ended up becoming the patron saint of the wool trade.

To keep things real and bring a bit of muddy-booted rusticity into town, a **farmers' market** is held in the village hall on the morning of the fourth Sunday of each month. This has all manner of local products like bread from Sparling and Faiers, pork products from Clavering Pigs and free-range eggs from Manor Farm. Sometimes the falcons, owls and hawks from Lavham Mews Falconry (01787 247215; www.lavhammewsfalconry.com) are on display outside – a rare opportunity to ruffle the feathers of a real-life raptor.

⑤ Angel Hotel Market Place ☎ 01787 247388. A refurbished diner's inn overlooking Lavenham's splendid market place and guildhall with East Anglian ales and a menu that changes daily.

Munnings Tea Room 29 High St ☎ 01787 24953 🖰 www.munningstearoom.com. Smart traditional tearoom serving good sandwiches and full afternoon cream tea.

Tickled Pink Tea Rooms 17 High St ☎ 01787 249517. Said to be haunted, this cosy tearoom in a 16th-century timber-framed cottage serves all manner of snacks, cakes and sandwiches.

⑲ Lindsey and Kersey

Like Worstead in Norfolk, both these modestly sized villages are associated with varieties of cloth. Lindsey gave its name to a coarse cloth of linen and wool known as linsey-woolsey, while Kersey describes a lightweight, coarse broadcloth of the sort used in military uniforms. **Kersey** is often widely regarded as one of the county's prettiest villages, with a lovely assortment of timbered weavers' cottages strung along its high street, a large wool-trade church and a quaint water splash at the bottom of the hill. **Lindsey** is even smaller – a hamlet with a modest rustic church that has no tower. There used to be two pubs in the parish, the White Rose at Rose Green and the Red Rose at Lindsey Tye. The White Rose has since closed and so the Lancastrians have been the victors this local 'war of the roses'. Near Rose Green are some earthworks and, hidden behind a hedge, the 12th-century chapel of St James, now in the care of English Heritage. The chapel was formerly the chantry of Lindsey Castle, of which the aforementioned earthworks are now the only reminder.

North of Lindsey, the village of **Monk's Eleigh** is home to **Suffolk Heritage Orchards** (The Hall, Church Hill ✆ 01449 740478), where George Hodgkinson grows a bewildering number of old varieties of apples, greengages and plums. These include the apple varieties St Edmund's Pippin from Bury St Edmunds and Sturmer Pippin from Sturmer near Haverhill, as well as Coe's Golden Cop, a classic Suffolk plum.

⑤ Bildeston Crown 132 High St, Bildeston IP7 7EB ✆ 01449 740510 ⌐🖯 www.thebildestoncrown.co.uk. This hostelry a few miles north of Lindsey and Kersey dates from 1529 but has had a sympathetic recent makeover that makes the most of the ancient beams, open fires and flagstones. Tasty food includes good sandwiches and an ambitious evening tasting menu; a range of Suffolk real ales are on offer.

⑤ Lindsey Rose Lindsey IP7 6PP ✆ 01449 741424 ⌐🖯 www.redroseinn.co.uk. With open beamed partitions and rich red décor, this 15th-century food-oriented inn has beef cut and cooked to order, beer-battered fish and Colchester oysters amongst its many offerings.

⑤ Swan The Street, Monks Eleigh IP7 7AU ✆ 01449 741391 ⌐🖯 www.monkseleigh.com. With an imaginative menu that will satisfy traditionalists as well as foodies, this bistro-like gastropub has a good range of wines, and Adnams on handpump.

⑳ Hadleigh

This market town has yet more timber-framed wool-trade buildings and is worth a diversion to look at its three-storeyed 15th-century Guildhall that once served as a poorhouse. A pleasant riverside stroll along the River Brett can start from the medieval Toppesfield Bridge, and another pleasant walk leads along a disused railway track that passes through Raydon Great Wood and serves as an alternative detour for National Cycle Route 1.

Boxford's lioness and the Wall of Death

Just west of Hadleigh, the old weaving village of Boxford was once the home of George 'Tornado' Smith, the son of a former landlord of the village's White Hart pub, who is acknowledged as being the first Englishman to perform the gravity-defying 'Wall of Death' on a motorcycle in this country. As well as taking his act to the Essex coastal resorts, he sometimes performed the feat in the pub garden for the amusement of villagers. To spice up his already spectacular act, he also sometimes carried a lioness in his sidecar. The lioness, Briton, who was taken for walks through the streets of Boxford, now lies buried in the pub garden; there's a plaque to her memory.

The Stour Valley – East Bergholt to Sudbury

Working east to west along the Stour Valley, Suffolk's southern border with Essex, I begin with what is one of Suffolk's best-known villages, East Bergholt, before following the valley west through Nayland to Sudbury.

㉑ East Bergholt

Forever famous as John Constable's birthplace, East Bergholt, and Flatford Mill in particular, are major honeypots for visitors to Suffolk. East Bergholt is both a beginning and an end: for walkers, the **Constable County Trail** starts here and passes past Flatford Mill and across the Stour on its way to Dedham in Essex. Flatford village is also the last place along the river's Suffolk bank before it widens to an estuary at Manningtree, although you might argue that the bridge at Cattawade, where the Stour starts to become tidal, has this honour.

East Bergholt is a largish village, just north of the river but close enough to Essex to have a Colchester postcode. Although the village also deserves a place in history for its tradition of Protestant radicalism in the 16th century, it is, of course, the painter John Constable who has really put the place on the map by not only being born here but also immortalising numerous local views in his paintings. You can no longer see the place of his birth – it was demolished years ago and now there is just a plaque where it used to be – but you can see a memorial window to the artist and his wife in the towerless church of **St Mary** (with its an unusual 16th-century wooden bell house) next door. If you venture down the high street towards the Red Lion, you can also see Constable's first studio next to a garage and engineering workshop. The cottage opposite the pub has a sign that says 'Dealer in Hatts' and another that says 'Ye Olde House', just in case you weren't sure. There's a handy bus stop by the pub with services to Colchester, Ipswich, Manningtree and Hadleigh.

Many visitors to East Bergholt head straight to **Flatford** by the river, down a narrow, leafy lane that follows a one-way system, a sensible precaution given the numbers that come here. At the end of the lane are a large car park and a path down to the river where you'll find a small Constable museum, a tearoom and, a little further along, **Flatford Mill** itself and **Willy Lot's cottage**. Both the mill and the cottage are immediately identifiable from the paintings. The best view of the mill is from across the river, so cross over on to the Essex bank and walk a little way along it. You are unlikely to be alone. **Rowing boats** for hire can be found at the bridge alongside, quite likely, aspiring artists with easels doing their own take on the Constable theme. Cud-chewing cows in the fields help complete the bucolic setting.

East Bergholt and John Constable (1776–1837)
Anne Locke

As a schoolboy, Constable would have crossed the Stour and walked through the meadows from East Bergholt to the Grammar School in the Square at Dedham. One of his earliest paintings is of the headmaster, who encouraged his pupil's artistic potential, though it is hard now to imagine that Constable's masterly landscape paintings were once so little appreciated that he sold only twenty in England in his lifetime, and had to wait until the age of 52 to be elected to the Royal Academy.

As a young man he loved to paint the details around his home of Flatford Mill – 'willows, old rotten planks, slimy posts and brickwork' – subjects so far from the more fashionable subjects of brooding forests, mountains and medieval ruins that they were scarcely considered picturesque at all. At the same time he was disinclined to emulate fellow Suffolk artist Thomas Gainsborough (see page 225), born some fifty years before and whom he much admired, in using his landscapes as the backgrounds to portraits of fashionable folk: he preferred (and was criticised for) showing farm workers and animals going unselfconsciously about their daily business in a real setting. As his own brother commented, 'When I look at a mill painted by John I see that it will *go round*, which is not always the case with those by other artists'.

Constable returned to East Bergholt each summer, renewing his happy associations with the place: 'I love every stile and stump, and every lane in the village', he remarked. It was here that he developed his very individual techniques for painting directly from nature: he was probably the first artist to sketch in oils in the open air, and he influenced many successors including the French Impressionists of the late 19th century. Constable's towering trees in full leaf and huge skies with rolling, stormy clouds are still a very recognisable part of the late summer scene.

㉒ *Stratford St Mary*

This village, which featured in many of Constable's paintings, is the most southerly village in Suffolk. It lies along the old London coaching road and so used to be a popular stop for herders marching their geese, turkeys and cattle south to market at London. Such was the volume of trade here in the past that the largest of the village's four inns was reputed to have extensive stabling for up to 200 horses, while another had 20 acres of pasture for cattle passing through. The trade has now gone, of course, but the through road remains – the frenetic A12, which unhappily divides the bulk of the village from its church. Stratford St Mary is certainly a pretty village, with plenty of splendid half-timbered Tudor buildings, but you cannot quite escape the rumble and swish of lorries and cars speeding past on their way to and from Colchester. These days, three pubs remain.

㉓ Stoke-by-Nayland and Polstead

Continuing west, either by road or on foot along the Stour Valley Path, you soon arrive in **Stoke-by-Nayland**, set away from the river on top of a hill. The church of **St James** here, with its 120-foot tower, is a beacon for miles around and Constable featured it in a number of his paintings, although not necessarily in exactly the same landscape. One of his most famous paintings, *Stoke-by-Nayland Church*, features the church illuminated beneath a dramatic rainbow. An earlier visitor, the puritan William 'Smasher' Dowsing, was less enthusiastic about art and destroyed countless 'superstitious' pictures within the church along with some 15th-century glass. Someone, perhaps Dowsing, perhaps another puritan, has also done their best to damage the alabaster tomb of Lady Anne Windsor, leaving a chipped nose and broken hand.

The village is peaceful and highly good-looking, glowing with Suffolk pink; the churchyard is a lovely spot to watch the swallows and house martins that swoop around the tower. Some handsome timbered houses opposite have a footpath leading between them and, if you ignore the sign pointing to 'Cherry Wood', you can continue across the tops of fields and enjoy an excellent view down to the valley below. Seen from here, you realise that Stoke-by-Nayland is quite an elevated village by East Anglian standards. If you retrace your steps and then follow the sign and footpath down to the valley, you'll eventually end up in Nayland, albeit by a rather circuitous route.

Just north of Stoke-by-Nayland, **Polstead** is infamous as the location of the Red Barn Murder of 1827 in which a local farmer's boy, William Corder, murdered his lover. The story captured the imagination of the people thanks to its publication in the penny dreadfuls and when Corder was later caught and subsequently hanged at Bury St Edmunds, his execution attracted a huge audience. Given the macabre tastes of the time, this wasn't the end of it: his skin was used to bind a copy of the trial proceedings (which can be seen along with his scalp in Moyses Hall Museum, Bury) and souvenir hunters squabbled over pieces of the hangman's rope, which sold for a guinea an inch, and even chipped away the victim's tombstone. A melodramatic play based on the events, *Maria Marten or The Murder in the Red Barn*, remained hugely popular throughout the mid 19th century and was resurrected as a 1935 British film.

A more cheerful association is the small sweet cherry variety, known as **Polstead Black**, that used to grow here and which is thought to have originally been brought to the area by Romans. Cherries are commemorated in several place names around here: Cherry Meadow, Cherry Farm, Cherry Billy's Lane; and there used to be a cherry fair too, on the village green each July. Cherry growing is, alas, no longer big business, although some local gardens still have their own Polstead Black cherry trees. There used also to be an ancient oak tree in the village – the **Gospel Oak** – that was considered to be the oldest tree in Suffolk at around 1,300 years old and the scene of Saxon worship back in the 7th century when it may have been planted by St Cedd or one of his followers. The oak collapsed in 1953 but its remains can still be seen between St Mary's Church and Polstead Hall near the war memorial. Given all this talk of ancient tradition, it's worth mentioning that the **community shop** on the green next to the village hall is the oldest in Suffolk and second oldest in England, dating from 1984. You can buy local **apple juices** here, made from Polstead apples from nearby Willow Farm, which also has its own farm shop at Polstead Heath north of the village.

S♥ The Crown Park St, Stoke-by-Nayland ✆ 01206 262001
🖰 www.crowninn.net. With low-ceilinged, rambling rooms, The Crown has a seasonal menu that sympathetically combines traditional and contemporary. There's an outstanding wine list, Adnams ales in the bar, and a sunny terrace for warm weather.

㉔ Nayland

Down in the valley itself on a lovely stretch of the Stour, Nayland is another fine village of timbered and colour-washed cottages. It's not quite Lavenham but it's not that far off in visual appeal, with timber-framed and colour-washed cottages everyway you look.

Across the Nayland Bridge, a footpath along the opposite bank follows the river west past a weir – part of the Stour Valley Path that leads to Wissington, with its Norman church, where the path crosses into Essex. As a reminder that you are still in Constable Country, if you take a look inside St James' Church you will see an altarpiece by the artist: *Christ Blessing the Bread and Wine*.

As has happened in other Stour Valley villages, gentrification seems to have had the effect of closing down pubs. When I visited the White Hart looked closed while the Queen's Head just up the road, which must once have been a coaching inn, has been converted to a dwelling. An obelisk-like milestone outside the village estate agents gives a clue as to why a village of this size cannot support more than one pub. With London just 55 miles away and Chelmsford 26 miles, we're firmly into commuter country here. This also explains why the place seems so quiet mid-week. At least, the Anchor Inn down by the bridge looks busy enough.

S♥ Anchor Inn 26 Court St, Nayland ✆ 01206 262313
🖰 www.anchornayland.co.uk. This traditional, yellow-washed pub has a delightful setting next to the bridge over the River Stour. There's plenty of local produce on offer like home-reared lamb, duck, pork and beef.

A walk in Constable Country

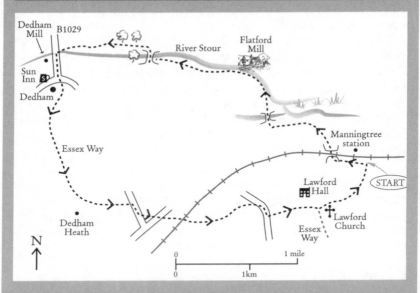

This seven-mile walk sneaks into Essex. Actually that's an understatement: most of it is in Essex, but it sums up the gentle charms of the Stour Valley so well that it's well worth the stray over the county border. Also, despite its requiring quite a bit of field-crossing, the southern part of the route follows the Essex Way, which is mostly waymarked (though it's still a good idea to take the OS map, Explorer sheet 196).

The route starts at Manningtree station, and heads out through the car park on the south side, where a rising path leads up to Lawton church. Here you join up with the Essex Way, which traces an intricate and nicely varied route past Lawford Hall, a Georgian-looking pile concealing an Elizabethan core, and over the Shir Burn and railway to reach Dedham. In this gorgeously handsome village street, the **SP Sun Inn** (01206 323351; www.thesuninndedham.com) is a very good stopping point; though it's a distinctly elegant (and much-liked) dining venue you can just pop in for a pint of Adnam's or one of the other regional brews, and they have their own tiny fruit and veg shop next door. Also in Dedham, **Castle House** (www.siralfredmunnings.co.uk) became the home of artist Alfred Munnings in 1919 and is open to the public on three or four afternoons a week in summer; it has the largest collection of Munnings' paintings anywhere.

Carry on north on the B1209, past Dedham Mill and over **Dedham Bridge**; here you follow the Stour Valley Path along the famous watermeadows of **Dedham Vale** immortalised by Constable; kingfishers make the occasional appearance, and snipe and redshank frequent the marshes. Recross the river just before Flatford Mill and follow the St Edmund Way back to Manningtree station.

The Stour Valley - west

㉕ Sudbury

The largest of the wool towns in this part of Suffolk, Sudbury is a busy place, with traffic streaming through its centre and local shoppers competing for parking spaces in the central square below the church. Among a rich mix of architectural styles Georgian buildings tend to dominate. One fine example of these is **Gainsborough's House** (01787 372958; www.gainsborough.org), the solid 18th-century house at 46 Gainsborough Street that now serves as a museum to the town's most famous son, Thomas Gainsborough, born here in 1727. A prominent bronze **statue** to the artist, palette and paintbrush in hand, stands at the top of the market square next to the church.

Thomas Gainsborough, landscape artist

Anne Locke

Although he is generally better known as a society portraitist, Gainsborough started his career as a Suffolk landscape artist: his early works such as *Cornard Wood* (now in the National Gallery), with its waving trees and stormy sky, were a great influence on the younger artist John Constable (see page 221). Gainsborough remained fond of including landscapes as backgrounds to his portraits: in *Mr and Mrs Andrews*, also in the National Gallery, the fashionably dressed sitters are off to one side of the painting, while their newly harvested cornfield – at the Auberies, a farm estate near Sudbury – glows equally prosperously alongside them.

The market square is host to a twice-weekly market on Thursdays and Saturdays. The tourist information centre has a **Town Trail** that describes the town's buildings, and the **Talbot Trail**, a series of small bronzes to follow around the centre of town, tells of Sudbury's past.

A stroll next to the **river** is hard to beat on a fine summer's afternoon. Continue down Gainsborough Street past the museum and you'll soon arrive at a footbridge across the River Stour from where you can wander south down to Ballingdon Bridge or north to Brundon Mill. At the Quay, south of Friars Street, you can take river trips on the Rosette, an electric boat run by the River Stour Trust (0845 8035787; www.riverstourtrust.org) on Sundays and Bank Holidays from Easter to October. These go downriver to Cornard, where there is a visitor centre, and on to The Swan at Great Henny.

Sudbury Farmers' Market takes place at St Peter's, Market Hill, on the last Friday of the month.

Granary Quay Lane ☎ 01787 313000. A tea room run by the River Stour Trust; open in summer on Sundays and bank holidays.
Secret Garden Tea Room 21 Friars St ☎ 01787 372030 🖰 www.tsg.uk.net. A quality tea room with a strong French theme and a blackboard with daily specials.

㉖ Long Melford

As you head north from Sudbury, Long Melford is almost like a continuation: a long, linear village of thatched Suffolk pink with more than a few antique shops and booksellers lining the high street. **Melford Hall**, an Elizabethan country house belonging to the National Trust, lies north of the village next to a large open green that was the site of a Whitsun horse fair, the largest in East Anglia, in the 19th century. The village's **Holy Trinity Church**, an enormous 15th-century Perpendicular edifice brimming with medieval stained glass, lies north of the green – you need to get quite close before it reveals itself fully. Here is living proof that Long Melford was once one of the very richest places in the land thanks to the success of the wool trade. The church contains chapels to three of its wool tycoon benefactors – the Cloptons, the Cordells and the Martyns – and with an attached Lady Chapel, it's effectively two buildings in one – more like a cathedral than a parish church. Simon Jenkins gives it a five-star rating in his book *England's Thousand Best Churches*, the only church in Suffolk to rate so highly.

A little way north of the church, you'll find **Kentwell Hall** (01787 310207; www.kentwell.co.uk), a moated Tudor mansion complete with a brick rose maze and a walled garden. There's also a rare-breed farm with Norfolk Horn sheep, Longhorn cattle and Suffolk Punch horses.

Black Lion The Green ☎ 01787 312356 🖰 www.blacklionhotel.net. On a corner of the village green, this 17th-century inn has classy dining in either a smart restaurant with antique fittings or a more informal front restaurant. For a special treat, it's the place to come for the ultimate cream tea.
Crown Hall St ☎ 01787 377666 🖰 www.thecrownhotelmelford.co.uk. A free house with a fine selection of ales and a daily changing seasonal menu with contemporary British cuisine, as well as sandwiches or baguettes in the bar.

㉗ Cavendish

Cavendish is exceptionally pretty and, understandably, perhaps just a little bit given to vanity, with neatly grouped thatched pink cottages facing a large village green with the church juxtaposed behind them. There's a handful of smart eating places along the high street, and another pub above the green, as well as an antique shop or two.

The village was not always so peaceful. During the Peasants' Revolt of 1381, John Cavendish, who came from the village, killed the rebel leader Wat Tyler with his sword at Smithfield in London. Irate local peasants decided to take their revenge on Cavendish's father, Sir John Cavendish, who was lord of the manor in the village. Sir John attempted to plead for sanctuary at **St Mary's Church** whilst hanging onto the door handle but was finally caught up with at Bury St Edmunds where he was beheaded by the mob. The very same handle supposedly hangs from the door of the village church today. Both Sue Ryder, who founded her international charitable organisation, the Sue Ryder Foundation, here and Leonard Cheshire, her husband, the World War II pilot who set up homes for disabled people, are buried in the village, and there's a small **Sue Ryder Foundation Museum** (01787 280252).

Bull Inn High St ☎ 01787 280245 🖰 www.thebullcavendish.co.uk. A traditional English pub with Adnams beers and reasonably priced food.

㉘ Clare

Another fine medieval wool town: I think this is my favourite of all the places along the Stour Valley. Particularly striking is the 15th-century **Ancient House**, which has luxuriant white pargetting like the sugar icing on a fancy cake. A date of 1473 on the wall no doubt refers to the date of the house itself rather than the pargetting, which would be at least a couple of centuries later. The house now serves as a **museum** with local history displays.

Directly opposite is the church of **St Peter and St Paul**, a fine Perpendicular building in which Henry VIII and Catherine of Aragon have bespoke pews bearing their crests. On the wall next to the porch is a sundial dated 1790 that is inscribed 'Go about your business', which might be interpreted as 'Back to work, peasants, now that you have paid your respect to God'. I found that the sundial seems to tell the time with uncanny accuracy (once you allow for correction to British Summer Time), as does the chiming clock on the tower. Inside the porch is a Green Man boss and, even more mysteriously, above the entrance to the church, an upside-down figure that some consider to be a rare example of a Green Woman.

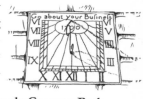

A couple of minutes' walk from the town centre, **Clare Castle Country Park** has the stone remains of a 13th-century castle keep on top of a mound overlooking the town. Clare's former railway station stands within the inner bailey of the castle; a small display on the town's railway history is inside a former goods shed. The park also serves as the gateway for a 3½-mile waymarked circular walk.

Bell Market Hill, Clare ☎ 01787 277741 🖰 www.thebellhotel-clare.com. A 16th-century coaching inn with a seasonal menu. Two bars serve local ales and bar snacks, and a conservatory leads on to a terrace.
Number One Delicatessen and Café 1 High St, Clare ☎ 01797 278392. With a central location, this has decent snacks and a nice range of fruit juices and cordials.

Sawday's Special Places to Stay

- **S28** Poplar Farm House
- **S29** Arch House
- **S30** The Westleton Crown

N

CHAPTER 8

0 — 4 miles
0 — 5km

THE SUFFOLK COAST

9. THE SUFFOLK COAST

Swoul, and Dunwich, and Walderswick
All go in at one lousie creek.
Suffolk coastal rhyme

It might be tempting to think that the two workaday towns of Lowestoft and Felixstowe typify this coastline, which stretches between the two. This couldn't be further from the truth, as both are exceptions and, from Kessingland all the way down to Bawdsey, the Suffolk coast is mostly rural and peaceful, with a couple of old-fashioned resorts interspersed by tiny villages up against the shingle. It is not an undiscovered coastline – far from it – but somehow Suffolk's unhurried, gentle pace of life has managed to persist without too much intrusion from the 21st century. Some things have changed quite dramatically over the past half century, of course, particularly the economy of the region and the incomers who have come to live here, but overall its character has survived without it ever becoming too much of a museum piece.

This coast has always attracted outsiders. The Scottish art nouveau architect and designer Charles Rennie Mackintosh came here to paint flowers when his architectural career was in the dumps. Benjamin Britten, having taken his leave of his home town of Lowestoft, made his home at Aldeburgh and wrote an opera about a fisherman, *Peter Grimes*. Southwold and Walberswick have always been popular with BBC television producers, authors and politicians, and you might even catch a glimpse of a vacationing rock star or Hollywood royalty at Aldeburgh's better hotels and restaurants. There is no doubt about it: the Suffolk coast exudes a certain type of understated glamour – classy and comfortable, like a pair of old but expensive shoes.

Between Lowestoft and Felixstowe, various inlets and estuaries punctuate the coastline. The Rivers Blyth, Dunwich, Minsmere, Alde, Ore, Deben, Orwell and Stour all flow into the North Sea along this stretch, and the larger of these once brought trade and prosperity to the wool villages of the Suffolk hinterland. These rivers were once far more important than they are today, and far more navigable too. Look at the River Ore that flows through Framlingham – a mere brook these days – and shake your head in disbelief that stone for building the town's castle was once shipped here all the way from the coast.

As well as the coast itself, this chapter also covers the immediate hinterland, roughly east of the A12 Lowestoft to Ipswich road. A good chunk of that terrain constitutes what's known as **The Sandlings**, which has light sandy soil akin to that of Breckland in the west of the region. The Sandlings has a similar history to Breckland too: early settlement by Neolithic peoples thanks to easily workable soil; medieval overgrazing by sheep; widespread gamekeeping and forestry in the first part of the 20th century; arable crops in the second half. Today, it is an area characterised by sandy heaths, forestry plantations and wide fields of grain.

The urban bookends of Lowestoft and Felixstowe only put in a token appearance but if you are at all interested in Southwold sailors, bedevilled Blythburgh or disappearing Dunwich, or are curious to experience the sensation of 'orfordness', then read on. I start by working down the coast north to south, detouring inland as seems appropriate. Away from the comfortable respectability of resorts like Southwold and Aldeburgh are some real oddities. Dunwich, now little more than a pub, a café and a car park, was one of England's great ports back in the 12th century. Orford Ness was a top-secret military research site that was firmly off limits until quite recently, while Snape Maltings, now an extensive arts and music complex, was a working maltings until not so very long ago

The Suffolk coast begins in the north at **Corton**, more or less a suburb of Lowestoft, which distinguishes itself by having a nude beach. **Lowestoft** itself has probably seen better days. In his book *The Rings of Saturn* W G Sebald describes being 'disheartened' by the town's deserted streets but, there again, he was always a writer whose glass was considerably less than half full. Like Great Yarmouth, just across the county boundary to the north, Lowestoft has seen service as both a fishing port and a resort and, rather like Cromer and Sheringham in Norfolk, the two towns have always been great rivals. Lowestoft's fleet of trawlers were decommissioned in 2002 and, like Yarmouth, it has seen tourist numbers dwindle during the last quarter of the 20th century. William A Dutt in his *Highways and Byways in East Anglia* published in 1900 writes of 'Clapham and Brixton primly disporting themselves on the south beach or placidly promenading the pier' back in the days when Clapham and Brixton themselves were solidly middle-class parts of London. Much has changed, and these days 'Loos-toff', as East Anglians tend to call it, is redolent of faded memories. If you are curious, you might want to check out the Ness, close to the Bird's Eye fish-finger factory, which is the most easterly point in the British Isles.

Head a little further south, past Kessingland with its holiday village and Africa-themed Suffolk Wildlife Park, and you reach Benacre with its isolated broad, a National Nature Reserve that lies within the Broads National Park. You soon encounter evidence of a rapidly disappearing coast. Covehithe was a small town in the medieval period but has been whittled down by North Sea erosion to a mere village these days, with the oddity of the partly dismantled church of St Andrew having a later, smaller church built within it. The coastline has retreated over a quarter of a mile here in the past two centuries and offers a taste of what is to come at Dunwich, beyond Southwold, a far more dramatically reduced place.

Getting around

There is no coast road as such. Away from the busy A12, plenty of minor roads veer off this towards the sea, although travelling between places along the coast itself, say between Aldeburgh and Orford for example, often involves circuitous journeys to get round estuaries. Southwold to Walberswick, which is really just a pleasant stroll on foot using the footbridge across the River Blyth, is a case in point and driving involves a long detour around the estuary to Blythburgh. Really, it's best to park up somewhere convenient and get your hiking boots on.

Public transport

This is so-so. Lowestoft is well connected to Norwich by a regular **train service**, while Felixtowe has trains to Ipswich. The East Suffolk Line, run by National Express, connects Lowestoft with Ipswich at roughly two-hour intervals stopping at Halesworth, Darsham, Saxmundham and Wickham Market along the way. You need the local **bus service** to reach the coast itself. The East Coast Explorer service 601 runs between Lowestoft, Southwold and Halesworth. Service 521 connects Halesworth with Beccles, Saxmundham and Leiston, and service 165 connects Leiston with Aldeburgh, Snape, Woodbridge and Ipswich. Service 71 operates between Woodbridge and Orford. With a bit of judicious timetable juggling you should be able to use these services to travel around the coast as long as you avoid Sundays. There's no regular service between Southwold and Leiston, although Coastlink provides a bookable service between Darsham railway station and the coast at Walberswick and Sizewell (01728 833526). This is wheelchair-friendly and carries a rack for two bicycles but needs to be pre-booked two days in advance.

Cycling

Cycling is generally enjoyable away from the A12. Although the narrow roads to the coast can get pretty busy in the summer months, most of the traffic is tourist vehicles that are not in any great hurry and are generally respectful to those on bikes. There are some excellent bridleways to explore too. The OS Landranger 156 map covers the area.

If you are arriving by train, bicycles may be picked up at Darsham station by arrangement with Byways Bicycles (01728 668764) or at Lowestoft at Streetlife (01502 585968). You can also transport your own bike using the National Express East Anglia rail services although, as there is usually only provision for four bikes per train; it is probably best to pre-book (0845 600 7245; www.national expresseastanglia.com). Darsham is perhaps the best station to use as a base, as it has both Dunwich and Minsmere within easy pedalling distance. Saxmundham station is reasonably convenient for Snape, Aldeburgh and Thorpeness.

Walking

This is very special country for walkers. As well as beach walks and quiet country lanes, the coastal region is criss-crossed by footpaths. Some of the most enjoyable hikes are along estuaries, such as that of the rivers Blyth and Alde, and you'll find plenty of scope for forest walks too, especially to the south in the extensive Tunstall and Rendlesham plantations. Those areas notated on the map as 'walks', such as The Walks near Leiston or Westleton Walks near Dunwich, refer to the old sheep 'walks' that ranged on the coastal hinterland but you can still walk there, even without a white woolly coat. There's a selection of downloadable circular walks on www.eastsuffolklinewalks.co.uk.

Tourist information

Aldeburgh 152 High St ☎ 01728 453637.
Lowestoft The East Point Pavilion, Royal Plain ☎ 01502 533600.
Southwold 69 High St ☎ 01502 724729.
Visit Suffolk Coast ☝ www.visit-suffolkcoast.co.uk.
Suffolk Coastal ☝ www.suffolkcoastal.gov.uk.
Walking in Suffolk ☝ www.walkinginsuffolk.co.uk.
East of England Tourism (☝ www.eet.org.uk) is in the process of producing a series of guides to sustainable tourism in the region. These will aim to reduce car dependency and encourage visitors to experience the local area. Currently, a guide to **Woodbridge** is available but look out for others in the future as a total of 50 will be published between 2010 and 2013.

Southwold, Dunwich and around

① Southwold

It's hard to imagine anyone not being seduced by Southwold: that this most bewitching of seaside towns manages to exude such easy charm without much trace of smugness is to its great credit. George Orwell (real name Eric Blair), who lived and taught in the town in the early 1930s, may have been critical of Southwold's comforting gentility but for most, this is actually its draw. Southwold is an iconic place that seems still to belong to the 1930s (in the nicest sense) in many ways. A lighthouse stands right in the middle of town, and there's a pier, lines of colourful beach huts and a brewery where casks are delivered locally by horse and cart. Despite all this, the town has more than enough grit to keep it real, and deeper layers exist here beneath the shiny veneer of cream teas, overpriced real estate, gleaming 4x4s and metropolitan accents. There are retired folk licking ice-cream cornets, kids making sandcastles on the beach, wet fish for sale at fishermen's huts along the Blyth River, and even a reading room for sailors.

The town's genteel feel is partly serendipitous thanks to a devastating fire that tore many of its buildings down in 1659. This created a handful of open areas that were left as fire breaks and never rebuilt upon, and it is these **greens** that contribute towards the town's wholesome air of uncluttered space. The best known of these is above the beach at Gun Hill, where cannon commemorate the Battle of Sole Bay fought just offshore from here, a rare contretemps in which the English and French fleets combined forces to fight the Dutch.

The town's ultimate landmark is its **lighthouse**, built in 1887 to replace three lighthouses threatened by coastal erosion. Tours are possible at certain times of year or you could simply contemplate its white pepper-pot form from one of the outside tables at the Sole Bay Inn just across the road. The lighthouse was automated in 1938 but before this, the keeper must have had the least lonely posting in the land, with the option of enjoying a pint in one of the town's hostelries whenever the fancy took him. The lighthouse's close neighbour, the **Adnams Sole Bay Brewery** was built in the same year (1890) that the lighthouse first went into operation. This replaced an earlier brewery on the same site, so the legend 'established 1660' that you see on bottles of Adnams ales is not mere hyperbole. The town is peppered with splendid Adnams houses all serving up delicious, well-hopped beer, a phenomenon that in this instance at least gives the word 'monopoly' a newfound respectability. The Sole Bay Inn is perhaps the best known but the Lord Nelson, Harbour Inn and others are equally good places to sup a pint.

Southwold Pier (www.southwoldpier.co.uk) re-opened for business in 2001 but the original structure dates from 1900 and stood until 1934 when a gale virtually destroyed it. The pier is proudly claimed to be the first to be built in Britain for over 45 years, which in itself is quite something. Take a stroll along it and you will find that it is not quite as run-of-the-mill as you might first have imagined.

Thanks to the wacky and inventive mind of Tim Hunkin, the pier's machine arcade has a wealth of bizarre but charming Heath-Robinson-like slot machines that put a smile on the most serious of faces. You might also wish to be present for the rather rude, half-hourly chiming of Hunkin's water clock, although it rarely seems to go off exactly when it should.

Southwold's **North Beach** lies beneath the pier with its wooden groynes jutting out to sea. There's sunbathing in deckchairs and sandcastle making a-plenty on the sand, while many more visitors are content to stroll the promenade above the beach huts. The town's beaches continue south of the town, too – along **The Denes** by the inlet of the River Blyth. If you head inland along the river's northern bank you will find a rowing-boat ferry across the river that has been operated by the same family since the 1920s and a handful of wooden huts selling very fresh fish at relatively low prices. There's a campsite here too, and a pub and a café a little further inland before you reach a footbridge across the river to the Walberswick bank.

The **Sailors' Reading Room** above the seaside promenade is a modest building that has photographs, newspaper cuttings and all manner of maritime memorabilia. Effectively, it serves as an informal museum and, sailor or not, you are free to enter, although photography is not allowed inside the building, presumably because it would interfere with the sailors' reading. The last time I visited, little reading was taking place and the sailors within were, instead, playing a spirited game of pool in the back room. If you are after a more formal museum then there's also the **Southwold Museum and Historic Society** (01502 726097; www.southwoldmuseum.org) in a Dutch-gabled cottage on Victoria Street. This covers the whole span of history of the town with a range of interactive displays. The museum, which has equal-access facilities, also organises Tuesday evening lectures throughout August at the Methodist hall on East Green.

Almost as well known as the lighthouse are the town's three hundred or so colourful **beach huts**. Those by the pier below Gun Hill are the most sought after. Other places along the East Anglia coast have similar huts, but none have quite the cachet that goes with owning one on Southwold beach. In truth, the huts are little more than well-appointed garden sheds but this has not prevented them from becoming highly prized *pieds-à-terre* in this neck of the woods. For about the same price as an east Midlands terrace house, you get a single wooden room next to a busy thoroughfare where local bylaws permit you to make tea, snooze in a chair and watch the sea. You are not permitted to sleep overnight in

Beer from the coast: the Adnams story

Adnams claim that beer was brewed on the same Southwold site back in the 14th century but the family themselves did not get involved until 1872 when George and Ernest Adnams bought the Sole Bay Brewery with help from their father. George wasn't cut out for the brewery business and soon upped sticks to Africa, where he met an unfortunate fate with a crocodile, but Ernest persisted with the enterprise to establish Adnams & Co Ltd in 1890.

Jack and Pierse Loftus bought themselves a stake in the business in 1902 and the company progressed modestly though the 20th century until 1970 when there was a substantial modernisation of the brewery. The same year also saw, perhaps a little counter-intuitively, the reintroduction of dray horses for deliveries around town. The brewery's 'Beer from the Coast' marketing campaign was launched in 2002, together with a charming set of posters, postcards and coasters which featured many Southwold icons – beach huts, the lighthouse and pebble beaches – all with cleverly disguised Adnams motifs hidden away somewhere in the scene.

Adnams has strong ties with its Southwold home, most notably through its charitable trust that was set up to provide assistance to organisations within a 25-

them, however. What can you expect for an asking price that might start as high as £70,000? Well, not running water and an electricity supply, obviously.

Away from the seafront, the town's high street heads inland past cafés, galleries and old-fashioned shops to **St Edmund's Church**, a towering 15th-century building constructed of imported Caen stone with flint dressing. Look up as you enter and you will see the forlorn-looking figure of a tied-up Edmund above the door. The church's interior is quite beautiful, with an exquisite angel-bedecked roof and intricate steeple-like font cover that is 24 feet high. There's also a figure called 'Southwold Jack', a soldier from the War of the Roses, who carries a sword and has an axe that rings a bell when the service is about to commence (there's another Southwold Jack figure on the wall of Adnams Brewery that also appears on the corporate logo). The east window, which is by Sir Ninian Comper, has scenes from St Edmund's martyrdom and is a 1954 replacement of an earlier window blown out by a German bomb landing just across the road in 1943.

For food in town, you are fairly spoilt for choice with so many tearooms and pubs, but there are plenty of places to buy quality do-it-yourself ingredients too. The High Street has the **Black Olive delicatessen** at 80a/80b (✆ 01502 722312), which has locally smoked fish, while the **Sole Bay Fish Company** (22e Blackshore ✆ 01502 724709) has its own boats with fish for sale at the harbour and at Southwold's **Monday market**. Both Crab Apple and Rose's Fruit Far and Salad Bowl at the Market Place have a good range of local seasonal produce.

mile radius of the town. The company's environmental commitment is also impressive. Adnams was awarded the Queen's Award for Enterprise: Sustainable Development in 2005 and in the following year constructed a new, ultra eco-friendly distribution centre. It was in this same year that the last of the brewery's dray horses were retired, as the road between the brewery and the new distribution centre was too busy and too far for the horses to travel. This was a sad day for Southwold, as the Adnams drays had become a familiar sight around town and had played a part in perpetuating the resort's old-fashioned image.

Ever keen to forge ahead on its sustainability route, Adnams went on to reduce the weight of its 500ml bottle by almost by half and set about constructing a new, energy-efficient brew house. This opened in 2007 to produce East Green, a new brew that would become the UK's first 'carbon neutral' beer, a feat achieved by using local high-yielding barley, aphid-resistant hops and lightweight beer bottles and by offsetting the tiny amount of CO_2 left over. It really amounts to something when you can claim that by supping beer you're doing your bit for the environment. The bonus is, East Green tastes good too. It's light, golden, hoppy and bitter – all the familiar characteristics of a traditional Adnams ale.

If it's afternoon tea you're after, Southwold has more tearooms and cafés than you can shake a buttered scone at. If you're looking for something more substantial and/or a beer then simply choose from any one of a number of Adnams houses in the town. Two other very well liked pubs in addition to those below are the **Harbour Inn** right by the boats on Blackshore and the friendly **Lord Nelson**, centrally placed in East Street.

S⃝ The Crown 90 High St, Southwold ☎ 01502 7222275 ⏚ www.adnams.co.uk. Of all the splendid Adnams establishments in the town, this is the most sought after and pre-booking is a very good idea, if not essential. The elegantly beamed interior oozes metropolitan sophistication, while the wood-panelled snug to the rear might appeal more to alehouse traditionalists. There's a good range of gutsy world-travelled dishes on offer and an excellent wine list in addition to Adnams ales.

S⃝ Randolph Hotel 41 Wangford Rd, Reydon ☎ 01502 723603. In a neighbouring village, just inland from Southwold, this late Victorian pub-hotel has a summer garden and modern good looks. There's excellent Adnams beer, of course, and local fish and game.

Sole Bay Inn East Green, Southwold ☎ 01502 723736. With the lighthouse rising behind it like a minaret, this is another Adnams favourite and about as close as you can get to the brewery. Do they have a direct beer pipe? Good solid unpretentious food and predictably excellent draught beer.

② Walberswick

Just across the water from Southwold, Walberswick is a former fishing village where the pace of life can make its neighbour seem almost frenetic in comparison. Long adopted by artists, Walberswick has slowly morphed over the years from bohemian to shabby chic. There's still a modicum of fishing taking place but most of the boats sloped in the estuary mud are of the hobby variety these days, and more than half of the properties in the village are holiday homes.

Historically, Walberswick took over where Dunwich left off as a trading port. When Dunwich harbour became irretrievably silted in the late 13th century, Walberswick exploited its position at the mouth of the River Blyth to become its replacement. Like Dunwich, it declined slowly over the years but managed to survive as a working port until the early years of the 20th century. What remains is the mere shadow of what was once a much larger place. The village has long attracted artists: in the 1890s and 1900s, the circle of English impressionists associated with Philip Wilson Steer came here to paint, and Charles Rennie Mackintosh made it his home in 1914 when, disillusioned with architecture, he came here to paint watercolours (it didn't all go smoothly for him though: he was arrested as a possible spy in 1915). The village remains inordinately popular with media types, with a number of actors and other celebrities maintaining homes here; there's a handful of famous Freuds too. As John Seymour dryly remarked when writing of the village in 1968: 'It is indeed, the haunt of ex-theatrical folk and lady watercolourists, but it is very attractive nevertheless.'

A stroll from Southwold

A fine **circular walk** can be made by following the west bank of the creek past the campsite as far as the derelict windmill, then striking northwest across East Hill as far as the B1387 and crossing this to Walberswick Common and the River Blyth beyond, returning to the village along the river's southern bank. If you are feeling particularly energetic, you could then cross over to Southwold by way of the ferry or the Bailey bridge a mile inland. The bridge is all that remains of the old **Southwold to Halesworth Light Railway** that ran its last train in 1929 after 50 years of service and was locally famous because its carriages had originally been intended for the Emperor of China. Reportedly, the forms of Chinese imperial dragons could just about be detected beneath the paintwork. Parts of the old railway route are still walkable, particularly between Blythburgh and Southwold.

S♪ The Anchor Main St ✆ 01502 722112 🖰 www.anchoratwalberswick.com. This Adnams house serves dishes to match the beer and uses produce from local butchers and organic vegetable growers. There's a sun terrace overlooking allotments and beach huts, and occasional summer barbeques out on the lawn.

③ Blythburgh

A few miles inland from Southwold at the head of the Blyth estuary, the village of Blythburgh clusters around the busy A12. The estuary itself is quite a sight, especially when the tide is in and its wading birds are squeezed in closer to view, but the major attraction here is undoubtedly the village's remarkable church. Just south of the village, at the junction of the B1387 is the Toby Walk's picnic site, named after the ghost of a dragoon drummer reputed to haunt the area.

Holy Trinity church

Like Cley in north Norfolk, Blythburgh's parish church is a reminder of prosperous times when the village served as an important wool port. The church, towering above reed beds close to the river, and sometimes 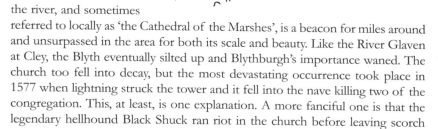 referred to locally as 'the Cathedral of the Marshes', is a beacon for miles around and unsurpassed in the area for both its scale and beauty. Like the River Glaven at Cley, the Blyth eventually silted up and Blythburgh's importance waned. The church too fell into decay, but the most devastating occurrence took place in 1577 when lightning struck the tower and it fell into the nave killing two of the congregation. This, at least, is one explanation. A more fanciful one is that the legendary hellhound Black Shuck ran riot in the church before leaving scorch marks in the north door and scurrying off to Bungay's St Mary's Church to create similar havoc there (see page 159). Despite spiteful mid 17th-century defacing by the arch-Puritan William 'Smasher' Dowsing (see page 205), the church is still a remarkable building, with carved angels flying across its roof space. In his *England's Thousand Best Churches*, Simon Jenkins calls it the 'queen of the Suffolk coast' (although he gives one more star to Southwold's St Edmund's) and it is by far the most evocative of the various settings used for summer concerts in the annual Aldeburgh Festival. Beneath the gaze of the benign angels overhead are poppyhead-carved pews that portray the Seven Deadly Sins. The church also has a wooden bell-striking figure, a brother to 'Southwold Jack' at St Edmund's, Southwold.

Henham Park

Just up the road from Blythburgh in the cleft of the A145 and A12 is Henham Park, a glorious estate set in lush parkland landscaped by Sir Humphry Repton in 1791, with ancient oaks, redwoods and even rare service trees and black poplars. Indeed the oaks seem so old and wide in girth here that you cannot help but wonder how they didn't end up as ships' timbers during the time of the Napoleonic wars at the start of the 19th century. The estate is currently in the ownership of Keith Rous, the Sixth Earl of Stradbroke, known as 'The Aussie Earl' because of his work as a sheep farmer in Australia prior to his inheriting the property. You can walk in the estate at certain times of year (www.henhampark.com) but most turn up for the **Latitude Music Festival** at the end of July, a family-friendly rock music festival that also features theatre, comedy, poetry, literature and cabaret. The estate is also occasionally used as the location for wild food safaris (01728 621380; www.foodsafari.co.uk). In case you thought that Adnams had a complete monopoly in these parts, the estate is also home to Hektor's Brewery.

White Hart Inn London Rd ☎01502 478217 ✆ www.blythburghwhitehart.co.uk. A 17th-century Dutch-gabled coaching inn that once served as the local courthouse and gaol but is now an Adnams house. Stirring views of the Blythburgh estuary.

④ Dunwich

A visit to Dunwich is not so much about what there is to see now – a pub, car park, café, a few ruins – but what has disappeared from view. As W A Dutt reports in *Highways and Byways of East Anglia*: 'the story of Dunwich seizes upon the imagination; though when one sees how little remains of what may once have been the chief city of East Anglia it is difficult to believe that Dunwich, too, was not a phantom city of a land of dreams'. That was in 1900 and almost nothing has changed – if anything the remaining village is even smaller today. Hard to believe, perhaps, but Dunwich was once the capital of East Anglia: a thriving port and shipbuilding centre with several churches, priories and even the seat of the East Anglia bishopric. With the confluence of the Blyth and Dunwich rivers forming a natural harbour, the town grew prosperous as a result of the wool trade in the early medieval period but, as has been the case elsewhere on this coastline, natural harbours are rarely permanent features. Today, the place is reduced to the status of a small village with a large beach car park. It's a popular place for day-trippers to take the air, eat fish and chips and stroll along the shingle – all pleasant enough, but the real thrill is to come here and contemplate what existed before.

Given that most of old Dunwich lies buried beneath the waves, it is perhaps inevitable that there's plenty of hyperbole describing the place as some lost Atlantis or Saxon Camelot. Old tales speak of 52 churches that used to exist here, and of tolling church bells heard out to sea during storms. However, Rowland Parker, author of the splendid *Men of Dunwich*, scoffs at such notions, saying that there were never more than six churches standing at any one time in the town, and that he has never heard any local talk of bells tolling out at sea. If you wish to learn more of the history of Dunwich and medieval Suffolk, Parker's book is highly recommended: although it contains a staggering amount of historical detail, it is as gripping as a good detective story.

Dunwich's early history has some grey areas, but what is certain is that, although the place was known to the Romans, it was Saxons who first developed it as a port. The Christian missionary St Felix of Burgundy founded the East Anglia bishopric here in the mid 7th century when the place was known as Dommoc. The bishopric moved to North Elmham in 870 before later transferral to Thetford and finally Norwich. Dunewic, a Saxonised version of its original name, is recorded as being a small town in 1060 with a single church. The Norman Conquest brought expansion to the port and within 20 years of the conquest, Dunwich had a population of around 3,000, a considerable number for those days. By the mid 13th century, it had become a vitally important port and shipbuilding centre. A conjectural map of the town and harbour of circa 1280 in Parker's book gives an idea of what might have been found here at that time: five churches, two priories, a guildhall, a market place, shipyards, a quay, town gates, a hospital, a leper hospital and even a bit of topography – Cock Hill and Hen Hill.

Dunwich's demise started in the same century. In 1286, a ferocious sea surge swept many of the town's buildings out to sea and the Dunwich River became partly silted up. The next century was no kinder. A storm in 1328 finished off Dunwich's harbour and this was the cue for Walberswick, just to the north, to take over the port trade. This resulted in such hostility between the two towns for the following century or so that confrontations often erupted into violence. That which remained was lost to the sea over the next few hundred years thanks to further coastal erosion.

All that can be seen today are the ruins of Greyfriars, the Franciscan priory, and fragments of the leper hospital (for a leper hospital in fine condition you might want to check out Lazar House along Sprowston Road in Norwich). The church that stands today, St James, is relatively recent, and dates from 1832. Marine archaeologist Stuart Bacon, who has been working here since 1971, has located the remains of two of the town's former churches, All Saints' and St Peter's, out to sea, and recent evidence of the town's shipbuilding industry has also been discovered. All Saints' was the last of Dunwich's medieval churches to be lost. It reached the cliff edge in 1904, although its tower did not collapse until 1922. Old postcards show the ruins of this church, a buttress of which was salvaged for incorporation into the structure of St James's Church. You can also see a brass taken from All Saints' inside the modern church.

Dunwich Museum on St James Street, open from April until September, has some fascinating displays outlining Dunwich's 1,500-year-old history. Even better, it's free to enter.

The Dunwich Dynamo

For a bicycle ride with a difference, you might want to consider participating in the annual Dunwich Dynamo. You'll need legs of steel, and night vision would be a distinct advantage too. The ride takes place each year on the Saturday night closest to the full moon in July – the next is on July 24th 2010. The 'Dynamo' leaves Hackney in London on the Saturday night and arrives in Dunwich the following morning – a gruelling 120-mile overnight ride, part of the way marked by decidedly low-tech tea lights in jam jars, and ending up with breakfast on the beach.

The event started back in 1993 when a group of London cycle messengers decided to go on a fun run to the coast. Since then, the route, planned by the London School of Cycling, has been organised on a turn up and go basis, with an increasing number of competitors taking place but less competition between them (if that makes sense). There were 700 participants on the 2006 run, or 'DD' as it is known, while the 2007 event had 450 participants of whom only 400 finished because of bad weather. The largest turnout yet was in 2009 when an estimated 1,000 riders started from Hackney, one of whom was riding a penny-farthing. This is no race – there's no official start time and no prize for arriving first to the coast. There's no safety car either, so participation is not to be taken lightly. It is certainly no picnic. It is 120 miles... at night... all the way through East London, Essex and Suffolk.

For FAQs and information concerning future DDs see the Southwark Cyclists website: www.southwarkcyclists.org.uk.

⑤ *Dunwich Heath and Minsmere*

North of Dunwich is the dense coniferous plantation of Dunwich Forest and a large marshy area – Dingle Marshes and Westwood Marshes – an uninterrupted squelch as far as Walberswick. A couple of footpaths lead across the marshes – consult the OS map – or alternatively you could trudge north along the shingle beach, but that would be hard work all the way to Walberswick. A more rewarding area for walkers is that to the south of the village – Dunwich Heath, Westleton Walks and the Minsmere RSPB nature reserve.

Dunwich Heath is National Trust-owned and above the cliffs a convenient car park looks down over the Minsmere reserve and on to the giant golf ball of the Sizewell B nuclear power station. The attractive white coastguard cottages next to the car park hold the National Trust visitor centre and a tearoom. Dunwich Heath itself is a rare example of typical, unimproved Sandlings habitat, with rare Dartford warblers lurking in the gorse bushes.

Sizewell nuclear power station can be seen from much of the Suffolk coast, certainly from as far away as Southwold and Orford Ness. Contaminated water leaked from Sizewell A in 2007 as the earlier power station was being decommissioned. Notwithstanding this, most locals are pretty blasé about its presence and some even prefer to swim on the beach near the water extraction pipes because 'the water's a bit warmer there'. The power station management has cultivated good relations with the nearby RSPB reserve over the years and has also provided employment for the residents of Leiston. It may be unpalatable to eco-warriors but the reality seems to be that nuclear power stations are becoming generally less controversial than wind farms.

Minsmere RSPB Nature Reserve (www.rspb.org.uk) is well known, a flagship reserve established in 1948 with year-round interest in its pools and reed beds. The reserve is a popular place with both twitchers and beginner birders and there's a wealth of information about the place in the visitor centre. Two circular trails around the reserve take you through a variety of habitats, and some of the seven hides are accessible to wheelchairs. Typical reed-bed species such as bittern, marsh harrier and bearded tit are all relatively common and it's pretty hard to miss the elegant black-and-white avocets that grace the ponds here. You might hear nightingales, too, in early summer in the woods close to the visitor centre.

><><><

Eels Foot Inn Eastbridge ☎01728 830154. A village pub, close to the Minsmere RSPB reserve, that has good Adnams beer and regular music nights.

Flora Tea Rooms Beach Car Park, Dunwich ☎01728 648433. Famous for their fish and chips as well as for location (you are at the mouth of what was once Dunwich's great harbour), this is a plain no-frills place serving good fish and chips, pots of tea and ice cream sundaes.

The Ship St James St, Dunwich ☎01728 648219 www.shipatdunwich.co.uk. This popular former smugglers' inn, virtually on the beach and well placed for walkers and birdwatchers, has excellent fish and chips and Adnams in the bar, as well as a modern dining room where generous portions of comforting traditional food are served.

⑥ Westleton and Middleton

These two villages sit between Dunwich and Yoxford on the A12. Westleton lies on the direct road to Dunwich and Minsmere RSPB reserve, while Middleton is just off it on another minor road. A third village, Theberton, lies just south of Middleton. All three are inviting, with scattered old houses that seem to determine the route of the road that curve around them rather than the other way round.

Westleton is a large attractive village with a green and St Peter's church, a thatched 14th-century church that was built by monks from Sibton Abbey, close to Peasenhall just across the A12. Legend has it that no grass can grow over the 'witch's stone' near the priest door of the church, and if you put your handkerchief in the grating of the wall and make an anti-clockwise circumambulation of the church you will hear the sound of the Devil clanking his chains beneath the grating. You may notice that this large church is lacking in one department – it has no tower or spire. The original tower collapsed in high winds in 1776. It was rebuilt but its replacement also collapsed during World War II, this time the result of a German bomb. The church stages occasional orchestral concerts as well as hosting Westleton's annual **Wild Flower Festival**.

Along the Westleton road, in Darsham just east of the A12, you'll find the **Emmerdale Farm Shop** (01728 668648; www.emmerdalefarmshop.co.uk), which stocks well-matured beef from a local herd of Suffolk Red Poll that are reared in the old-fashioned way, grazing on marshes in spring and summer, as well as locally grown vegetables like potatoes and asparagus and products from other local suppliers; it also has a coffee shop.

Middleton, straddling a road that goes nowhere in particular, has the distinction of being the only village in Suffolk that has its own moor, actually just a big field a mile from the village centre. There's an old tradition here called the **Cutty Wren Hunt** that is based on an ancient tradition in which a wren is captured on the evening of St Stephen's (ie: Boxing Day) for purposes of divination. The custom finally died out at the beginning of the 20th century, but a modified version of it was resurrected in 1994. Originally, a wren would be captured and killed, and then fastened to a holly and ivy-bedecked broomstick to be taken around the village by boys who would demand gifts from the householders. These days, real live wrens are spared and the ritual consists of a lantern-lit procession bearing a wooden wren that goes from the village hall to the Bell Inn where the Old Glory Molly Dancers perform. The ritual may have prehistoric origins but is a curious one, as wrens are generally considered unlucky birds to kill. There may be a connection here with the midwinter tradition of topsy-turveydom in which the usual rules of behaviour are turned upside down, and the wren's perceived association with the underworld is symbolically challenged. Although similar traditions exist in Ireland and Britain's Celtic fringe, the one at Middleton appears to be unique for England. All this bird abuse so close to Minsmere!

Molly Dancing in East Anglia

Molly dancing is the East Anglian version of Morris dancing, a more earthy tradition that is altogether scarier and might even be described as 'Morris dancing with menace'. Molly involves a type of dance traditionally performed by ploughboys in midwinter. It mostly existed in the Midlands and East Anglia and, before the recent revival, the tradition was last witnessed in Cambridgeshire in the 1930s. Molly dancing is usually associated with Plough Monday, the first Monday after Epiphany ('Twelfth Night'), a day on which ploughboys would tour their village and offer to dance for money for local landowners, meting out 'trick or treat' style mischief to those who refused to pay. The commonest penalty would be to plough a furrow across the lawn or garden of the offending party. Anonymity was vital, as it would be these same landowners who would provide employment once the farming season got under way. Consequently, faces would be blackened with soot, Sunday best clothes modified with coloured scarves and one of the team would cross-dress as a woman.

The revived tradition incorporates all of these elements with a modern twist. East Anglia has several Molly 'teams': Old Glory, who also perform the Cutty Wren Hunt at Middleton (page 242), Ouse Washes Molly Dancers and Gog Magog Molly.

As well as Plough Monday and the Cutty Wren Hunt, Old Glory Molly can also sometimes be seen dancing at Southwold and Walberswick on Christmas Eve. Whatever the occasion, the proceedings usually have a solemn, dark edge. Old Glory don't smile or talk when they perform, and they don't perform outside winter. They do tend to scare small children though. It's a serious business that seems both primordial and quintessentially English. In fact, one witness is reported to have said that the Molly experience was 'so English, it brought tears to my eyes'.

Theberton is another village with a pretty, thatched church; in this case, a much smaller one than at Westleton but at least complete with tower. A Zeppelin airship was shot down here during World War I and 16 German airmen perished in the crash. There is a memorial in the cemetery across the road from the church, and a piece of the airship itself mounted in a glass case in the porch. Fragments of the Zeppelin were recycled into all sorts of new uses such as keepsake brooches made from bits of recycled airship brass, and it's thought various bits and pieces, handed down through the generations, survive in the area today.

Bell Inn Middleton ☎ 01728 648286. A cosy thatched Adnams pub with a small dining area and a relaxed bar with sofas; limited choice of food.

⑤ Westleton Crown The Street, Westleton ☎ 01728 648777
⌂ www.westletoncrown.co.uk. This former coaching inn claims to have provided 800 years of continuous service to travellers. There's an open fire for chilled walkers and a huge map of the locality on the wall. The extensive menu is mostly sourced from local butchers or Lowestoft fishing boats.

Aldeburgh, Orford and Britten country

⑦ Aldeburgh

Aldeburgh is the Suffolk coast's other main resort: a former shipbuilding and fishing town that went into decline when fishing boats became too large to drag up the beach and other, more suitable ports were favoured for the construction of ships. Before this happened though, ships as illustrious as Sir Francis Drake's *Pelican* (famously later renamed as *Golden Hind*) were built here. There's still some fishing done from Aldeburgh's shingle beach and one of the town's great pleasures is to buy ultra-fresh **fish** from one of the huts on the beach and go off and cook it. Of course, you could have fish from the very same catch cooked for you instead – more on this later.

This town these days is a place of wealth and refinement, with barely a rough edge apart from the workaday fishing huts and 'punts' on the beach. As you might expect, there is a considerable number of incomers and those that live here year round tend to know that they are on to a good thing, which gives the place just the slightest hint of self-satisfaction. Aldeburgh's connections with the composer **Benjamin Britten** (actually a Lowestoft man) and the annual **Aldeburgh Festival** bring such kudos to the town that you wonder what a real-life Peter Grimes might make of it – a little hifalutin perhaps?

Despite the widespread fame of its fish-and-chip shops, it is immediately obvious that Aldeburgh is as much about pan-fried sea bass on a big square plate as it is about fish and chips in paper. It is undeniably lovely though, with bracing sea-scented air, a Blue Flag shingle beach, some interesting buildings and, of course, fantastic fresh fish.

The most striking building is the **Moot Hall**, a Tudor timber-framed building that looks a little odd sitting right next to the beach, and holds a museum of the town's history. Its current location is thanks to longshore drift rather than eccentric town planning as it used to sit smack dab in the town centre. As elsewhere on this coastline, the relentless North Sea has shaved great chunks off what was once the original medieval town.

A better-known landmark these days is **The Scallop**, a large stainless steel sculpture in the shape of a shell that stands on the northern beach close to the car park. The sculpture, the work of Suffolk artist Maggi Hambling, was unveiled in 2003 to much controversy. It is dedicated to Benjamin Britten and the upright shell bears the words: 'I hear those voices that will not be drowned', taken from Britten's *Peter Grimes*. Some clearly consider The Scallop to be an eyesore and a despoilment of a beautiful natural setting. As a result, the work has received a lot of flak since it was first erected, with graffiti, paint splattering and petitions all brought to bear in the case against. It is hard to see why the sculpture has been quite so vilified in some quarters; it is, after all, a natural, seaside form – a shell.

Such protest may be nothing new. The poet George Crabbe who was born in the town and in 1810 wrote *The Borough*, the lengthy poem in which the solitary character of Peter Grimes first surfaced, notes a certain philistinism in the local character:

> *... a wild, amphibious race,*
> *With sullen woe displayed in every face;*
> *Who far from civil arts and social fly,*
> *And scowl at strangers with suspicious eye.*

Thankfully, there's not really that much scowling going on these days, nor a lot of flying away from civil arts. It's not always that highbrow either: most who come to see The Scallop seem to prefer to have their photographs taken sitting on it rather than contemplating its verse.

Aldeburgh's ultimate chippie

Walk one minute inland from the seafront to the High Street and if it's lunchtime or early evening you will probably come across a lengthy queue. The chances are that this is a hungry crocodile patiently waiting for service at **The Fish and Chip Shop** at number 226. The Fish and Chip Shop – yes, that's its name – has been listed as one of the country's top ten by the *Observer* and eulogised by chefs like Rick Stein and Nigel Slater. The secret, according to the owner Margaret Thompson, is that no flour is added to the batter and that vegetable oil, not beef dripping, is used for frying. It has been a family business since 1967. Some even claim it to be the best in the country. A place that can prosaically call itself The Fish and Chip Shop rather than 'The Codfather', 'This is the Plaice' or something similar just has to be good. There's another branch further along the High Street that is run by the same concern but this one is the original. By the time you get your fish supper you'll undoubtedly be very hungry. Walk back to the sea wall to enjoy your food by the sea but beware of local gulls that have become very adept at aerial fish theft.

Aldeburgh's 14th-century flint church of **St Peter and St Paul** on a low hill above the town has further local artistic interest. Here, there's a memorial bust of local poet George Crabbe and a gorgeous stained glass window by John Piper that depicts three Britten parables of the Curlew River. Benjamin Britten and his partner Peter Pears are both buried in the churchyard.

Just south of the town past **Slaughden**, once an important centre for boat building, now a yachting marina, you reach a narrow spit with a **Martello tower**. This is the most northerly of a string of 103 squat defensive towers that stretch from here south as far as Seaford, East Sussex. Twenty-nine of these were built in Suffolk and Essex between 1808 and 1812 as defences against possible invasion by Napoleon, and as well as being the most northerly the one at

Slaughden is also the largest, effectively four towers combined into one in a quatrefoil form. The spit pushes south with the River Alde on one side and the sea on the other to become Orford Ness – a very long trudge along the shingle and best visited on the National Trust ferry from Orford Quay (see page 250).

The **Aldeburgh Arts Festival** (www.aldeburgh.co.uk), an annual June festival of mainly classical music founded by Benjamin Britten in 1948, has become famous over the years. Most of the action takes place along the estuary at the purpose-built concert hall at Snape Maltings but some events use other venues like Blythburgh church. The town has become the home of two more festivals in recent years: the **Aldeburgh Poetry Festival** (www.aldeburghpoetry festival.org) in November and the **Aldeburgh Food and Drink Festival** (www.aldeburghfoodanddrink.co.uk) in September. The latter, in part sponsored by Adnams Brewery and Suffolk County Council, has been running since 2006 and takes place both in the town and at Snape Maltings. The festival's purpose is to celebrate the abundance of local produce and to help people reconnect with the local countryside and the food it produces – all very consistent with the Slow philosophy. There's a different slant to proceedings each year: 2009 focused on education and helping children and their parents reconnect with food, where it comes from and how it is produced.

For food in town, as well the very obvious fish huts on the beach, there's Hall Farm Shop on the Saxmundham road (☎ 01728 453666), which has Aldeburgh saltmarsh beef and lamb and other local foods. The high street has a couple of good delicatessens, and a **farmers' market** is held on the morning of the 3rd Saturday of each month at Aldeburgh Church Hall.

Cross Keys Crabbe St ☎ 01728 452637 ⌨ www.aldeburgh-crosskeys.co.uk. Ideally placed for a most authentic Southwold experience: a pint of Adnams outside this pink, cottagey 16th-century place, sitting by the beach and tucking into local fish.

⑧ Thorpeness

Heading north from Aldeburgh along the coast, you soon reach the village of Thorpeness, an odd place that was created from scratch by a Scottish barrister, Glencairn Stuart Ogilvie, in the Edwardian period. A hamlet had existed before but it was Ogilvie who decided to build a private holiday village here as a place where his friends and family could spend their summers. Work commenced in 1910, with a country club, a golf course and holiday homes in Tudor and Jacobean styles all appearing over the next decade or so. The village remained largely in the ownership of the Ogilvie family until 1972 when much of it was sold off to pay death duties.

The village's most iconic sight – it appears on Suffolk guidebooks as readily as Cley-next-the-Sea's windmill does to represent Norfolk – is the **House in the Clouds**, a wooden house on a high, five-storey plinth. The plinth was originally a disguised water tower but once mains water had been installed in the village, it was converted into further living accommodation and a games room. You can rent it should you choose to – very expensively. The views must be quite something. Thorpeness's other main sight is its artificial boating lake called **The Mere** that was inspired by *Peter Pan*, whose author J M Barrie was an Ogilvie family friend. A regatta takes place here each August in the week after Aldeburgh Carnival.

Whether you like Thorpeness or not tends to depend on your taste for mock Tudor. In some ways, the village is rather like Portmeirion in Wales, albeit without the Italianate architecture and the cult appeal of the Portmeirion-set TV series *The Prisoner*. Like that place, it feels rather like a film set, although Thorpeness is still waiting for the definitive film.

⑨ Snape

Snape is a small village a few miles inland from Aldeburgh, close to the Alde estuary, although most people tend to think immediately of **Snape Maltings** (01728 688303; www.snapemaltings.co.uk) at the head of the estuary itself. The Maltings are an impressive collection of shops and galleries converted from an assortment of Victorian riverside malthouses and granaries. Malt production finally ceased here in 1965 and since then a slow restoration and conversion of the buildings has been taking place. A bespoke Concert Hall was built in 1967 and the slow process of conversion of the existing buildings has been taking place ever since. Currently, its businesses include craft shops, home and garden stores, restaurants, art galleries, jewellery and fashion and even old-fashioned children's toys. At the time of writing, plans were afoot to lease some of the converted buildings for residential use. The Concert Hall, which serves as the centrepiece for the Aldeburgh Arts Festival, finds use all year round as a concert venue. It is a lovely venue, although as something of a cathedral in wood it can be uncomfortable if you are sitting for any length of time. It is probably best to do as Snape regulars do and bring your own cushion. The Maltings are also used the venue for the annual Aldeburgh Food and Drink Festival. A **farmers' market** is held here on the first and third Saturday of each month.

The Maltings sit in a superb natural environment that is virtually surrounded by reed beds. The RSPB, who have an office here in the small Virginia-creeper-clad building by the quay, provide guided walks every Thursday and also put on a range of activities for children and families. For a brief glimpse of the river and estuary, the *Cormorant* makes 30-minute **river trips** in summer; these can be booked at the craft shop by the quay. Alternatively, you might prefer to strike out along a **riverside footpath**. One of these leads to the village of Iken and its isolated church on the south bank (the boat trip sails past here too), while another that links up with the Suffolk coast and Heath Path at Snape village leads north of the estuary to Aldeburgh and the coast.

A couple of miles west of The Maltings lies the village of **Blaxhall**, where writer George Ewart Evans, author of *Ask the Fellows who Cut the Hay*, used to live; and where he did just that – ask the fellows etc – in the pursuit of oral history. **The Ship Inn** (01728 688316; www.blaxhallshipinn.co.uk) here has always been an important place for local folk song and this tradition is continued to this day, with regular 'sing, say or pay' events and even the odd competition. John Seymour reports that here (in the 1960s) you could hear men sing folksongs like *The Dark Eyed Sailor* and *The Larks They Sang Melodious*. You still can.

SP **Crown Inn** Bridge Rd, Snape IP17 1SL ☎ 01728 688324. This Adnams inn is also a smallholding that raises all of its own livestock, so has menus that take advantage of very local meat as well as locally landed fish. There are Adnams ales and wines to choose from, and families and dog walkers are most welcome.

SP **Golden Key** Priory Rd, Snape IP17 1SQ ☎ 01728 688510. A 15th-century cottage-style pub close to The Maltings that has daily menus featuring an abundance of locally sourced produce.

⑩ Saxmundham

This small market town is just to the north of Snape. It is not really on the coast at all but since it lies just east of the A12, and on the road to Sizewell, Leiston and Aldeburgh, it might be best to include it here. In some ways, it is a bit like Framlingham (see page 199) but without the castle and the gentle buzz. What Saxmundham does have is a functioning station on the East Suffolk coastal railway line, a handy link to Lowestoft and Ipswich. Mostly though, 'Sax' is a quiet, old-fashioned place with ironmongers, bakery and barbers' shops clustered cosily alongside each other in the centre – the classic small market town. It tends to come more alive on Wednesday market days but otherwise most of the excitement seems to emanate from the car park of Waitrose down near the church. Sad to say, the opening of a new supermarket appears to be more of a magnet for local shoppers, and to provide more Sax-appeal, than any number of quality second-hand bookshops or organic farm shops. To its credit, Saxmundham does have some representatives of both, notably Sax Books (01728 605775) and the Peakhill Organic Farm Shop (01728 605918) next door to each other on the High Street. The farm shop stocks organic meat and vegetables from its own farm in addition to cheeses, preserves and honey from other local producers.

St John the Baptist Church, just up the hill from the Waitrose car park, has an intriguing font with a pair of **woodwoses** on opposite sides. The woodwose – a hairy, wild-looking man with a club – is sometimes referred to as 'The Old Man of Suffolk', but for my money, it is really just another expression of what many would call 'the green man'. Of the pair here, one has his club raised, the other lowered. The church literature puts it politely: 'clubs raised by the unregenerate, lowered by the regenerate' without venturing red-faced into any explanation as to what the symbolism of the club might actually be. I'll leave you to draw your own conclusions, although its seems a little topsy-turvy to me; as Freud observed, 'sometimes a cigar is just a cigar'. If you are more interested in medieval carpentry than prurient symbolism, look upwards to the fine hammerbeam roof. The graveyard has a highly unusual headstone, that of one John Noller, which takes the form of a sundial.

Not far from the town, a little way to the east, **Peakhill Farm** (01728 602248; www.peakhillfarm.co.uk) is a long-established organic establishment based at Theberton near Leiston. The farm run by Rob and Karen White has a herd of South Devon cattle, some sows and a field of vegetable and salads, all of which are cultivated organically. There's a good range of Peakhill products on sale at the friendly farm shop in Saxmundham (see above).

Bistro at the Deli 26a High St ✆ 01728 605607 🖥 www.thedeli.biz. A deli selling continental and local produce, and home-baked pies and quiches made from local, seasonal ingredients. It also doubles as a café, with daily specials, good sandwiches, cakes and coffee.

S Crown Inn Great Glemham ✆ 01728 663693. In a village southwest of Saxmundham, close to Parham, this 17th-century redbrick pub serves locally sourced food such as Benhall venison and Creasey's meats from Peasenhall. There's a selection of Adnams and Earl Soham ales along with a regular guest beer.

⑪ Orford

To reach Orford from Aldeburgh means a detour around the Alde estuary at Snape. Coming from the west, several minor roads lead through the wide coniferous expanse of **Tunstall Forest**, passing through quiet, tucked-away villages like **Chillesford** and **Butley**, both of which have decent pubs and are worth a stop. Butley, with its jolly yellow daffodil village sign, is perhaps the more distinguished, with a Norman church and the remains of an Augustinian priory. After the fairly nondescript forestry village of Sudborne with its mix of bungalows and old terrace cottages just up the road, arriving at Orford's central square next to the church is a real pleasure, although there is little sense yet of being at the coast. For that, you will need to walk or drive the short distance down to the quay where all will be revealed.

Orford is very much a village of two halves: the village centre is a charming conglomeration of cottages around what was once a market square and hemmed in by the village church to the north and a 12th-century castle keep to the south. **St Bartholomew's Church** dates mostly from the 14th century, although there are traces of a Norman chancel. Of **Orford Castle**, which now belongs to English Heritage, only the keep remains but it is an impressive one and it is almost worth paying the entry fee just to climb up the spiral staircase for the view alone. Built by Henry II in 1165, at a time when they tended not to do things by halves, the keep has ten-foot-thick walls and is 90 feet high – a citadel that would be hard to breach with modern weaponry let alone longbows and maces. This, of course, is only a fraction of the fortifications that once stood here, which does raise the question as to what happened to all the stone that was shipped in to construct the original building.

Market Hill, around which much of the village clusters, is not much of a hill and no longer has a market but it's here you'll find a few shops, the Town Hall and the post office. There's a trio of narrow alleyways leading off Market Hill that connect with Broad Street and along the one next to Butley Orford Oysterage, you'll find the **Butley Orford Oysterage Shop** (01394 450277; www.butleyorfordoysterage.co.uk) where they have all manner of fresh and smoked fish and naturally, ultra-fresh oysters. The Butley Orford Oysterage itself has a sign depicting a merman, which relates to the tale of a wild man-like creature that turned up in someone's fishing nets in the 12th century. In good medieval fashion, the poor creature was tortured but did not, or could not, talk and eventually managed to escape back to sea.

A five-minute stroll along Quay Street brings you to a large car park opposite the **Jolly Sailors** pub and then the **Quay**. Suddenly it becomes maritime, with sailing dinghies bobbing around on the river. The village, like many others on this seaboard, was once a thriving port but the growth of **Orford Ness**, the huge sand spit opposite, eventually denied Orford its ready access to the sea. However, judging by the number of yachts and pleasure boats here, the river seems a perfectly acceptable substitute for most modern-day sailors. There's not much else: a small National Trust shed selling tickets for the ferry across to the Ness, Brinkley's shed selling wet fish and, next door, a tearoom. There's no electricity so Mrs Brinkley keeps her fish on ice – she has cod, skate and sea bass, or at least that was what she had on the day when I visited. 'There's just two boats that fish from here these days – us and another boat,' she told me. 'My husband catches the fish and I clean and sell it, so we do alright together.'

High House Fruit Farm Sudbourne IP12 2BL ☎ 01394 450450
🖥 www.high-house.co.uk. Pick your own fruit or buy ready-picked at this traditionally managed farm north of Orford. They also make their own apple juice, and camping is available.

⑫ Orford Ness

If you are not at Orford Quay for the sailing, your eyes will no doubt be drawn across the water to Orford Ness, which exudes an air of mystery typical of places associated with forbidden territory. From 1913 to the mid 1980s, the spit was firmly closed to the public, a top secret, no-go area dedicated to military testing and radar research. The links with its secret past are part of its appeal; otherwise, it's undeniable that Orford Ness is quite a remarkable bit of topography.

Though hardly pretty, this long shingle spit is undoubtedly evocative. Signs warn about unexploded ordnance, and everywhere you'll see tangles of tortured metal and wire netting among the teasels in the shingle. Overall, it's a rather melancholy landscape and you might begin to wonder if Orford Ness should actually be 'orfordness', a state of mind, rather than the name of a wayward landform.

To get there, you must take the National Trust boat. The *Octavia* runs across to Orford Ness roughly every half an hour between 11am and 2pm, with the last boat back around 5pm. 'Please don't miss the last boat back,' the NT boatman will inevitably warn you. 'It gets pretty nippy out there at night and there's only one loo for the whole of the spit.'

Seen from Orford Quay, Orford Ness has the appearance of being an island, and the ferry trip across the River Ore simply adds to this impression, but it's not – it's actually a long sand spit that begins just south of Aldeburgh and gradually widens as it follows the coast south. It is the largest shingle spit in England (nearly ten miles long) and it is only when you disembark at the jetty that you can really appreciate the scale of the place. The National Trust has a number of recommended waymarked routes to follow but the reality is that you won't see much unless you are prepared to walk some distance. Concrete roads lead around the spit and you have to trudge along these some way before you get to see anything of much interest. Bicycles are not permitted.

The Red Trail leads along the road and across a central dyke to the Bomb Ballistic Building, where you can climb to the roof terrace and survey the surroundings. A track leads across from here to a lighthouse on the shoreline, where there are also some ruined, boarded-up buildings. You might be lucky enough to see porpoises out to sea from the beach here (someone had done so the day before my visit) but you are more likely to spot gulls and terns, and nervous rabbits and hares flitting across the shingle. From the lighthouse, you can walk along the shingle as far as the Police Tower, where another track leads to Lab 1, the first of the military 'pagodas' that are clearly visible from the mainland. If post-apocalyptic landscapes are not your thing then you'd be better off choosing the Green Trail. This follows a circuit around King's Marshes on the landward side of the spit, where you should find plenty of waders feeding in the pools and lagoons. You could just about do both Red and Green trails if you came across on an early boat but you would have to get a move on, as that would constitute a total walk of around ten miles.

Halvergate Island, an RSPB reserve, lies a little further south between Orford Ness and the mainland. It's well known for its breeding avocets and there are occasional boats from Orford Quay.

Butley Orford Oysterage Market Hill, Orford ☎ 01394 450277. This long-popular seafood restaurant serves Orford-caught fish and oysters grown at nearby Butley Creek.

⑤ The Froize The Street, Chillesford IP12 3PU ☎ 01394 450282 ⌂ www.froize.co.uk. En route to Orford, this remote village restaurant set in converted 18th-century keepers' cottages specialises in local game and retro rustic cooking, and serves local Adnams beer and Aspall's cider.

Jolly Sailor Inn Quay St, Orford ☎ 01394 450243. Just before Orford Quay, this traditional inn has fresh homemade food and a beer garden.

Riverside Tearoom Orford Quay ☎ 07794 551530 ⌂ www.riversidetearoom.co.uk. This is a good place for tea and scones whilst waiting for the ferry to Orford Ness. There's an outside sun terrace overlooking the River Ore.

South of Orford

To reach Shingle Street, the next settlement south along the Suffolk coast, requires a diversion inland from Orford around the River Butley via Chilesford and Butley. A minor road skirts Rendlesham Forest to reach Hollesley, with its HM Young Offenders Institution, before the road peters out completely at Shingle Street.

⑬ Rendlesham Forest

Rendlesham Forest is a vast coniferous expanse with a smattering of picnic places and forest walks. Gnarled old Scots pines scratch at the sky but plenty of plantations are relatively new, planted to replace the losses brought about by the 1987 October 'hurricane' that wreaked havoc across southern England. I visited the area just after the event and I remember being shocked by the extent of the damage: huge shattered trunks, branches split like matchwood – the aftermath of the sort of extreme weather event that we are not supposed to experience in mild, moderate Britain.

The forest has experienced even stranger events than this if you can believe all that you hear. The so-called **Rendlesham Forest Incident** occurred over three successive nights during Christmas 1980, and was probably the most publicised example of a UFO incident ever to have occurred in the UK. It involved a series of unexplained sightings of lights and even the alleged landing of an alien spacecraft in the forest. There were two airbases in the area at the time, RAF Bentwaters and RAF Woodbridge, both of which were being used by the US Air Force. Although witnesses of the event were encouraged to believe that the pulsating lights they witnessed were simply those of Orford Lighthouse, there were those who insisted that they had seen a conical metallic object landing in a forest clearing. As with all events of this sort, the incident provided fertile ground for conspiracy theorists and the Ministry of Defence was accused of engineering a news cover-up after the event. The incident did not make national news until three years later when the *News of the World* published the story beneath the headline: *UFO lands in Suffolk – and that's official.*

For those intrigued by these extra-terrestrial claims, the Forestry Commission (www.forestry.gov.uk) has helpfully marked a three-mile 'UFO Trail' for walkers that begins at the **Rendlesham Forest Centre** and includes the main locations of the incident (two bicycle trails are marked from here too). Inevitably there's more on the internet: see www.rendlesham-incident.co.uk.

Back to earth, Rendlesham Forest provides important habitat for woodlarks and nightjars – 20 per cent of the national breeding population, in fact – and three types of deer, as well as badgers and adders lurking in the woods.

⑭ Shingle Street

This really does feel like the end of the road. On a blustery winter's night, it probably seems like the end of the world. There's really not much to Shingle Street: a row of coastguard cottages and holiday lets, a phone box, a car park and an awful lot of shingle. It does have a certain rather desolate charm; the beach is more or less empty, with wonderful views north towards Orford Ness and the mouth of the River Ore. At the southern end of this short strip of beachside houses stands a Martello tower, and you can see three more of them looking south from here framed by the distant silhouettes of Scots pines. There's virtually nothing else along this coast until you reach the Deben River estuary with Felixstowe sitting on its opposite bank. Standing on the shingle here with the coast curving south to vanishing point it seems hard to believe that Ipswich is only a dozen miles away.

If you want to keep going as far as the River Deben, you'll need to retrace your steps back to Hollesley (pronounced 'Hosely') then head south through Alderton to Bawdsey and then Bawdsey Manor, where there's a passenger ferry across the estuary mouth to Felixstowe. The **Suffolk Coast and Heaths Path** goes this way too, clomping along the shore south from Shingle Street, across the Deben by way of the ferry then past another two Martello towers before reaching the outskirts of the town that is home to Britain's largest container port, **Felixstowe**.

⑮ Woodbridge

This is not on the coast as such but on an estuary, and I confess to having overlooked Woodbridge in the past. A medium-sized town, very close to Ipswich, it didn't sound too inspiring. Then came the impetus: 'You really must go to Woodbridge,' my mother's neighbour insisted, 'It's a smashing little place.' This was, after all, the first port of call, after Ipswich, of William A Dutt's turn-of-the-century *Highways and Byways* journey. He referred to Woodbridge as 'a delightful little town – one of the prettiest little country market towns in England.' I am pleased to report that he was quite right.

Woodbridge stands at the head of the River Deben estuary. The estuary is where you'll find yourself if you arrive by train – and perhaps by car too, as there's a big, convenient car park down here by the railway lines. From here, there's a footbridge across the railway and a riverside path that leads south along the estuary past reed beds and rowing clubs. If you head in the opposite direction and walk around the back of the riverside theatre you'll soon reach a quay that has one of the town's most distinctive buildings, the **Tide Mill** (01728 746959; www.tidemill.org.uk). This elegant, white-planked 18th-century building operated until the 1950s and, as its name suggests, harvested the power of the incoming tide to turn a waterwheel. The mill still works and can be visited but the pond that used to store the tidal water has been replaced by a much smaller one while the original has morphed into a kidney-shaped **yacht harbour** that is closed to the general public  unless you are wearing the right kind of sailor's hat. Much less fancy but, I think, more characterful, boats are moored at the quay beside the tide mill. Some of these look as if they have been here a long time and you can detect a real sense of community in the slightly battered craft with pot plants and bicycles on their decks moored in the boatyard beyond the yacht harbour.

Away from the riverside, central Woodbridge is delightfully traffic-free, with the pedestrianised streets of Quay Street, Church Street, New Street and The Thoroughfare combining to provide a compact shopping and strolling area. One of the glories of Woodbridge is that there are so many small retailers and so few chain stores: the Woodbridge Town Centre Management Group has come up with the slogan, 'Choose Woodbridge for real shopping', and it kind of makes sense. The Thoroughfare, in particular, has several independent bookshops and tearooms. In fact, the town as a whole has so many coffee houses and tea rooms you suspect that the town council may have shares in Twinings.

Woodbridge's **historic core** lies a little further uphill. Woodbridge is surprisingly hilly and slopes sharply away from the river. Melton Hill, which has St John's Church, is claimed by some to be the inspiration for the *Grand Old Duke of York* nursery rhyme although there is no historical evidence of 10,000 soldiers marching up and down this particular hill. Other Woodbridge hills have been suggested, as has Ipswich, which has an actual Grand Old Duke of York pub. The Duke of York in question, Frederick Augustus, the second son of George III, actually had far more than 10,000 men under his command in his Napoleonic campaign, and he wasn't old either – just 31 at the time. The song more than likely came about following an unsuccessful campaign in Flanders, and that is probably where the hill in question is.

Returning to terra firma in Woodbridge, Church Street and New Street merge at Market Hill where the imposing Dutch-gabled **Shire Hall** has pride of place. Built by Thomas Seckford in1575, this once served as the town's corn exchange but now is used as the **Suffolk Punch Heavy Horse Museum** (01394 380643;

www.suffolkhorsesociety.org.uk) with informative displays on the history of the breed. The **Woodbridge Museum** (01394 380502), with its exhibits detailing the history of the town and its people, especially local luminaries Thomas Seckford and Edward FitzGerald, lies just opposite. You can get a great view of the rooftops of the town by climbing up the steps to the small balcony on the southern side of the Shire Hall. North of the Shire Hall, there's a pleasant shady square, a surprisingly tranquil spot to find right in the centre of town. Keep going along Theatre Street and you reach **Buttrum's Mill**, a nicely restored six-storey tower mill, which is open for visitors on summer weekends and bank holidays.

Woodbridge has a couple of excellent delis in town. **Loaves and Fishes** (☎ 01394 384040) at 52 Thoroughfare has a great selection of cheese, smoked fish and organic produce, while **Woodbridge Fine Food Company** (☎ 01394 610000 🖱 www.woodbridgefinefoodcompany.co.uk) at 2a New St has fresh shellfish, wines, picnic foods and their 'world famous pies'.

Cherry Tree Inn 73 Cumberland St ☎ 01394 384627 🖱 www.thecherrytreepub.co.uk. A traditional inn with home-cooked food and a good selection of cask ales and wines.
Georgian Coffeehouse 47a Thoroughfare ☎ 01394 387292 🖱 www.georgiancoffeehouse.co.uk. One of several traditional tea rooms serving light meals and afternoon teas.
Waterfront Café Tide Mill Way ☎ 01394 610333 🖱 www.thewaterfrontcafe.co.uk. A stylish café and seafood restaurant next to the Tide Mill.
Whistlestop Café Station Rd ☎ 01394 384831. A conveniently situated café right next to the station.

⑯ Sutton Hoo

Just across the Deben estuary from Woodbridge is the **Sutton Hoo Burial Site** (01394 389700; www.nationaltrust.org.uk), which was unearthed in 1939 to reveal a large Anglo-Saxon ship which had been buried stuffed with treasure that included magnificent garnet-set gold jewellery, silver, drinking horns and armour: Anglo-Saxon notables tended to leave this world in great style. Ship burials seem to have been a Suffolk speciality: there were others here, and one in nearby Snape, but treasure-hunters raided the Sutton Hoo mounds in the 16th century and only missed finding this one by a few inches. The notable in question here is most probably Raedwald, who was King of East Anglia in the early 7th century. As famous as the ship-burial is the beautiful silver and gold ceremonial helmet found at the site that has become a Sutton Hoo icon. The discovery is a saga in itself: the landowner, Mrs Edith Pretty, a widowed spiritualist, commissioned a self-taught local archaeologist, Basil Brown, to excavate some grassy mounds which she somehow sensed had some significance. To his everlasting credit, rather than simply digging down for treasure, Brown recognised that the lines of metal rivets in the sandy soil represented all that was left of a ship's hull, still in position, and excavated with great skill. But once the discovery became national news, he was sadly sidelined by the 'professionals' directed by the British Museum. The mounds, with their pagan associations, were later used as a place of execution: join one of the tours led by local volunteers to get the best sense of what happened here. Run by the National Trust, the site is set in a 245-acre estate with attractive woodland and estuary walks. The exhibition hall has a full-size reconstruction of the burial chamber and displays that tell the story, describing Sutton Hoo as 'page one of English History', which somewhat overlooks the Romans and Iceni tribes that came before.

⑰ Boulge

You may struggle to find Boulge on the map, as it is very small. The village – more just a collection of lanes – does have an interesting story to tell though. Across the A12 from Woodbridge and a little further north, there's a minor road that leads west to the village of Bredfield. If you take this, after less than a mile you will come to a junction with a water pump and some fancy wrought ironwork that has finger signs pointing in every direction. Take the one that says 'Boulge, Debach and Clopton' and just after Partridge Farm you should notice a crude hand-painted sign pointing along a rough track to Boulge Church. Take this and you'll soon come to **St Michael Church** hidden away on the edge of a small wood, a delightfully peaceful spot that seems much further from the A12 than it really is. The graveyard here is the resting place of Edward FitzGerald, a slightly oddball Victorian polymath who was responsible for translating Omar Khayyam's Rubaiyat poems from the Persian. FitzGerald's family owned the Boulge Estate to which the church belongs – the hall was destroyed in the 1950s – and he lies buried in the graveyard here under a simple carved granite slab. Some straggly rose bushes around the grave are rather more special than they might first appear, having been planted by admirers from the Omar Khayyam Club in 1893, ten years after FitzGerald's death. The original rose was raised from seed brought from the grave of Omar Khayyam in Nishapur, Persia, and more have been planted since, although none of them appears to be doing very well. Nevertheless, their oriental origin provides an exotic touch to what might seem a perfectly ordinary, half-forgotten Suffolk graveyard.

Edward FitzGerald lived a life somewhat at odds with the rest of his family, and that his grave lies separate from the large family tomb is probably indicative of the alienation he felt. FitzGerald disliked the stuffy life of the estate and spent much of his adult life at Woodbridge where he dressed in odd clothes and befriended herring fishermen at the quay. One in particular, Joseph 'Posh' Fletcher, had a long-term relationship with FitzGerald that was most probably not entirely platonic – quite scandalous at the time. Ironically, FitzGerald's Woodbridge boat was named *Scandal* too. If you think Edward FitzGerald sounds like a typical W G Sebald character, then you are right. Sebald passed this way in *The Rings of Saturn* and wrote movingly of FitzGerald's predicament.

⑱ Ipswich

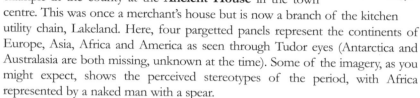

Ipswich, Suffolk's largest town by far, does not readily fit with the notion of Slow and so I will not say that much. I should mention a couple of things though. For pargetting aficionados, the town has what is perhaps the very best example in the county at the **Ancient House** in the town centre. This was once a merchant's house but is now a branch of the kitchen utility chain, Lakeland. Here, four pargetted panels represent the continents of Europe, Asia, Africa and America as seen through Tudor eyes (Antarctica and Australasia are both missing, unknown at the time). Some of the imagery, as you might expect, shows the perceived stereotypes of the period, with Africa represented by a naked man with a spear.

There's an interesting story regarding the bells at the church of **St Lawrence** too, which is in the centre of Ipswich and is currently used as a community centre. In September 2009, the church's five bells were returned to their place in the tower for the first time in 25 years. Cast in the mid-15th century, they are the oldest circle of bells in the world. They were removed in 1985, but have now been overhauled and reinstalled. Their sound is reckoned to be unique and beautifully mellow by those able to judge these things. Whatever the quality of this genuinely medieval sound, it is humbling to think that when these bells first chimed in the streets of Ipswich, Columbus had not yet discovered America.

Back from the brink: Jimmy's Farm saves the Essex Pig

Jimmy Doherty's farm is one of the best known in the country thanks to a 2009 BBC2 television series that documented the trials of raising rare-breed pigs. Jimmy's business goes under the name of the Essex Pig Company and you might be fooled into thinking that the farm stands on the wrong side of the River Stour. It doesn't – it's in Suffolk, just south of the A14 near a village called Wherstead. The pigs, however, have an impeccable Essex pedigree.

The Essex Pig is a direct descendant of the breed that once foraged East Anglia's wildwood. Modernisation brought about a dramatic decline in their numbers following World War II, and by 1967 the breed was considered extinct. Luckily, one farmer, John Crowshaw, managed to keep his pedigree Essex bloodline pure. Although the Essex Pig remains officially extinct, Jimmy Doherty is currently hard at work building up the numbers of this rare animal. Jimmy's Essex porkers are in suitably aristocratic company, having both Saddlebacks and hefty Gloucestershire Old Spots as farmyard neighbours.

Jimmy's Farm Pannington Hall Lane, Wherstead IP9 2AR ☎ 08444 938088 ◌ www.essexpigcompany.com. Rare-breed pig farm with shop, woodland trail, events and courses, a butterfly house, a vegetable garden, special activities for children, and a farmers' market on the first Saturday of the month.

Index

Page numbers in **bold** refer to main entries